Marriage and the Economy

Theory and Evidence from Advanced Industrial Societies

Marriage and the Economy explores how marriage influences the monetized economy as well as the household economy, the value of all goods produced in households. Marriage institutions are to the household economy what business institutions are to the monetized economy, and marital status is clearly related to the household economy. Marriage also influences the economy as conventionally measured via its impact on labor supply, workers' productivity, savings, consumption, and government programs such as welfare and social security. The macroeconomic analyses presented here are based on the microeconomic foundations of cost/benefit analysis, game theory, and market analysis. A number of specialists in various areas of economics present microeconomic analyses of marriage, divorce, and behavior within marriages.

Western values and laws have been very successful at transforming the way the world does business, but their success at maintaining individual commitments to family values is less impressive. It is worth trying to approach family values with the same tools that have accomplished so much in other areas: the tools of logic, reason, and recognition of the existence of market forces.

Shoshana A. Grossbard-Shechtman is Professor of Economics at San Diego State University. Her books include *On the Economics of Marriage* (1993) and *The Expansion of Economics* (2002), and her articles have appeared in economics, sociology, and anthropology journals. Professor Grossbard-Shechtman is founding editor of the new journal *Review of Economics of the Household* and serves on the editorial board of the *Journal of Socio-Economics* and the *Journal of Bioeconomics*. A past Fellow at the Center for Advanced Studies in the Behavioral Sciences in Palo Alto, she served as a visiting scholar at Columbia University for the academic year 2002–3.

Marriage and the Economy

Theory and Evidence from Advanced Industrial Societies

Edited by

SHOSHANA A. GROSSBARD-SHECHTMAN

San Diego State University

Foreword by

JACOB MINCER

Columbia University

CAMBRIDGE UNIVERSITY PRESS

PUBLISHED BY THE PRESS SYNDICATE OF THE UNIVERSITY OF CAMBRIDGE
The Pitt Building, Trumpington Street, Cambridge, United Kingdom

CAMBRIDGE UNIVERSITY PRESS
The Edinburgh Building, Cambridge CB2 2RU, UK
40 West 20th Street, New York, NY 10011-4211, USA
477 Williamstown Road, Port Melbourne, VIC 3207, Australia
Ruiz de Alarcón 13, 28014 Madrid, Spain
Dock House, The Waterfront, Cape Town 8001, South Africa

http://www.cambridge.org

First published 2003

Printed in the United States of America

Typeface Times Ten 10/13 pt.   *System* LATEX 2_ε [TB]

A catalog record for this book is available from the British Library.

Library of Congress Cataloging in Publication Data
Marriage and the economy : theory and evidence from advanced industrial
societies / edited by Shoshana A. Grossbard-Shechtman.
p. cm.
Includes bibliographical references and index.
ISBN 0-521-81454-5 – ISBN 0-521-89143-4 (pb.)
1. Marriage – Economic aspects – Developed countries. 2. Married people –
Employment – Developed countries. 3. Family – Economic aspects – Developed
countries. 4. Social values – Developed countries. 5. Industrialization – Developed
countries – History – 20th century. 6. Economics – Developed countries – History –
20th century. I. Grossbard – Shechtman, Shoshana, 1948–
HQ518 .M325 2003
306.81′09–dc21   2002073690

ISBN 0 521 81454 5 hardback
ISBN 0 521 89143 4 paperback

This book is dedicated to the memory of one of this book's authors, Leslie Whittington. Leslie, her husband, and their two young children were killed when terrorists hijacked their plane on September 11, 2001, well after she had completed her chapter with James Alm. Leslie worked toward the construction of a better society. Her research in the field of economic demography has made a difference. Leslie continues to live in our hearts and memories. This book is also dedicated to my children, Michal Hanna, Zev Mordechai, Chaim Joshua, and Esther Eve.

Contents

Figures

Tables

Contributors

James Alm is Professor and Chair of the Department of Economics in the Andrew Young School of Policy Studies at Georgia State University in Atlanta, Georgia. Much of his research has examined the responses of individuals and firms to taxation, in such areas as tax reform, the tax treatment of the family, the line item veto, social security, housing, indexation, tax and expenditure limitations, and tax compliance. He has also worked extensively on fiscal and decentralization reforms in Bangladesh, Indonesia, Jamaica, Grenada, Turkey, Egypt, Hungary, China, the Philippines, the Russian Federation, Nigeria, and Uganda. He is currently on the Advisory Board of the National Tax Association and the editorial boards of *Economic Inquiry* and *Review of Economics of the Household*, and he is also Associate Editor of *Public Finance Review*. More information and links to publications can be found at http://www.gsu.edu/~ecojra.

Andrea H. Beller is a professor of family economics at the University of Illinois at Urbana–Champaign (UIUC). She coauthored *The Economics of Child Support* (Yale University Press, 1993). Beller is on the editorial boards of *The Quarterly Review of Economics and Finance* and the *Review of Economics of the Household*, the board of the Committee on the Status of Women in the Economics Profession, and Illinois' Child Support Advisory Committee. She received the Senior Faculty Award for Excellence in Research in the College of Agricultural, Consumer and Environmental Sciences at UIUC in 2001 and the Distinguished Alumni Award from Case-Western Reserve University in 2000. Her Web address is http://www.ace.uiuc.edu/faculty/bellerah.html.

Michael J. Brien is an economist in the Economics Consulting Group of Deloitte & Touche LLP. Prior to joining Deloitte & Touche, he was an assistant professor of economics at the University of Virginia. He has also served as a senior economist on the President's Council of Economic Advisers, specializing in labor and social policies. His research interests include the economics of marriage, the impact of teen childbearing, and the analysis of social programs.

Shirley Burggraf is a professor of economics at Florida A&M University in Tallahassee and a recent Bunting Fellow at Radcliffe College. She is the author of the *Feminine Economy and Economic Man*, published by Addison Wesley in 1997.

Rachel Connelly is an associate professor of economics at Bowdoin College. She has written extensively on the subject of the economics of childcare. Connelly is currently involved in research on the value of employer-subsidized childcare in the United States, turnover and wages of childcare workers in the United States, and the demand for childcare arrangements in Minnesota.

Linda N. Edwards is Associate Provost and a professor of economics at the Graduate Center of the City University of New York and serves on the Advisory Board of the City of New York Independent Budget Office. Edwards has written extensively (with Elizabeth Field-Hendrey) on home-based work and is currently researching wage differentials between home-based and on-site women workers.

Elizabeth Field-Hendrey is Chair of the Department of Economics at Queens College and a professor of economics at Queens College and the Graduate Center of the City University of New York. Her research interests include labor economics and economic history. She is engaged in a long-term collaboration with Linda Edwards on home-based work; they are currently investigating wage differentials between home-based and on-site workers. She is also doing research into the substitutability of male and female labor, and she is completing a project on the relative efficiency of slave labor in the antebellum United States.

John Fitzgerald is a professor of economics at Bowdoin College. He has written articles on determinants of time on welfare, home production, attrition in panel surveys, and earnings instability. Current projects include a study of the impact of welfare reform on female headship and the impact of income variability on food stamp use.

John W. Graham is a professor of economics at Rutgers University. He coauthored *The Economics of Child Support* (Yale University Press, 1993). His Web address is http://newark.rutgers.edu/~jwgraham.

Shoshana Grossbard-Shechtman is a professor of economics at San Diego State University and past Fellow at the Center for Advanced Studies in the Behavioral Sciences at Stanford. Her books include *On the Economics of Marriage* (Westview Press, 1993) and *The Expansion of Economics* (M. E. Sharpe, 2002). Her articles have appeared in economics, sociology, and anthropology journals. She is founding editor of the *Review of Economics of the Household* (forthcoming, Kluwer Academic Publishers) and serves on the editorial board of the *Journal of Socio-Economics* and the *Journal of Bioeconomics*. More information and links to publications can be found at http://www-rohan.sdsu.edu/faculty/sgs/index.html.

Joni Hersch is a lecturer on law at Harvard Law School, where she teaches a course on empirical methods for lawyers. She has published numerous articles on gender differences in labor market outcomes, the economics of home production, the stock market effects of litigation, smoking regulations, and risk-taking behavior. Hersch has taught at the California Institute of Technology, Duke, Northwestern, and Harvard. She was Professor of Economics at the University of Wyoming until December 1999. She has served on the board of the American Economic Association's Committee on the Status of Women in the Economics Profession and was a recipient of the National Science Foundation Visiting Professorship for Women grant.

Duncan Ironmonger is an associate professor of economics and director of the Households Research Unit at the University of Melbourne. He is known internationally for his research on the reactions of consumers to new commodities and for his pioneering work on household input-output tables for measuring and valuing household productive and leisure activities. In this field, he has been a consultant to the United Nations and official statistical offices in Australia, Canada, Finland, New Zealand, Norway, and Sweden.

Jean Kimmel is an associate professor of economics at Western Michigan University in Kalamazoo, Michigan. Prior to joining the faculty at WMU in August 2001, she was Senior Economist at the W. E. Upjohn Institute for Employment Research, where she was a researcher for twelve years. She is a labor economist whose research interests include childcare, welfare-to-work policies, employment-related health and disability issues, and multiple-job holding. Her research papers have been published in a number of journals in economics and labor relations. She is currently serving as board member and Midwest representative to the Committee on the Status of Women in the Economics Profession (CSWEP).

Evelyn L. Lehrer is a professor of economics at the University of Illinois–Chicago. She has written extensively on union formation and dissolution, women's labor supply, fertility, childcare arrangements, family income distribution, and the economics of religion. More information on her research, which has been published in economic and demographic journals, may be found at http://www.uic.edu/~elehrer.

Joseph P. Lupton is an economist at the Board of Governors of the Federal Reserve System in Washington, DC. He has worked as a research associate for both the Panel Study of Income Dynamics and the Health and Retirement Study since 1997. His research focuses on household wealth accumulation and the various state dependencies of saving behavior.

Jacob Mincer is the Buttenweiser Professor of Economics Emeritus at Columbia University. He is an elected member of the National Academy of Sciences and a distinguished Fellow of the American Economic Association. Mincer is a member of the editorial board of the *Journal of Labor Economics* and the *Economics of Education*. He is the author of *Schooling, Experience, and Earnings*, published by Columbia University Press in 1974, and *Collected Studies in Human Capital and Labor Supply*, published by Edward Elgar in 1993.

Shoshana Neuman is an associate professor of economics at Bar-Ilan University, Israel. She is a research Fellow at the Center for Economic Policy Research in London, a research Fellow at the Institute for the Study of Labor (IZA) in Bonn, Germany, and a participant in the European Union's project on Labor Demand, Education, and the Dynamics of Social Exclusion. She is the author of many articles on labor supply, earnings, marriage, fertility, and education.

Michelle E. Sheran is an assistant professor of economics at the University of North Carolina at Greensboro. She is currently working on a theoretical and empirical study of women's life-cycle career and family decisions. Her research interests include marriage, childbearing, foster care, and women's labor supply.

James P. Smith is Senior Economist in the Labor and Population Program at Rand. He is a member of the Committee on Population at the National Academy of Sciences, a member of the Advisory Council at the Public Policy Institute of California, and a past member of the board of editors of the *American Economic Review.* Smith has written many books and articles. His books include the recent *The New Americans: The Economic, Demographic, and Fiscal Effects of Immigration* (National Academy Press, 1997) and *Female Labor Supply: Theory and Estimation* (Princeton University Press, 1999).

Faye Soupourmas is a research Fellow in the Households Research Unit, Department of Economics, at the University of Melbourne. As part of the Households Research Unit, Soupourmas has worked on a number of projects related to the measurement of the economic value of the household economy. She has made a valuable contribution to the innovative research undertaken by the Households Research Unit on the valuation of household production in Australia.

Leslie Whittington was an associate professor of public policy and formerly associate dean of policy studies at Georgetown University. She had published numerous articles exploring the impact of public policy on family structure and decision-making in leading economic and demographic journals. She died with her family when their plane was hijacked and crashed into the Pentagon on September 11, 2001. She was on her way to spend a sabbatical in Australia at the Australian National University.

Frances Woolley is an associate professor of economics at Carleton University in Ottawa, Canada. She has written extensively on the economics of family decision making, public policy toward families, and feminist economics. She is on the editorial board of *Feminist Economics,* a vice-president of the International Association for Feminist Economics, and a former member of the Canadian Economics Association Executive Council. She was recently awarded the Doug Purvis Memorial Award for her work on taxing Canadian families. More information and links to publications can be found at http://www.carleton.ca/~fwoolley.

Foreword

Jacob Mincer

Beginning students of economics learn about the circular flow of the economy in which households and business firms are the major sectors, with government in the background as participant and setter of rules. Households provide labor to business firms from which they receive income. This income returns to the firms as consumption expenditures and financial investments (savings). In the basic economic analysis that follows, households are the decision makers in consumer demand and in labor supply. Financial transactions receive less attention in elementary treatments. Economists ignored decisions about formation, dissolution, and size of the household prior to the latter half of the twentieth century.

These omissions are understandable. The traditional treatment of the household as consumer and worker becomes awkward when it recognizes that most households contain more than one person. Indeed, historically, the prototypical household was the extended family, and the economy (Greek for *household*) was coextensive with it. Moreover, in order to face the issue of decisions about household formation and size, it was necessary to abandon the fallacy that non-market activities are not subject to economic analysis. The New Home Economics (NHE) is the development that followed this recognition.

The New Home Economics is no longer new, but its many insights into the role of the household in the economy are continuously augmented by researchers in economics and in the other social sciences. A brief listing of knowledge acquired by the NHE approach indicates its scope and power: *Labor supply* analyzed in the family context permits the estimation of income and price effects on labor supply. This contributes to an explanation of the secular growth of the female labor force as a corollary of economic growth. *Fertility behavior* is affected by growth of wages, non-market productivity, contraceptive technology, and family instability. The *trade-off between quantity and human capital investments ("quality") of children* is a factor in economic growth and in the demographic transition, now ubiquitous. *Gender differentials in the labor market* (wages, turnover, unemployment) in part mirror the intrafamily allocation of time and of human capital investments. Similarly, the latter affect *family migration decisions.*

Researchers in modern household economics continue to analyze many other issues. *Marriage and the Economy* is the latest sampling of research currently conducted by the second and third generations of NHE economists. Much of the research is related, at least by implication, to the questions (and answers) raised by the work of predecessors. That the received knowledge is put through more thorough analytical and empirical scrutiny is to be expected of a field nearing maturity. Focus on determinants and consequences of marriage is timely, especially as, in historical perspective, we have moved from the extended family to the nuclear and now to the subnuclear (single-parent, or just single) household. It is not clear whether this trend represents a viable adaptation to economic growth or a potential obstacle to it. Both the trend and its consequences require a great deal of further research. A single volume cannot cover all one would like to learn, but the readers will be more than compensated by the rich and stimulating work in this book.

New York City, March 2003

Acknowledgments

I am very grateful to my professors, parents, and other people who have triggered my interest in the economics of marriage. Professor Gary Becker deserves special credit for inspiring my work. I also thank Professor Clive Granger from the University of California–San Diego for giving me the idea of editing a book in my area of expertise and my editor at Cambridge University Press, Scott Parris, for his encouragement and helpful advice. Most importantly, I thank the authors who entrusted me with their work.

San Diego, February 2003

Marriage and the Economy

Theory and Evidence from Advanced Industrial Societies

ONE

Marriage and the Economy

Shoshana Grossbard-Shechtman

The institution of marriage is found in nearly all human societies. This fact clearly reflects the importance of sexual and reproductive functions in human life. Marriage entails commitment between sexual partners. Why do societies develop marital institutions that encourage commitment between spouses? In her presidential address to the Population Association of America in 1995, Linda Waite, a professor of sociology at the University of Chicago, emphasized how commitment in marriage can benefit earnings. Married workers may earn more because they are more productive.[1] *Marriage and the Economy* extends the work by Waite and others by exploring more in depth how marriage possibly influences labor supply and workers' productivity and by presenting analyses of other channels by which marriage may have an impact on the economy: savings, consumption, and government programs such as welfare programs and social security.

This book is an economics book because it deals with the "economy," the part of society that centers around exchanges of goods and services. The "economy" is an aggregate and involves a macroeconomic perspective. Until recently it was standard practice to focus on monetized transactions when calculating the value of an economy, and to overlook the

[1] Waite also discussed the benefits of marriage from the perspective of health (including mental health), children's achievements, and sexual satisfaction. Space limitations led me to exclude the topic of health and marriage from this book (see Waite and Maggie Gallagher 2000).

I thank James Alm, Edward Balsdon, Andrea Beller, Michael Brien, Shirley Burggraf, John Fitzgerald, Joni Hersch, Duncan Ironmonger, Evelyn Lehrer, Jacob Mincer, Zev Shechtman, Leslie Whittington, and Frances Woolley for useful comments.

value of the non-monetary household economy. Marriage influences the household economy at least as much as it affects the monetized economy. *Marriage and the Economy* adds to our understanding of how marriage influences both the monetized economy and the household economy. Marriage institutions are to the household economy what business institutions are to the monetized economy.

The study of the economics of marriage includes analyses of how marriage influences the economy (a macro perspective) as well as economic analyses of marriage, divorce, and behavior within marriages (a micro perspective). Let us start with an overlook of the microeconomics of marriage.

MICROECONOMIC THEORETICAL TOOLS

Economic theories of marriage can accommodate a wide range of assumptions and institutional constraints, including a variety of assumptions regarding the roles of men and women, ideals about love, and biological constraints. To better understand how these various dimensions can be incorporated into an economic analysis of marriage, let us look at the basic theoretical constructs that economists use when analyzing marriage. Most economic analyses of marriage have been part of applied microeconomics, and they have relied on the same theoretical tools that economists use in all microeconomic applications of economics: cost/benefit analysis, game theory, and market analysis.[2]

- The most basic economic theory of marriage is *cost/benefit analysis*.[3] Costs and benefits can be compared whether one searches for lasting romantic love, or for a companion who will replace the maid. Men and women may all perform such analyses, even if the factors that they consider as costs and benefits may differ somewhat. Cost/benefit theories of marriage are rational choice theories.[4]
- *Game theory* is a second theoretical tool that economists of marriage commonly use. Game theories apply whenever behavior is strategic. Whether its goal is holy matrimony or the satisfaction of biological needs, marriage involves strategic behavior and therefore game the-

---

[2] Market analysis is really a particular type of game theory.

[3] All three theoretical tools have been used in Gary S. Becker's seminal articles (Becker 1973, 1974).

[4] Such rational choice theories have become increasingly popular among sociologists.

ory is applicable.[5] If strategies differ by gender, economists can use game theories to model gender wars or cooperative behavior between husbands and wives.

- *Market analysis* applies whenever choices are available on a demand side or a supply side.[6] The existence of any possible substitute opens the door to potential competition. If there can be competition, there is a market, even if the competitive spirit is totally eradicated, and if the workings of a market for mates are not so obvious to most observers. The process of competition for potential mates can be observed universally, but takes different forms from one culture to the next. In the West, it can be observed at bars, church socials, proms, and such. In India it is more likely to take the form of a list of available grooms and brides printed in the local newspaper. In Japan and Korea, the need to compete drives parents to circulate numerous copies of the resumé of their marriageable children.

Reactions to the Microeconomics of Marriage

Economists started paying more attention to the institution of marriage after Jacob Mincer and Gary S. Becker started the New Home Economics (NHE) in the early 1960s, when they were both professors of economics at Columbia University. The NHE brought the analysis of household production into formal economic analysis.[7] In the 1970s, Becker pioneered

---

[5] Game-theoretical analyses of marriage were pioneered by Marilyn Manser and Murray Brown (1980) and Marjorie B. McElroy and Mary Jean Horney (1981). See also Elizabeth H. Peters (1986), McElroy (1990), Paul S. Carlin (1991), and Chapter 5 in this book.

[6] The insight that marriage market conditions influence many individual decisions follows from Becker's (1973) competitive market model, which originally appeared in the first part of his theory of marriage published by the *Journal of Political Economy*. Becker (1981) later reproduced this model in the second chapter of his *Treatise on the Family*, a chapter dealing with polygamy. Becker's (1973, 1974, 1981) explanations of marriage also contain a matching model that is very different from the competitive market model (see Chapter 2 in this book). Other market theories of marriage include Amyra Grossbard (1976), Michael C. Keeley (1977), David M. Heer and Amyra Grossbard-Shechtman (1981), and Robert Cherry (1998). Economic analyses of marriage can also be found in Bertrand Lemennicier (1988), Alejandro Cigno (1991), Grossbard-Shechtman (1993), Yoram Weiss (1997), and Francisco Cabrillo (1999).

[7] Mincer's econometric applications provided insights into the secular growth in women's participation in the labor force and into changes in fertility behavior. For more on the history of the NHE, see Grossbard-Shechtman (2001b). Earlier economic analyses of household decisions include the work of Hazel Kyrk and Margaret Reid (see Andrea H. Beller and Elizabeth D. Kiss 1999 and Yun-Ae Yi 1996). The NHE was also enriched by the work of Robert A. Pollak (1985) emphasizing similarities between firms and households.

the economics of marriage.[8] It is in part for his work in this area that he received the Nobel Prize in economics in 1992. Thirty years after the start of the study of the economics of marriage, business and money institutions – not marriage and other family institutions – still frame most of the ideas that economists write about.[9]

The reasons why the economics of marriage is unpopular relative to other applications of economics include unpopular positions regarding gender, economists' tendency to focus on materialistic concerns, and resistance from other disciplines.

Gender. The economics of marriage as developed by Becker and other NHE economists assumed that men and women behave according to traditional gender roles.[10,11] The underlying assumption that homemaking is a woman's job has come under criticism by feminist economists such as those in the United States, Canada, and France.[12] In fact, it is a misconception to think that the economics of marriage depends on any particular assumptions regarding gender differences.

Materialism. Most existing economic analyses of marriage have emphasized the materialistic dimensions of marriage, in contradistinction with the idealistic beliefs leading most Westerners to want to marry: romantic love and holy matrimony. It is data limitations that lead economists to focus on the mundane and the materialistic, not the essence of our theories. Matters of love, happiness, and soulfulness are difficult to measure. Throwing out economic analyses of marriage because of their emphasis on measurable and more materialistic dimensions of life is like throwing out the baby with the bath water. Economic analyses of marriage are applicable even if people approach marriage out of pure idealism. They will still be faced with some mating choices for themselves or their children.

---

[8] An earlier Marxist tradition also included economic analyses of gender roles (see Grossbard-Shechtman 1999).

[9] While most microeconomists ignore the institution of marriage, even power macroeconomists pay attention to marriage institutions.

[10] An instance of a NHE-based model making old-fashioned assumptions about gender roles is Reuben Gronau (1977). Consider for instance, Gronau's conclusion that the increase in the divorce rate in the United States followed the entry of women into the labor force. The reasoning goes like this: Women are supposed to be homemakers; their homemaking creates stable marriages; if they enter into the labor force, less is produced in marriage and divorce increases.

[11] Such reasoning is also found in Becker (1981).

[12] An example of a U.S. economist who has been critical of Becker's work on marriage is Barbara Bergmann (1995). Canadian and French examples are Frances Woolley (1996) and Catherine Sofer (1985).

Even those who dream of romance or get elevated by ideas about holy matrimony cannot remain totally oblivious of the hard realities involved in breadwinning and housecleaning. As long as there is work involved, cost/benefit analysis taking account of opportunity costs applies. As long as there is a choice between two potential recipients of romantic love, or at least two potential soul mates, a market analysis applies.

Biology and Sociology. A third possible objection to economic analyses of marriage could come from those who believe that biological theories matter more than economic theories. Economists have in fact incorporated many biological assumptions in their theories.[13] Traditionally, sociologists have been doing most of the research on marriage and divorce. Since the 1990s, Becker's theory of marriage has become influential among sociologists of the family. Sociologists studying marriage do not bring an economic approach to their analyses to the same degree that economists do. Exceptions include Waite and Maggie Gallagher (2000) and sociological studies of marriage markets.[14]

MARRIAGE MARKETS AND THE ECONOMY

Practically every idea in this book contains a macroeconomic side to it. In economics, one way to establish a connection between micro and macro is by way of market analysis. A market is basically an abstract concept that brings together many small (micro) decision makers by aggregating them into market demands and supplies, and recognizing that demand and supply interact.

Macroeconomists aggregate markets for all products and then analyze how these are connected to markets for monetized labor and capital. They occasionally recognize that a household economy exists side by side with the monetized economy, as is evident from Chapter 13.[15] However, macroeconomists typically ignore marriage markets.

The household economy is linked to the monetized economy due to the following connections: (1) Labor supply is jointly determined with the

---

[13] See, for example, Theodore C. Bergstrom's (1997) review article in the *Handbook of Population Economics* and a special issue of the *Journal of Bioeconomics*.

[14] More on market theories of marriage by sociologists can be found in Grossbard-Shechtman (1993, Chapter 2). For a more comprehensive comparison between economic and sociological analyses of marriage, see Grossbard-Shechtman (2001a), Chapters 8 and 9.

[15] Some macroeconomic analyses that deal with fertility are found in William Lord (2002).

supply of work in household production; and (2) commercial consumption of goods and services (also savings) is jointly determined with the consumption of goods and services produced in the home. Given that most household production occurs in marriages, and that marriage markets affect not only decisions about marriage and divorce but also the allocation of time and income to household production, marriage markets play an important role in both of these connections between the monetized economy and the household economy.

The link between marriage markets and supply of labor is especially potent. This connection is based on an essential principle: Household production is time-intensive. If the household is a married household, time in household production may take the form of labor to the extent that household production time is not the individual's preferred activity. Let us call "Work-in-Marriage" the time in marital household production that is work in the sense of time that has an opportunity cost, that is, there is a more valuable activity that was forgone. Next, markets for Work-in-Marriage can be modeled along the lines used to model other labor markets.[16] The analysis starts with individual supply and demand.

Individual Supply of Work-in-Marriage

The supply of Work-in-Marriage is conceptually very similar to the supply of paid labor. In both cases, individuals make a decision about working for others – a firm in the case of labor, and a spouse in the case of Work-in-Marriage. In both the cases of labor and Work-in-Marriage, the opportunity cost of labor is the value of the most valuable foregone opportunity, and both labor and Work-in-Marriage are assumed to be less valuable activities than other forms of household production that are more self-satisfying.[17, 18]

---

[16] This follows Grossbard-Shechtman (1984), which also includes a macroeconomic perspective. The idea of applying analyses from labor markets to the study of marriage can also be found in microeconomic analyses of marriage such as Grossbard (1976) and Keeley (1977). The marriage markets found in Becker's theory of marriage are quite different from labor markets.

[17] The idea that husbands and wives may possibly negotiate their leisure in marriage does not fit in simple models of leisure and labor, such as the classical Lionel Robbins (1930) model, which ignores household production. What activities actually are considered as Work-in-Marriage will vary from one individual to the next, although there are certain activities that most people consider to be chores.

[18] Individual supplies of work and of Work-in-Marriage are a function of an individual choice between three uses of time: work, production of self-consumed goods, and Work-in-Marriage. Three uses of time are also found in Gronau's (1977) labor supply model, but his definitions of leisure and household production time differ from mine.

Personnel economics teaches us that there are three kinds of incentives that possibly motivate workers to supply labor: threat, non-pecuniary reward, and compensation:

- *Threat.* Workers may be forced to work if the employer threatens to punish them, or if the threat is hunger or other undesirable results. This is a motive based on fear.
- *Non-pecuniary rewards.* Such rewards include the satisfaction from doing one's duty, loyalty, or the enjoyment out of supplying the product or doing the activity (the intrinsic reward).[19]
- *Compensation.* This incentive takes the form of barter or pay.

These incentives can apply to any kind of work, including Work-in-Marriage. When it comes to non-pecuniary rewards, work and Work-in-Marriage are similar. One can serve one's family out of love, which is reminiscent of loyal service to a firm and of military service motivated by patriotism. The two forms of work differ significantly in the degree to which people supply them for the other two incentives: expected compensation and threat.

In the case of Work-in-Marriage, compensation often takes the form of barter – for instance, an agreement whereby a husband washes dishes if his wife cooks. Such barters are also found in the labor force, as in the case of a barter deal between an accountant and a stockbroker within a firm. A major difference between the two forms of labor is that paid compensation in the form of wages is the norm in the case of work, whereas monetary compensation for Work-in-Marriage is a rare occurrence.

While there is no institutionally supported wage for Work-in-Marriage that is the equivalent of wages in the labor market, a closer look reveals some interesting parallels between monetary compensations for work and Work-in-Marriage.[20] Most workers in the labor force receive a pay

---

[19] Others, such as children, may also benefit from this work.

[20] In a historical perspective, the differences between work and Work-in-Marriage become even less obvious. Wages are a relatively new invention. Until a few centuries ago, most workers were agricultural workers who were trading goods for protection services offered by their feudal lord. I am struck by some of the parallels between this feudal system and the way that husbands have traditionally treated women supplying Work-in-Marriage in many parts of the world. This feudal system also characterized the way that industrialists often treated workers in the early stages of industrialization. In all these feudal-style systems, workers had very limited power relative to the power of those who benefited from their work and owned most productive resources. Under feudalism, fear of hunger and need for physical protection played an important role in motivating workers. Agricultural

package consisting of their wage earnings and pecuniary benefits – that is, benefits that have a clear monetary value, such as health insurance. Similarly, compensation for Work-in-Marriage suppliers often includes benefits of a pecuniary nature, such as access to goods purchased with a spouse's income or access to a spouse's retirement benefits.[21] Other possible benefits offered to suppliers of Work-in-Marriage include payments made prior to marriage (such as dowry or bridewealth) or after the marriage ends (such as alimony payments, transfers of assets after divorce, or cashing of a life insurance policy after the death of a provider). We can call *quasiwages* contemporaneous benefits that can be considered as compensation for Work-in-Marriage.

An individual labor supply is the willingness to work at different wage levels. Economists assume that a competitive labor market establishes wage levels, and they investigate how an individual responds to various wage levels. The law of supply applied to labor markets implies that the higher the wage, the more people are willing to work.[22] In the case of Work-in-Marriage, wages are not in evidence but we can model an individual supply of Work-in-Marriage as the willingness to supply Work-in-Marriage at various quasiwage levels. Both men and women can have such supply, and one expects the law of supply to apply here as well: The higher the quasiwage, the more people will supply Work-in-Marriage.

---

workers' power was limited by the lack of alternative opportunities for employment: lack of alternative professions and lack of alternative employers within their profession. Likewise, until recently, married women in the West could barely find employment outside the homemaking profession, and the lack of divorce opportunities led them to be stuck to their husband, even if he was abusive. Fear of hunger and need for protection from rape and other dangers were major reasons why women supplied Work-in-Marriage. This situation still exists in some segments of industrialized societies, and is found on a large scale in many of the world's agriculture-based societies.

[21] This quasiwage can be related to Becker's concept of implicit price in marriage and can be defined as a share of the gain from marriage. The difference between the approach presented here and Becker's implicit price in marriage is that Becker's theory of marriage does not have a supply of work in married household production in the sense that economists define labor supply: a positive relationship between the amount of labor an individual supplies and the reward for that labor. For a similar and more recent theory in sociology, see Grossbard-Shechtman (2001a, Chapter 8). Intramarriage allocation of goods can be analyzed as the result of a quasiwage payment for Work-in-Marriage. Alternative economic models of intramarriage allocation of goods assume that no goods are produced in marital household production and all goods are purchased from commercial firms (see, for instance, Pierre-Andre Chiappori 1992).

[22] There are rare exceptions to this law, as in the case of the backward-bending labor supply.

Individual Demand for Work-in-Marriage

Individual demand for Work-in-Marriage is similar to the demand for labor by firms and governments in the sense that it is a derived demand based on the productivity of labor and the value of the products of that labor. The gains from marriage to the employer of Work-in-Marriage – that is, the beneficiary of Work-in-Marriage – limit the amount that is likely to be transferred in return for work in this kind of household production. In the case of paid labor, it is easier to place a dollar value on labor than in the case of Work-in-Marriage. As is suggested by Chapters 9 and 13 in this book, it may not be easy, but there are some ways to estimate the value of labor in household production, including marital household production. It is an additional empirical challenge to estimate which portion of an individual's time in household production is actually Work-in-Marriage as opposed to household production that benefits only the self. Luckily, the usefulness of a market analysis of Work-in-Marriage does not depend on our ability to measure actual amounts of Work-in-Marriage, but on our ability to predict how factors influencing Work-in-Marriage markets influence the economy.

Demand for Work-in-Marriage varies with productivity, which is in turn a function of productive skills, or what economists call human capital. Factors influencing Work-in-Marriage productivity will therefore influence the demand for Work-in-Marriage. Some of these productive skills are spouse-specific – that is they benefit only one spouse and have zero value in case of divorce and remarriage. Other skills are forms of general marital human capital. One expects certain forms of education to contribute to marriage-general human capital – that is, human capital valuable in any marriage – embodied in an individual if the result is higher productivity in Work-in-Marriage.

Other factors that are likely to affect productivity in Work-in-Marriage and therefore demand for Work-in-Marriage include the amount of capital used in household production, and determinants of the value of the product. For instance, if Work-in-Marriage is work in parenting, the value of the children born to the marriage or of the quality of these children that is obtained with Work-in-Marriage will influence a provider's willingness to pay for a homemaker's Work-in-Marriage.[23]

---

[23] On the demand for women as baby producers, see, for example, Becker (1981) and Lena Edlund and Evelyn Korn (2002).

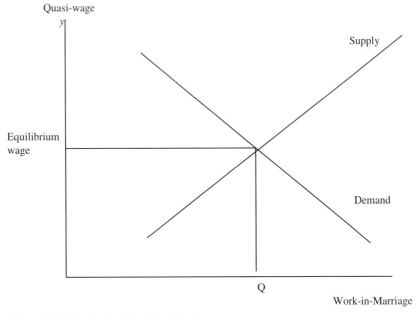

Figure 1.1. Market for Work-in-Marriage

The Market for Work-in-Marriage

Supply and demand by individual men and women willing to supply or demand goods produced in marriage are at the basis of aggregate demands and supplies of Work-in-Marriage and will establish equilibrium conditions for Work-in-Marriage suppliers – including a quasiwage y – and an aggregate level of employment in Work-in-Marriage. A marriage market conceived as a market for Work-in-Marriage is shown in Figure 1.1. Employment in Work-in-Marriage and quasiwages for labor in married household production are determined simultaneously with other aspects of production, including quantity and price in markets for labor, capital, and goods and services.[24] Economists call that a general equilibrium.

As in most models of the economy, it is assumed that the market process operates and that there is competition.[25] Competition in this case

---

[24] This involves a general equilibrium process. For a general equilibrium model including markets for married household production, see Grossbard-Shechtman (1984).

[25] The assumption that a (possibly implicit) price mechanism functions in marriage markets has the advantage of connecting marriage market analysis to other useful economic models of marriage that assume a price mechanism, such as search models (Keeley 1977;

is between various potential suppliers of Work-in-Marriage interested in marriage to the same person, and between various potential employers of Work-in-Marriage interested in marriage to the same Work-in-Marriage supplier. A constraint not found in regular labor markets is that monogamy is often imposed, implying matches between one employer and one supplier. Another constraint is that where one spouse does not specialize in Work-in-Marriage, a match between two given individuals, typically a man and a woman, has to involve matching supplies and demands of both persons' Work-in-Marriage.

We cannot perceive the workings of competitive markets for Work-in-Marriage by following market signals such as wage fluctuations or wage differences, as we can do in the case of labor markets. However, the assumptions behind competition appear to apply to markets for Work-in-Marriage as much as they do to regular labor markets. In both cases, prior to an employment or marriage relationship, workers and employers are interchangeable. In the case of labor supply, workers can join various firms; in the case of Work-in-Marriage, individuals can unite with various potential spouses. Related to this substitutability is the concept of general human capital that also applies to both work and Work-in-Marriage. If firm-related human capital can benefit various firms, it is called general human capital.[26] If marriage-related human capital can benefit various potential spouses, let us call it marriage-general human capital. Other productive skills of use in marital household production are spouse-specific – that is, they benefit only one spouse and have zero value in case of divorce and remarriage, which is the equivalent of firm-specific human capital in the case of work for firms.

Whenever aggregate supply or demand shifts in a market for Work-in-Marriage, the quasiwage for Work-in-Marriage is likely to change too. Here are a number of applications of this Work-in-Marriage market analysis:

Poor market conditions for Work-in-Marriage suppliers could explain why few people supply Work-in-Marriage and marriage is on the decline. Why do most industrialized nations experience a decline in marriage such as the one documented for the United States in Chapter 2? In large

---

see Chapter 2 in this book) and models about compensating differentials (see Grossbard-Shechtman 1984, 1993).

[26] Becker (1964) defines general human capital in contradistinction to firm-specific capital. Marital human capital – general or spouse-specific – was called marriage-specific human capital in Becker, Elizabeth M. Landes, and Robert T. Michael (1977). The term "spouse-specific" is introduced in Chapter 3 by Evelyn Lehrer.

numbers, contemporary young women are avoiding traditional marriage. Many young Western women, especially in Sweden and France and increasingly so in the United States, choose to cohabit rather than marry, and sometimes prefer to have children out of wedlock. Even though the divorce rate has not increased in recent years, it remains very high. It is possible that the decline in the popularity of marriage observed in the West resulted from increasing numbers of women in industrialized countries voting with their feet and walking away from supplying the Work-in-Marriage that previous generations of women had been supplying under conditions of low compensation. Traditionally, women were expected to supply this work out of love or fear, and the compensation they were offered played a small role.[27] They had no alternatives; no other jobs were available and there was no possibility of changing husbands. Women started walking away from marriage with the creation of earning opportunities outside marriage. In recent years, the decrease in the stigma of divorce has contributed to the divorce rate,[28] and more often than not women initiate divorces in the United States and many other Western countries. Low quasiwages for Work-in-Marriage may also lead some women to conclude that having children out of wedlock is a desirable option relative to having them in marriage. Others blame a defunct welfare program for high rates of out-of-wedlock births in the United States.[29]

Low remarriage rates for women could partially be the result of women's low willingness to supply Work-in-Marriage at existing quasiwages. Remarriage rates are much higher for men than for women. The traditional explanation for this differential is that men find it easier to remarry, as society places a greater premium on women's youth than on men's youth. This could be true. Another possible explanation is that men are more likely to find remarriage beneficial than is the case with women. It is well documented that men's earnings benefit from marriage (see Chapter 10) and it is also the case that marriage benefits men's health (see Waite and Gallagher 2000). In contrast, marriage does not benefit women's earnings or health. In fact, according to a number of indicators, married women appear to be less healthy than their single counterparts. Such benefits of marriage for men are consistent with the traditional role of women

---

[27] Shirley Burggraf (1999) has a similar explanation.

[28] Most of these are Western countries, but recently Japanese women have joined their Western counterparts in the industrialized world.

[29] An example is James Q. Wilson, formerly from UCLA and now at Pepperdine University (see Wilson 2002)

as Work-in-Marriage suppliers. However, why would women want to remarry in order to supply Work-in-Marriage unless they receive adequate
compensation? If both men and women are rational, and quasiwages for
remarrying women are too low, it would make sense for women to be less
interested in remarriage than men.

*To get people to supply more Work-in-Marriage requires higher quasi-
wages.* An economic approach leads to the recognition of possible ways
of raising the compensation for Work-in-Marriage and thereby lead both
men and women to work more in marriage and make happier families.
It may require new kinds of marriage contracts, for instance. Labor contracts help regulate labor relations in firms and specify wages and work
benefits.[30] Similarly, marriage contracts help regulate Work-in-Marriage
and specify elements of the compensation for Work-in-Marriage. It may
be more complicated in the case of Work-in-Marriage relations than in
the case of labor relations, given the more frequent instances of dual exchange of Work-in-Marriage and the absence of a wage system. (Labor
relations are often complex as well, especially in recent decades when
workers are increasingly paid in terms of ownership rights, which blurs
the distinction between worker and employer.)

*Egalitarian marriage is one way to get both spouses to supply Work-in-
Marriage.* One increasingly observes intramarriage exchanges between a
male homemaker and a female breadwinner, and between spouses who
both are homemakers and breadwinners. More and more men and women
moonlight in the sense that they are active in both paid labor and Work-
in-Marriage. In contemporary marriages, it is frequently the case that
Work-in-Marriage is supplied by both men and women, and it can be
supplied part-time or full-time. This form of egalitarianism may well en-
tice educated women into marriage, as it is a popular form of marriage
among the educated classes in the United States (see Myra H. Strober
and Agnes Miling Kaneko Chan 1998). Egalitarian marriage implies a
higher quasiwage for women's Work-in-Marriage than traditional marriage, where women do most of the work and often get very limited compensation. Even though the egalitarian lifestyle has been around for a
few decades, it does not seem to have been adopted by large numbers
of people. It may be hard to maintain when biological differences are
obviously relevant, such as when women are pregnant or nursing. Other

---

[30] More on the economics of marriage contracts can be found, for example, in
Leonore Weitzman (1981), Katharine Silbaugh (1996), and Grossbard-Shechtman and
Lemennicier (1999).

means of improving the happiness of Work-in-Marriage suppliers may be needed.

Education may be valued in markets for Work-in-Marriage. Competitive markets for marriage establish a premium for the skills (human capital) that individuals can apply to marital household production and that are of a general nature; that is, these skills will be valued by any substitutable man or woman who potentially participates in the same marriage market. In the case of labor demand, we know that education adds to general capital and therefore leads to higher wages. Likewise, in the case of Work-in-Marriage, we expect a Work-in-Marriage supplier's education to add to her or his quasiwage for Work-in-Marriage. If we recognize that women tend to be homemakers more than men, and that homemakers appreciate promises of stability more than providers, the finding that in the United States educated women are less likely to divorce, reported in Chapter 3, can be interpreted as an indication that education raises a woman's quasiwage for Work-in-Marriage, and therefore suggests that educated women are more productive in household production than their less educated counterparts. The same conclusion can be derived for Guatemalan women. In Guatemala, it was found that years of schooling increased an unskilled woman's chances of being in a formal union (relative to an informal union). In the context of poor villages in Guatemala, where job opportunities for women are very limited, women prefer a formal union to an informal one, and a formal union can be viewed as an aspect of the compensation for Work-in-Marriage. Years of schooling thus seem to raise the quasiwage for Work-in-Marriage in Guatemala as well as in the United States.[31] In the context of a polygamous society, a woman's higher quasiwage may take the form of exclusive access to a husband. A study of polygamy in Nigeria indicated that educated women are less likely to live in a polygamous household, again an indication that education tends to raise women's productivity in Work-in-Marriage.[32] One expects both men and women's productivity in Work-in-Marriage to benefit from education, although it is possible that not all levels of schooling equally contribute to productivity in Work-in-Marriage.[33]

---

[31] See Grossbard-Shechtman (1982) and Olivia Ekert-Jaffé and Catherine Sofer (1996).

[32] Grossbard (1976) shows that each year of schooling increases a Nigerian woman's likelihood of being the only wife in her household, while it decreases a Nigerian man's likelihood of having only one wife. The latter effect may involve an income effect.

[33] Casual observations lead me to conclude that higher education contributes considerably to productivity in Work-in-Marriage. To the extent that higher levels of education do not benefit women's marriageability, given the fact that so many highly educated women are

Next, I discuss how markets for Work-in-Marriage connect to the monetized economy.

Marriage Markets and the Monetized Economy

If more goods and services are produced within marriage, the aggregate demand for goods and services (which includes demand for substitutes for home-produced goods) will decrease. A macroeconomic model taking account of markets for Work-in-Marriage can affect the (monetized) economy via effects on the supply of paid labor or via effects on the demand for goods and services, including savings. Here are a few examples. They are illustrated with the help of Figure 1.1 depicting a market for Work-in-Marriage.

Example 1: Change in Taste for Parental Childcare. Consider an autonomous increase in a society's standards for parental supervision. This will cause an increase in demand for parental supervision produced by a spouse, one form of Work-in-Marriage that has a demand on the part of people who want children, know they need caretaking, and prefer to have a spouse who takes care of their children. Accordingly, there will be a shift to the right in the aggregate demand for Work-in-Marriage in Figure 1.1. In turn, this shift will cause more employment in the marital household economy and an increase in the quasiwage y. That is, spouses who want to benefit from increased household production without putting in the effort now need to pay more to obtain any level of household production. This result follows from the fact that the supply of Work-in-Marriage is upward sloping.[34]

Production in the monetized economy is a function of the supply of labor. As workers choosing between Work-in-Marriage and labor force

unmarried, this may not be for lack of marriage-related productivity of higher education but for lack of institutions that make quasiwages for Work-in-Marriage more proportional to the productivity of the worker. As a result, many educated women choose to stay unmarried. Certain countries are more adept at getting college-educated women to form couples (and supply Work-in-Marriage) than others, possibly as the result of a system that compensates Work-in-Marriage more according to its productivity. For instance, in France, women are more likely to be married, to bear children, and to participate in the labor force (a function of education) than in other European countries (Jeanne Fagnani 2000).

[34] The supply is expected to be upward sloping for the same reasons that the supply of monetized labor is upward sloping. These reasons include opportunity costs in terms of foregone leisure and a variety of entry points; some individuals are willing to work at very low compensation levels, while others have higher reservation wages.

participation react to an increase in y, they are expected to reduce their paid labor supply. As a result, aggregate production in the economy contracts. At the same time, the people who plan to use a spouse's household production work need to "pay" more for that work (higher y) and will have to work more in the monetized economy to afford to pay the higher y. It is likely that the net effect on the aggregate supply of paid labor and aggregate production is a decrease in monetized production, for the higher quasiwage to Work-in-Marriage suppliers can be offered not only in monetized form but also in the form of reciprocated Work-in-Marriage. Furthermore, increased taste for parental childcare in marriage causes a decrease in the demand for market substitutes for parental childcare, thus causing a decrease in demand for monetized consumption and consequently a decrease in aggregate demand. It thus follows that the monetized economy will contract as a result of higher standards for parental involvement in childcare.

Example 2: Change in Sex Ratio. The sex ratio is the ratio of men to women interacting in the same marriage markets. In an economy with traditional roles where only women are homemakers and men providers in marriage, an increase in the sex ratio (with no change in population size) causes an increase in demand for women's Work-in-Marriage and a decrease in the supply of women's Work-in-Marriage.[35] This leads to a higher quasiwage y for women interested in homemaking and therefore to a reduction in women's paid labor supply.[36] At the same time, an increase in sex ratio causes those who want to obtain Work-in-Marriage to have to work harder to earn the income enabling them to pay the higher y, and this may lead to increased labor supply, especially in the case of men who often are on the demand side in this market.[37] If the net effect is a decrease in aggregate hours of work in the monetized economy, aggregate production will shrink. Furthermore, the increase in sex ratio causes a

---

[35] It is assumed that the total population interacting in the marriage market remains constant, so an increase in the number of men is accompanied by a decrease in the number of women.

[36] This conclusion does not hold if success in marriage markets does not translate into more attractive conditions in household production in marriage relative to the opportunities available in the labor force. In Chapter 10, Shoshana Neuman and I examine some variations in women's labor supply that may be related to this factor.

[37] Aggregate demand is not likely to change if the change in quasiwage causes a change only in the composition of consumption, but not in total consumption. More on the distribution of consumption within marriage is found in Chapter 7.

redistribution of income from men to women, and this redistribution may also influence aggregate consumption.

If the net result is a decrease in aggregate production, it follows that if two economies are the same (for example, in terms of the same gender roles regarding marital household production), except for differences in sex ratio, the economy with the higher sex ratio will have a smaller monetized sector. Household production will not necessarily be different. In a traditional system, female homemakers will receive a larger share of the pie relative to male providers. These implications of sex ratio effects on the economy follow from the integration of marriage markets into macroeconomic analysis.

Example 3: Imposition of Monogamy. Some societies prohibit polygamy, whereas others do not. Comparing two traditional societies where women are homemakers and men are not, if polygamy is prohibited, this prohibition will reduce the demand for women's Work-in-Marriage. Therefore, the introduction of monogamy laws will reduce an economy's equilibrium quasiwage for women's Work-in-Marriage.[38] This explains why in polygamous countries it is more common that men pay bridewealth to women's guardians than is the case in monogamous countries.[39] This does not mean that women are better off under polygamy, for the higher value of women's Work-in-Marriage may lead men in polygamous societies to impose stricter limits on women's freedom.[40,41] In a society with traditional gender roles, the introduction of monogamy cuts the total employment of women in Work-in-Marriage and is likely to push some women into the paid labor force. This will cause higher aggregate production.

Macroeconomists typically would not have thought of how marital institutions such as polygamy laws or divorce laws could possibly affect aggregate production in the monetized economy, and total production including household production. It would not have occurred to them that sex ratios in marriage markets could have any effect on the economy.

---

[38] See Becker (1973, 1981), Grossbard (1978), and Grossbard-Shechtman (1993).

[39] See Grossbard (1978).

[40] Bergmann (1995) has criticized Becker for arguing that women are better off under polygamy. On the idea that polygamous societies are more likely to have men restricting the freedom of young people to marry with mates of their own choice, see Marcia Guttentag and Paul F. Secord (1983). To test economic models of marriage, we need to compare societies giving their young the same freedom to choose a mate, or at least restricting that freedom to the same extent.

[41] Religions have much to say on these matters. Islam permits polygamy, while Christianity does not.

Toward an Institutional Economics of Marriage

So far we have seen how marriage institutions can affect production. Production and other aspects of the economy can also influence the choice of marriage institutions. Economists have become increasingly aware of the calculus involved in collective behavior, much of their research categorized as "public choice economics." As recognized by the New Institutional Economics (see, for example, Douglass North 1981), institutions – including political and legal institutions – are changed by people with interests in these institutions. Societal norms regarding (gendered) marital roles at home and at work evolve from individual decisions regarding the use of time and income in the household and monetized economies. More and more people opt out of the traditional marriages that often forced women into supplying Work-in-Marriage. Accordingly, new marriage institutions are replacing the marriage institutions that framed such traditional marriages. Eventually, some of these changes may take the form of new laws about divorce or age at marriage. Religious institutions may also change, including customs and religious regulations regarding divorce. Economic analysis of collective behavior can help us explain changes in marital roles and in the relative importance of marriage versus cohabitation.[42] Economic analysis can also help individuals navigate within existing institutions and can help intellectuals in designing institutions that better serve the interests of society.

HOW THIS BOOK IS ORGANIZED

This book is organized according to four types of economic analyses of marriage: the economics of marriage formation and divorce, effects of marriage on spending, effects of marriage on work, and macrolevel analyses.

The Economics of Marriage and Divorce

In Chapter 2, Michael J. Brien and Michelle E. Sheran describe some recent historical trends on marriage and divorce in the United States They then survey economic theories of marriage other than the Work-in-Marriage theory presented in this chapter. They also review some empirical models that economists use primarily to explain the decision to marry, and they examine how the decision to marry interacts with related decisions (such as childbearing and labor supply).

---

[42] See Heer and Grossbard-Shechtman (1981) and Nancy Folbre (1994).

In Chapter 3, Evelyn L. Lehrer reviews the factors that influence the probability that a marriage will be dissolved. These include the characteristics of the spouses and their match, as well as the nature of the investments made by each partner during the course of their union. She notes that both premarital cohabitation and early entry into first marriage raise the odds of marital breakup, which poses a dilemma as young men and women who delay their first marriage tend to enter informal unions. Lehrer also compares the stability of remarriages to that of first unions, and finds that some variables influence the probability of divorce very differently depending on whether the union is a first or a higher-order marriage. She also discusses the importance for marital stability of certain factors that are specifically associated with remarriage, namely, the presence of stepchildren and non-transferable claims on assets accumulated during a previous union.

Another interesting conclusion of Lehrer is that, consistent with Becker et al.'s (1977) theory, prophecies of divorce tend to be self-fulfilling. Women who anticipate a high probability of divorce orient their efforts to labor force activities, thereby increasing the risk of an eventual breakup. Similarly, couples who have reasons to believe their marriage is unstable (such as interfaith couples) limit their investments in spouse-specific human capital, a behavior that raises the probability of a subsequent dissolution.

Three paths through which government policies influence marital choices are examined by Leslie Whittington and James Alm in Chapter 4: cash transfers to the poor, income taxes, and divorce laws. It turns out that in the United States many public policies are some distance from a neutral treatment of marriage. This is mostly unintentional, as lawmakers clearly did not mean to discourage marriage when they enacted policies that increased taxes on married couples or that rewarded welfare mothers for the absence of a spouse.

Effects of Marriage on Income Uses

Marriage institutions can affect the economy because so many decisions regarding consumption and savings are made in marriages. This section of the book covers how people spend their income, and accumulate wealth, and deals with one particular kind of government spending.

Chapter 5, by Frances Woolley, examines how marriage affects personal finances, her focus being a particular question: Who in a marriage controls the money? The chapter also contains a useful survey of recent developments in the study of intrahousehold resource allocation. Using a new Canadian survey of families with children, Woolley does not find a systematic pro-male or pro-female bias in household finances. However she does find that, as predicted by theory, partners with greater incomes have greater control over money, younger spouses do better, and less income pooling occurs when one partner, especially the man, has been married before.

Chapter 6, by Joseph P. Lupton and James P. Smith, explores the relationship between marital status and asset accumulation. The authors report large positive marital differentials in assets and savings. Married couples apparently save significantly more than other households, a fact that is not solely related to their higher incomes nor to the simple aggregation of two individuals' wealth. As a result, married couples have significantly more household wealth than all other household types. If marriage is related to household savings, the sharp decline in the fraction of American households who are married may be part of the reason for the secular fall in U.S. private savings rates.

If children are an important reason why people marry and stay married, it follows that divorce will have important consequences for household spending. In Chapter 7, Andrea H. Beller and John W. Graham write about the economic determinants and consequences of child-support payments. This includes an analysis of child-support payments as an income source over time, the underlying economic behavior of custodial and non-custodial parents that determines whether and how much child support is paid, and the economic consequences for the parents and children of receiving child support. Beller and Graham find that marriage dramatically increases the chances that a child-support payment will be obtained in case of separation. This is one of the gains from marriage from the perspective of a prospective custodial parent. It is puzzling that even though only 17 percent of never-married mothers of one-year-olds received any child support, large numbers of never-married mothers are having children in the United States. Even though the proportion of out-of-wedlock births has recently decreased, it remains high by international standards.[43]

At least one finding reported by Beller and Graham suggests that marriage market conditions influence the likelihood of receiving child support: Custodial mothers who receive child support have higher incomes than mothers who do not have an award.[44] With respect to consequences

---

[43] See Grossbard, Ekert-Jaffé, and Lemennicier (2002).

[44] In terms of a marriage market theory, this finding could indicate that women with higher incomes are also more likely to obtain a positive quasiwage for their Work-in-Marriage

of child support, Beller and Graham report that child support benefits children, especially their educational attainment, above and beyond its role as income.

Modern states invest in their children in many ways. Many government programs transfer funds directly to families with children. In recent decades, such cash welfare programs have primarily benefited unmarried mothers. In Chapter 8, John Fitzgerald shows how in the United States women with better marriage prospects have spent less time on welfare, thereby providing evidence of a macrolevel link between marriage markets and the macroeconomy. Marriage prospects are measured in terms of ratios of marriageable men and women (sex ratios). To the extent that it is negatively related to marriage prospects and likelihood of marriage, and that much household production occurs in marriage, government spending on welfare programs for single parents may discourage consumption of non-commercial home-produced goods. It is possible, however, that single parents spend more time in household production than some married parents, at least in Australia (see Chapter 13).

Effects of Marriage on Time Uses

This part of the book examines effects of marriage on time uses: work and leisure, work being either Work-in-Marriage or work devoted to the production of market goods and services. Chapter 9 deals with household production, while Chapters 10 through 12 deal with paid work.

In Chapter 9, Joni Hersch examines labor market and legal issues associated with time spent on household production. Married women's willingness to incur an opportunity cost when performing household production is one of the indications that housework has real economic value.

Since economic loss in the event of disability or wrongful death includes the value of lost home services, valuing household production time is an essential component of personal injury litigation. Similarly, in many divorce cases, the wife's main claim to the assets accumulated during marriage is her contribution to household production. To demonstrate the salient legal issues involved in the impact of household production on divorce, Hersch discusses the *Wendt v. Wendt* divorce case, in which Lorna Wendt claimed that her role as a corporate wife entitled her to a larger share of the marital assets than conventionally awarded.

if we interpret the actual payment of child support as compensation for childcare Work-in-Marriage paid after divorce.

Three chapters – Chapters 10 to 12 – deal with the link between household production, mostly by married women, and labor markets. The authors' findings carry implications both for policy and for business strategies regarding workers' recruitment. In Chapter 10, Shoshana Neuman and I present some recent facts on marriage and the labor force participation of men and women in the United States. We report on marital differentials in the labor force participation of men and women of childbearing age. Marital differentials tend to be negative for women – that is, married women participate less in the paid labor force than their unmarried counterparts, whereas the opposite is true for men. Marital differentials are larger among those employed full-time year-round than among workers with less commitment to the labor force. Reinforcing the conclusions of Chapter 8 on exit and entry from and into welfare recipiency, we also find that sex ratios affect women's labor supply: Better marriage prospects discourage women's labor supply.

Chapter 10 also reports some recent findings on marriage and wages. Marital differentials in men's wages tend to be positive, and research indicates that at least some of those differentials result from the effects of marriage on earnings. Most research does not find marital differentials in women's wages.

Chapter 11 by Rachel Connelly and Jean Kimmel discusses marriage, labor supply, and childcare. Based on their analysis of the Survey of Income and Program Participation (SIPP), Connelly and Kimmel report important marital differentials in the propensity to use childcare by relatives, the probability of working part-time, the amount paid for childcare, and the sensitivity of employment to changes in the cost of childcare.

In Chapter 12, Elizabeth Field-Hendrey and Linda N. Edwards present an economic analysis of marriage and home-based work. They analyze a subsample of the 1990 Census of population of the United States and find that compared to unmarried women, married women are more likely to choose home-based paid work. The greater home responsibilities that married women often take upon themselves, creating more scope for combining the needs of the home and family with home-based work, may explain some of this marital differential. Field-Hendrey and Edwards also find that married women tend to have personal characteristics that are associated with high costs of working – small children, living in a rural area, living on a farm – and that these characteristics also correlate with the probability that they will choose to work at home. Marriage does not raise the probability of home-based work for black women, possibly because black women face a less advantageous marriage market than

with the existing statistics of Gross National Product (GNP). That chapter presents estimates of Gross Household Product (GHP). It is estimated that in Australia in the mid-1990s, married households produced 75 percent of GHP. It is logical to assume that Australia is not so different from other countries, and that much household production occurs in marriages in most of the world.[46]

Divorce and Marriage Laws. There is much concern with the high levels of divorce currently observed in the United States and many other countries. This concern is one of the factors explaining a growing interest in the study of divorce laws, principally by legal scholars. Chapters 3 and 4 report on some of the effects of divorce laws on divorce rates. Chapter 3 presents an impressive list of factors that influence divorce rates based on microlevel studies. Most of these studies do not explore the effects of divorce laws. In contrast, the macrolevel studies reported in Chapter 4 take account of variations in divorce laws but consider very few microlevel factors that may affect aggregate numbers and need to be controlled when assessing the impact of divorce laws. The comparison of divorce laws is mostly about the effect of passage to no-fault divorce in the United States. Economic analysis can be applied to comparisons of other aspects of divorce laws, as well as to comparisons between countries.[47] Divorce laws need to consider possible implications for household production as argued in Chapter 9. Chapter 7 dealing with child support is also relevant to this issue.

The U.S. legal system currently regulates transactions in marriage very differently from the way it regulates other transactions. By analyzing the institutions regulating marriage and divorce in ways that are more similar to the ways that the Western world approaches business issues, we may considerably enrich the level of national discussion about marriage and family values. One of the reasons why marital institutions are treated so differently from business institutions is that U.S. law assumes that production in marriage is motivated primarily by emotions rather than by economic forces. The similarities between firms and marriages emphasized in this book and its economic logic lead one to question our current

[46] As a country with a legal system based on common law, it is even possible that in Australia less household production is produced in marriage than in comparable countries with community property systems of division of assets at divorce (see Grossbard-Shechtman, Ekert- Jaffé, and Lemennicier 2002).

[47] See Yoram Weiss and Robert T. Willis (1993) and Jeffrey S. Gray (1998) for comparisons of other aspects of divorce laws in the United States, and Grossbard-Shechtman, Ekert-Jaffé, and Lemennicier (2002) for a preliminary comparison across countries.

white women. As a result, they have less of an incentive to engage in married home production and to find home-based paid work compatible with such production.

Marriage and the Macroeconomy

In Chapter 13, Duncan Ironmonger and Faye Soupourmas present national accounts of household production for Australia. They report that in Australia in the mid-1990s, the unmonetized household economy produced about 20 percent more valuable economic output than the monetized market economy, and that the imputed income resulting from household production was 67 percent more than household disposable income. They show that married households contained 74 percent of the adult population and produced 75 percent of GHP (Gross Household Product). A very large contribution to GHP from single-parent households explained the high proportion of GHP produced by unmarried households. Chapter 13 also discusses the comparative contributions of women and men at various stages of life – with and without children, younger and older, and married and unmarried. It concludes that marriage makes for only small differences in total work, independent of life stage and the number of adults. The apparent positive effect of marital status on market work can be explained by age and gender structural differences between married and unmarried households. The differences between men and women in paid work are balanced by compensating differences in unpaid work.

Given that in most countries traditional national accounting practices include only paid labor and ignore work devoted to household production, it follows that a switch from household labor to paid labor will be associated with an increase in official measures of national production. Had Western countries routinely taken account of the contribution of household production to their national product, less economic growth would have been observed as a result of the dramatic increase in the labor force participation of married women noted in recent decades.

Parental investments in children are an important reason why people save. Children are also a major motivator of people's household production and a major reason why people marry.[45] In Chapter 14, Shirley

[45] This is also widely recognized by economists writing on marriage, including Becker (1973) and Richard A. Posner (1992).

Burggraf explores some implications of parental investments for macro-economic theory and policy. What if macroeconomic modelers focused as much on family investment as on business investment? This chapter presents an argument for taking the investment role of parental partner-ship very seriously and for economic policies that support marriage com-mensurately with its contribution to economic performance. The financial dimensions of parental investment are outlined in a way that highlights the family's role as a major institution regulating investments. The chapter highlights the enormous gap between macroeconomic consequences of parental investment versus private economic signals to parents, a discon-nection that helps account for the limited significance of family institutions in macroeconomics. The chapter discusses the role of marriage in facili-tating parental investment and sketches some thoughts about modeling marital partnership into macroeconomic models.

PRACTICAL IMPLICATIONS

This book is unique in its emphasis on practical implications from eco-nomic analyses of marriage. Readers will find implications regarding taxes, savings, social security, employment, poverty, national accounting, and divorce laws. Guidelines for national accounting implications for busi-ness are also included.

Implications for Policy

Taxes. Chapter 4 shows how in the U.S. income taxation is not neutral with respect to marriage. Instead, the tax code often creates penalties or sub-sidies for marriage. Other chapters in this book that contain implications for tax policy include Chapters 9, 13, and 14 on household production. Treated implicitly in Chapter 13 is the important question of taxing the household economy relative to the monetized economy. Given that time in household production is not taxed, current policies probably subsi-dize household production. From the chapters on labor supply, we can also infer insights on the effect of tax laws that differentially target vari-ous forms of employment, such as taxes differentiating between full-time and part-time work (these forms of work are contrasted in Chapter 10), and between home-based and on-site work (forms of work covered in Chapter 12). Inferences on the advantages and disadvantages of tax de-ductions for at-home childcare can be derived from Chapter 11, a chapter that can also help policy makers decide whether childcare subsidies are desirable, and if so, help them decide the optimal form for such subsidies.

Government Programs. Many parts of this book are relevant to policy makers interested in alleviating poverty. The following are a few examples. The U.S. government has spent considerable effort to save welfare funds by getting non-custodial fathers to pay child support. Chapter 7 can help in assessing the effectiveness of this effort, designing new ways to encourage non-custodial parents to meet their support obligations, and establishing guidelines for child-support payments that more closely approximate the true costs of raising a child.

Chapter 8 can help us conceive of ways to reduce welfare programs by encouraging marriage. It mentions two policy implications. First, it follows that one does not need to resort to purely cultural explanations to explain racial differences in welfare use: African American women face lower po-tential spouse availability, and this helps explain why African American women tend to stay on welfare longer than white women. Second, since higher rates of low-income male employment improve the marriageable pool for low-income women, policies that improve men's labor market prospects have the indirect effect of reducing welfare use by single and married mothers. Chapter 4 reminds us that welfare policies involve not only direct fiscal costs but also indirect costs due to their effects on house-hold production and marriage.

Savings and Investments. A strong economy needs investments. Personal savings are a major source of financing for such investments. Chapter 6 reports a generally overlooked positive effect of marriage on savings. If Lupton and Smith, the authors of Chapter 6, are right, it may be desirable to institute pro-marriage policies in order to encourage savings. A related policy recommendation is found in Chapter 14: It may be wise for a na-tion to promote marriage to the extent that compared to single parents, married couples invest more in their children and that such investments benefit the nation's human capital.

National Accounting. As stated in Ironmonger (1989),

Households work. Yet the work that they do and the very large volume of eco-nomic production that results from this work are consistently ignored in national statistics. Households employ more people for more hours in useful productive work than do business and government. However, the most commonly used na-tional measures of employment and work exclude unpaid employment and work in households, not because it is without value, but merely because it is not paid.

Chapter 13 presents plenty of ammunition to those who want regu-lar official statistics of the value of household production to compare

divorce laws in a more fundamental sense than most previous discussions steeped in the world of religion or law. Western values and laws have been very successful at transforming the way the world does business, but its success at maintaining individual commitments to family values is less impressive. It is worth trying to approach family values with the same tools that have accomplished so much in other areas – the tools of logic, reason, and recognition of the existence of market forces.

Implications for Firms

Firms depend on what households decide with respect to consumption, labor supply, and investments, so they also have to gain from a better understanding of the effects of marriage institutions on individual behavior. Firms depend on households for the supply of labor and other factors of production, as well as for the purchase of their products. As far as labor supply is concerned, managers want to know how many workers with particular productivity-related characteristics can be expected to enter certain occupations or comply with certain job requirements. These supply factors influence both firms' ability to fill vacancies and the wages they can expect to pay. For instance, to the extent that certain categories of workers earn more when married due to a productivity-enhancing contribution of marriage (see Chapter 10), firms may be justified in preferring married workers for such jobs. Also, firms may want to pay more attention to the variety of work arrangements they offer to their workers in terms of compatibility with housework and other household production responsibilities.

One of the most important issues relating marriage to labor supply is the issue of childcare. The relative availability of childcare facilities and subsidies to married and unmarried parents is an important factor affecting not only individual parents and policy makers, but also the firms that depend on the supply of workers with different characteristics. Chapter 11 reports that the employment of single mothers is more sensitive to the price of childcare than that of married mothers. This implies that personnel recruiting strategies such as the building of cheap day care centers may be more successful in attracting single mothers than in attracting married mothers. Depending on whether the type of worker the firm is recruiting is more likely to be married or single, a firm's childcare strategy will vary in effectiveness.

A strategy that may work better for firms trying to attract the labor supply of married women is a strategy encouraging home-based work, because compared to unmarried women, married women are more likely to choose home-based rather than on-site wage work (see Chapter 12). Businesses may want to calibrate their recruiting strategies not only on the basis of marital status, but also taking account of marriage market conditions. As far as marital status is concerned, if businesses want to attract married women, they may offer more home-based work, especially in an area with a traditionally minded population; home-based work is more compatible with the kind of married household labor that women provide in traditional marriages, and where such marriages are more common it is more likely that women will be interested in home-based work. Given that firms are aiming at married workers, they may want to take account of marriage market conditions; if these conditions favor women, it may take higher salaries or better benefit packages to attract female workers. If these conditions favor men, it may take higher male wages and more benefits such as male-oriented workplace amenities to attract male workers who would be less eager to sacrifice their quality of life in order to earn the income often needed to attract and keep a wife.

This book also offers interesting implications for the supply of capital. Readers interested in financial issues will be most interested in Chapter 6 which deals with savings. From a macroeconomic perspective, interest rates are a function of both the demand and the supply of capital. Economies accustomed to encouraging premarital savings as preparation for marriage will benefit from a larger supply of capital, which brings down interest rates. The popularity of this custom in Italy and Belgium helps explain why these two countries have higher savings rates than most other Western countries.[48]

Marriage institutions also have a major impact on consumption patterns. If marriages involve extensive home cooking, for instance, restaurants can expect less business. The higher the quality of home-cooked meals, the more restaurants have to excel in order to attract customers. This book touches only the surface of how marriage influences consumption patterns, the chapters most relevant to these concerns being Chapters 5–7 and 9.

Broader Implications

This book also carries implications for individual decision making and for institutional and cultural change. When placing emphasis on romantic

---

[48] See Grossbard-Shechtman (forthcoming). This article also presents a few interesting ideas on marriage and consumption.

love, Western societies promote simplistic theories of marriage such as those behind the tale of Cinderella and Prince Charming. These fantasy-based theories foster the illusion that when it comes to marital love, there is no need to try one's best and possibly compete. People develop ideas that they are forever irreplaceable, that their foot is as unique as Cinderella's, and that only one shoe will fit. People who erect such illusionary barriers to competition from alternative candidates for marriage are more likely to give up on marriage if they do not get what they want or to fall apart if problems arise after marriage. Fairy tale addicts and other naïve thinkers will tend to underinvest in the skills that help marriages work, such as communication skills, a generous character, or a willingness to grow and listen. Furthermore, people become careless when choosing a mate, losing track of the qualities that really make a marriage work and using suboptimal search strategies. As a result, in the United States and most other Western countries, people undermarry: They stay single too long and their marriages break up with unnecessary easiness, often harming a couple's children.[49]

The same danger lurks behind lofty theories encouraged by religions, such as theories about soul mates who are uniquely meant for each other and nobody else. Again, the danger with such theory is that it may discourage a person from investing in the skills that make marriages work and help identify an optimal match.

Excessive idealism and lack of recognition of basic economic forces such as the law of supply also characterize some Western legal scholars specializing in marriage and divorce. For instance, legal scholars who deplore "opportunistic" behavior in marriage delay the long overdue rationalization of divorce laws (see Chapter 9).[50] They consider it a problem if people respond to economic incentives in the case of household production, but not in the case of production occurring outside the home. Those who criticize opportunistic behavior in marriage ignore some powerful universal forces: people's deep-seated desire to better their lives – the motivation of self-interest – and the forces of competition, another motor driving people to better themselves.

Relative to Western societies, Eastern societies encourage their youth to be more careful in choosing a mate and to prepare themselves more systematically for the competitive search process that typically helps people find mates that suit them better. This often requires major parental involvement, as is typically the case even in Westernized families in

---

[49] See Waite and Gallagher (2000).
[50] See, for example, Lloyd Cohen (1987).

Japan, Korea, or India. Segments of Western societies behave more like people in the Far East than average Westerners. This includes natives from the Far East living in the West. It also includes segmented religious groups such as Torah-observant Jews in the United States. The latter often rely on matchmaking services and parental help in choosing a mate, indicating a more economic approach than that prevalent among secularized Jews.[51]

IN CONCLUSION

I hope that this book will open the eyes of policy makers and firms as to how marriage affects the economy. Most of all, I hope that *Marriage and the Economy* helps more people realize that like all other productive activities, what people produce in marriage requires hard work and thoughtful planning. It has become a cliché to complain that people can get a marriage license with less difficulty than they can get a driver's license or a gun permit, even though bad marriages can be toxic and occasionally frame behavior that endangers society. This book offers readers some new ideas as to how to address the decline of marriage without expecting a return to some of the quasifeudal marriage institutions of the past. Until a century ago, most Western women had very few options other than supplying their Work-in-Marriage to a man who would become their husband for life. If their husband was abusive, they had very limited options under a system that made divorce almost impossible. In country after country, laws regulating employment and divorce have been liberalized, and women are voting with their feet by asserting their claims for happiness, increasingly rejecting traditional marriage. This trend is expected to continue and to spread to continents where women currently live in conditions similar to those found in the West a hundred years ago.

I personally have a stake in the institution of marriage and see no real alternative to it. It is this concern for marriage that led to my own involvement with the economics of marriage and to my appreciation of the economic analyses performed by the other authors contributing to

---

[51] Traditional Judaism encourages exclusive monogamous marriage and discourages extramarital relations, which places Judaism on the idealistic side of the crosscultural spectrum, together with the other major religions. At the same time, traditional Judaism encourages investment in skills that make people more marriageable and that lead to a more systematic search for a mate, two elements of an economic approach. Traditional Jewish sources call these two components of the process of marital preparation *hishtadlut*, which in Hebrew means a time investment (see Yehudah Lebovits 1987).

this book. The following pages will be of interest not only to those who share my commitment to the institution of marriage, but also to those who oppose marriage. There are ideas for policy makers and ideas for businesses interested in selling products or hiring workers. There is fruit for thought for those who plan to marry or to divorce, those who want their children to marry well and wonder what they can do to help them be prepared, and those who are currently married and are trying to make their marriage work.

Academia has not given the economics of marriage much room to develop. In the last thirty years, those of us who entered this specialty have encountered many difficulties. One of the reasons that I remained in this field is my conviction that the economic analysis of marriage has much to offer to those who try to build a better world. I am glad that my colleagues who contributed to this book participated in this project, even though they may not necessarily share all the views expressed in this introduction. It is our hope that the various ideas and themes developed in this volume will encourage additional research on the economics of marriage and divorce.

REFERENCES

Becker, Gary S. *Human Capital.* New York: Columbia University Press, 1964.
———. "A Theory of Marriage: Part I." *Journal of Political Economy*, 1973, *81*, pp. 813–46.
———. "A Theory of Marriage: Part II." *Journal of Political Economy*, 1974, *82*, pp. 511–26.
———. "Altruism, Egoism, and Genetic Fitness: Economics and Sociobiology." *Journal of Economic Literature*, 1976, *14*, pp. 817–26.
———. *A Treatise on the Family*, 1st ed., Cambridge, MA: Harvard University Press, 1981.
Becker, Gary, Landes, Elizabeth M. and Michael, Robert T. "An Economic Analysis of Marital Instability." *Journal of Political Economy*, 1977, *85*(6), pp. 1141–87.
Beller, Andrea H. and Kiss, D. Elizabeth. "On the Contribution of Hazel Kyrk to Family Economics." Paper presented at the meetings of the Society for the Advancement of Behavioral Economics, San Diego, June 1999.
Bergmann, Barbara. "Becker's Theory of the Family: Preposterous Conclusions." *Feminist Economics*, 1995, *1*, pp. 141–50.
Bergstrom, Theodore C. "A Survey of Theories of the Family," in Mark R. Rosenzweig and Oded Stark, eds., *Handbook of Population and Family Economics*, New York, NY: Elsevier Science, 1997.
Burggraf, Shirley P. *The Feminine Economy and Economic Man.* Reading, MA: Perseus Books, 1999.

Cabrillo, Francisco. *The Economics of the Family and Family Policy*. London: Edward Elgar, 1999.

Carlin, Paul S. "Intra-Family Bargaining and Time Allocation." *Research in Population Economics*, 1991, *7*, pp. 215–43.

Cherry, Robert. "Rational Choice and the Price of Marriage." *Feminist Economics*, 1998, *4*, pp. 27–49.

Chiappori, Pierre-Andre. "Collective Labor Supply and Welfare." *Journal of Political Economy*, 1992, *100*, pp. 437–67.

Chiswick, Carmel and Lehrer, Evelyn. "On Marriage-Specific Capital: Its Role as a Determinant of Remarriage." *Journal of Population Economics*, 1990, *3*, pp. 193–213.

Cigno, Alejandro. *Economics of the Family*. Oxford, UK: Clarendon Press, 1991.

Cohen, Lloyd. "Marriage, Divorce, and Quasi Rents; or, 'I Gave Him the Best Years of My Life.'" *Journal of Legal Studies*, 1987, *16*, pp. 267–303.

Edlund, Lena and Korn, Evelyn. "A Theory of Prostitution." *Journal of Political Economy*, 2002, *110*(1), pp. 181–214.

Ekert-Jaffé, Olivia and Sofer, Catherine. "Formal versus Informal Marriage: Explaining Factors," in *Evolution or Revolution in European Population*, Actes du IXème Congrès de l'EAPS, 1996.

Fagnani, Jeanne. *Un Travail et des Enfants*. Paris: Bayard, 2000.

Folbre, Nancy. *Who Pays for the Kids? Gender and the Structures of Constraint*. London: Routledge, 1994.

Gray, Jeffrey S. "Divorce-Law Changes Household Bargaining, and Married Women's Labor Supply." *American Economic Review*, June 1998, *88*(3), pp. 628–42.

Gronau, Reuben. "Leisure, Home Production, and Work – The Theory of the Allocation of Time Revisited." *Journal of Political Economy*, 1977, *85*, pp. 1099–124.

Grossbard, Amyra. "An Economic Analysis of Polygamy: The Case of Maiduguri." *Current Anthropology*, December 1976, *17*, pp. 701–7.

_____. "Towards a Marriage between Economics and Anthropology and a General Theory of Marriage," *American Economic Review*, 1978, *86*, pp. 33–7.

Grossbard-Shechtman, Amyra. "A Theory of Marriage Formality: The Case of Guatemala." *Economic Development and Cultural Change*, 1982, *30*, pp. 813–30.

_____. "A Theory of Allocation of Time in Markets for Labor and Marriage." *Economic Journal*, 1984, *94*, pp. 863–82.

Grossbard-Shechtman, Shoshana Amyra. *On the Economics of Marriage: A Theory of Marriage, Labor, and Divorce*. Boulder, CO: Westview Press. 1993.

_____. "Marriage Market Models," in M. Tommasi and K. Ierulli, eds., *The New Economics of Human Behavior*. Cambridge, UK: Cambridge University Press, 1995.

_____. "Theories of Marriage," in Janice Peterson and Margaret Lewis, eds., *The Elgar Companion to Feminist Economics*. London: Edward Elgar, 1999.

_____. "Economics and Sociology of Work and Marriage," in Shoshana Grossbard-Shechtman and Christopher Clague, eds., *The Expansion of Economics*. M. E. Sharpe, 2001a.

———. "The New Home Economics at Columbia and Chicago." *Feminist Economics*, 2001b, *7*, pp. 103–30.

———. "A Consumer Theory with Competitive Markets for Work in Marriage." *Journal of Socio-Economics*, forthcoming.

Grossbard-Shechtman, Shoshana, Olivia Ekert-Jaffé and Lemennicier, Bertrand. "Property Division at Divorce and Demographic Behavior: An Economic Analysis and International Comparison." Paper presented at the American Economic Meetings, Atlanta, January 2002.

Grossbard-Shechtman, Shoshana and Lemennicier, Bertrand. "Marriage Contracts and the Law and Economics Movement: A Critical View from an Austrian Perspective." *Journal of Socio-Economics*, 1999, *28*, pp. 665–90.

Guttentag, Marcia and Secord, Paul F. *Too Many Women: The Sex Ratio Question.* Beverly Hills, CA: Sage Publications, 1983.

Heer, David M. and Grossbard-Shechtman, Amyra. "The Impact of the Female Marriage Squeeze and the Contraceptive Revolution on Sex Roles and the Women's Liberation Movement in the United States, 1960 to 1975." *Journal of Marriage and the Family*, 1981, *43*, pp. 49–65.

Ironmonger, Duncan. "Preface," in Duncan Ironmonger, ed., *Households Work: Productive Activities, Women and Income in the Household Economy.* Sydney: Allen & Unwin, 1989.

Keeley, Michael C. "The Economics of Family Formation." *Economic Inquiry*, 1977, *15*, pp. 238–50.

———. "An Analysis of the Age Pattern of First Marriage." *International Economic Review*, 1979, *20*, pp. 527–44.

Lebovits, Yehudah. *Shidduchim and Zivugim.* Spring Valley, NY: Targum/Feldheim, 1987.

Lemennicier, Bertrand. *Le Marché du Mariage et de la Famille.* Paris: Presses Universitaires de France, 1988.

Lord, William. *Household Dynamics: Economic Growth and Policy.* Oxford, UK: Oxford University Press, 2002.

Manser, Marilyn and Brown, Murray. "Marriage and Household Decision Making: A Bargaining Analysis." *International Economic Review,* February 1980, *21*(1), pp. 31–44.

McElroy, Marjorie B. "The Empirical Content of Nash-Bargained Household Behavior." *Journal of Human Resources,* 1990, *25*, pp. 559–83.

McElroy, Marjorie B. and Horney, Mary Jean. "Nash Bargained Household Decisions: Toward a Generalization of the Theory of Demand." *International Economic Review,* June 1981, *22*(2), pp. 333–49.

North, Douglass C. *Structure and Change in Economic History.* New York: W. W. Norton, 1981.

Peters, Elizabeth H. "Marriage and Divorce: Informational Constraints and Private Contracting." *American Economic Review*, 1986, *76*, pp. 437–54.

Pollak, Robert A. "A Transaction Cost Approach to Families and Households." *Journal of Economic Literature,* 1985, *23*, pp. 581–608.

Posner, Richard A. *Sex and Reason.* Cambridge, MA: Harvard University Press, 1992.

Robbins, Lionel. "On the Elasticity of Demand for Income in Terms of Efforts." *Economica*, 1930, *10*, pp. 123–9.

Silbaugh, Katharine. "Turning Labor into Love: Housework and the Law." *Northwestern University Law Review*, 1996, *91*(1), pp. 1–86.

Sofer, Catherine. *La Division du Travail entre Hommes et Femmes*. Paris: Economica, 1985.

Strober, Myra H. and Chan, Agnes Miling Kaneko. "Husbands, Wives, and Housework: Graduates of Stanford and Tokyo Universities." *Feminist Economics*, 1998, *4*(3), pp. 97–128.

Waite, Linda J. and Gallagher, Maggie. *The Case for Marriage*. New York: Doubleday, 2000.

Weiss, Yoram. "The Formation and Dissolution of Families: Why Marry? Who Marries Whom? and What Happens Upon Divorce," in Mark Rosenzweig and Oded Stark, eds., *Handbook of Population and Family Economics*. New York: Elsevier, 1997, pp. 81–123.

Weiss, Yoram, and Willis, Robert T. "Transfers among Divorced Couples: Evidence and Interpretation" *Journal of Labor Economics*, October 1993, pp. 629–79.

Weitzman, Leonore. *The Marriage Contract: Spouses, Lovers and the Law*. New York: Free Press, 1981.

Wilson, James Q. "The Decline of Marriage." "Insight" section, *San Diego Union-Tribune*, February 17, 2002, pp. G1, G6.

Woolley, Frances. "Getting the Better of Becker." *Feminist Economics*, 1996, *2*, pp. 114–20.

Yi, Yun-Ae. "Margaret G. Reid: Life and Achievements." *Feminist Economics*, 1996, *2*, pp. 17–36.

PART I

THE ECONOMICS OF MARRIAGE AND DIVORCE

TWO

The Economics of Marriage and Household Formation

Michael J. Brien and Michelle E. Sheran

The institution of marriage plays a central role in the lives of most people. It is therefore understandable that the decisions of who and when to marry are usually afforded careful deliberation. Social scientists have long been interested in this behavior in part because the decision to form a relationship is a fundamental aspect of human behavior. Virtually everyone in our society has contact with the institution. In the United States, for example, less than 5 percent of persons aged sixty-five and above have never been married (U.S. Bureau of the Census 1998). Marriage has also been of interest to researchers and policy makers because of its strong connection to other important actions taken by individuals. Some have argued that marriage is like an insurance policy in that it offers protection against poor health, financial insecurity, and deviant behaviors (Linda Waite 1995). The decision to marry, and to remain married, is highly intertwined with other choices, such as how many children to have and whether to work in the labor market.

For a number of reasons, the study of marriage is particularly interesting at this point in time. One primary reason is the large changes in demographic behavior that have taken place in recent decades. Some have suggested that the institution of marriage changed in the second half of the twentieth century. Demographic trends make a strong case for this point. The timing and manner in which relationships are formed and dissolved have changed dramatically. Individuals are marrying later in life, are more likely to live with a partner outside of a formal marriage,

We thank Shoshana Grossbard-Shechtman for many detailed comments and suggestions.

and are more likely to end a marriage. Behaviors related to marriage have also changed. The most notable change has been the large increase in the fraction of children born out of wedlock. Given these changes, the theoretical and empirical analysis of marriage and related behaviors has become even more important.

This chapter surveys several theoretical and empirical models used primarily by economists to explain the decision to marry. Economists have brought to the study of marriage analytic tools that have traditionally been applied to other economic behaviors. Specific attention is given to the role of marriage markets and the interaction of marriage with related decisions (such as childbearing and labor supply). To provide context for this study, we begin by surveying some of the demographic trends in this area.

DEMOGRAPHIC TRENDS

Around the world, there have been dramatic changes in marriage and divorce patterns over the past fifty years. This section begins by describing two of the major changes in marriage that occurred in the United States: Men and women spend a smaller proportion of their lives married, and increasing numbers are choosing to live together outside of a formal marriage. Because of its central place, we also describe the changes in fertility behavior. While much of the data covered in this chapter are from the United States, it is important to recognize that there is considerable variation across cultures. We conclude this section with a brief discussion of this crosscultural variation.

Delayed Marriage

In the United States, a pronounced trend toward delayed marriage emerged during the second half of the twentieth century. In the 1950s, the first-marriage rate for women was approximately 160 per 1,000 unmarried women. This rate declined only slightly over the next twenty years. In the early 1970s, however, the first-marriage rate began to drop rapidly. By the mid-1990s, this rate was only above half of what it was fifty years earlier. As shown in Figure 2.1, between 1950 and 1998, the percentage of never-married women age twenty to twenty-four more than doubled, from 32.3 percent to 70.3 percent. The percentage of never-married women age twenty-five to twenty-nine almost tripled, from 13.3 percent to 38.6 percent. Over the same period, the percentage of never-married

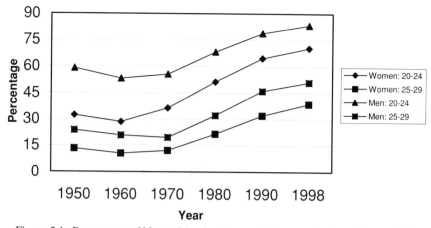

Figure 2.1. Percentage of Never-Married Men and Women, by Age. *Sources:* U.S. Bureau of the Census 1998; Spain, Daphne and Bianci, Suzanne M. 1996.

men age twenty to twenty-four increased 70 percent (59 percent to 83.4 percent), and the percentage of never-married men age twenty-five to twenty-nine more than doubled (23.8 percent to 51 percent).

In the last fifty years, changes in the age at which American men and women first marry have paralleled changes in marriage rates. Figure 2.2 shows that the median age at first marriage has increased since 1950. In 1950, one-half of American men were married by age twenty-three, and one-half of American women were married by age twenty. By 1998, the median age at first marriage rose to nearly twenty-seven for men and twenty-five for women. While the age at first marriage has changed over the century for both men and women, men have consistently married later in life than women have. However, the gap between the age at first marriage for men and women has narrowed from a four-year age difference at the turn of the century to a less than two-year age difference in 1998 (U.S. Bureau of the Census 1998).

Within the United States, marriage behavior between blacks and whites varies tremendously . The age at first marriage has risen more rapidly for blacks than whites (Julie DaVanzo and M. Omar Rahman 1993). Consequently, a significantly larger percentage of blacks have never been married. In 1950, the percentages of blacks and whites never married were similar. Since 1950, the percentage of never-married whites has increased slightly, while the percentage of never-married blacks has increased dramatically. Between 1950 and 1998, the percentage of never-married women increased 2 percent for whites, compared to 95 percent

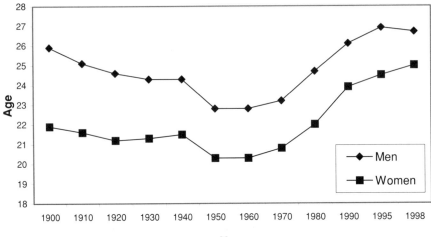

Figure 2.2. Median Age at First Marriage by Sex. *Source:* U.S. Bureau of the Census 1998. Figures for 1947 to 1997 are based on Current Population Survey (CPS) data. Figures for years prior to 1947 are based on decennial censuses. CPS data comes from U.S. Bureau of the Census, Current Population Reports, Series P20-514, "Marital Status and Living Arrangements: March 1998 (update)," and earlier reports.

for blacks; the percentage of never-married men increased 12 percent for whites, compared to 64 percent for blacks.

Rise in Non-Marital Cohabitation

Cohabitation has become increasingly common in the United States. Between 1960 and 1998, the number of unmarried couple households increased almost tenfold. The proportion of the population who cohabited before first marriage increased from 11 percent in the 1970s to almost 50 percent in the 1980s. The proportion of remarrying individuals who cohabited increased from one-third to two-thirds over the same period (Larry L. Bumpass and James A. Sweet 1989; Bumpass, Sweet, and Andrew Cherlin 1991).

Despite declining marriage (and remarriage) rates, people are still forming unions at approximately the same rate and age due to increasing cohabitation. Table 2.1 shows that while the proportion of men and women married before the age of twenty-five fell across birth cohorts, the proportion in unions did not substantially change. Bumpass and Sweet (1989) estimate that increases in cohabitation offset 67 percent of the decline in marriage for people under age twenty-five. Moreover, they find

Table 2.1 *Life Estimates of Cohabitation and Marriage before the Age of Twenty-Five (%)*

Birth Cohort	Males			Females		
	Cohabit	Marry	Union	Cohabit	Marry	Union
1960–64	33	38	67	37	61	76
1955–59	29	51	66	26	67	76
1950–54	24	55	68	16	72	78
1945–49	11	66	70	7	79	82
1940–44	8	68	70	3	82	83

Source: Bumpass and Sweet 1989.

that cohabitation offsets the drop in marriage before a given age more among females than males and blacks than whites.

Changes in Fertility Behavior

One of the main reasons social scientists and policy makers study marriage is the relationship between marriage and childbearing behavior. Several prevalent trends in fertility in the United States during the past fifty years are important to note in any study of marriage. First, the total fertility rate, or the number of children a hypothetical woman has over her lifetime if she experiences the observed age-specific birth rates, has been declining since its all-time high of 3.6 children per woman in 1955.[1] By 1996, the fertility rate had fallen to 1.9 children per woman, a 7 percent decrease from only 1990 (Center for Disease Control and Prevention 1997, 1998).

Second, age-specific fertility rates, or the ages at which most childbearing occurs, indicate that increasing numbers of woman are delaying childbearing. For example, birth rates for women in their twenties have been relatively stable over the past two decades. In contrast, birth rates for women in their thirties have increased consistently since the mid-1970s (Center for Disease Control and Prevention 1998).

Third, and most significantly, the incidence of births outside of wedlock has been increasing for the past five decades. This increase can be attributed in part to declining marriage rates, increases in the age at first marriage, rising divorce rates, and increasing cohabitation, which have resulted in an increasing number of unmarried women in their

[1] An exception to this decline occurred in the late 1980s. Fertility rates rose 8 percent between 1986 and 1990 (Center for Disease Control and Prevention, 1997). This rise can be attributed to increases among women in their thirties and early forties, "indicating 'catch-up fertility' by women who postponed childbearing" (DaVanzo and Rahman 1993).

reproductive years. Between 1940 and 1995, the non-marital birth ratio, or the proportion of all births occurring to unmarried women, grew from less than 4 percent to almost one-third of all births. In addition, out-of-wedlock birth rates for black women have been consistently higher than for white women over the same period. However, differences in the non-marital birth rate among blacks and whites have greatly diminished since 1980. This is due to increases in out-of-wedlock births among white women. For example, between 1980 and the early 1990s, the non-marital birth rate rose 94 percent for white women, compared to only 7 percent for black women (Center for Disease Control and Prevention 1995).

Crosscultural Variation

Across the globe there are large variations in many aspects of marriage formation, including age at marriage and cohabitation, the two aspects that we principally discussed in the U.S. context. Societies also differ in incidence of plural marriage, celibacy, courtship practices, and frequency of monetary payments at marriage. As Table 2.2 demonstrates, age at marriage varies widely across the globe. In most agrarian societies, where life expectancy is low, there is a high premium on large families and women marry very young. In addition, in societies where polygamy is prevalent, women marry much earlier than men (Shoshana Grossbard-Shechtman 1993).

Cohabitation rates and proportions of out-of-wedlock births also vary dramatically across continents. Cohabitation rates are particularly high in Latin America. In 1974, a time when cohabitation in the United States was rare and the ratio of cohabitation to marriage was 0.02, that ratio was larger than that in Honduras and Guatemala. In other words, there were more cohabiting couples than married couples (Grossbard-Shechtman 1993).

Table 2.2 further reveals the substantial variation in out-of-wedlock birth rates across countries. In 1995 in Europe, the proportion of out-of-wedlock births varied from a high of 59.6 percent in Iceland to a low of 2.9 percent in Greece. With a third of births occurring out of wedlock, the United States is comparable to the United Kingdom, Finland, and France. Other than Iceland, only the rest of Scandinavia and the former East Germany had more than 40 percent of births occur out of wedlock in 1995. Besides Greece, the only other European countries where that proportion was in the single digits were Switzerland and Italy (Kathleen Kiernan, Hilary Land, and Jane Lewis 1998). In the Far East, cohabitation

Table 2.2 *Marriage and Out-of-Wedlock Childbearing in Developed Countries*

Country	Average age at marriage, 1991–7		% births out-of-wedlock, 1994–98
	Women	Men	
Australia	27	29	23
Austria	26	29	30
Belgium	25	28	18
Canada	26	29	37
Denmark	30[1]	32[1]	45
Finland	29	32	37
France	28	30	40
Germany	28	30	19
Greece	25	29	4
Iceland	30	32	64
Ireland	28	29	30
Italy	27[1]	30[1]	9
Netherlands	28	31	21
New Zealand	27	29	41
Norway	29	31	49
Spain	26	28	12
Sweden	31	33	55
Switzerland	27	30	9
United Kingdom	26	28	38
United States	25[1]	26[1]	32

Note: [1] Average age at first marriage.

Source: The World's Women 2000: Trends and Statistics.

rates and proportions of out-of-wedlock births tend to be very low, as is the case in Japan (World Bank 1994).

On a global scale, marriage institutions also vary along other dimensions. Some societies, for example, permit polygamy, while others do not (Hanan Jacoby 1995). Marriage institutions also differ in terms of courtship practices and incidence of arranged marriages. Finally, there is crosscultural variation in forms of premarital monetary payments, both bridewealth (paid by the groom) and dowry (paid by the bride).

ECONOMIC DETERMINANTS OF MARRIAGE

Obviously individuals choose to be married for a multitude of reasons – the companionship of a partner, the desire to raise children in a two-parent household, and the legal protections associated with joint assets.

For some reason, many individuals are better off when married. To help better understand the behavioral process, economists have attempted to discover the underlying source of these benefits. One mechanism could be specialization in market and non-market activities. If the husband, for example, has a comparative advantage in the labor force, the couple may benefit if the wife specializes in home work (such as the rearing of children) while the husband focuses his attention on market work. This specialization may allow each person to perform those tasks more efficiently and generate greater output for the family. This could help explain, for instance, the empirical observation that married men earn more in the labor market even when one is able to control for non-random selection into marriage (Waite 1995). There are a number of other potential sources for the benefits to marriage. These could include the extension of credit markets, risk pooling, and the sharing of collective goods.[2]

The notion that economic factors affect the decision to marry and other aspects of marriage has been long considered. In the *Wealth of Nations*, which was published in 1776, Adam Smith discussed how poverty can serve to discourage marriage in the working class. Researching why, when, and whom individuals marry using the tools and techniques of economics is generally a more recent movement. David Gale and Lloyd Shapley (1962) first advanced a matching model of marriage. Gary Becker's works, "A Theory of Marriage: Part I and II" (1973, 1974) combined matching models based on the work of Tjalling Koopmans and Martin Beckman (1957) and competitive market models into what has become the standard economic approach.[3]

Becker's framework is one of household production in which family members allocate time and resources to market and home work with the goal of producing goods from which they receive utility. The basic marriage model is based on the premise that a potential couple compares the utility they would receive if married with the combined utility each individual would receive if single. Participants in the marriage market will marry only if the utility they receive when married – based on their share of the family output – exceeds the utility they receive when single. The difference between the combined utility of the married couple and the sum of the utilities when single is the gain to marriage. This, for example, might be the higher wages that a married man receives because he is able to specialize in market work.

---

[2] See Yoram Weiss (1997) for a rigorous treatment of these examples.
[3] See Chapter 1 for further discussion of Becker's model.

Using this framework, Becker is able to derive a market relationship between the output or utility received in the marriage market and the number of participants in the market – the prices and quantities in a standard supply-and-demand analysis. Assuming that all men are identical and all women are identical, he argues that an equilibrium will occur in this market when equal numbers of men and women wish to marry and when the utility received by someone who chooses to marry is at least as great as that which they could have received if they chose not to marry. Becker is able to use this model to derive implications about how changes in the relative availability of men and women affects who marries and the distribution of the benefits to marriage (that is, who has market power).

One could also think of a marriage market in which men and women differ in characteristics, such as intelligence, race, education, and religion. Each individual identifies the set of persons within the marriage market with whom he enjoys a positive gain to marriage. He then seeks to maximize his share of the marital gain by choosing his best mate. In a competitive framework, the marriage market ensures a situation that maximizes the sum of the gains over all marriages. This implies that each participant may not be paired with the partner who provides him his highest utility. Rather, an optimal pairing of all individuals results in the sense that persons not married to each other could not marry to make one better off without making the other worse off.

Becker uses this model to derive implications about sorting within the marriage market. Positive assortative mating is the tendency for people with similar traits to marry. Becker's matching model predicts that we should observe positive assortative mating on traits that are complements because these traits reinforce each other in the production and/or consumption of household commodities. For example, people with similar educational levels, religious preferences, intelligence, and ages may have similar preferences for certain consumption activities. As a result, the couple's shared participation in these activities increases their gain from marriage.

Negative assortative mating is the tendency for people with opposite traits to marry. Becker's matching model predicts that we should observe negative assortative mating on traits that are substitutes since these traits offset each other in the production and/or consumption of household commodities. For example, individuals with a comparative advantage in labor market activities (that is, a higher wage) benefit from marrying individuals with a comparative advantage in household activities, to the extent that the production of household commodities may be increased through the specialization of labor.

The prediction of negative sorting by wage can also be derived from a competitive market model that assumes that women who earn more in the labor force are less productive in marriage. Women who are high earners would then be considered the equivalent of unskilled wives in the marriage market and would marry men who earn less and cannot afford the more productive and expensive skilled wives.

Many economists have built upon Becker's marriage models. David Lam (1988), for example, extends Becker's matching model by incorporating a household public good. Becker's (1973) model assumes that spouses derive utility only from the consumption of a private good that is produced using time and market inputs. Gains from marriage, therefore, derive entirely from the specialization of labor in market work and home production. By allowing utility to depend upon a public good that is produced in the home, Lam allows spouses to derive gains both from joint consumption of the public good as well as from the specialization of labor. Lam finds that possibly offsetting forces determine the direction of assortative mating on wages. Specifically, joint public good consumption leads to positive assortative mating on wages since spouses with similar wages share similar preferences for consumption. However, household production of the public good leads to negative assorting on wages since it creates a return to the division and specialization of labor. Lam's results, therefore, may explain why there has been little empirical support for Becker's prediction of negative assortative mating on wages.

Michael Keeley (1977) extends Becker's theory of marriage by adapting it to a search model, a framework more commonly applied to the job hunting process. Becker's model assumes that the production of the household good and its division between spouses depend upon spouses' characteristics. Therefore, Keeley argues that single individuals have incentives to use resources to search within the marriage market for their most "suitable" mate.[4] A potential mate's suitability is measured by what Keeley terms his or her "marital wage," or the share of the marital output that a searcher expects to receive if married to the potential mate.

---

[4] An individual does not observe a potential mate's suitability unless he is in the marriage market. Moreover, he enters the marriage market only if he expects the benefit of search to outweigh its costs. Both the cost of search and the potential gains to marriage depend upon his characteristics.

Marital wages are not observed with certainty during the search. Instead, a potential mate observes only a marriage "offer," or a draw from the marital wage distribution. An offer is accepted only if the offer exceeds the expected income from future search.

Theodore Bergstrom and Mark Bagnoli (1993) use a matching model of marriage to explain why high-wage men marry later in life than low-wage men. Theirs is a two-period matching model of marriage. In each period, individuals choose whether to marry or remain single. Individuals vary in their attractiveness to members of the opposite sex, or their "quality." Traditional gender roles determine this quality. Men are valued for their role as economic providers, while women are valued as homemakers and childbearers. A man's quality is revealed only after he has worked for a period of time in the market. In contrast, the passage of time reveals relatively little about the quality of a woman. Equilibrium is determined by the following simple matching rule: Each female is paired with a male of equal expected quality. Bergstrom and Bagnoli show that this rule generates the result that high-quality men marry later in life because they choose to wait until after their quality is revealed in order to get matched with a high-quality woman. The model implies that high-quality women gain nothing from waiting. As a result, the model predicts that women marry younger than men, with the most desirable women marrying successful older men and the less desirable women marrying younger men who do not expect to be as successful.

EMPIRICAL MODELS OF MARRIAGE

Marriage markets influence many aspects of marriage, including the assignment of partners, the timing and frequency of marriage, and the division of marital gains. Testing these influences requires an empirical definition of what constitutes an individual's marriage market. Various definitions appear in the literature that vary in the level of geographic aggregation and in the economic and demographic characteristics of the market participants.

The level of geographic aggregation is an assumption about the size of a geographic area in which respondents will search for a potential partner. Empirically there is a trade-off between the accuracy of the data used in the construction of the marriage markets and the hypothesized scope of the marriage market. From a theoretical point of view, it may be appropriate to define marriage markets at a more disaggregated level. However, disaggregate data are often very limited or unavailable.

Instead of defining marriage markets geographically, an individual's marriage market may be defined by the quality of mates, as measured by economic and demographic characteristics, such as race, age, education, and income. Two common measures of the quality of marriage partners used by researchers are labor market opportunities and earning potential. For example, William Wilson and Kathryn Neckerman (1986) examine the relationship between marriage and the economic status and availability of males. They construct a "male marriageable pool index" from the ratio of employed civilian men to women in the same age and race category. The purpose of this index is to reflect the number of "good" mates available to women of a certain race. They find, particularly for younger age groups, a "long-term decline" in the number of available black men, in contrast to the stable, or possibly increasing, number of available white men.

Robert Wood (1995) also examines the effect of changes in the marriageable pool on changes in the marriage rate, using income- and employment-based measures of the marriage market. A significant problem with these measures is the fact that male employment decisions are jointly determined with marriage decisions. Wood uses methods to control for this and finds that the decline in the black marriageable pool, while not insignificant, accounts for "only 3 to 4 percent of the decline in black marriage rates in the 1970s." He also finds that the economic-based measures are not significant predictors of the changes in the white marriage rates over this same period.

Researchers have also attempted to link the *timing* of marriage to the number and suitability of available mates. This includes the work of Daniel Lichter et al. (1995), which finds that mate availability and the economic/employment status of potential male partners significantly influence the waiting time to marriage and explain a significant portion of the racial differences in the timing of marriage. Michael Brien (1997) uses a variety of measures of the marriage market, and finds that the availability of mates and economic factors, such as joblessness, appear, on some level, to influence the timing of marriage for whites and blacks. Specifically, residing in a state with a favorable marriage market will shorten the waiting time to marriage. Moreover, Brien finds support for the hypothesis that racial differences in the timing of marriage are due to differences in the availability of "marriageable" mates.

Finally, David Loughran (1998) uses a search model to test whether the timing of marriage for women is related to the distribution of male wages. Search theory predicts that the expected return from marital search will be greater the larger the differences in earnings among men, and will, consequently, lead women to delay marriage. Loughran finds evidence that the "rising male wage inequality is responsible for a significant proportion of the rise in female age at first marriage between 1970 and 1990."

MARRIAGE AND RELATED BEHAVIORS

Although it is widely recognized that marital status, fertility, and labor supply decisions are jointly determined, few economic frameworks of marriage explicitly model this interrelationship. Moreover, most of these models are one-period models that cannot explain dynamic phenomena such as marriage timing and spacing. Dynamic models, which explicitly model the intertemporal evolution of choices over an individual's lifetime, are the exception.

George Akerlof, Janet Yellen, and Michael Katz (1996) explore the relationship between marriage and non-marital childbearing decisions. The authors argue that abortion and effective birth control methods are responsible for the increases in the number of unwed births that have occurred in the United States since the early 1970s. They hypothesize that abortion and contraception have made transforming a pregnancy into childbearing a choice, and therefore have made marriage a less automatic response to unwed pregnancy. While their model is not dynamic, it captures the sequential nature of non-marital conception and marriage decisions by modeling the decision to have a child out of wedlock as a sequence of decisions about sexual activity, birth control, and marriage.

Brien, Lee Lillard, and Waite (1999) also explore the relationship between marriage and non-marital conception, focusing on the dynamic processes that link marriage, cohabitation, and non-marital conception events. Specifically, the authors empirically model the timing of each of these three events, taking into account their simultaneity. Each event may occur multiple times over the period of observation for any particular woman, and the outcome of one event may influence the risk of another event or the risk of a repeat of the same event. Among their results, Brien et al. find evidence that a young woman more likely to be involved in one of those events is also more likely to be involved in the others. The most striking positive correlation appears for marriage and non-marital conception. This suggests that those couples nearing marriage are less vigilant about preventing pregnancy because of their approaching nuptials, or, more likely, that couples facing an accidental pregnancy marry quickly for that reason.[5] In addition, their results show that marriage is a much more frequent outcome of a non-marital conception than is cohabitation, at least for whites.

Although many studies have addressed the importance of the interdependence between marriage and labor supply decisions, few have explicitly modeled the two decisions jointly. Wilbert Van der Klaauw (1996) develops a dynamic structural model of women's marriage and labor supply decisions. In each period, each woman simultaneously chooses whether to marry a potential mate and whether to work in the labor force. A woman is assumed to make marriage and labor supply decisions in order to maximize her lifetime utility. Therefore, she considers the impact that her choices today will have on her decisions in the future. The utility each woman enjoys every period depends on her marital status, consumption of market goods, and the presence of children. Although childbearing decisions are not explicitly modeled, Van der Klaauw's model includes childbearing as a random variable that depends upon a woman's characteristics and marriage decisions.

Clearly, individual decisions about marriage and cohabitation are interrelated. Couples consider both options when deciding to cohabit, to marry without cohabiting, and to move from cohabitation to marriage. If cohabitation is a step on the way to marriage, individuals most likely to cohabit will also be most likely to marry. To the extent that cohabitation substitutes for marriage, people most likely to cohabit will be least likely to marry. Some research suggests that the role of cohabitation in family formation differs by racial and ethnic groups, acting as a stepping-stone to marriage for some and as a substitute to marriage for others (Wendy Manning and Nancy Landale 1996; Laura Loomis and Landale 1994).

Brien, Lillard, and Waite (1999) hypothesize that if cohabitation acts as a stage in the courtship process, then couples who cohabit should have a higher probability of marriage than comparable single couples. However, if cohabitation acts primarily as a substitute for marriage, then couples who cohabit should have a lower probability of marriage. Among their results, they find that young women who enter a cohabitation show a jump in the probability of marriage at that point, with dramatic increases for whites and much smaller increases for blacks. This pattern suggests that, for whites especially, living together is a step on the road to marriage.

---

[5] Since they lack accurate information on abortion, Brien, Lillard, and Waite's measures of non-marital conception include only those pregnancies carried to term.

For black women, the much smaller increase in the likelihood of marriage that accompanies the start of a cohabitation suggests that for this group, cohabitation acts more as a substitute for marriage than a step on the way.

Brien, Lillard, and Steven Stern (1999) develop and estimate an economic search model of non-marital cohabitation, marriage, and divorce. Their research explicitly models the information gathering process within a relationship. In their theoretical model, individuals do not fully realize the quality of their match with a potential partner upon an initial meeting. Based on an imperfect observation of match quality, however, agents must decide whether to form a coresidential relationship with that partner and must also choose whether the relationship will be a formal marriage that may be relatively costly to dissolve, or a more informal, non-marital cohabitation that may not have some of the benefits associated with a formal marriage. This decision is based on the expected value of each type of relationship and the expected value of continued search. Once a couple enters into a relationship, the quality of the match becomes clearer over time. As information becomes known, individuals must decide whether to dissolve the relationship or, if it is an informal union, whether to convert the relationship into a formal marriage.

CONCLUSION

The goal of this chapter was to provide an overview of the theoretical and empirical models that have been used to examine marriage behavior. Studying why, when, and who people marry is important for a number of reasons. One of the primary reasons, and one that was not stressed in this chapter, is the application of these models for guiding public policy. These types of models can help us understand whether certain public policies either intentionally or unintentionally affect the decision to marry. The large demographic changes that have been recently observed have brought considerable interest in this line of research, and the further testing and refinement of these models will help further our understanding of this important institution.

REFERENCES

Akerlof, George A., Yellen, Janet L. and Katz, Michael L. "An Analysis of Out-of-Wedlock Childbearing in the United States." *Quarterly Journal of Economics,* 1996, *61*(2), pp. 277–317.

Becker, Gary S. 1973. "A Theory of Marriage: Part I." *Journal of Political Economy,* 1973, *81*, pp. 813–46.

———. "A Theory of Marriage: Part II." *Journal of Political Economy,* 1974, *82*, pp. 511–26.

———. *Treatise on the Family.* Cambridge, MA: Harvard University Press, 1991.

Bergstrom, Theodore C. "A Survey of Theories of the Family," in Mark R. Rosenzweig and Oded Stark, eds. *Handbook of Population and Family Economics.* New York: Elsevier Science, 1997.

Bergstrom, Theodore C. and Bagnoli, Mark. "Courtship as a Waiting Game." *Journal of Political Economy,* 1993, *101*(1), pp. 185–202.

Brien, Michael J. "Racial Differences in Marriage and the Role of Marriage Markets." *Journal of Human Resources,* 1997, *32*(4), pp. 741–78.

Brien, Michael J., Lillard, Lee A. and Stern, Steven. "Cohabitation, Marriage, and Divorce in a Model of Match Quality." Unpublished manuscript, 1999.

Brien, Michael J., Lillard, Lee A. and Waite, Linda J. "Interrelated Family-Building Behaviors: Cohabitation, Marriage, and Non-Marital Conceptions." *Demography,* 1999, *36*, pp. 535–52.

Bryant, W. Keith. *The Economic Organization of the Household.* New York: Cambridge University Press, 1990.

Bumpass, Larry L., Raley, R. Kelly and Sweet, James A. "The Changing Character of Stepfamilies: Implications of Cohabitation and Nonmarital Childbearing." *Demography,* 1995, *32*(3), pp. 425–36.

Bumpass, Larry L. and Sweet, James A. "National Estimates of Cohabitation." *Demography,* 1989, *26*(4), pp. 615–25.

Bumpass, Larry L., Sweet, James A. and Cherlin, Andrew. "The Role of Cohabitation in Declining Rates of Marriage." *Journal of Marriage and the Family,* 1991, *53*, pp. 913–25.

Center for Disease Control and Prevention. *Vital and Health Statistics Series 21, No. 53, Highlights of a New Report from the National Center for Health Statistics, 1995.* U.S. Department of Health and Human Services.

Center for Disease Control and Prevention. *Monthly Vital Statistics Report, Volume 45, No. 11, Supplement, Report of Final Natality Statistics, 1995.* U.S. Department of Health and Human Services, 1997.

Center for Disease Control and Prevention. *Monthly Vital Statistics Report, Volume 46, No. 11, Supplement, Report of Final Natality Statistics, 1996.* U.S. Department of Health and Human Services, 1998.

Cherlin, Andrew. *Marriage, Divorce, Remarriage.* Cambridge, MA: Harvard University Press, 1992.

DaVanzo, Julie and Rahman, M.Omar. "American Families: Trends and Policy Issues." RAND, 1993.

Epstein, Elizabeth and Guttman, Ruth. "Mate Selection in Man: Evidence, Theory and Outcome." *Social Biology,* 1984, *31*, pp. 243–78.

Gale, David and Shapley, Lloyd S. "College Admissions and the Stability of Marriage." *American Mathematical Monthly,* 1962, *69*(1), pp. 9–15.

Goldin, Claudia. "The Meaning of College in the Lives of American Women: The Past Hundred Years." Working paper no. 4099. Cambridge, MA: NBER, 1992.

Grossbard, Amyra. "An Economic Analysis of Polygamy: The Case of Maiduguri." *Current Anthropology,* 1976, *17,* pp. 701–11.

Grossbard-Shechtman, Amyra. "Marriage Squeezes and the Marriage Market," in Kingsley Davis in association with A. Grossbard-Shechtman, ed., *Contemporary Marriage: Comparative Perspectives on a Changing Institution.* New York: Russell Sage Publications, 1985.

Grossbard-Shechtman, Shoshana. *On the Economics of Marriage.* Boulder, CO: Westview Press, 1993.

Heer, David M. and Grossbard-Shechtman, Amyra. "The Impact of the Female Marriage Squeeze and the Contraceptive Revolution on Sex Roles and the Women's Liberation Movement in the United States, 1960 to 1975." *Journal of Marriage and the Family,* 1991, *43,* pp. 49–65.

Jacoby, Hanan. "Economics of Polygyny in Sub-Saharan Africa: Female Productivity and the Demand for Wives in Cote d'Ivoire." *Journal of Political Economy,* 1995, *103*(5), pp. 938–71.

Johnson, Robert A. *Religious Assortative Marriage in the United States.* New York: Oxford University Press, 1980.

Keeley, Michael. "The Economics of Family Formation." *Economic Inquiry,* 1977, *15,* pp. 238–50.

Kiernan, Kathleen, Land, Hilary and Lewis, Jane. *Lone Motherhood in Twentieth-Century Britain.* Oxford, UK: Clarendon Press, 1998.

Koopmans, Tjalling C. and Beckman, Martin. "Assignment Problems and the Location of Economic Activities." *Econometrica,* 1957, *25*(1), pp. 53–76.

Korenman, Sanders and Neumark, David. "Does Marriage Really Make Men More Productive?" *Journal of Human Resources,* 1991, *26*(2), pp. 282–307.

Lam, David. "Marriage Markets and Assortative Mating with Household Public Goods." *Journal of Human Resources,* 1988, *23*(4), pp. 462–87.

Lerman, Robert I. "Employment Patterns of Unwed Fathers and Public Policy," in R. I. Lerman and T. J. Ooms, eds., *Young Unwed Fathers: Changing Roles and Emerging Policies.* Philadelphia, PA: Temple University Press, 1993.

Lichter, Daniel T., Anderson, Robert N. and Hayward, M. D. "Marriage Markets and Marital Choice." *Journal of Family Issues,* 1995, *16,* pp. 412–31.

Loomis, Laura S. and Landale, Nancy S. "Nonmarital Cohabitation and Childbearing among Black and White American Women." *Journal of Marriage and the Family,* 1994, *56,* pp. 949–62.

Loughran, David S. "Does Variance Matter? The Effect of Rising Male Wage Inequality on Female Age at First Marriage." Unpublished manuscript, 1998.

Manning, Wendy D. and Landale, Nancy S. "Racial and Ethnic Differences in the Role of Cohabitation in Premarital Childbearing." *Journal of Marriage and the Family,* 1996, *58,* pp. 63–77.

Mare, Robert and Winship, Christopher. "Socioeconomic Change and the Decline of Marriage for Blacks and Whites," in C. Jencks and P. Peterson, eds., *The Urban Underclass.* Washington, DC: Brookings Institute, 1991.

Mortensen, Dale T. "Matching: Finding a Partner for Life or Otherwise." *American Journal of Sociology,* 1988, *94,* pp. S215–40.

Pierret, Charles R. "Why Has the Marriage Rate Declined in the United States? An Economic Analysis of the Marriage Market." Working paper. Washington, DC: Bureau of Labor Statistics, 1998.

Smith, Adam. *An Inquiry into the Nature and Causes of the Wealth of Nations.* London: Strahan & Cadell, 1776.

Spain, Daphne and Bianci, Suzanne M. *Balancing Act: Motherhood, Marriage and Employment among American Women.* New York: Russell Sage Publications, 1996.

U.S. Bureau of the Census. *Current Population Reports, Series P20, No. 514, Marital Status and Living Arrangements: March 1998.* Washington, DC: U.S. Government Printing Office, 1998.

Van der Klaauw, Wilbert. "Female Labour Supply and Marital Status Decisions: A Life-Cycle Model." *Review of Economic Studies,* 1996, *63*, pp. 199–235.

Waite, Linda. "Does Marriage Matter?" *Demography,* 1995, *32*(4), pp. 483–507.

Weiss, Yoram. "The Formation and Dissolution of Families: Why Marry? Who Marries Whom? and What Happens upon Divorce," in Mark Rosenzweig and Oded Stark, eds., *Handbook of Population and Family Economics.* New York: Elsevier Science, 1997.

Wilson, William J. and Neckerman, Kathryn M. "Poverty and Family Structure: "The Widening Gap between Evidence and Policy Issues," in Sheldon H. Danziger and Daniel H. Weinberg, eds., *Fighting Poverty: What Works and What Doesn't.* Cambridge, MA: Harvard University Press, 1986, pp. 232–59.

Wood, Robert G. "Marriage Rates and Marriageable Men: A Test of the Wilson Hypothesis." *Journal of Human Resources,* 1995, *30*(1), pp. 163–93.

World Bank. *World Development Report,* 1994.

Wu, Zheng and Balakrishnan, T. R. "Dissolution of Premarital Cohabitation in Canada." *Demography,* 1995, *32*(4), pp. 521–32.

THREE

The Economics of Divorce

Evelyn L. Lehrer

The far-reaching implications of the dissolution of a marriage for all family members are well known. The wife, who typically retains custody of the children, generally undergoes a significant decline in financial well-being following divorce (Saul D. Hoffman and Greg J. Duncan 1988). Growing up in a single-parent household deprives children of important inputs of parental time and money, and also limits their access to other family and community resources, with adverse effects both short term and long term (Sheila Krein and Andrea Beller 1988; Beller and John W. Graham 1993; Sara McLanahan and Gary Sandefur 1994). It is thus important to understand how various factors influence the probability that a union will be dissolved. This chapter reviews the evidence on this issue, focusing primarily on determinants at the micro level. These include the characteristics of each of the spouses and the quality of their match, the behaviors of each partner during and before the marriage, and the role of new information and events that were unanticipated at the time of the marriage. I also discuss differences between first unions and remarriages.

This chapter first outlines the theory on the economic gains from marriage and the process of marital search, which is essential to understanding the determinants of divorce. Within this framework, I then discuss the empirical evidence on how various factors affect the risk that a union will eventually be dissolved. The emphasis is on microlevel factors, although I mention some macrolevel factors such as divorce laws at the end of this

I am indebted to Shoshana Grossbard-Shechtman for many helpful comments and suggestions on earlier drafts of this chapter.

chapter (see also Chapter 4). The closing section highlights important areas where additional research is needed.

GAINS FROM MARRIAGE AND THE PROCESS OF MARITAL SEARCH

From an economic perspective, marriage may be viewed as a partnership formed to coordinate and facilitate production and consumption activities, including the production and raising of the couple's children (Gary Becker 1991). Division of labor and specialization within the family increase the couple's productivity, and represent a key source of gains from marriage. Other sources include (a) the pooling of risks (for example, one spouse may increase the level of work in the labor force if the other becomes unemployed); (b) economies of scale (for example, renting a large apartment costs less than renting two small apartments); (c) public goods (for example, all members of a household can enjoy the beauty of pictures hanging on the walls); and (d) positive externalities (for example, watching a television program may yield more enjoyment if done with someone else rather than alone, if utility is derived from the partner's consumption or mere presence).

For all these reasons, marriage may lead to higher levels of production and consumption. The amount of the gain, however, varies across couples, depending on the characteristics of each partner and the quality of their match. Becker (1991) develops implications about the matching of individuals with various characteristics. The optimal sorting is characterized by negative assortative mating for traits that are substitutes, and positive assortative mating for those that are complements.

In practice, many matches are not "ideal" – in the sense that better matches might have resulted had searching continued – because the search process is costly. The costs include the foregone gains from marriage, as well as various time and out-of-pocket expenses (such as expenditures on personal appearance and dating). The best choice of the reservation offer (the minimum level of match quality) is that which equates at the margin the costs of marital search and the present value of the future benefits associated with search (Michael C. Keeley 1977).

A union between two individuals may seem optimal from the perspective of both partners at a certain point in time. However, this assessment may subsequently change if one or both spouses discover that their expectations about their own characteristics or those of their partner were incorrect, or if major changes that were not anticipated at the time of the marriage take place. If one or both spouses assess the costs of terminating the union as sufficiently small, the marriage may be dissolved.

DETERMINANTS OF THE PROBABILITY OF DIVORCE

The preceding discussion suggests that marriage dissolution is more likely if the characteristics of the partners or their match, or the behavior of the spouses before and during the union, imply (a) relatively low gains from marriage and/or (b) relatively low costs of divorce. In addition, major unanticipated events that take place during the course of a marriage may be destabilizing. The sections that follow examine the empirical evidence on various factors that are related to these circumstances.

Characteristics of the Spouses and Their Match

The Husband's Permanent Earnings. A high level of husband's potential earnings is expected to generate a positive income effect that increases marital stability. More resources in the household imply a higher standard of living and may alleviate sources of marital tension associated with economic difficulties. In addition, as Becker (1991) notes, high-income men are likely to gain more from marriage insofar as they can compete more effectively in the marriage market and more easily attract wives with the desired characteristics. Empirically, there is strong evidence in the literature that men with a higher earning potential have more stable unions (Robert Michael 1979, 1988; Yoram Weiss and Robert J. Willis 1997).

The Wife's Earning Potential. An increase in the wife's earning capacity would be expected to generate an income effect similar to that discussed in connection with the husband's earnings. However, because women's wages are usually lower than men's, an increase in the wife's wage (holding the husband's income constant) may reduce the benefits from the division of labor within marriage, increasing the likelihood of separation. An "independence effect" reinforces this influence: A higher wage rate increases a woman's ability to support herself and her children outside of marriage. Thus, among unhappily married women, those with a higher earning potential can more easily terminate their unions. The empirical findings in the literature differ across studies partly because of differences in the point in time at which female earning capacity is measured (Evelyn L. Lehrer 1988). In addition, studies differ widely in the extent to which

other variables that are correlated with female wages are controlled –
including education, current hours of work, and years of experience. The
weight of the evidence, however, suggests that, other factors held constant, an increase in the wife's earning capacity has a destabilizing effect
(Michael 1979, 1988; Marianne A. Ferber and William Sander 1989; Weiss
and Willis 1997).

Interaction between the Husband's and Wife's Earning Capacity. In
Becker's model (1991), gains from marriage are highest when the spouses
have different productivity characteristics and can enjoy the benefits from
specialization and division of labor. This theory implies that the optimal
sorting is characterized by negative assortative mating on wages, individuals with high wages being matched to mates with low wages who have incentives to specialize in home production. However, as David Lam (1988)
has pointed out, joint consumption of public goods is another source of
gains from marriage. This represents an offsetting force that generates
a tendency for positive assortative mating on wages, due to the returns
from the spouses having similar demands for public goods.

The empirical evidence on the relative strength of these forces is
mixed. James P. Smith (1979) finds a correlation of 0.10 between the
husband's and wife's earning capacities for white couples, and 0.41 for
black couples. Lehrer and Marc Nerlove (1984) report a correlation between 0.10 and 0.17 for white couples, and between 0.11 and 0.25 for their
black counterparts, depending on life-cycle stage. These marriage patterns suggest positive, albeit weak, assortative mating in this dimension,
implying that complementarities between the husband's and wife's earning capacities dominate.[1] At the same time, Weiss and Willis (1997) report
a very wide gap between the predicted earnings of husbands and wives
($25,005 versus $11,606, based on data from 1985); they also find that the
earning capacities of the spouses interact positively in a divorce equation.
The authors interpret these results as evidence that complementarities
stemming from the consumption of public goods are not sufficient to offset the substitution effects associated with the division of labor.

Educational Attainment. Holding constant the spouses' earning capacities, education is a complementary trait within the context of marriage,

---

[1] As Lam (1988) discusses in detail, the interpretation of the correlation between the
spouses' wages is complicated by problems of reciprocal causality and the intraregional
correlation of wages, among other factors.

as it has an impact on a wide range of activities in which husband and wife are jointly involved. Education affects the daily communication and interactions within a marriage; education also influences decisions regarding child-rearing approaches, the level of human capital investments in children, and the allocation of time to home production and leisure activities.

Empirically, studies with various data sets and from different time periods consistently report a high correlation coefficient between the spouses' schooling levels, between 0.5 and 0.6 (see, for example, Richard Layard and Antoni Zabalza 1979; Lehrer 2001). Analyses of the determinants of divorce generally find that high levels of the husband's and wife's education have a stabilizing effect (Jessie M. Tzeng and Robert D. Mare 1995; Weiss and Willis 1997). In addition, the interaction between the spouses' schooling levels reveals strong complementarities: The higher the husband's level of schooling, the higher is the contribution of the wife's education to the stability of the marriage (Weiss and Willis 1997).

Intelligence. Like education, intelligence is a trait for which positive assortative mating is optimal, as it affects virtually all aspects of a relationship between marital partners. Evidence on simple correlations between the spouses' level of ability supports this view (Arthur R. Jensen 1978). It also appears that individuals of unusually high ability may have a relatively high divorce rate (Becker, Elizabeth M. Landes, and Robert T. Michael 1977). Being a genius is a rare trait, and it is difficult for such people to find partners of comparable ability; their tendency to be mismatched along this dimension would be a factor leading to marital instability.

Age. Jensen (1978) cites age as the trait for which positive assortative mating is strongest. In the United States, a gap of about two years between husband and wife is typical, with the husband usually the older partner. Large differences in age, especially when the wife is older than the husband, have been found to be destabilizing. The precise patterns vary across studies, however, and the effects appear to differ by race and marriage order (Lehrer 1996a).

Religious Affiliation. Religion is a complementary trait within marriage. It affects many activities beyond participation in religious observances at home and at church. Religion influences the education and upbringing of the children, the allocation of time and money, the cultivation of social relationships, and often even the choice of place of residence. Thus households in which the partners differ in religious affiliation are expected to have reduced efficiency, more conflict, and a higher likelihood of dissolution.

Religious heterogamy has indeed been found to have an adverse impact on marital stability (Michael 1979; Lehrer 1996a). Intermarriage, however, comes in different shades and forms, and not all interfaith unions are equally unstable. The destabilizing effect of intermarriage is most pronounced in two cases: first, when the spouses are affiliated to religions that have highly dissimilar religious beliefs and practices (such as, a Jew and a Christian); and second, when the affiliation of one or both partners is exclusivist in nature, with sharply drawn boundaries and membership criteria (for example, Mormons and fundamentalist Protestants) (Lehrer and Carmel Chiswick 1993).

Other dimensions of religion are also important. Among couples in religiously homogamous unions, it used to be that those affiliated to the Catholic and Jewish faiths were especially stable (Michael 1979; Frances Kobrin Goldscheider 1986), but it appears that this is no longer the case. By the late 1980s, homogamous Mormon marriages stood out as the most stable of intrafaith unions (Lehrer and Chiswick 1993). Having some affiliation as opposed to none has a positive effect on marital stability (Lehrer and Chiswick 1993), and higher levels of religious participation also have a favorable influence (Tim B. Heaton and Edith L. Pratt 1990).

Race and Ethnicity. It is well known that levels of marital instability are substantially higher among blacks than among whites, primarily for reasons related to pronounced differences in socioeconomic status between the two groups (Steven Ruggles 1997). Another contributing factor is the narrower male–female wage rate in the black population (Paul F. Secord and Kenneth Ghee 1986), which decreases gains from marriage associated with division of labor. In addition, the ratio of marriageable men to marriageable women is lower in the black population. This difference in the sex ratio implies that compared to their white counterparts, black women have a less advantageous position in the marriage market. The risk of union dissolution is thus higher in the black population, as women generally place a higher priority on marital stability than men (Grossbard-Shechtman 1984, 1985; Marcia Guttentag and Secord 1983). There is also evidence that the way in which various factors influence the probability of divorce varies systematically across these two racial groups (Jay D. Teachman 1986; Lehrer 1996a).

Much less is known about patterns of marital stability for Hispanics, Asians, and other racial and ethnic groups in the United States. In addition, little research has been done on the implications for marital stability of intermarriage across various racial and ethnic lines.

Nonintact Family Background. Individuals raised in broken homes may have a higher risk of divorce for several reasons. First, such individuals generally begin their unions with an economic disadvantage, and they tend to do so at an early age. Both of these factors increase the odds of an eventual divorce. Second, gains from marriage may be lower for such individuals, to the extent that they have had fewer opportunities to learn some of the interpersonal skills that are essential to a successful union. Third, for persons brought up in nonintact families, the perceived costs of a marital breakup may be lower, as they have seen that divorce is a viable solution to an unhappy marital situation. Paul R. Amato (1996) reports evidence suggesting that the first two factors play an important role in explaining the intergenerational transmission of marital instability; he finds little support for the third channel. Research by Sara McLanahan and Larry Bumpass (1988) suggests that the timing of the disruption matters. Compared to individuals who experienced a parental divorce in middle childhood, the adverse effects are stronger for those who experienced it before the age of five or during the adolescent years.

Investments in Marriage-Specific Human Capital

The behaviors of each spouse during the course of the marriage have an important impact on the stability of the union. Becker et al. (1977) emphasize the role of investments in marriage-specific human capital, that is, those investments that decline substantially in value following the termination of a marriage. Chiswick and Lehrer (1990) refine this notion by distinguishing marriage-specific investments that are transferable among unions from those that are specific to a particular spouse. After the dissolution of a union, the value of the former can be restored through remarriage; in contrast, the decline in the value of the latter is irreversible.

Spouse-Specific Human Capital. Couples who invest in spouse-specific capital enhance the stability of their marriage because, by definition, dissolution of the union would cause an irreversible decline in their value. Examples of spouse-specific investments might include acquiring knowledge about the spouse's culture, learning about leisure activities that the spouse particularly enjoys (such as, a specific hobby or sport), and learning to get along with members of the spouse's family. However, by far, children shared with a spouse represent the single most important type of investment in spouse-specific capital. The value of investments in children declines after a divorce, in part because of the tendency for the level of expenditures on children to fall to an inefficiently low level (Weiss and Willis 1985). Underprovision of the couple's collective good, child expenditures, is likely to occur because of the father's lack of control over the allocation of resources by the mother, who is typically the custodial parent. To the extent that both parents value their children's welfare, both would suffer.

Several other adverse changes in connection with the children usually happen after the breakup of a marriage. First, the non-custodial parent has much less contact with the children, and the connection between parent and child is weakened (Frank F. Furstenberg et al. 1983). Second, from the custodial parent's perspective, the presence of a child from a previous union makes remarriage more difficult and also has an adverse effect on the stability of a future union (Chiswick and Lehrer 1990; Lehrer 1996a). A third consideration is related to the fact that children generate consumption externalities flowing between the parents (Lehrer 1996a). This is one of the important psychic returns from children. For instance, a child's first steps yield utility to the mother and the father, and each parent derives utility from the other's enjoyment. This component of utility disappears following divorce.

For all of the preceding reasons, the value of investments in children declines irreversibly after marriage dissolution. Thus the presence of a couple's children provides strong incentives for both partners to continue their union. Empirically, most studies find that such children are indeed a stabilizing force within a marriage (Becker et al. 1977; Lehrer 1996a).

Because the value of investments in spouse-specific human capital falls irreversibly after the dissolution of a union, individuals who anticipate a high likelihood of marital breakup have incentives to make fewer investments in such capital. Consistent with this view, Becker et al. (1977) find that couples who differ in race or education, two traits for which positive assortative mating is optimal, have indeed lower levels of fertility. In addition, religiously heterogamous couples have been found to have lower intended fertility (Lehrer 1996b) and a smaller completed family size (Lehrer 1996c). Along similar lines, in a model that treats fertility and marital stability as jointly dependent, Lee Lillard and Linda J. Waite (1993) find that the risk of marital disruption has a negative impact on the probability of marital childbearing. All these results lend support to the notion emphasized by Becker (1991) that prophecies of divorce are self-fulfilling. Couples who anticipate a high probability of divorce make few investments in spouse-specific capital, and thereby increase the likelihood that their marriage will eventually fail.

Although the effect of a couple's offspring on marital stability is generally positive, it is not always of the same magnitude, and in some cases the impact is actually adverse. The nature of the influence depends on various factors, including the child's age, health status, and gender.

Waite and Lillard (1991) focus on variations by the child's age. They find that children ages five or younger greatly decrease the risk of divorce. The effect is particularly pronounced for the firstborn, confirming previous findings that the birth of the first child solidifies a marriage (Waite, Gus W. Haggstrom, and David E. Kanouse 1985). The effects associated with children become insignificant for the six to twelve age group, and turn positive afterward; that is, the presence of teenage children actually raises the probability of marital breakup. One possible explanation for this pattern is that unhappily married couples often avoid divorce while the children are very young, because the costs of a marital breakup may be particularly high at this life-cycle stage. Alternatively, this result may be related to the substantial strains on parenthood that teenagers often pose: The presence of a difficult, rebellious child in the household may reduce gains from marriage. It would be useful to extend this research to study how marital stability is affected as children grow up and begin to leave the home. Recent efforts in this direction suggest that the impact of the transition to the empty nest varies with marriage duration (Bridget Hiedemann, Olga Suhomlinova, and Angela M. O'Rand 1998).

The challenges of parenthood are especially stressful when a child is in poor health, suffering from an illness or disability that makes daily life difficult. Jane Mauldon (1992) finds that various indicators of children's ill health are associated with a high risk of divorce, suggesting that the quality of the marriage indeed suffers as a result. The adverse effects of poor health on marital stability are stronger for children age six to nine than for younger children. The increased risk of divorce associated with the older age group may be due in part to the fact that the costs of divorce fall as the child grows up. School systems are required to educate all children over age five, regardless of handicap. Thus the task of raising a child in poor health as a single parent may appear more manageable after the child reaches school age. In addition, gains from marriage may decrease over time: The strains of raising the child may be exacerbated as the handicap becomes more apparent and the permanency of the problem clearer.

Regarding the child's gender, Philip Morgan, Diane N. Lye, and Gretchen A. Condran (1988) find that the risk of marital instability is lower in raising sons than daughters. They interpret this result as reflecting the greater involvement of fathers with sons than with daughters, and a correspondingly higher level of spouse-specific investments in male offspring.

While children from the current union generally have a stabilizing influence, children from a previous union tend to have an adverse impact on marital stability (Becker et al. 1977; Lynn K. White and Alan Booth 1985; Waite and Lillard 1991). The reasons for this pattern have been the subject of some controversy. Andrew Cherlin (1978) interprets this result as reflecting the fact that remarried couples lack institutionalized guidelines for solving problems in their remarried life, particularly in connection with children from their previous unions. Becker et al. (1977, p. 1155) suggest that the presence of stepchildren may be destabilizing because they are "a source of friction; that is, positive specific capital in one marriage could be 'negative' specific capital in a subsequent marriage." More recently, an alternative interpretation has been advanced: Children from a previous union have an adverse impact on marital stability because they make their *custodial parent*, typically the mother, a less attractive partner. The presence of such children indicates that, ceteris paribus, she embodies less human capital that would be relevant to a new union; it also signals that many of her future investments of time, energy, and other resources will be diverted from her new partnership (Chiswick and Lehrer 1990).

Transferable Marriage-Specific Human Capital. During the course of a union, an individual may also invest in transferable marriage-specific capital. This concept refers to household management and production skills – investments that are more valuable within marriage than in the single status, but which are transferable from one union to another. These include not only those skills typically associated with homemaking, such as cooking and cleaning, but also knowledge about local markets and resources, the development of networks within the community, and other investments oriented to increasing allocative efficiency in household management that enhance the consumption of all family members.

These investments are more valuable in the married status largely because of specialization within marriage, which raises the efficiency of time-intensive home production activities. In addition, another adult in the household implies higher consumption returns to specialized investments in home production.

For a previously married woman, marriage-specific capital constitutes an important component of gains from marriage, as entry into a new union would restore its value. Using the length of the first union as a proxy for the value of these investments (in analogy to the conventional interpretation of years of labor market experience as a proxy for general on-the-job training), Chiswick and Lehrer (1990) find empirical support for the proposition that the higher the value, the faster the remarriage. Similarly, there is support for the hypothesis that the level of these investments, as proxied by the duration of previous unions, has a positive influence on the stability of a subsequent marriage (Lehrer 1996a).[2]

Investments That May Be Transferable or Spouse-Specific. Some skills that are acquired during the course of a marriage may be either transferable or spouse-specific, depending on the circumstances. For instance, there is evidence that women make investments that increase the earning capacity of their husbands (Grossbard-Shechtman 1993; Waite and Maggie Gallagher 2000). The skills acquired by the woman in the process of doing so may be of value only in the particular occupation of her husband, or they may be quite general and potentially transferable to another spouse. The same can be said about skills acquired in the process of teaching religious practices and beliefs to a spouse (Grossbard-Shechtman and Shoshana Neuman 1993). The expected effects on the probability of divorce would differ, depending on whether the investments are spouse-specific or transferable.

Wage-Enhancing Human Capital Investments during Marriage

While men typically work on a full-time basis after completing their education, there is much more variation in labor force attachment among women. The extent to which a married woman orients her time and effort

---

[2] The length of previous marriages may also be an indicator of unobserved gains from marriage. Chiswick and Lehrer (1990) and Lehrer (1996a) provide empirical tests for these alternative interpretations.

to work outside of the home has several opposing influences on marital stability. On the one hand, female employment decreases gains from marriage stemming from division of labor and specialization. In addition, women who have accumulated experience in the labor force are in a better financial position to leave an unhappy marriage, and may also have had more opportunities to meet alternative potential partners. On the other hand, gains associated with the pooling of risks may be higher when both spouses are employed and have skills that are useful in the labor force (Valerie Oppenheimer 1997). Gains associated with positive externalities and the consumption of public goods may also be higher if both partners work outside the home and develop similar interests.

Empirically, the evidence is very mixed, partly because of differences across studies in the specification of the female employment variables and in the extent to which related factors are controlled. Additionally, few studies consider the fact that causality also runs from the expectation of divorce to female employment. The theoretical interrelationships between these two variables are developed by Grossbard-Shechtman and Keeley (1993). William R. Johnson and Jonathan Skinner's (1988) econometric analysis finds that when the possibility of reciprocal causality is taken into account, there is no significant effect of female employment on the probability of divorce, but the influence in the opposite direction is strong. That is, women who anticipate a high probability of divorce respond by orienting their investments to the labor force. Along similar lines, Weiss and Willis (1997) report evidence that women who are unhappy about their marriages invest more in labor force activities. Further supporting this view is evidence that women in interfaith unions tend to display higher levels of employment, possibly in anticipation of their elevated risk of marriage dissolution (Lehrer 1995, 1999). This behavior again points to the self-fulfilling nature of divorce prophecies. As women who anticipate a divorce enhance their ability to be financially independent, the chances that they will indeed choose to terminate an unhappy marriage increase.

Behaviors of the Partners before the Marriage

The past decades have witnessed a major increase in the prevalence of cohabitation. It has been noted that at certain stages of the life cycle, the cohabitation option may indeed have some attractive features compared to marriage. Efficient search in the marriage market is hindered when there is considerable uncertainty about traits relevant to assortative mating, as would be the case for an individual who is a long way from the transition to a fairly stable career. As Valerie K. Oppenheimer (1988, pp. 583–4) notes:

Cohabitation gets young people out of high-cost search activities during a period of social immaturity but without incurring what are, for many, the penalties of either heterosexual isolation or promiscuity, and it often offers many of the benefits of marriage, including the pooling of resources and the economies of scale that living together provide. It also facilitates the kind of interaction that increases the knowledge of oneself and of a potential marriage partner and of the kind of mutual adaptations that are so essential to stable relationships.

In addition, by providing a great deal of information about the characteristics of the partner, cohabitation would be expected to improve the chances for subsequent marital stability, as presumably only those matches that are "proven" to work out are formalized into a marriage. However, the empirical evidence overwhelmingly shows that cohabitation before marriage is linked with a higher, not a lower, risk of an eventual divorce (David Popenoe and Barbara Dafoe Whitehead 1999). The most pronounced adverse effects are associated with a pattern of serial cohabitation (Teachman and Karen A. Polonko 1993; Alfred DeMaris and William L. MacDonald 1993); at the other extreme, a brief period of prenuptial cohabitation may have no adverse influence on the stability of the subsequent marriage (Susan L. Brown 1998).

The generally negative association between cohabitation and marital stability may partly reflect the fact that the process of cohabitation per se leads to changes in attitudes and behaviors that undermine union stability (William G. Axinn and Arland Thornton 1992; Axinn and Jennifer S. Barber 1997). Selectivity factors also play a role. Those who choose cohabiting arrangements include a disproportionate number of people who have less commitment to the institution of marriage, who are poor "marriage material," or who thought their unions were at a relatively high risk of dissolution in the first place (Robert Schoen 1992; Neil G. Bennett, Ann Klimas Blanc, and David E. Bloom 1988; Alan Booth and David Johnson 1988). A recent analysis finds that correcting for adverse selection eliminates the negative effect of cohabitation on subsequent marital stability (Lillard, Brien, and Waite 1995).

While premarital cohabitation is generally linked with a higher risk of marital instability, it is also well known that an early entry into first marriage strongly increases the probability of divorce. Indeed, this relationship is one of the most robust results in the literature on the determinants of marriage dissolution (Teresa Castro-Martin and Bumpass 1989; Lehrer 1996a). A very early age at marriage may imply that the union was contracted at a time of substantial uncertainty about the individual's own characteristics; it may also indicate that the period of marital search was unusually short, leading to little information about the spouse's traits. The trade-offs for marital stability between the timing of the first marriage and whether it is preceded by cohabitation are complex, and have not been quantified in the literature to date.

Unexpected Events

Becker et al.'s (1977) model implies that any major departure from the conditions that prevailed at the initiation of a marriage – both negative and positive – may trigger the breakup of the union. The authors interpret observed effects of extreme values of certain covariates on the divorce probability as consistent with this hypothesis. In particular, the adverse influence on marital stability of an additional child at high parities is viewed as reflecting unexpectedly high fertility. Similarly, the destabilizing impact of unusually high male earnings is interpreted as reflecting the influence of an income level much higher than that anticipated at the time of marriage. Along the same lines, Weiss and Willis (1997) report that an unexpected increase in the wife's earning capacity raises the risk of divorce. However, the authors also find that an unanticipated increase in the husband's earning capacity has a stabilizing impact.

If in a particular couple the gains from marriage and the costs of divorce are high – because of the characteristics of the spouses and their match, or their patterns of human capital investments – their union can be expected to withstand the winds of major unanticipated changes.

Differences between First Marriages and Remarriages

Some special considerations that affect the stability of remarriages have been noted already, namely, investments in transferable and spouse-specific human capital made during the course of a previous union. Other factors also play a role. On the one hand, divorce may be more likely for people in second or third marriages, because individuals who have been previously divorced are not a random group. They may have traits that make them more susceptible to a future divorce – perhaps they are less efficient searchers, or have unobserved characteristics that decrease their gains from marriage (Becker 1991). On the other hand, there may be a learning effect: A failed marriage may provide an experience that increases the chances of success in a future union.

The facts on this matter are not clear. Studies have often dealt with this issue by including a dummy variable for marriage order in a divorce equation (Becker et al. 1977; Cherlin 1977). However, subsequent research has shown that this approach is problematic, because certain variables affect marital stability very differently in first and higher-order marriages. In addition, factors come into play in remarriages that are not relevant to first marriages, especially stepchildren and previous investments in transferable marriage-specific skills (Lehrer 1996a). Moreover, the distribution of important variables, including education and age at union formation, varies considerably by marriage order (Castro-Martin and Bumpass 1989).

Recent evidence suggests that the probability of divorce is similar for the typical couple in their first union and the typical couple in a higher-order union. But in the case of remarriages, there is an extremely high variance in the risk of marital breakup, depending on the length of the first union, the woman's age at remarriage, and whether she had children in her first union (Lehrer 1996a).

One variable that appears to influence divorce probabilities very differently depending on whether the marriage is a first or a higher-order union is the woman's age at the time of marriage. Other factors held constant, first marriages that are begun at early ages are at a higher risk of divorce than those begun later in life, by a very wide margin. Exactly the opposite is the case for remarriages (Lehrer 1996a).

This finding may be related to the fact that higher-order unions that begin early in the life cycle are similar to first marriages in an important way. The spouses typically enter the union with few assets, and over time the husband and the wife contribute to building the family's financial position. Even if the wife fully specializes in home production, there is a partnership between the spouses in raising the children and increasing the net worth of the family. In contrast, individuals remarrying later in life are likely to begin their new union with a significant stock of assets. And while the level of such assets would have a favorable impact on gains from marriage, decisions with regard to the intrafamily distribution of the assets and related streams of income may have a destabilizing influence. This negative effect is likely to be especially pronounced if the initial distribution is uneven and/or if one of the marital histories includes a divorce with considerable dispute over economic matters. An adverse impact is also likely to be observed if there are non-transferable claims on some of the assets (for example, child support payments that the wife may be receiving from a previous husband). The problem of "mine," "yours," and "ours" may be an important factor leading to marital instability. To date, no study has examined empirically how these factors related to the financial status of each partner at the time of remarriage affect the probability of union dissolution.

Influences at the Macro Level

Although this review has focused on the determinants of marital disruption at the micro level, it is important to note that characteristics of the demographic, economic, and legal environment have also been found to play a role. Specifically, research has noted that the divorce rate generally tends to be higher when there is a surplus of marriageable women (Grossbard-Shechtman 1993), when relative economic status is low (Richard Easterlin 1987), and when public transfer programs are more generous (Michael 1988). Although there has been considerable debate regarding the effects of no-fault divorce laws (Elizabeth H. Peters 1986; Douglas W. Allen 1992), recent research suggests that the incidence of marital breakup has been higher in states that have adopted such laws (Leora Friedberg 1998; Margaret F. Brinig and Frank H. Buckley 1998; Chapter 4 in this book).

CONCLUDING REMARKS

Since the seminal work of Becker et al. (1977), we have learned a great deal about which marriages are at a high risk of divorce and why. But many areas remain where our understanding of both the theoretical and empirical relationships is still weak. For instance, additional research is needed on the structural differences between first marriages and remarriages, and on the trade-offs for marital stability between the timing of the first union and whether it takes the form of cohabitation or legal marriage. Although a pattern of intergenerational transmission of marital instability has been documented, the role that economic factors play in this process has received little attention. To date, the vast majority of studies have focused on patterns of marriage dissolution early in the life cycle. We know considerably less about disruptions later in life, as the children grow up and begin to leave their parents with an empty nest. Finally, as the demographic landscape in the United States continues to change, it will be increasingly important to improve our understanding of patterns of union dissolution for the various demographic groups, as well as the implications for marital stability of intermarriage across racial, ethnic, and religious lines.

REFERENCES

Allen, Douglas W. "Marriage and Divorce: Comment." *American Economic Review*, 1992, *82*(3), pp. 679–85.

Amato, Paul R. "Explaining the Intergenerational Transmission of Divorce." *Journal of Marriage and the Family*, 1996, *58*, pp. 628–40.

Axinn, William G. and Barber, Jennifer S. "Living Arrangements and Family Formation Attitudes in Early Adulthood." *Journal of Marriage and the Family*, 1997, *59*, pp. 595–611.

Axinn, William G. and Thornton, Arland. "The Relationship between Cohabitation and Divorce: Selectivity or Causal Influence?" *Demography*, 1992, *29*, pp. 357–74.

Becker, Gary. *A Treatise on the Family*. Cambridge, MA: Harvard University Press, 1991.

Becker, Gary, Landes, Elizabeth M. and Michael, Robert T. "An Economic Analysis of Marital Instability." *Journal of Political Economy*, 1977, *85*(6), pp. 1141–87.

Beller, Andrea and Graham, John W. *Small Change: The Economics of Child Support*. New Haven, CT: Yale University Press, 1993.

Bennett, Neil G., Blanc Klimas, Ann and Bloom, David E. "Commitment and the Modern Union: Assessing the Link between Premarital Cohabitation and Subsequent Marital Stability." *American Sociological Review*, 1988, 53, pp. 127–38.

Booth, Alan and Johnson, David. "Premarital Cohabitation and Marital Success." *Journal of Family Issues*, 1988, *9*, pp. 255–72.

Brinig, Margaret F. and Buckley, Frank H. "No-Fault Laws and At-Fault People." *International Review of Law and Economics*, 1998, *18*, pp. 325–40.

Brown, Susan L. "Cohabitation as Marriage Prelude versus Marriage Alternative: The Significance of Psychological Well-Being." Presented at the annual meeting of the American Sociological Association, San Francisco 1998.

Castro-Martin, Teresa and Bumpass, Larry L. "Recent Trends in Marital Disruption." *Demography*, 1989, *26*(1), pp. 37–52.

Cherlin, Andrew. "The Effect of Children on Marital Dissolution." *Demography*, 1977, *14*(3), pp. 265–72.

———. "Remarriage as an Incomplete Institution." *American Journal of Sociology*, 1978, *84*(3), pp. 634–50.

Chiswick, Carmel and Lehrer, Evelyn. "On Marriage-Specific Capital: Its Role as a Determinant of Remarriage." *Journal of Population Economics*, 1990, *3*, pp. 193–213.

DeMaris, Alfred and MacDonald, William L. "Premarital Cohabitation and Marital Instability: A Test of the Unconventionality Hypothesis." *Journal of Marriage and the Family*, 1993, *55*, pp. 399–407.

Easterlin, Richard. *Birth and Fortune – The Impact of Numbers on Personal Welfare*. Chicago, IL: University of Chicago Press, 1987.

Ferber, Marianne A. and Sander, William. "Of Women, Men, and Divorce: Not by Economics Alone." *Review of Social Economy*, 1989, *47*(1), pp. 15–26.

Friedberg, Leora. "Did Unilateral Divorce Raise Divorce Rates? Evidence from Panel Data." *American Economic Review*, 1998, *88*(3), pp. 608–27.

Furstenberg, Frank F., Nord, Christine Winquist, Peterson, James L. and Zill, Nicholas. "The Life Course of Children and Divorce: Marital Disruption and Parental Contact." *American Sociological Review*, 1983, *48*(10), pp. 656–68.

Grossbard-Shechtman, Amyra. "Review of Guttentag and Secord's Too Many Women." *Sociology and Social Research*, 1984, *68*, pp. 390–1.

———. "Marriage Squeezes and the Marriage Market," in Kingsley Davis, ed., in association with Amyra Grossbard-Shecthman, *Contemporary Marriage: Comparative Perspectives on a Changing Institution*. New York: Russell Sage Publications, 1985, pp. 375–96.

Grossbard-Shechtman, Shoshana. *On the Economics of Marriage: A Theory of Marriage, Labor, and Divorce*. Boulder, CO: Westview Press, 1993.

Grossbard-Shechtman, Shoshana and Keeley, Michael. "A Theory of Divorce and Labor Supply," in Shoshana Grossbard-Shechtman, ed., *On the Economics of Marriage: A Theory of Marriage, Labor, and Divorce*. Boulder, CO: Westview Press, 1993, pp. 182–213.

Grossbard-Shechtman, Shoshana and Neuman, Shoshana. "Religiosity and Investments in Spousal Productivity," in Shoshana Grossbard-Shechtman, ed., *On the Economics of Marriage: A Theory of Marriage, Labor, and Divorce*. Boulder, CO: Westview Press, 1993, pp. 290–302.

Guttentag, Marcia and Secord, Paul F. *Too Many Women: The Sex Ratio Question*. Beverly Hills, CA: Russell Sage Publications, 1983.

Heaton, Tim B. and Pratt, Edith L. "The Effects of Religious Homogamy on Marital Satisfaction and Stability." *Journal of Family Issues*, 1990, *11*(2), pp. 191–207.

Hiedemann, Bridget, Suhomlinova, Olga and O'Rand, Angela M. "Economic Independence, Economic Status, and Empty Nest in Midlife Marital Disruption." *Journal of Marriage and the Family*, 1998, pp. 219–31.

Hoffman, Saul D. and Duncan, Greg J. "What Are the Economic Consequences of Divorce?" *Demography*, 1988, *25*(4), pp. 641–5.

Jensen, Arthur R. "Genetic and Behavioral Effects of Nonrandom Mating," in R. Travis Osborne, Clyde E. Noble and Nathaniel Weyl, eds., *Human Variation: The Biopsychology of Age, Race, and Sex*. New York: Academic Press, 1978, pp. 51–102.

Johnson, William R. and Skinner, Jonathan. "Labor Supply and Marital Separation" *American Economic Review*, 1988, *76*(3), pp. 455–69.

Keeley, Michael C. "The Economics of Family Formation." *Economic Inquiry*, April 1977, pp. 238–50.

Kobrin Goldscheider, Frances. "Family Patterns among the U.S. Yiddish–Mother Tongue Subpopulation: 1970," in Steven M. Cohen and Paula E Hyman, eds., *The Jewish Family: Myths and Reality*. New York: Holmes and Meir, 1986, pp. 172–83.

Krein, Sheila and Beller, Andrea. "Educational Attainment of Children from Single-Parent Families: Differences by Exposure, Gender, and Race." *Demography*, 1988, *25*(2), pp. 221–34.

Lam, David. "Marriage Markets and Assortative Mating with Household Public Goods: Theoretical Results and Empirical Implications." *Journal of Human Resources*, 1988, *23*(4), pp. 462–87.

Layard, Richard and Zabalza, Antoni. "Family Income Distribution: Explanation and Policy Evaluation." *Journal of Political Economy*, 1979, *87*(5), pp. S133–61.

Lehrer, Evelyn L. "Determinants of Marital Instability: A Cox-Regression Analysis." *Applied Economics*, 1988, *20*(2), pp. 195–210.

———. "The Effects of Religion on the Labor Supply of Married Women." *Social Science Research*, 1995, *24*, pp. 281–301.

———. "The Determinants of Marital Stability: A Comparative Analysis of First and Higher Order Marriages," in T. Paul Schultz, ed., *Research in Population Economics*, 1996a, *8*, pp. 91–121. Greenwich, CT: JAI Press.

———. "Religion as a Determinant of Fertility." *Journal of Population Economics*, 1996b, *9*, pp. 173–96.

———. "The Role of the Husband's Religion on the Economic and Demographic Behavior of Families." *Journal for the Scientific Study of Religion*, 1996c, *35*(2), pp. 145–55.

———. "Married Women's Labor Supply Behavior in the 1990s: Differences by Life-Cycle Stage." *Social Science Quarterly*, 1999, *80*(3), pp. 574–90.

———. "The Impact of Women's Employment on Family Income Distribution: A Comparison between 1973 and 1992–1994." *Quarterly Review of Economics and Finance*, 2001, *40*, pp. 295–301.

Lehrer, Evelyn and Chiswick, Carmel. "Religion as a Determinant of Marital Stability" *Demography*, 1993, *30*(3), pp. 385–404.

Lehrer, Evelyn and Nerlove, Marc. "A Life-Cycle Analysis of Family Income Distribution." *Economic Inquiry*, 1984, *22*, pp. 360–74.

Lillard, Lee, Brien, Michael J. and Waite, Linda J. "Pre-Marital Cohabitation and Subsequent Marital Dissolution: Is It Self-Selection?" *Demography*, 1995, *32*(3), pp. 437–58.

Lillard, Lee, and Waite, Linda J. "A Joint Model of Marital Childbearing and Marital Disruption." *Demography*, 1993, *30*(4), pp. 653–83.

Mauldon, Jane. "Children's Risks of Experiencing Divorce and Remarriage: Do Disabled Children Destabilize Marriages?" *Population Studies*, 1992, *46*, pp. 349–62.

McLanahan, Sara and Bumpass, Larry. "Intergenerational Consequences of Family Disruption." *American Journal of Sociology*, 1988, *94*, pp. 130–52.

McLanahan, Sara and Sandefur, Gary. *Growing Up with a Single Parent: What Hurts, What Helps*. Cambridge, MA: Harvard University Press, 1994.

Michael, Robert. "Determinants of Divorce," in Louis Levy-Garboua, ed., *Sociological Economics*. London: Russell Sage Publications, 1979, pp. 223–69.

Michael, Robert. "Why Did the U.S. Divorce Rate Double within a Decade?" *Research in Population Economics*, 1988, *6*, pp. 367–99.

Morgan, Philip, Lye, Diane N. and Condran, Gretchen A. "Sons, Daughters, and the Risk of Marital Disruption." *American Journal of Sociology*, 1988, *94*(1), pp. 110–29.

Oppenheimer, Valerie K. "A Theory of Marriage Timing." *American Journal of Sociology*, 1988, *94*, pp. 563–91.

_____. "Women's Employment and the Gain to Marriage: The Specialization and Trading Model." *Annual Review of Sociology*, 1997, *23*, pp. 431–53.

Peters, Elizabeth H. "Marriage and Divorce: Informational Constraints and Private Contracting." *American Economic Review*, 1986, *76*, pp. 437–54.

Popenoe, David and Whitehead, Barbara Dafoe. "Should We Live Together? What Young Adults Need to Know about Cohabitation before Marriage." Unpublished manuscript, Rutgers, State University of New Jersey, 1999.

Ruggles, Steven. "The Rise of Divorce and Separation in the United States, 1880–1990." *Demography*, 1997, *34*(4), pp. 455–66.

Schoen, Robert. "First Unions and the Stability of First Marriages." *Journal of Marriage and the Family*, 1992, *54*, pp. 281–4.

Secord, Paul F. and Ghee, Kenneth. "Implications of the Black Marriage Market for Marital Conflict." *Journal of Family Issues*, 1986, *7*(1), pp. 21–30.

Smith, James P. "The Distribution of Family Earnings." *Journal of Political Economy*, 1979, *87*(5, part 2), pp. S163–92.

Teachman, Jay D. "First and Second Marital Dissolution: A Decomposition Exercise for Whites and Blacks." *Sociological Quarterly*, 1986, *27*(4), pp. 571–90.

Teachman, Jay D. and Polonko, Karen A. "Cohabitation and Marital Stability in the United States." *Social Forces*, 1993, *69*, pp. 207–20.

Tzeng, Jessie M. and Mare, Robert D. "Labor Market and Socioeconomic Effects on Marital Stability." *Social Science Research*, 1995, *24*, pp. 329–51.

Waite, Linda J. and Gallagher, Maggie. *The Case for Marriage*. New York: Doubleday, 2000.

Waite, Linda J., Haggstrom, Gus W. and Kanouse, David E. "The Consequences of Parenthood for the Marital Stability of Young Adults." *American Sociological Review*, 1985, *50*, pp. 850–7.

Waite, Linda J. and Lillard, Lee A. "Children and Marital Disruption" *American Journal of Sociology*, 1991, *96*(4), pp. 930–53.

Weiss, Yoram and Willis, Robert J. "Children as Collective Goods." *Journal of Labor Economics*, 1985, *3*, pp. 268–92.

_____. "Match Quality, New Information, and Marital Dissolution." *Journal of Labor Economics*, 1997, *15*(1), pp. S293–329.

White, Lynn K. and Booth, Alan. "The Quality and Stability of Remarriages: The Role of Stepchildren." *American Sociological Review*, 1985, *50*, pp. 689–98.

FOUR

The Effects of Public Policy on Marital Status in the United States

Leslie A. Whittington and James Alm

Marriage is an institution that deeply affects many aspects of economic and cultural life, some of which are discussed extensively in other chapters of this book. The striking changes in marital behavior among the U.S. population have therefore launched numerous investigations into their root causes, many of which have focused upon economic factors as one type of determinant of marital decisions. Unemployment rates, female labor force opportunities, female wages, the presence of adequate "marriageable" partners, and educational attainment have all been found to play a role in explaining the trends in marital behavior.[1]

Public policy decisions that have altered economic incentives may also have contributed to the changes that we have observed over the past three decades. Many features of public policies in the United States have implicit subsidies or penalties for marriage and divorce. In particular, government tax and transfer policies are seldom *marriage-neutral*; that is, the magnitude of taxes paid or transfers received may change solely because of a change in marital status. Further, legal policies that alter the relative costs or benefits of marriage also have the potential to influence marriage patterns, especially through their effects on marital dissolution. These government policies may therefore create incentives for family formation in some cases and disincentives in others. The scope of these policies may not always be deliberate but is nonetheless pervasive. The

---

[1] Some recent examples include William Sander (1992); Shoshana Grossbard-Shechtman (1993); Valerie K. Oppenheimer and Vivian Lew (1995); Arland Thornton, William G. Axinn, and Jay D. Teachman (1995); and Michael J. Brien (1997). See also the previous chapters by Michael Brien and Michelle Sheran (Chapter 1) and Evelyn Lehrer (Chapter 2) in this book.

United States General Accounting Office (1996) has identified 1,049 laws at the federal level alone that may have implicit penalties or subsidies for marriage. State laws and programs can also affect marital decisions.

In this chapter, we examine three paths through which government policies in the U.S. may influence marital choices: cash transfers for the poor, the so-called marriage tax or marriage subsidy in the federal individual income tax, and changes in divorce law. Each of the following sections discusses these issues. The final section presents some conclusions.

WELFARE, MARRIAGE, AND DIVORCE

The U.S. welfare system has probably generated more controversy about how public policy affects human behavior than any other program. Policy makers and their constituents have expressed concerns about the size of the welfare system, its growth, and especially the perverse incentives inherent in the system that may encourage welfare dependency (Robert A. Moffitt 1992). One ongoing issue is the impact of welfare programs on family structure decisions, including marriage, divorce, and cohabitation.

Disincentives for Marriage in the Structure of the U.S. Welfare System

Many features of the U.S. welfare system may influence marital status, but most research has been directed toward understanding behavioral responses to the former Aid to Families with Dependent Children (AFDC) program. AFDC provided cash benefits to children in low-income families headed by women. It was first established under the Social Security Act of 1935, and has now been replaced by Temporary Assistance for Needy Families (TANF) as a result of the sweeping welfare reform adopted in 1996.

AFDC was a means-tested entitlement program targeted toward unmarried female heads of household, mainly women with children under the age of eighteen, with eligibility for AFDC benefits based largely on income and family assets. Moreover, before 1968 many states expressly disallowed the presence of any adult male in an AFDC household. The common view was that a woman would become ineligible for AFDC benefits if she cohabited with a man, whether he was her legal husband or not, a feature that would clearly create a disincentive for marriage.

As pointed out by Moffitt, Robert Reville, and Anne E. Winkler (1998), this view was not entirely accurate, because eligibility for AFDC benefits did not always require the absence of a cohabiting partner or spouse.

There are several reasons for this. First, from 1961 onward, AFDC programs for unemployed parents (AFDC-UP) allowed cash benefits to two-parent families, whether married or not. To be eligible, the designated principal earner in the family simply had to be unemployed, but there was no requirement that the male be absent from the household. The states were not always required to offer AFDC-UP programs, however, and twenty-two states did not adopt them until the Family Support Act of 1988 mandated that they do so (Winkler 1995).

Second, in 1968 the U.S. Supreme Court threw out the state requirement that disallowed the presence of any adult male in an AFDC household. After this ruling, males were allowed to co-reside with women receiving AFDC benefits if they were not deemed parents (actual or substitute) of the children, even though any income contributed by the co-residing male to the financial support of the family was considered part of the overall family income in determining eligibility and benefit levels. The Supreme Court went further in 1981 and required states to consider at least a portion of stepfather income as family income; however, co-habiting and non-parental males were still allowed to co-reside without necessarily affecting the family's eligibility or benefit amount.

These seemingly contradictory rulings, in combination with inconsistent applications of the rules across states, make it difficult to conclude that AFDC was an unambiguously "anti-marriage" program. Nevertheless, as Moffitt, Reville, and Winkler (1998) emphasize, the AFDC program tended to treat households with a cohabiting male who was not the natural father of the children much more leniently than those with a resident spouse or father of the children. This feature created a clear disincentive for marriage and also a clear incentive for divorce, because women who married faced the reduction or loss of their AFDC benefits. In their entirety, then, the various features of the AFDC program suggest that AFDC benefits should be positively associated in empirical studies with the probability that a woman is a female head of household, either because she has never married or because she has divorced her spouse.

Other major welfare programs in the United States also frequently have marriage penalties. Medicaid, which provides health benefits for the poor, was a program closely linked to AFDC. Almost all eligibility for Medicaid was determined by AFDC receipt, and by the early 1990s two-thirds of all Medicaid recipients were from AFDC families (Moffitt 1992). The same marriage penalties therefore applied to Medicaid as well as to AFDC, because loss of AFDC benefits almost necessarily meant loss of Medicaid benefits.

The Food Stamp program provides an in-kind benefit in the form of coupons that can be exchanged in grocery stores for eligible food items. Although the Food Stamp program is means tested, there is no categorical requirement for eligibility, so that the marital status of the family does not by itself factor into the receipt of benefits. Stacy Dickert-Conlin (1999, p. 220) points out that "separation may increase the joint benefits of two low-income individuals because the sum of the maximum payment for a single-person household exceeds the maximum payment for a two-person household." Therefore, the receipt of food stamps might discourage marriage and facilitate separation or divorce.

Researchers have often bundled welfare benefits into a single "commodity" in their empirical analyses. The research question then is frequently the broad one, "Do welfare benefits affect marital status?" rather than simply, "Do AFDC programs affect marital status?"

Has Welfare Affected Marriage Behavior?

Many researchers across a host of academic disciplines have tried to determine the precise impact of AFDC, or more broadly, welfare programs, on household structure in the United States. Table 4.1 summarizes some of the more recent studies exploring the impact of AFDC and other welfare benefits on marital status. The results of these studies are decidedly mixed. T. Paul Schultz (1994), Neil G. Bennett, David E. Bloom, and Cynthia K. Miller (1995), and Saul D. Hoffman and Greg J. Duncan (1995) offer evidence that welfare has had a negative influence on marriage probabilities. The effect is not trivial but is generally modest. Hoffman and Duncan (1995), for example, estimate that a 25 percent increase in the level of AFDC benefits would generate an increase in the short-term divorce rate (or those in years one to three) of about one-quarter of a percentage point. The impact on the divorce rate of couples married five years or more is even smaller.

Winkler (1994, 1995), Moffitt (1994), and Diane K. McLaughlin and Daniel T. Lichter (1997) sometimes find a similar effect, but they also demonstrate that the estimated impact is quite fragile and can often be eroded by slight changes in the empirical specification.[2] This work tends

---

[2] For example, Winkler (1994) finds that the negative impact of welfare on the probability of marriage is greatly diminished by the inclusion of community-specific variables capturing conservatism, because AFDC levels and conservative community attitudes are negatively correlated. Moffitt (1994) shows that the negative effect of AFDC on female headship is eliminated by the inclusion of state-specific controls.

Table 4.1 *Some Recent Studies of the Effect of Welfare on Marital Status and Family Headship*

Authors	Research question	Welfare measures	Principal findings
T. Paul Schultz (1994)	Does AFDC, Medicaid, and/or AFDC–UP affect the probability that a woman is currently married?	• AFDC benefits, equal to the cash equivalent of the combined monthly AFDC and Food Stamp benefits, by state • Average monthly Medicaid reimbursement per AFDC family, by state • Monthly expenditures on AFDC–UP per AFDC family, by state	• AFDC decreases the probability of a recipient being currently married and living with her spouse, especially for young women. • Relative to AFDC, Medicaid exerts a larger and more statistically significant negative impact on the current marriage probability. • AFDC–UP programs are not significant determinants of current marital status.
Robert A. Moffitt (1994)	Does the inclusion of state-specific effects alter the findings about the impact of welfare on female headship?	• Welfare benefits, equal to the sum of AFDC, Medicaid, and Food Stamp benefits, by state • Indicator of the presence of an AFDC–UP program, by state	• Without controls for state of residence, welfare benefits have a positive, significant correlation with female head-of-household status. • Controls for state of residence generally cause welfare benefits either to become insignificant or to reverse in sign, thereby exerting a negative influence on the probability of female headship.

(continued)

Table 4.1 (*continued*)

Authors	Research question	Welfare measures	Principal findings
Anne E. Winkler (1994)	Do welfare programs explain marital status when there is control for community values?	Maximum combined AFDC and Food Stamp benefit for a family of three	AFDC has a negative effect on probability of marriage, but the magnitude and statistical significance of the effect are reduced when the model includes a strong measure of community values.
Neil G. Bennett, David E. Bloom, and Cynthia K. Miller (1995)	Does AFDC affect the probability of women marrying if they have a child outside of marriage? Does AFDC affect expectations of marriage?	Dummy variable for the receipt of any AFDC payment in a specified period	The receipt of AFDC decreases the probability of marriage for women with out-of-wedlock births, but the receipt of AFDC does not affect the expectation of a future marriage.
Anne E. Winkler (1995)	Do AFDC–UP programs encourage two-parent households?	• Maximum AFDC and Food Stamp benefit for a family of three with no income • Interaction term between the AFDC guarantee and a dummy variable for the presence of an AFDC program in the state	• Neither the AFDC guarantee nor the AFDC–UP program has a significant impact on the probability of being a two-parent household. • The AFDC–UP program has a marginally significant negative effect on the probability of being married, counter to theoretical expectations.

| Saul D. Hoffman and Greg J. Duncan (1995) | Does AFDC income affect the probability of divorce? | • AFDC guarantee for relevant family size with no income, both the current year and a five-year moving average, with an alternate measure of the benefit level for a family of four
• Dummy variable for the presence of an AFDC–UP program | • AFDC benefits are associated with a small increase in the probability of divorce.
• The AFDC–UP program has no significant effect on the probability of divorce. |
| Diane K. McLaughlin and Daniel T. Lichter (1997) | Does welfare receipt influence the probability of a first marriage? | • Dummy variable for the receipt by the woman of any welfare (AFDC, Food Stamps, or a housing allowance) during the year preceding the observation period
• Average annual welfare payment to women in the local area | • The receipt of welfare does not significantly affect the probability of a first marriage.
• The average welfare payment in the area has a significant negative effect on the probability of marriage for poor women, but not on the probability of marriage for women who are not poor. |

to confirm the earlier conclusions of Moffitt (1992), who surveyed the work of economists through the early 1990s.[3] He concluded that empirical studies consistently found that welfare programs positively influenced the probability of female headship and thus by extension put downward pressure on marriage rates and upward pressure on divorce rates. However, he also concluded that the effects were not particularly large, certainly not large enough to explain the rise of female headship that occurred in the late 1960s and the early 1970s. We conclude similarly that the empirical evidence suggests a noticeable but not dramatic influence of AFDC (and more broadly, welfare) on marriage probabilities in the United States.

The cash transfer system was overhauled in 1996, and AFDC was replaced with Temporary Assistance to Needy Families (TANF). One frequently expressed goal of welfare reform was to strengthen the institution of marriage in the United States (Laura Wheaton 1999). There are two aspects of the new program that in particular may mitigate the marriage disincentives of the former AFDC. First, and probably most consequential, is that cash benefits are time-limited. This removes the long-term marriage disincentive generated by an ongoing income stream of welfare payments. Second, states have been given significant leeway in designing their welfare programs. Many have substantially liberalized assistance to two-parent families by relaxing the work requirements of the AFDC-UP, thereby also alleviating the marriage disincentive.

It is too early to determine conclusively the impact of the TANF program on marital behavior. In an early glimpse of possible results, David Fein (1999) finds that eighteen months into the new program in Delaware, marital cohabitation has increased among some groups of women. He also finds that women with relatively low levels of education had higher expectations of marriage.

INCOME TAXES AND MARITAL DECISIONS

A striking feature of the federal individual income tax is that tax burdens sometimes change solely due to a change in marital status. Many couples pay more in taxes as married than their combined taxes as singles, while many others pay less in taxes as married than as singles. This lack of *marriage neutrality* in the income tax is not the result of

---

[3] For earlier surveys, see John Bishop (1980) and Lyle Groenveld, Michael Hannan, and Nancy Tuma (1983).

any explicit or deliberate statutory feature of the tax, but arises because of two fundamental principles underlying the design of the federal income tax: the use of the family (rather than the individual) as the taxable unit, and the imposition of progressive (rather than proportional) tax rates.

The existence of the marriage tax/subsidy means that there are marital incentives – and disincentives – in the tax system. Taxes are blamed for many social woes. Is it possible that taxes have also contributed to the decline in marriage and rise in divorce in the United States?

A simple example from James Alm, Dickert-Conlin, and Leslie A. Whittington (1999) illustrates how the tax burden of a married couple may differ from the combined taxes of the same couple were they not married. Consider a couple whose 1998 combined adjusted gross income (AGI) is $80,000 in total, with the earnings split equally across both partners. If these two people remain legally single, they each have a tax liability equal to $5,958, giving them a combined liability of $11,916. If the couple were to legally marry, the couple can no longer use the "Single" taxpayer features, but instead must pay taxes as either "Married, Filing Separately," or as "Married, Filing Jointly." There is rarely any significant difference in one method versus the other of married filing, and the vast majority of married taxpayers file a joint return.[4] If our hypothetical couple files jointly, their combined income is now $80,000, and their marital tax liability is $13,394. This is $1,478 *more* than they would owe as single individuals, and arises solely because of their marital status. The additional tax caused by marriage is referred to as the marriage tax or marriage penalty of the U.S. individual income tax.

Although it is not as widely recognized, marriage does not always cause couples to incur a penalty. Couples in which one person makes substantially more money than the other will generally incur a "marriage subsidy" or "marriage bonus," meaning that their tax liability falls with marriage. If our couple had a single earner making $80,000 while the other person had no income, then their marital tax burden would be $13,394 as before, but their combined single tax burdens would be $17,508. In this case, they would pay $4,114 *less* if married than if they remained single. Table 4.2 shows these combinations of spousal income and their resulting marriage tax/subsidy.

---

[4] There is generally no gain from filing separately, because such items as the tax bracket widths and standard deduction for married individuals filing separately are exactly one-half of those for married couples filing jointly.

Table 4.2 *1998 Tax Treatment of a Couple Earning $80,000 as Single versus Married*

Taxes when single, equal income		Taxes when married, equal earners	
Income of each person	= $40,000	Income of couple	= $80,000
Less standard deduction	= 4,250	Less standard deduction	= 7,100
Less personal exemption	= 2,700	Less 2 personal exemptions =	5,400
Taxable income	= $33,050	Taxable income	= $67,500
Tax liability of each person =	$5,958		
Total tax liability of both people	= $11,916	Tax liability of couple	= $13,394

MARRIAGE TAX = $13,394 − 11,916 ⇒ $1,478 *MORE* TAXES PAID AS MARRIED THAN AS SINGLE

Taxes when single, one earner		Taxes when married, one earner	
Income of earner	= $80,000	Income of couple	= $80,000
Less standard deduction	= 4,250	Less standard deduction	= 7,100
Less personal exemption	= 2,700	Less 2 personal exemptions =	5,400
Taxable income	= $73,050	Taxable income	= $67,500
Tax liability of earner	= $17,508		
Tax liability of person with no income	= $0		
Total tax liability of both people	= $17,508	Tax liability of couple	= $13,394

MARRIAGE SUBSIDY = $13,394 − 17,508 ⇒ $4,114 *LESS* TAXES PAID AS MARRIED THAN AS SINGLE

The mechanics of why income tax liabilities are influenced by marriage are relatively simple in this case.[5] First, there are different statutory features of the income tax for married persons than for single persons. For example, the standard deduction allowed two taxpayers as married persons is larger than that allowed a single person, but it is not twice as large. Also, the tax rates that a married couple faces are drawn from a different tax schedule than those of single taxpayers. Second, the tax rates are imposed at progressive levels, so that the marginal tax rate increases with income. In some sense, the secondary earner is taxed as though his or her income is added on top of the primary earner, and the equal-earning

[5] Many aspects of the individual income tax generate marriage non-neutralities. The U.S. General Accounting Office (GAO) (1996) identified fifty-nine provisions in the federal personal income tax code alone that create penalties or subsidies. We highlight only the major features of the income tax that result in changes to tax liability due solely to marriage.

couple therefore has a higher marginal tax rate than if each partner's income were taxed at the appropriate single rate.

The Earned Income Tax Credit (EITC) is another important source of marriage non-neutrality for low-income households, because marital status can affect the size of the credit received. The EITC is a refundable tax credit allowed to low-income taxpayers with earned (or labor market) income. It increases with earnings up to a point, then declines, and is finally phased out with income over a cutoff point.[6] The value of the EITC to a taxpayer does not explicitly hinge on marital status, but it does depend on total family income. As Dickert-Conlin and Scott Houser (1998) illustrate, the EITC can either increase or decrease with marriage depending upon the distribution of family earnings and the total income of the family.

It is important to recognize that the marriage tax does not result from an explicit or even intended policy of taxing marriage. Instead, as noted earlier, it is the result of two other goals of the income tax: treating families with equal income equally (or "horizontal equity across families"), and imposing tax rates that rise with income (or "progressivity"). Income tax systems can be marriage-neutral if one of these two principles of taxation is relaxed. For example, the individual is the unit of taxation in many European countries, and as a result the tax non-neutralities imposed by marriage do not exist, at least not in the same form (Joseph A. Pechman and Gary V. Engelhardt 1990).[7]

There has not always been a tax penalty for marriage. Until 1948, the individual was the unit of income taxation in the United States, so that the tax was largely marriage-neutral. However, in 1948, the tax code introduced income splitting for couples, in which a spouse was taxed on half of the couple's joint income. This change meant that a couple's tax liability was essentially the same as the combined taxes of two individuals, each with half of the couple's total income. With progressive tax rates, nearly all couples now received a marriage subsidy, one that grew substantially over time, and by 1969 a single taxpayer's tax burden could be as much as 40 percent higher than that of a married couple with equal income (Harvey S. Rosen 1977). A separate tax schedule for single taxpayers was

---

[6] In 1998, the maximum EITC was $2,271 for a family with one qualifying child, $3,756 for a family with more than one qualifying child, and $341 for a family without a qualifying child. The respective income ceilings were $26,473, $30,095, and $10,030.

[7] If the individual, rather than the family, is the taxable unit, marital status has no impact on the taxes on that person's earnings. Individual income rather than marital income is the relevant consideration, and tax features would not differ due to marital status.

enacted in the Tax Reform Act of 1969 to address the perceived inequity between single and married taxpayers, but the marriage tax was the perverse result of changing the relative position of married taxpayers. Alm and Whittington (1996) estimate that by 1994 roughly 60 percent of families paid an average penalty of $1,200, while about 30 percent of families received a subsidy that averaged $1,100. The remaining 10 percent of taxpayers were unaffected by marital status.[8] Those most likely to incur a penalty are families with two earners and with children. Families with a single earner nearly always receive a large marriage subsidy.

The numbers of families incurring a marriage penalty or receiving a marriage subsidy, as well as the magnitudes of the tax/subsidy, have changed over time as a result of changing tax statutes and family demographics. Many tax features have changed over the past thirty years and thereby changed the average size of the marriage tax. Alm and Whittington (1996) estimate that the average marriage tax has tended to rise, fall, and then rise again since 1969 in response to these tax and demographic changes. They also demonstrate that these changes are largely the result of climbing labor force participation on the part of U.S. women.

Tax Incentives and Marriage and Divorce Decisions

Extending the basic economic model of marriage to include income taxes is straightforward (Alm and Whittington 1997, 1999). Taxes may affect the gains to marriage via two paths. First, differential income tax treatment of married couples may alter the total taxes paid by the couple relative to taxes paid as single individuals. If total taxes paid increase with marriage, ceteris paribus, then the gains to marriage unambiguously decline. Second, marriage may change the marginal tax rate faced by the couple relative to that faced as singles. A higher marginal tax rate with marriage increases the tax liability of the couple and so lowers the benefits of marriage. However, a higher marginal tax rate lowers the after-tax wage rates of the individuals, thereby reducing the opportunity cost of household production work and increasing the gains from marriage. The impact of the marginal tax rate on the gains to marriage, and therefore on the probability of marriage, is thus an empirical issue. However, it is clear that the tax system both creates incentives for those marriages that involve specialization

[8] Other estimates of average penalties and subsidies can be found in Daniel R. Feenberg and Rosen (1995) and the Congressional Budget Office (1997). Also, see Alm and Whittington (1996) for a discussion of some of the difficulties in estimating the marriage tax.

in household production (such as marriages organized along traditional gender lines) and discourages those marriages with two wage earners.

Table 4.3 summarizes the recent empirical work on income taxes and marriage. This work has used both aggregate and individual panel data, and has tended to find that the marriage tax has a small but statistically significant impact on marriage and divorce probabilities (Alm and Whittington 1995, 1999; Whittington and Alm 1997; Dickert-Conlin 1999).[9] The income tax may also affect the timing of marriage. Several studies have found that couples in the United States (David L. Sjoquist and Mary Beth Walker 1995; Alm and Whittington 1997) and in Canada, England, and Wales (A.M.G. Gelardi 1996) have timed their marriages to avoid one year of the tax penalty. The magnitude of these effects appears to be quite small; one estimate finds that doubling the tax penalty increases the probability that a couple delays its marriage to the next tax year by 1 percent (Alm and Whittington 1997). There is little evidence that the tax penalty/subsidy affects the timing of divorce (Whittington and Alm 1997). In sum, there is some consistent evidence that taxes affect marital status and its timing, but this evidence also shows that taxes are not large contributors to these decisions.

NO-FAULT DIVORCE AND MARITAL CHOICES

One of the most controversial policy topics concerning marital behavior is the move to unilateral divorce law in the United States. The legal requirements for a couple to seek a divorce have changed dramatically across the states during the last several decades, at the same general period during which divorce rates were climbing steeply. The conventional wisdom suggests that the increases in divorce were in fact caused by public policies that made divorce more easily obtained than earlier in the century. However, the empirical evidence is much more clouded.

One factor that contributes to the puzzle is purely semantic. There is some confusion on the precise legal requirements for divorce, and this has in turn created some confusion in subsequent empirical work. There are four basic divorce terms used in the discussion of divorce law: fault, no-fault, mutual, and unilateral divorce. A *fault* divorce requires

---

[9] For example, Alm and Whittington (1999) use individual longitudinal data from the Panel Study of Income Dynamics. Their estimation results suggest that at the mean values of the variables, a 10 percent rise in the marriage penalty leads to a 2.3 percent reduction in the possibility of first marriage, while at the level of the maximum tax penalty, a 10 percent rise in the marriage penalty leads to a 12.5 percent fall in the probability of first marriage.

Table 4.3 *Some Recent Studies on the Effects of the Income Tax on Marital Status*

Authors	Research question	Data	Principal findings
James Alm and Leslie A. Whittington (1995)	Does the average marriage tax in the individual income tax affect the percentage of women who are married in the United States?	Aggregate time series for the United States, 1947–88, with the dependent variable the percentage of women aged 18 to 44 who are married and the independent variables including the average marriage tax	The average marriage tax has a negative and statistically significant impact on the percentage of women who are married, with a marriage-tax elasticity of −0.05.
David L. Sjoquist and Mary Beth Walker (1995)	Does the average marriage tax in the individual income tax affect either the aggregate marriage rate or the timing of November–December versus March–April marriages in the United States?	Time series for the United States, 1948–87, with the dependent variable in the rate equation the fraction of unmarried women older than age 18 who marry each year, the dependent variable in the timing equation the ratio of November–December marriages to March–April marriages, and the independent variables in both equations including the marriage tax	• The marriage tax does not have a significant impact on the fraction of women who marry each year. • The marriage tax has a negative and statistically significant impact on the timing of marriages, with a marriage tax elasticity of −0.02.
A. M. G. Gelardi (1996)	Do changes in the tax benefit of marriage affect the timing of marriages in Canada and in England-Wales?	Time series for Canada, 1960–91, and for England-Wales, 1960–91, with the dependent variable the percentage of annual marriages occurring in each month and the independent variables including a dummy variable for a legislated change in the tax benefit of marriage	The percentage of marriages occurring by month is significantly affected by changes in the tax benefits of marriage.

88

Study	Research question	Data and method	Findings
Leslie A. Whittington and James Alm (1997)	Does the marriage tax in the United States affect the probability of an individual's divorce?	Individual panel data for men and women, 1968–92, with the dependent variable the probability of making the transition from married to divorced and the independent variables including the marriage tax	The marriage tax has a small, positive, and statistically significant impact on the probability of divorce for women but not for men.
James Alm and Leslie A. Whittington (1997)	Does the marriage tax in the United States affect the timing of an individual's marriage or divorce?	Individual panel data, 1967–89, with the dependent variables the probability of a couple choosing to marry or to divorce in the last versus the first quarter of the year and the independent variables including the marriage tax	The marriage tax has a small, positive, and statistically significant impact on the probability that a marriage is delayed from the last quarter of the year to the first quarter of the next year, but the marriage tax does not have an impact on the probability of divorce.
Stacy Dickert-Conlin (1999)	Do the marriage tax penalty and the marriage transfer penalty in the U.S. tax and transfer systems affect the probability of separation?	Individual data for women married in 1990, with the dependent variable the probability of separation and the independent variables including the marriage tax penalty and the marriage transfer penalty	The marriage tax penalty has a positive and statistically significant impact on the probability of separation, while the marriage transfer penalty has a positive and statistically significant impact on the probability of separation.
James Alm and Leslie A. Whittington (1999)	Does the marriage tax in the United States affect the probability that an individual marries?	Individual panel data for men and women, 1968–92, with the dependent variable the probability of making the transition from single to married and the independent variables including the marriage tax	The marriage tax has a small, positive, and statistically significant impact on the probability of marriage for women but not for men.

that one party be blamed for the breakup of a marriage, and also requires that the other spouse be found completely innocent of damaging the marriage; accepted faults include adultery, cruelty, desertion, impotency, conviction of a felony, drunkenness, non-support, drug addiction, and mental illness (Thomas A. Marvell 1989). In contrast, a *no-fault* divorce does not require the establishment of either partner as a guilty party; instead, the court allows the divorce simply on the grounds that the marriage is no longer viable. *Mutual* divorce requires that both spouses agree to the dissolution of the marriage, while *unilateral* divorce merely requires one party to desire a divorce. These divorce requirements are not necessarily mutually exclusive. For example, a state can simultaneously have both fault and no-fault grounds for divorce. Quite a few states allow no-fault divorce but require mutual consent, and even more states have no-fault grounds for obtaining a divorce but fault grounds for property settlements.[10]

In part because of these legal definitions, there is a substantial amount of disagreement over how to categorize some states. If, for example, a state allows divorce but only after a long period of living separately, does this legal feature constitute unilateral or mutual divorce? Differing interpretations of the definitions of divorce law have blurred some of the views about the effects of legal changes (Leora Friedberg 1998).

The Move from Mutual to Unilateral to No-Fault Divorce

Until the early 1970s, divorce law was largely fault-based. A fault-based structure made the dissolution of a marriage difficult; Paul A. Nakonezny, Robert D. Shull, and Joseph Lee Rodgers (1995) suggest that this was precisely the intent of fault-based divorce law. In cases where malfeasance did not necessarily have to be explicitly established, mutual consent was required, a requirement that also obviously complicated the divorce process.

A few states moved toward a no-fault divorce standard during the 1960s, and Nevada had essentially already been a no-fault divorce haven for decades (Ira Mark Ellman and Sharon L. Lohr 1998). However, the real sea change occurred in the early 1970s when a "landslide of liberalizing legislation was passed" (Marvell, 1989, p. 544). Over 60 percent of

---

[10] Leora Friedberg (1998) illustrates some of these seeming contradictions in state policy.

the states enacted no-fault divorce requirements between 1970 and 1973 (Ellman and Lohr 1998). Many states also did away with mutual consent requirements in favor of a unilateral divorce process.[11]

All states now have some form of no-fault divorce law. However, in recent years several states have considered revising their divorce laws to move back toward a mutual or fault-based divorce system (Friedberg 1998). Most prominent among these is Louisiana, which has established a "covenant" marriage as an alternative to a traditional marriage. A covenant marriage is not as easily dissolved as a traditional marriage; it requires the establishment of fault and a two-year waiting period before a divorce is allowed. Legislators in Louisiana enacted covenant marriage with the belief that stricter divorce requirements would lead to a reduced divorce rate.

Divorce Law and Incentives to Divorce. Many policy makers and their constituents accept as fact that easing divorce requirements necessarily leads to increasing marital dissolutions. However, empirical evidence is not largely supportive of this conclusion. Economic models of divorce (Gary S. Becker, Elisabeth M. Landes, and Robert T. Michael 1977; Becker 1981; H. Elizabeth Peters 1986) assume that divorce will occur when the gains to marriage are less than the combined gains as unmarried individuals; put differently, if divorce is "efficient," it will occur. The important consideration for our discussion here is whether divorce law actually changes the benefits or costs of married versus single status. As shown by Becker (1981), the Coase Theorem implies that legal changes by themselves do not fundamentally alter the benefit/cost calculus of divorce and so should not be expected to alter divorce rates. Peters (1986) tests this hypothesis, and finds empirical evidence to support it. However, she also concludes that legal changes likely result in a redistribution of goods within the marriage. Under the mutual divorce requirement, the spouse who wants the divorce would have to "buy" the divorce by compensating the other member for the divorce. In contrast, under a unilateral regime, the spouse who wants to stay married has to compensate the unsatisfied partner in order to keep the divorce from occurring. Consequently, the change in divorce law would not generate any increase in "inefficient" divorces, as commonly asserted, but it would alter the relative wealth and well-being of partners.

---

[11] Douglas W. Allen (1998) notes that most European nations also reformed their divorce laws in the same period, as did Australia.

For the Coase Theorem to hold, however, there must be clearly defined property rights and relatively low transaction costs. Douglas W. Allen (1992) argues that neither assumption regularly holds in the case of divorce. For example, Marvell (1989) suggests that the move to no-fault or unilateral divorce will decrease the legal expenses associated with divorce; he further argues that the necessity of publicly establishing some faulty marital behaviors involves psychic costs and, perhaps, loss of personal income due to reputational effects on one's business or career. Certainly, there is frequently a large time cost associated with divorce. These factors imply that the transaction costs associated with divorce are potentially large. If so, the Coase Theorem may not hold, and a shift in regime could in principle affect the probability of divorce.[12] Marvell (1989), however, argues that formalizing no-fault and unilateral divorce actually represented little real change in the actual practice of divorce. Most divorces prior to the legal changes of the early 1970s were uncontested and rarely investigated by judges assigned to the cases.

Evidence on the Impact of No-Fault Laws on Divorce Rates. We have summarized in Table 4.4 some recent empirical studies on divorce laws and divorce rates. Clearly, no consensus exists among academic researchers about the significance or magnitude of the effect. Marvell (1989), Nakonezny et al. (1995), Allen (1998), and Friedberg (1998) all determine that divorce law has affected divorce rates, although they do not concur in the importance of the effect relative to the steep rise in divorce rates. On the other hand, Jeffrey S. Gray (1996), Norvell D. Glenn (1997), and Ellman and Lohr (1998) find no evidence of a significant causal relationship between divorce law and subsequent divorce rates. It is interesting that Gray does find that divorce settlements are significantly lower in unilateral divorce states that recognize community property.

These researchers use very different methodologies in their work, from relatively simple "view-the-trends" approaches to more sophisticated econometric modeling, and these differences account for much of the variation in results. The work utilizing more advanced statistical analysis typically finds that divorce law does influence the divorce rate in a meaningful way (Friedberg 1998; Allen 1998; Gray 1996). Friedberg (1998), for example, estimates that the divorce rate would have been 6 percent

---

[12] Marvell (1989) notes other factors that both support and discount the possibility that divorce law significantly influences the divorce rate.

Table 4.4 *Some Recent Studies on the Effects of Changes in Divorce Laws on Marital Status*

Authors	Research question	Data	Principal findings
Thomas A. Marvell (1989)	Did adoption of no-fault divorce lead to an increase in divorces?	State-level data for 38 states over the period 1961–86.	Overall time series, crosssection analysis finds that no-fault laws increased divorces. State-by-state analyses find a significant effect in 16 of 38 states in the sample. In those states, no-fault increased divorces by an average of 20–5 percent after a one-year delay.
Paul A. Nakonezny, Robert D. Shull, and Joseph Lee Rodgers (1995)	Did no-fault divorce law increase the divorce rate in states?	State-level data for 50 states; one observation per state.	Divorce rates climbed significantly following adoption of no-fault divorce, as a direct result of the legal changes. Divorce increased by .8 divorces per 1,000 people in the state.
Norvell D. Glenn (1997)	Were the results of Nakonezny, Shull, and Rodgers (1995) strong enough to make definitive conclusions about the impact of no-fault divorce on divorce rates?	State-level data for the period 1965–79.	The adoption of no-fault divorce did not have a large direct impact on divorce rates. The adoption of no-fault law was probably a response to an already climbing divorce rate.

(continued)

Table 4.4 (continued)

Authors	Research question	Data	Principal findings
Jeffrey S. Gray (1996)	Does unilateral divorce law affect marital stability or property settlement?	Current Population Survey 1979 March/April Match File	Unilateral divorce law has no significant effect on state divorce rates. Alimony awards are significantly lower in common law marriage states with unilateral divorce. Divorce settlements are significantly lower only in those unilateral states that have community property statutes.
Douglas W. Allen (1998)	Did the move to no-fault law increase divorce rates in Canada?	1984 Canadian Family History Survey and aggregate data from the period 1950–92	Adoption of no-fault divorce increased "inefficient" divorces, meaning one partner used the law to the disadvantage of the other partner.
Ira Mark Ellman and Sharon L. Lohr (1998)	Were there changes in divorce rates after enactment of no-fault divorce?	State-level time series data on 47 states	In most cases, state divorce rate increases began before any changes in divorce law. Some short-run increases in divorce rates are noted after the move to no-fault divorce, but no long-term effects.
Leora Friedberg (1998)	Did the move to unilateral divorce increase the divorce rate?	Longitudinal data on 50 states and the District of Columbia, 1968–88	The divorce rate would have been 6 percent lower in 1988 if states had not moved to unilateral divorce. Unilateral divorce accounts for 17 percent of the increase in divorce rates over the 20-year period 1968–88. The effect is permanent, not temporary.

lower in 1988 if the country had not moved to unilateral divorce. However, despite the conflicting findings, it seems apparent from this range of findings that changes in divorce law were not the principal cause of the rise in divorce (or the decline in marriage) rates experienced over the past several decades.

CONCLUSIONS

It is difficult to determine the effects of public policies in the United States on marital decisions. Estimating the effects of policy on marital behavior is not a simple empirical process, for several reasons. Family decisions are made in multiple, interconnected dimensions – childbearing, marriage, labor supply, and living arrangements – and disentangling these decisions is an immensely difficult task. The behavior of households may strongly influence policy decisions, rather than causality being firmly in the other direction. Data problems are also quite severe. A particularly subtle issue in the marriage decision is that the researcher cannot know all the available marriage options facing an individual; the researcher knows only the spouse whom the individual actually chooses to marry, not the different possible spouses whom he or she chooses not to marry.[13] These various challenges have been addressed in different ways, giving rise to disputes over appropriate methodology, data, and conclusions.

It is not possible for us to resolve these disputes. Rather, our intent here is the simpler one, to summarize the findings of the empirical research on public policies and marital decisions. Our main conclusions here are threefold.

First, it is clear that many public policies are some distance from a neutral treatment of marriage. This result seems an obvious shortcoming. In particular, discouraging marriage or encouraging divorce could not have been the intent of policy makers when they enacted policies that increased taxes on married couples or that rewarded families for the absence of a spouse. Perhaps most important, the existence of programs that penalize marriage and/or encourage divorce can weaken the family as a basic societal institution, thereby contributing to many well-documented social ills. On narrower efficiency grounds, marriage penalties – even marriage subsidies – can distort decisions along multiple dimensions of behavior. By lessening respect for public institutions, these policies can generate a range of illegal and undesirable behaviors.

---

[13] See T. Paul Schultz (1994) and Alm and Whittington (1999) for a detailed discussion of this issue and an empirical strategy to deal with it.

Second, and as a result, we believe that the most reliable studies consistently show that policy can influence fundamental family choices such as marriage and divorce. Welfare, income taxes, and unilateral divorce law clearly change the economic calculus of marriage and divorce, and individuals respond to these changed incentives.

In fiscal matters, marriage neutrality is achievable, if not easily so, and mainly requires facing the many trade-offs inherent in public policies.[14] Consider tax policy as an illustration. In the recent 106th Congress, legislators introduced numerous amendments, resolutions, and bills, motivated in large part by a desire to reduce the marriage tax. This push toward eradicating the marriage penalty continued into the 107th Congress, and was a focal point of the tax reform package introduced by President George W. Bush early in his administration. Table 4.5 summarizes the main features of many of the major bills introduced in the 106th Congress. As the table shows, the proposed legislative cures tend to fall into one of several categories: adjusting specific items such as the standard deduction or the Earned Income Tax Credit for married taxpayers; reintroducing a two-earner deduction for married couples; adjusting marginal tax rates or brackets to reduce the marriage tax; allowing married taxpayers to file separately; and combining some of these features. None of these plans achieves full marriage neutrality, although several take large steps toward that end, and none of these bills was passed and signed into law during the 106th Congress. The Economic Growth and Tax Relief Reconciliation Act of 2001, passed by the 107th Congress in June 2001, explicitly deals with the marriage penalty by gradually increasing the standard deduction of married couples to 200 percent of the standard deduction of singles, increasing the start and finish of the phase-out range of the EITC, lowering tax rates, and increasing tax brackets. Ironically, some of these moves will have the effect of decreasing the relative tax advantage of marriage to single-earner couples (Whittington and Alm 2001).

Still, and last, if there is any comfort to be found in our discussion of public policies, it is that to the extent that these effects can be uncovered, they almost always are quite small. In short, we believe that the policies

---

[14] For example, achieving marriage neutrality in the individual income tax requires eliminating either of the two conditions that generate a marriage penalty or subsidy: imposing taxes based on household resources, and imposing them at different marginal tax rates. Similar actions are required in the transfer system, especially changes that would introduce a proportional rate structure or that would make the individual the unit instead of the family. For a detailed analysis of various proposals, see the Congressional Budget Office (1997).

Table 4.5 *Some Marriage Tax Relief Proposals Introduced in the 106th Congress*

Bills	Sponsor	Main features of proposed legislation
H.R. 108 H.R. 725 H.R. 2020 H.R. 2085 H.R. 2574 H.R. 2646 S. 284 S. 1160	Rep. Knollengerg (R-MI) Rep. Kleczka (D-WI) Rep. Johnson (R-CN) Rep. Hooley (D-OR) Rep. Maloney (D-CN) Rep. McCarthy (D-NY) Sen. McCain (R-AZ) Sen. Grassley (R-IA)	Increases the standard deduction for married couples filing jointly to double the standard deduction for single taxpayers.
H.R. 1453 S. 8	Rep. Lampson (D-TX) Sen. Daschle (D-SD)	Allows a deduction for two-earner married couples, specified as a percentage of the earned income of the spouse with lower earnings.
S. 2053	Sen. Jeffords (R-VT)	Gives marriage tax relief for recipients of the Earned Income Tax Credit.
S. 2305 S. 2403	Sen. Bayh (D-IN) Sen. Bayh (D-IN)	Gives marriage tax relief for recipients of the Earned Income Tax Credit, and gives a nonrefundable marriage tax credit to married couples filing jointly.
H.R. 767	Rep. Thune (R-SD)	Increases the tax brackets for married couples filing jointly to double the brackets of single taxpayers.
S. 1379	Sen. Dominici (R-NM)	Reduces the tax rates for all taxpayers, and further reduces the tax rates for low- and middle-income married couples filing jointly.
S. 799	Sen. Campbell (R-CO)	Increases the standard deduction for married couples filing jointly to double the standard deduction for single taxpayers, and reduces the tax rates for all taxpayers.
H.R. 2350 H.R. 2414 S. 12	Rep. Johnson (R-TX) Rep. Tancredo (R-CO) Sen. Hutchinson (R-TX)	Increases the standard deduction for married couples filing jointly to double the standard deduction for single taxpayers, and increases the tax brackets for married couples filing jointly to double the brackets of single taxpayers.
H.R. 6	Rep. Weller (R-IL)	Gives marriage tax relief for recipients of the Earned Income Tax Credit, increases the standard deduction for married couples filing jointly to double the standard deduction for single taxpayers, and expands the 15 percent tax bracket for married couples filing jointly.

(continued)

Table 4.5 *(continued)*

Bills	Sponsor	Main features of proposed legislation
S. 2346	Sen. Roth (R-DE)	Gives marriage tax relief for recipients of the Earned Income Tax Credit is given, increases the standard deduction for married couples filing jointly to double the standard deduction for single taxpayers, expands the 15 and 28 percent tax brackets for married couples filing jointly, and protects family tax credits from the Alternative Minimum Tax.
H.R. 2488 S. 1429	Rep. Archer (R-TX) Sen. Roth (R-DE)	Gives marriage tax relief for recipients of the Earned Income Tax Credit, increases the standard deduction for married couples filing jointly to double the standard deduction for single taxpayers, and reduces the tax rates for all taxpayers.
S. 15	Sen. Hutchinson (R-TX)	Allows income splitting and separate filing for married couples.

reviewed have not generated large, catastrophic, or consistent behavioral effects, so that it is difficult to conclude that U.S. public policies have in their entirety either encouraged or discouraged marriage. This does not mean that public policies should not be changed to lessen any of their potentially adverse effects on marriage decisions. Instead, it may well mean that the failure to achieve complete marriage neutrality in all public policies is more a nuisance than a crisis.

REFERENCES

Allen, Douglas W. "Marriage and Divorce: Comment." *American Economic Review*, September 1992, *82*(3), pp. 679–85.

_____. "No-Fault Divorce in Canada: Its Cause and Effect." *Journal of Economic Behavior and Organization*, March 1998, *37*(1), pp. 129–49.

Alm, James, Dickert-Conlin, Stacy and Whittington, Leslie A. "The Marriage Penalty." *Journal of Economic Perspectives*, Summer 1999, *13*(3), pp. 193–204.

Alm, James and Whittington, Leslie A. "Income Taxes and the Marriage Decision." *Applied Economics*, 1995, *27*(1), pp. 25–31.

_____. "The Rise and Fall and Rise . . . of the Marriage Tax." *National Tax Journal*, December 1996, *49*(4), pp. 571–89.

_____. "Income Taxes and the Timing of Marriage Decisions." *Journal of Public Economics*, June 1997, *64*(2), pp. 219–40.

———. "For Love or Money? The Impact of Income Taxes on Marriage." *Economica*, 1999, *66*(4), pp. 297–316.

Becker, Gary S. *A Treatise on the Family*. Cambridge, MA: Harvard University Press, 1981.

Becker, Gary S., Landes, Elisabeth M. and Michael, Robert T. "An Economic Analysis of Marital Instability." *Journal of Political Economy*, 1977, *85*(6), pp. 1141–87.

Bennett, Neil G., Bloom, David E. and Miller, Cynthia K. "The Influence of Nonmarital Childbearing on the Formation of First Marriages." *Demography*, 1995, *32*(1), pp. 47–62.

Bishop, John. "Jobs, Cash Transfers, and Marital Instability: A Review and Synthesis of the Evidence." *Journal of Human Resources*, 1980, *15*(3), pp. 301–34.

Brien, Michael J. "Racial Differences in Marriage and the Role of Marriage Markets." *Journal of Human Resources*, 1997, *32*(4), pp. 741–78.

Congressional Budget Office. *For Better or for Worse: Marriage and the Federal Income Tax*. Washington, DC: Congress of the United States, 1997.

Dickert-Conlin, Stacy. "Taxes and Transfers: Their Effects on the Decision to End a Marriage." *Journal of Public Economics*, 1999, *73*(2), pp. 217–40.

Dickert-Conlin, Stacy and Houser, Scott. "Taxes and Transfers: A New Look at the Marriage Penalty." *National Tax Journal*, 1998, *51*(2), pp. 175–217.

Ellman, Ira Mark and Lohr, Sharon L. "Dissolving the Relationship between Divorce Laws and Divorce Rates." *International Review of Law and Economics*, 1998, *18*, pp. 341–59.

Feenberg, Daniel R. and Rosen, Harvey S. "Recent Developments in the Marriage Tax." *National Tax Journal*, 1995, *48*(1), pp. 91–101.

Fein, David. "Will Welfare Reform Influence Marriage and Fertility? Early Evidence from the ABC Demonstration." Bethesda, MD: ABT Associates working paper, 1999.

Friedberg, Leora. "Does Unilateral Divorce Raise Divorce Rates? Evidence from Panel Data." *American Economic Review*, September 1998, *88*(3), pp. 608–27.

Gelardi, A. M. G. "The Influence of Tax Law Changes on the Timing of Marriages: A Two-Country Analysis." *National Tax Journal*, 1996, *49*(1), pp. 17–30.

Glenn, Norvell D. "A Reconsideration of the Effect of No-Fault Divorce on Divorce Rates." *Journal of Marriage and the Family*, November 1997, *59*, pp. 1023–5.

Gray, Jeffrey S. "The Economic Impact of Divorce Law Reform." *Population Research and Policy Review*, 1996, *15*(2), pp. 275–96.

Groeneveld, Lyle, Hannan, Michael and Tuma, Nancy. "Income and Marital Events: Review of Previous Research," in *Final Report of the Seattle–Denver Income Maintenance Experiment*, Volume 1: *Design and Results*. Menlo Park, CA: SRI International, 1983.

Grossbard-Shechtman, Shoshana Amyra. *On the Economics of Marriage: A Theory of Marriage, Labor and Divorce*. Boulder, CO: Westview Press. 1993.

Hoffman, Saul D. and Duncan, Greg J. "The Effect of Incomes, Wages, and AFDC Benefits on Marital Disruption." *Journal of Human Resources*, 1995, *30*(1), pp. 19–41.

Marvell, Thomas A. "Divorce Rates and the Fault Requirement." *Law and Society Review*, 1989, *23*(4), pp. 543–67.

McLaughlin, Diane K. and Lichter, Daniel T. "Poverty and the Marital Behavior of Young Women." *Journal of Marriage and the Family*, 1997, *59*, pp. 582–94.

Moffitt, Robert A. "Incentive Effects of the U.S. Welfare System: A Review." *The Journal of Economic Literature*, 1992, *30*(1), pp. 1–61.

_____. "Welfare Effects on Female Headship with Area Effects." *Journal of Human Resources,* 1994, *29*(2), pp. 621–36.

Moffitt, Robert A., Reville, Robert and Winkler, Anne E. "Beyond Single Mothers: Cohabitation and Marriage in the AFDC Program." *Demography*, 1998, *35*, pp. 259–78.

Nakonezny, Paul A., Shull, Robert D. and Rodgers, Joseph Lee. "The Effect of No-Fault Divorce Law on the Divorce Rate across the Fifty States and Its Relation to Income, Education, and Religiosity." *Journal of Marriage and the Family*, 1995, *57*(2), pp. 477–88.

Oppenheimer, Valerie K. and Lew, Vivian. "American Marriage Formation in the 1980s: How Important Was Women's Economic Independence?" in Karen Oppenheim Mason and An-Magritt Jensen, eds., *Gender and Family Change in Industrialized Countries.* Oxford, UK: Clarendon Press, 1995, pp. 105–38.

Pechman, Joseph A. and Engelhardt, Gary V. "The Income Tax Treatment of the Family." *National Tax Journal*, March 1990, *43*(1), pp. 1–22.

Peters, H. Elizabeth. "Marriage and Divorce: Informational Constraints and Private Contracting." *American Economic Review*, 1986, *76*(3), pp. 437–54.

Rosen, Harvey S. "Is It Time to Abandon Joint Filing?" *National Tax Journal*, 1977, *49*(4), pp. 423–8.

Sander, William. "Unobserved Variables and Marital Status." *Journal of Population Economics*, 1992, *5*, pp. 217–28.

Schultz, T. Paul. "Marital Status and Fertility in the United States." *Journal of Human Resources*, 1994, *29*(2), pp. 637–69.

Sjoquist, David L. and Walker, Mary Beth. "The Marriage Tax and the Rate and Timing of Marriage." *National Tax Journal*, December 1995, *48*(4), pp. 547–58.

Thornton, Arland, Axinn, William G. and Teachman, Jay D. "The Influence of School Enrollment and Accumulation on Cohabitation and Marriage in Early Adulthood." *American Sociological Review,* 1995, *60*(4), pp. 762–74.

United States General Accounting Office. *Income Tax Treatment of Married and Single Individuals.* Washington, DC: Government Printing Office, 1996.

Wheaton, Laura. "Low-Income Families and the Marriage Tax," number 1 in the series, in Elaine Sorenson, ed., *Strengthening Families.* Washington, DC: Urban Institute, 1999.

Whittington, Leslie A. and Alm, James. "'Til Death or Taxes Do Us Part: The Effect of Income Taxation on Divorce." *Journal of Human Resources*, 1997, *32*(2), pp. 388–412.

_____. "Tax Reductions, Tax Changes and the Marriage Penalty." *National Tax Journal*, 2001, *54*(3), pp. 455–72.

Winkler, Anne E. "The Determinants of a Mother's Choice of Family Structure: Labor Market Conditions, AFDC Policy or Community Mores?" *Population Research and Policy Review*, 1994, *13*(3), pp. 283–303.

_____. "Does AFDC-UP Encourage Two-Parent Families?" *Journal of Policy Analysis and Management*, 1995, *14*(1), pp. 4–24.

PART II

EFFECTS OF MARRIAGE ON INCOME USES

FIVE

Control over Money in Marriage

Frances Woolley

The traditional economic view of the household is that, although there are differences in the roles men and women play in marriage, these differences represent an efficient division of labor, and both equally enjoy the rewards from cooperation. To put it another way, it is assumed that income received during marriage is "pooled" in a common pot. In economic theory, this assumption is made whenever a married couple is treated as if they have a common budget constraint. At the policy level, this assumption is reflected in, for example, measurements of low income or income inequality that are based only on family income, or the use of a married couple's total income to determine tax liabilities or eligibility for government benefits.

Yet a growing body of research casts doubt on the traditional economic view of marriage. More and more, scholars are beginning to see marriage as a "cooperative conflict" (Amartya Sen 1990). Spouses gain when they cooperate in raising children, sharing a home, or dividing labor so work can be done more efficiently. Yet spouses are in conflict over how the gains from marriage are to be distributed. For example, who gets to spend the money saved by preparing meals at home?

The chapters in this book describe several theories about marriage, and their predictions as to how the conflict will be resolved. For example,

I would like to acknowledge the financial support of the Social Sciences and Humanities Research Council of Canada and a Carleton University GR-6 research grant. Judith Madill was instrumental in the design and implementation of the survey. Shoshana Grossbard-Shechtman, Jon Kesselman, and Bob Pollak provided helpful comments on earlier versions of this paper.

Shoshana Grossbard-Shechtman (1993, this volume), argues that the "wage" each spouse receives for his or her part of the marriage is the outcome of a "marriage market" process. The supply and demand for husbands' and wives' spousal labor determines who gets what within marriage. Anything that affects supply and demand – for example, the ratio of women to men, the availability of substitutes for spousal labor, government programs such as "Bridefare" (Robert Cherry 1998), or the attractiveness of alternatives to marriage – will change how spouses share resources.

Another approach, described by Joni Hersch (Chapter 9 in this volume) is to imagine a husband and wife bargaining over the gains to coopera-tion. In bargaining models, anything that improves a person's bargaining position – such as greater earning power (Zhiqi Chen and Frances Woolley 1999; Shelly Lundberg and Robert Pollak 1993), more favorable treat-ment under divorce law (Marjorie B. McElroy and Mary Jean Horney 1981), or even physical strength and capacity for violence – will increase that person's share of the gains from marriage.

Studies testing the traditional economic view against newer approaches almost invariably find that the new approaches are better able to explain people's behavior. Factors that should have no real effects according to the traditional model, such as who receives government benefits, do in fact change families' expenditures patterns or labor force behavior. The implications of these findings go far beyond prescriptions for economic theorizing. The policy implications are profound. Measures of poverty that assume equal sharing within the household will mismeasure the true extent of poverty (Shelley Phipps and Peter Burton 1995). The same is true for inequality measures (Woolley and Judith Marshall 1994). Target-ing transfers such as Earned Income Tax Credits on the basis of family income may miss people in "secondary poverty" – those without access to other family members' resources. It matters which family member re-ceives government benefits. A family allowance paid to mothers may have quite different impacts from a tax deduction for dependants claimed by the higher-earning spouse.

The basic question addressed in this chapter is "Who gets what in a marriage?" The problem is shown in Figure 5.1. The curve PP shows the gains to cooperation in marriage, and all possible divisions of those gains between the husband and the wife. Divisions in the upper-left of Figure 5.1 are favorable to husbands, divisions in the lower-right favor wives. In this framework, two issues emerge. First, where on Figure 5.1 is a couple located? For example, are most marriages egalitarian in their

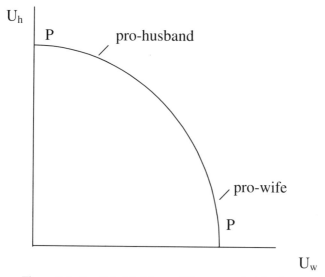

Figure 5.1. Possible Divisions of Resources in Marriage

distribution of individual utility, that is, located toward the center of Figure 5.1? Are the terms of marriages more favorable to one partner or the other? Second, what factors influence how the gains are shared? For example, do women who work for pay outside the home enjoy a greater share of the gains from marriage?

Economists rarely observe directly what happens within marriages. As a result, those wishing to understand marriage have generally used individual men's and women's consumption and work decisions, which are more readily observable, to infer how couples share resources. In the next section, I survey the contributions of some of this research, lessons we have learned, and some of the limitations of this research.

This paper answers the "Who gets what?" question in a new way: by using data on who controls family finances. Household finance data have been used extensively by sociologists, but very rarely by economists (one exception is Simone Dobbelsteen and Peter Kooreman 1997). I describe how much control each partner has over the family finances and household decision making, based on a survey of three hundred families with children in the Ottawa–Hull area carried out by the author, with Judith Madill. I then examine the factors underlying marital outcomes. Do partners with earnings of their own have a greater say in household decision making? Do younger couples have more equal relationships than older couples? What impact do children have?

WHAT DO ECONOMISTS KNOW?

While North Americans cherish the ideal of egalitarian marriage, studies in developing countries show that family members frequently share unequally in the household's resources. In poor countries, unequal access to resources can mean having less food or medical care, and the evidence of inequality is higher morbidity and mortality, or stunted growth. Lawrence Haddad, John Hoddinott, and Harold Alderman (1997) provide a comprehensive survey of the literature. Some of the recurring findings from this literature are that an increase in men's income is associated with more spending on tobacco, alcohol, and men's clothing, while transfers to women are significantly more likely to be spent on education, health, and household services, and women are more likely to spend money on children (Duncan Thomas 1990).

In rich countries, however, the question of "who gets what?" rarely takes the form of "who will have enough to eat?" Rather, it involves larger, more discretionary, expenditures. A number of studies have examined expenditures, such as clothing, which can be assigned to men, women, or children, as shown in Table 5.1. Martin Browning, Francois Bourguignon, Pierre-Andre Chiappori, and Valerie Lechene (1994) and Lundberg, Pollak, and Terence Wales (1997) find a positive relationship between women's share of family income and expenditures on women's or children's clothing, even after controlling for other factors that might affect clothing expenditures, such as labor force participation. Phipps and Burton (1998) study expenditures in more general terms, and find personal care, restaurant meals, women's clothing, and childcare expenditures increase as women's share of household income increases, holding total household income constant. Tobacco and alcohol expenditures, home food expenditures, and men's clothing expenditures increase with men's share of household income. Unfortunately many of these studies are based on the small number of goods that can unambiguously be assigned to one family member, such as clothing. Other expenditure information, such as spending on tobacco and alcohol, is unreliable.

An alternative approach is to use information on how much paid labor each household member supplies to infer how resources are shared in marriage. Shoshana Grossbard-Shechtman (1993) has used the term "spousal labor" to describe household production for the benefit of a partner. Remuneration for spousal labor is a "quasiwage." She has estimated the quasiwage received by women in marriage using labor supply data, hypothesizing that a decrease in the quasiwage in marriage will

Table 5.1 *Studies Based on Family Expenditure Data*

Authors	Study	Findings
Browning et al. (1994)	Canada, Family Expenditure Survey 1978, 1982, 1984, 1986, married couples in full-time employment without children	Expenditure on women's clothing increases with • Women's share of total household income • Total household expenditures • Husband's age less wife's ages
Lazear and Michael (1986)	United States, 1970 and 1979 Current Population Surveys, families with children	Results estimated from spending on adult clothing, tobacco, and alcohol. Income available to children higher in more educated male-headed households, lower in Southern, rural households, *not* controlling for total household income. Children receive on average 40 percent as much of household income as does an adult.
Lundberg, Pollak, and Wales (1997)	United Kingdom, Family Expenditure Survey, before and after 1979 child benefit change	Child benefit reforms transferring on average £400 from husbands to wives increased expenditures on children's clothing by £54 and women's clothing by £39.
Phipps and Burton (1998)	Canada, Family Expenditure Survey, 1986; couples with both partners in full-time employment	Personal care, restaurant meals, women's clothing, and childcare expenditures increase as women's share of household income increases. Tobacco and alcohol expenditures, home food expenditures, and men's clothing expenditures increase with men's share of household income.

increase women's paid labor force participation. She argues, using U.S. and Israeli data, that worsening marriage market conditions – for example, the relatively large number of marriageable women relative to men in the 1960s and 1970s – tended to be associated with faster increases in female labor participation and feminism, "a reflection of the growing frustration among women who were having a difficult time achieving the standard of living their mothers and older sisters had reached [through marriage] in the past" (1993: 98–9). In Chapter 10 of this book, Grossbard-Shechtman and Shoshana Neuman provide further evidence on the interaction between marriage and labor markets.

A number of other authors have also used information on paid work to estimate how resources are shared inside families. For example, Patricia Apps and Elizabeth Savage (1989) and Apps and Ray Rees (1993) find that men and women do share unequally in the benefits of marriage. Their estimates of "who gets what" are sensitive to several assumptions, particularly assumptions on how much unpaid work is done by each spouse. Chiappori, Bernard Fortin, and Guy Lacroix (1998) use a similar technique to Apps and Rees. They find, like Grossbard-Shechtman, that the "sex ratio," the number of men relative to women in an age group, is a key determinant of sharing. A 1 percent increase in the sex ratio raises transfers from husbands to their wives by around $2,500 per year. However, their methodology makes strong assumptions about the efficiency and consistency of marital decision making, and ignores household production.[1]

These findings suggest that family income is not a common pool that all family members access equally. The traditional division of labor with men in the market and women at home is not benign. It is better understood as a transaction, where love and care, time and money, are exchanged. Yet little is known about transactions inside households. Are there financial flows inside households that even out disparities in earnings and unpaid work? Perhaps one of the simplest ways of answering this question is just to ask couples how they manage their financial resources.

HOW FAMILIES MANAGE THEIR MONEY

Sociologists have studied money and marriage extensively (Jan Pahl 1983, 1989; Gail Wilson 1987; David Cheal 1989, 1998; Judith Treas 1993; Viviana Zelizer 1994). Their work is informative, and also reveals the complexities and tensions that arise when studying a couple's finances.

Financial decision making is double-edged. On the one hand, control over the family's finances is a source of power. For example, in Gary Becker's (1974) "rotten kid theorem," other family members act as the altruistic head of the household wishes, because the household head controls the family's finances. On the other hand, day-to-day money

---

[1] I am grateful to Shoshana Grossbard-Shechtman for pointing this out to me.

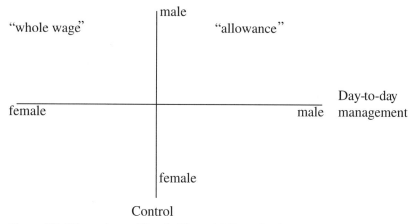

Figure 5.2. Dimensions of Family Financial Organization

management can be time-consuming, and even tedious. Sociologists have come up with various phrases to mark this distinction. For example, Christina Safilios-Rothschild (1976) uses the terms "orchestration power" and "implementation power" to distinguish between two types of decision-making authority:

Spouses who have "orchestration" power have, in fact, the power to make only the important and infrequent decisions that do not infringe upon their time but that determine the family life style and the major characteristics and features of the family. They also have the power to relegate unimportant and time-consuming decisions to their spouse who can, thus, derive a "feeling of power" by implementing those decisions within the limitations set by crucial and pervasive decisions made by the powerful spouse (p. 359).

Safilios-Rothschild's work suggests that there are two key characteristics of a couple's financial management system: who has control, or orchestration power, over major financial decisions, and who manages finances on a day-to-day basis. Figure 5.2 puts control and management together in one diagram. The horizontal axis shows who does the day-to-day financial management: Is it done by the male, by the female, or by both? The vertical axis shows control: Is it exercised by the husband, wife, or do both partners have an equal say? These four quadrants in Figure 5.2 capture a wide range of family financial systems. In the upper-left, for example, is the traditional British or American working-class arrangement known as the "whole wage" system, described in Pahl (1983) or Zelizer (1994). The husband hands over most of his paypacket to his wife for housekeeping. She manages the households' finances, but he usually makes the all-important decisions of how much of his paypacket to reserve for his own personal spending money. In the upper-right are the more upper-class traditional arrangements (again documented by Pahl 1983 and Zelizer 1994), whereby husbands both manage and control the family's finances, sometimes giving wives a set "allowance" for housekeeping. In the center are "shared management" systems, where both partners share in the management of family finances.

Other studies have shown that there are wide variations across cultures and, within a given country, across social classes, in how couples manage their money. For example, studies of Asian family financial management, such as Hanna Papanek and Laurel Schwede (1988), have found that wives dominate financial decision making. In 70.5 percent of the Indonesian couples surveyed by Papanek and Schwede, the wife decided all money matters, possibly consulting with her husband or other household members. Low-income British families show a similar pattern. For example, Wilson (1987) found that three-quarters of the low-income families she surveyed had one person managing the household finances, and that person was usually the wife, while Pahl (1983) found wife-controlled management systems in 70 percent of the British low-income families she studied. However in the high-income families surveyed by Pahl (1983), three-quarters had husband-controlled financial management systems. By way of contrast, Treas's study of nine thousand American couples, based on the Survey of Income and Program Participation, found that 64.4 percent had only joint accounts, and so "merge their individual interests into a single economic collective" (Treas 1983: 723).

The wide variation in forms of financial management used by couples suggests that evidence on family financial management can be used to test the various models of marriage described in this volume. For example, the marriage market approach suggests that a partner working inside the home should receive some form of quasiwage, some form of remuneration, for their spousal labor. Family financial management patterns testify to the existence – or absence – of remuneration for spousal labor. A couple with a traditional division of labor can institutionalize equal sharing by depositing all incomes into a joint account to which both have access. Alternatively, a wage earner can institutionalize unequal access to resources by, for example, keeping all financial accounts in his or her name. Patterns of access, and information about who has control over the financial resources, provide some evidence about "who gets what" inside a marriage. Where, in terms of Figure 5.2, do most couples fall?

Among our respondents, the ideal of marriage as an equal partnership is strong. In the couples we surveyed, 56 percent of men and 48 percent of women when asked, "Who would you say really controls the money which comes into this household?" responded that they controlled the money together. Yet, at the same time, we found differences between patterns of orchestration and patterns of implementation. When asked "Who would you say makes the day to day spending decisions in this house?" the most common response was again joint decision making, chosen by 43 percent of respondents, but a substantial minority – 38 percent – of respondents said the woman was mostly responsible for day-to-day spending. Less than 7 percent of respondents identified the male partner as responsible. However, when it comes to orchestration, "Who . . . does the overall planning of money matters in this house?" there is jointness, but much more male, involvement. Although 49 percent of couples report joint decision making, over a quarter of respondents said the male partner was mostly responsible, with around 17 percent identifying the female partner.

Yet how reliable are these subjective perceptions of household decision making? At one level, it seems reasonable to expect people to know which partner has greater influence on household outcomes. But as Bina Agarwal (1997: 15) argues, differences (and inequalities) in men's and women's roles inside marriages may be accepted as a natural and self-evident part of the social order. The male "head of the household" will not have to demand the best and largest portion of meat if all family members unquestioningly accept his privilege as "tradition." For this reason, we place less emphasis in this chapter on subjective measures of decision making, for example, "Who would you say really controls the money?" Ideals of equality are so strong that we are overwhelmed with joint responses, and it is hard to know exactly what these joint responses mean. Instead, we focus on less subjective measures of access and control over money – who makes cash withdrawals, who reconciles the accounts, who writes checks – questions couples can more easily answer objectively.

The project is different from that of Treas (1993). Treas models couples' decisions to merge or keep separate their family finances on the presumption that, when money is kept in a joint bank account, both partners can access the money equally. The findings of this study call Treas's presumptions into question. I will show that, even when couples have joint bank accounts, they play separate and often unequal roles in the management of the family's finances. At the same time, I will call into question the "separateness" of separate bank accounts. Treas, for example, speculates that a wife's account "may be more collective in character" (1993: 729–30) than a husband's. I am able to provide evidence on the accuracy of this assertion with information on how much access and control partners have over "separate" bank accounts.

Our research is based on a sample of three hundred couples in the Ottawa–Hull region in Canada during 1995. The interviews consisted of one joint interview lasting about twenty minutes, two individual interviews lasting about forty minutes, and two individual self-completion questionnaires. The interviews were carried out in the respondents' homes. The individual interviews were carried out in privacy whenever possible; this was facilitated by having the other partner fill out the questionnaire while the individual interview was being carried out.

The survey was limited to English-speaking couples with children under eighteen. Initial contact was made through a telephone call. In this initial phone call, the potential respondent was asked prescreening questions, the nature of the survey was explained, a time was agreed upon for the initial interviews. Of those surveyed, 88 percent are married and 11 percent are living in common law relationships. The median length of the relationship is ten and half years, 15.7 percent of male and 15.3 percent of female respondents have been married before, the median age of female respondents is thirty-six, the median age for male respondents thirty-eight. We obtained income data from both male and female respondents independently; males reported a median household income in the $65,000 to $69,999 range (in Canadian dollars), while the median household income reported by females was $70,000 to $74,999; however, the differences between male and female reported incomes were not statistically significant (Pearson chi squared $= 0.79$).

Material Equality?

The starting point for the analysis was a sketch of who has access to, and control over, various financial resources. Respondents were asked "How many bank, credit union, trust company or other similar accounts do you have?" then asked a series of questions about access to and control over each account, for a maximum of six accounts. Table 5.2 shows, for accounts one through six, responses to the question "Whose name or names is the account in?" Recorded are the percentage of accounts held by males and females, by other family members (such as children), as well as the percent jointly held, and the total number of couples having such an account.

Table 5.2 *Accounts Held by Men and Women Separately and Joint Accounts,*
in Percentages

Account	Male	Female	Joint	Other	N =	Active
1	13.7	20.0	63.3	1.7	300	96.7
2	15.6	24.7	53.8	4.4	275	93.1
3	21.1	26.8	31.9	18.8	213	86.4
4	28.1	19.9	20.5	28.8	146	87.7
5	30.9	12.8	21.3	28.7	94	84.0
6	18.0	24.0	22.0	24.0	50	82.0

Note: Figures calculated by the author from own survey data. Percentages do not add up to 100 because of refusals. Accounts are designated as active if they have been used in the last twelve months.

The major conclusion from Table 5.2 is that stated ownership of bank accounts is most often joint. The primary account (the one mentioned first by the respondents) is, for 63.3 percent of couples, a joint account. The percentage of accounts that are held separately by one spouse, either the male or the female, rises as we move from the primary account into additional accounts, reaching a maximum of almost half of all "fourth" accounts. The accounts mentioned last are more likely to be in another family member's name.

When accounts are separate, women are as likely to hold them as men. The total number of "female" accounts is greater than the total number of "male" accounts (238 as opposed to 208). The impression of femaleness in Table 5.2 is reinforced by a "ladies first" convention, as women's accounts are reported prior to men's accounts.

One possible reason that women have more accounts is that they may be more involved in the households' day-to-day financial management. This would mean, in terms of Figure 5.2, that the average couple would be toward the center, or slightly to the left, of the diagram. A more detailed analysis of financial management practices supports the hypothesis that women have more day-to-day involvement. Tables 5.3 through 5.5 show who performs a range of activities according to whether the accounts are male-name, female-name, or joint. The data given in these tables are for the account designated as "account 1" by the respondents. Similar data were collected for up to six bank accounts, but the basic pattern that emerges for accounts two through six is similar to the data for account one presented in Tables 5.3 through 5.5. (Respondents were not instructed as to which account they should consider as "first." I have used account

Table 5.3 *Who Does What in Male-Name Accounts, in Percentages of All Male-Name Accounts*

	Cash withdrawals	Writes checks	Records	Keeps track of balance	Reconciles
Male always (1)	61.0	67.6	38.5	66.7	33.3
Male more (2)	2.4	8.1	0	0	0
Equal (3)	7.3	0	10.3	7.7	2.6
Female more (4)	8.9	2.7	0	2.6	0
Female always (5)	2.4	8.1	7.7	7.7	2.6
Mean value	1.68	1.39	1.91	1.64	1..40
(standard error)	(0.21)	(0.22)	(0.31)	(0.23)	(0.29)
Nobody/not done	9.8	13.5	43.5	15.4	61.5
N =	N = 41	N = 37	N = 39	N = 39	N = 39

Note: Figures calculated by the author from the family financial management survey. Figures refer to "account 1" only.

Table 5.4 *Who Does What in Female-Name Accounts, in Percentages of All Female-Name Accounts*

	Cash withdrawals	Writes checks	Records	Keeps track of balance	Reconciles
Male always (1)	1.7	0	4.9	6.6	4.9
Male more (2)	1.7	1.7	1.6	0	0
Equal (3)	5.0	1.7	0	1.6	1.6
Female more (4)	10.0	0	1.6	1.6	3.3
Female always (5)	75	78	52.5	73.8	42.6
Mean value	4.66	4.80	4.57	4.63	4.50
(standard error)	(0.11)	(0.12)	(0.20)	(0.16)	(0.22)
Nobody/not done	5.0	16.9	39.3	16.4	47.5
N =	N = 60	N = 59	N = 61	N = 61	N = 61

Note: Figures calculated by the author from the family financial management survey. Figures refer to "account 1" only.

one information to avoid clouding the picture with data on little used, relatively unimportant accounts.)

The key conclusion from Tables 5.3 and 5.4 is that if a bank account is in the name of one partner, that partner in most cases will have primary access to and control over that account. For both male- and female-held accounts, and for the five key activities identified, the account holder carried the activity in the majority of cases. However, there is female involvement in managing male-name accounts, as well as male involvement in female-name accounts. Women more often or mostly withdraw

Table 5.5 *Who Does What in Joint Accounts, in Percentages*

	Cash withdrawals	Writes checks	Records	Keeps track of balance	Reconciles
Male always (1)	13.2	13.4	20.8	26.9	27.4
Male more (2)	21.1	11.8	0.5	5.4	5.9
Equal (3)	33.7	15.5	10.4	14.5	8.1
Female more (4)	17.9	27.3	10.4	10.8	3.8
Female always (5)	8.9	25.1	36.6	36.0	37.1
Mean value	2.88	3.36	3.43	3.25	3.21
(standard error)	(0.09)	(0.11)	(0.13)	(0.13)	(0.15)
Nobody/not done	4.7	6.4	21.3	6.5	17.7
N =	190	187	183	186	186

Note: Figures calculated by the author from the family financial management survey. Accounts are designated as "account 1."

cash in 11.3 percent of male-name accounts, and women write checks in 10.9 percent of such accounts. Men are involved in managing female-name accounts too, with the greatest involvement being in reconciling and recording transactions.

One might wonder how one partner can make withdrawals or write checks on an account in the other's name. However, partners may share bank cards for making cash withdrawals, or the account holder may sign checks filled out by the other spouse. Another possibility is that respondents are identifying as "separate" joint accounts where one person is the first-named account holder, main contributor, or most active user.

Tables 5.3 and 5.4 also show the average "male-ness" of male accounts and the average "female-ness" of female accounts. A value of 3 represents equality, values below 3 pro-male, and values above 3 are pro-female. Women's accounts are more "female" than male accounts are "male," although these differences are not statistically significant at $p = 0.05$. Yet because there are substantially more female-held accounts (20.0 percent of primary accounts) than male-held accounts (13.7 percent), when finances are separate, financial management is more often in the hands of women.

Table 5.5 shows the same information for joint accounts. Table 5.5 shows that, even in nominally joint accounts, one person acts as "financial manager," carrying out managerial activities such as recording transactions, keeping track of the balance, and reconciling the account. The male partner always or mostly conducts these activities in 20 to 30 percent of the households, and the female partner does so in 40 to 50 percent of

households. The mean value is pro-female (above 3.0) for all of these activities, and statistically significantly so (at $p = 0.05$) for writing checks,
recording, and keeping the account balance. The most female-dominated
activity is check writing. Women are responsible for check writing in over
50 percent of joint accounts, a fact no doubt linked with women's performance of grocery shopping and other tasks. The managerial activity that
men are most involved in is reconciling the accounts.

Of the five activities identified in the survey, the only one that both
partners carried out equally in a substantial number (33.7 percent) of
households, and the only activity that men do more often than women, is
making cash withdrawals. Cash withdrawals are special for a number of
reasons. First, cash is not easily accounted for. Cash leaves no paper trail,
in contrast to, credit cards, for example. Cash use may reflect a partner's
freedom not to account for expenditures. Second, cash is particularly
convenient for small, discretionary expenditures, such as buying lunch
at work, buying beer, or spending on leisure activities. Historically, in
British whole wage systems, men's cash allowance was often referred
to as "beer money." The pattern of cash withdrawals may reflect each
partner's levels of discretionary expenditures. Third, cash is easy to carry,
compared to a checkbook, for example. Men may use cash rather than
checks because men do not carry handbags. Finally, and most importantly,
cash withdrawals confer access and control over family resources, but not
time-consuming administration and management. The high level of male
involvement in making cash withdrawals indicates that family financial
management is a less female-dominated activity than we would think if
we looked only at who writes most of the checks.

A detailed analysis confirms the initial impression: In terms of
Figure 5.2, the average household is more likely to be on the left, with
the wife slightly more involved than the husband in day-to-day financial
management. Yet is this a cause for feminist celebration? Financial management is a double-edged sword. It can confer power, but it also involves
work. Is managing the household's finances like being a CEO, deciding
what happens when, holding the orchestration power? Or is it more like
being a cleaner, tidying up the mess that others have left, implementing
decisions made by others? In the next section of this chapter, I carry out
tests that help to decide between these two interpretations. The idea behind these tests is that, if managing finances is a form of orchestration
power, we would expect it to be carried out by the spouse with more bargaining power – that is, the partner with the higher income, more options
outside the relationship, and so on.

Determinants of Male and Female Control

In this section, I use regression analysis to explain the patterns of control documented in the preceding section. The hypothesis being tested is that the "male-ness" or "female-ness" of a family's financial management is influenced by each partner's economic position and opportunities, both inside and outside marriage.

Formally, I take as a dependent variable the control over money (CM), measured from 1 (male always) to 5 (female always), as in Tables 5.2 to 5.5. All accounts designated as "account 1," whether male, female or joint, were included in the analysis. It is hypothesized that each partner's economic position and opportunities affect how money is controlled in marriage, that is, $CM = f(X) + e$, where X is a vector of economic and other variables, and e a random component, assumed to be normally distributed.

If control over money confers and reflects power, we would expect partners with better bargaining positions to have greater control. The literature identifies a number of factors that affect the allocation of resources in marriage. First, theoretically, a higher income enhances a person's bargaining position (Chen and Woolley 1999). A higher income improves a person's fall-back position – the well-being that one partner can achieve without the cooperation of the other partner. Previous empirical work has found that income matters, as surveyed in this study. Given that CM measures the "femaleness" of control, we would predict a negative coefficient on male income and a positive coefficient on female income.

Second, the better a person's "outside options," or the options available outside the current relationship, the better her bargaining position (Woolley 1999). We use three variables to measure outside options. If the couple has a common law relationship, instead of being legally married, this will alter the options available to each of the spouses if the relationship breaks down. For example, the couple can part without going through formal separation and asset division proceedings. It is not obvious from a theoretical point of view whether a common law relationship favors men or women, but it may matter.

The spouses' ages and their age difference also affect their outside options. As a person gets older, his or her probability of remarrying decreases, diminishing the number of options outside the present relationship. However, if remarriage prospects for both partners diminish with age, we would not expect age to affect *relative* bargaining positions much. However, the greater the age difference between the spouses, the better, relatively, the outside options of the younger spouse. For this reason, we included the age difference, calculated as male age less female age, as an explanatory variable. As well as having theoretical support, this variable has been found by Grossbard-Shechtman and Shoshana Neuman (1988) to affect the presumed quasiwage of women in marriage, and by Browning, Bourguignon, Chiappori, and LeChene (1994) to shift the "sharing rule" inside marriage in women's favor. The predicted coefficient on male age–female age is positive.

Education is another influence on outside options, as the educated have more employment and other opportunities. Yet there are other possible interpretations of education. Education, to a certain extent, measures socioeconomic status. There is also a liberal notion that education, particularly university education, exposes people to a wide range of ideas and attitudes, and makes their behavior less subject to tradition and custom. Because education captures so many influences, I include "years schooling" in the regression equation, without having a strong prior on its sign.

Yet managing the household's finances involves work as well as conferring control. If the "work" aspect of financial management is relatively more important than the "control" aspect, we would expect managing money to be part of an overall division of labor within the household. One theory of marriage (see, for example, Francine Blau, Marianne Ferber, and Anne Winkler 1998) suggests that spouses can divide work efficiently by specializing where they are relatively more productive, for example, if one spouse specializes in paid work and the other unpaid. We include two variables intended to measure the division of labor. The first is "full-time," a dummy variable indicating whether or not the female partner is in full-time paid employment. We used full-time rather than part-time employment because Canadian evidence suggests that women's part-time work permits couples to retain a traditional division of labor within the household (Statistics Canada 1995). Women employed full-time are more likely to challenge – because of time pressure if for no other reason – the traditional division of labor within the household. If managing money is part of the work of grocery shopping and everyday household tasks, we would expect women employed full-time to do less money management. The one caveat to this prediction is that people employed in managerial or financial positions may be more likely to have knowledge, such as bookkeeping or spreadsheet skills, that make them good financial managers. However, the effect of skill should be captured, at least in part, through the education variable.

Table 5.6 *Descriptive Statistics on Explanatory Variables*

	Minimum	Maximum	Mean	Median	n
Male income	No income (1)	150,000 and above (37)	38,000 to 39,999 (19.41)	45,000 to 49,999 (21)	297
Female income	No income (1)	120,000 to 129,999 (34)	20,000 to 21,999 (10.92)	20,000 to 21,999 (10)	292
Male age	19	63	38.99	38	273
Male–female age	17	–13	1.99	2.0	273
Male schooling	4	30	16.35	16	300
Female schooling	9	32	15.53	16	300
Male married before	0	1	0.157	0	299
Female married before	0	1	0.153	0	299
Common law	0	1	0.111	0	296
Female full-time	0	1	0.463	0	300

Note: Calculated by the author from the Family Financial Management data set.

Two other variables, "male – married before" and "female – married before," also capture division of labor within the household. As Treas (1993: 728) argues, an individual whose previous marriage ended in divorce or widowhood has less reason to expect permanence. Yet the traditional division of labor renders the partner specializing in household production extremely vulnerable in the event of divorce. When a partner has been married before, we would expect to see less specialization, either toward men or women. "Married before" may, however, also proxy a number of other variables, for example, attitudes toward marriage.

Some explanatory variables could not be included because of the nature of our sample. The entire sample is composed of people who have children, so we cannot compare those with and without children. Although we did experiment with, for example, family size, that variable had little explanatory power. Broad population or geographic characteristics, such as sex ratios, could not be included because the sample is drawn from a single geographic area.

Table 5.6 summarizes the explanatory variables used, along with their descriptive statistics. Most of the information in the table is straightforward; however, some points should be noted. First, the sample is well educated, with a mean sixteen years of schooling. In part, this reflects the nature of the sample area: Ottawa's two main industries, government and the high technology sector, attract highly educated employees. However, it may reflect some sample selection bias. Second, the income variable is the respondent's self-reported total income, reported separately by each partner. It is categorical, ranging from 1 (no income) to 37 ($150,000 or above). The income variable was formulated in categorical terms to increase response rates and make respondents feel as if their privacy was being protected. Actual income data would be useful; however, nothing can be done now to change the data collected. Other income measures are available in the data set. However, none fit so well as total income. Because the income measure used is unconventional, it is not obvious that the magnitude of the regression coefficients has any meaningful interpretation. Yet given that the dependent variable is simply a scalar, one-to-five measure of "female-ness" in money control, the sign and significance of the coefficients are our foci of concern.

Table 5.7 provides summaries of the linear regression results. The one striking finding is the significance of male income: Males with higher incomes exert more control over money. This is yet another blow for the traditional economic view of the family as a unitary entity, treating their financial resources as a common pool. Part of the explanation for the findings may be comparative advantage. Men with higher incomes are more likely to have managerial or professional jobs that require knowledge of financial management. This may explain the particularly strong effect of male income on "who reconciles." Yet the comparative advantage explanation is unlikely to be the whole story. Making cash withdrawals hardly requires managerial or professional skills, yet men with higher incomes are still more likely to do so. Also, the coefficient on male schooling, while insignificant, is positive, suggesting more educated men are more likely to have joint or female control of family finances. Instead, the strong effect of male income supports bargaining models of the family, which predict that greater incomes will be associated with greater control.

The coefficient on female income is of the expected sign – that is, a higher income increases the degree of female control. Yet the sign on female income is insignificant. The most likely explanation of this finding is that women are more likely than men to keep their incomes in separate accounts. Thirty-four percent of the women surveyed put their earnings into an account in their own name, as opposed to only 22 percent of men. Because the analysis is for the account labeled "account 1" only, a number of these separate, female bank accounts may be excluded from

Table 5.7 *Determinants of Control over Money*

	Who makes cash withdrawals	Writes checks	Who records	Who keeps track of balance	Who reconciles
Constant	2.18***	2.74***	3.772***	3.166***	3.886***
	(0.717)	(0.819)	(1.048)	(0.939)	(1.125)
Male income	−0.0225**	−0.0268**	−0.021**	−0.0343***	−0.040***
	(0.011)	(0.012)	(0.014)	(0.014)	(0.016)
Female income	0.0171	0.0237	0.0487	0.0270	0.0463
	(0.015)	(0.017)	(0.021)	(0.021)	(0.022)
Male age	0.0167	0.0217	0.0216	0.0091	−0.0025
	(0.015)	(0.016)	(0.020)	(0.018)	(0.022)
Male–female age	0.0498**	0.0347	−0.0167	0.0118	0.0578
	(0.024)	(0.028)	(0.034)	(0.032)	(0.038)
Male years schooling	0.0360	0.0152	−0.0208	0.0340	0.0003
	(0.028)	(0.031)	(0.037)	(0.035)	(0.040)
Female years schooling	−0.0043	−0.0297	−0.190	−0.0182	0.0143
	(0.033)	(0.040)	(0.049)	(0.043)	(0.052)
Male married before	−0.418	−0.612*	0.233	−0.318	−0.939**
	(0.292)	(0.064)	(0.437)	(0.390)	(0.477)
Female married before	0.145	−0.151	−0.505	−0.208	−0.116
	(0.270)	(0.306)	(3.90)	(0.352)	(0.799)
Common law	0.662**	0.888**	1.025**	0.968**	1.178**
	(0.313)	(0.362)	(0.442)	(0.396)	(0.024)
Female full-time	−0.264	−0.0817	0.151	−0.258	0.081
	(0.244)	(0.270)	(0.332)	(0.429)	(0.348)
n	244	235	232	233	178
Significance	0.025	0.060	0.064	0.127	0.022
R^2	0.083	0.075	0.091	0.065	0.114
Adjusted R^2	0.043	0.034	0.040	0.023	0.062

Note: Regression coefficients, standard errors in parentheses. *** indicates significance at $p = 0.01$, ** significance at $p = 0.05$, * significance at $p = 0.10$.

the analysis. Yet the fact that the coefficient on female income is of the expected sign provides tentative support for the economic theories of the family.

The significance of the spouses' age difference in explaining cash withdrawals is another interesting finding supporting, as outlined earlier, the idea that younger women are in a relatively more advantageous bargaining position. It is noteworthy that the age difference is significant only for cash withdrawals, which, I argued previously, involve more discretion and less work than other aspects of financial management.

One thing that is striking about the results in Table 5.7 is the consistent significance of the marital status variables, particularly "male married before" and "common law." Men who have been married before have more control over money, as is also the case of women in common law relationships. In order to understand why these variables mattered, I ran a multinomial logit regression, using the variables in Tables 5.6 and 5.7 to explain couples' choice of "male," "female," or "joint" accounts as "account 1." The results of the regression are reported in Table 5.8. The way to interpret these results is as follows. A negative coefficient, such as the coefficient on male schooling in the "male account" regression, means that when men are more educated, "account 1" is less likely to be only in their name. Because the coefficient on male schooling in the female regression is negative also (though insignificant), we would conclude that when men are more educated, they are less likely to have a first account under their own name, and more likely to have a joint first account.

Table 5.8 sheds some light on the marital status findings. When the male partner has been married before, the first account is more likely to be in the man's name, and less likely to be a joint account. This explains the results found in Table 5.7. When a man has been married before, "account 1" is more likely to be a separate account in the man's name, over which he is likely to have primary control. These results are consistent with Treas's (1993) finding that people who have been married before are less likely to have joint finances. It may be, as Treas suggests, that people who have been married before expect less permanence from their relationship. Alternatively, when child or spousal support must be paid to a former partner, the new partner may well wish to keep finances separate, rather than having her income go to support another family.

Table 5.8 also reveals that when people live in a common law relationship, "account 1" is more likely to be in the woman's name. I would suggest that this is because common law couples tend to be less likely to have a traditional division of labor, where men specialize in market work, and women in home work. Entering into a traditional relationship is more risky for the partner giving up paid work without protection of a marriage contract.

The multinomial logit methods used to create Table 5.8 can also be used to provide categorical, not linear, analysis of control over money. I ran multinomial logit regressions on the five control-over-money variables. Theoretically, the multinomial logit analysis is superior to the linear

Table 5.8 *Multinomial Logit Regression Results*

	Male account	Female account
	β	β
	(s.e.)	(s.e.)
Constant	3.71**	–1.01
	(1.77)	(1.41)
Male income	–0.0039	–0.0666***
	(0.030)	(0.026)
Female income	–0.0240	0.0621**
	(0.041)	(0.032)
Male age	–0.0855**	0.0091
	(0.040)	(0.028)
Male–female age	0.0282	0.100**
	(0.055)	(0.048)
Male years schooling	–0.170**	–0.0425
	(0.076)	(0.058)
Female years schooling	0.0347	0.0109
	(0.087)	(0.065)
Male married before	1.476**	0.476
	(0.610)	(0.527)
Female married before	0.474	0.220
	(0.581)	(0.498)
Common law	–0.607	1.318***
	(0.776)	(0.523)
Female full-time	–0.185	–0.232
	(0.606)	(0.485)

Note: n = 256, Pseudo r-squareds: Cox and Snell, 0.209; Nagelkerke, 0.256; McFadden, 0.139. Significance at $p = 0.01$ indicated by ***, $p = 0.05$ by **, $p = 0.10$ by *.

regression model. The linear model imposes an artificial cardinality on what are essentially categorical variables. Unfortunately, with five categories and a fairly small data set, the multinomial logit procedure encountered difficulties, and the validity of the model fit is uncertain.

Because of questions about the model's robustness, and because of space constraints, this chapter does not report the results in full. However, the basic findings of the multinomial logit model replicate the linear model. Higher male incomes lead to a significantly greater probability of male control over withdrawing cash, writing checks, recording transactions, keeping track of the balance, or reconciling accounts. Female income was also significant in some of the multinomial logit regressions, being associated with more female control over, for example, cash withdrawals. Males who have been married before are more likely to control "account 1"; however, the parameter estimates in some cases are very large (tending toward infinity), and standard errors cannot be calculated. Education was significant in some regressions; for example, male education was associated with higher levels of "female more" responses to "who writes checks" and "who keeps track of the balance," while female education was positive and significant in "equal" recording of transactions.

In general, an inspection of the multinomial logit results reveals that the linear results are primarily driven by higher levels of male control associated with higher male incomes, male education, or a previous marriage, and by lower levels of male control associated with common law relationships. Equality is extremely difficult to predict; only one coefficient was statistically significant in all of the "equal" regressions.

CONCLUSIONS

This chapter presented a first analysis of a rich new Canadian data set. Although much more work remains to be done, even this analysis reveals much of significance. The family cannot be viewed as a separate entity, a model of harmony and sharing in a world of discord. People's economic and social circumstances shape how they live their family lives. The effects are not limited to who does the dishes. Access to, and control over, the family's financial resources is shaped by each family member's circumstances. Who has the most control over money? Women are more involved than men with every aspect of managing money. The area with the greatest male involvement is making cash withdrawals. Those with higher earnings have more control over money. Do couples pool their money? Most pool at least part of their financial resources. People who have been married before are more likely to keep their finances separate. Living in a common law relationship is less likely to be associated with traditional financial management patterns. The results here are a challenge to anyone who believes the family can be treated as one for purposes of economic theory or public policy.

REFERENCES

Agarwal, Bina. *A Field of One's Own: Gender and Land Rights in South Asia.* Cambridge, UK: Cambridge University Press, 1994.
Apps, Patricia and Rees, Ray. "Labour Supply, Household Production and Intra-Family Welfare Distribution." University of Guelph Working Paper, 1993.

Apps, Patricia and Savage, Elizabeth. "Labour Supply, Welfare Rankings and the Measurement of Inequality." *Journal of Public Economics*, 1989, pp. 335–64.

Becker, Gary S. "A Theory of Social Interactions." *Journal of Political Economy*, 1974, *70*, pp. 1–13.

Blau, Francine, Ferber, Marianne and Winkler, Anne. *The Economics of Women, Men and Work,* 3rd ed. Upper Saddle River, NJ: Prentice Hall, 1998.

Browning, Martin, Bourguignon, Francois, Chiappori, Pierre-Andre and Lechene, Valerie. "Incomes and Outcomes: A Structural Model of Intra-Household Allocation." *Journal of Political Economy,* 1994, *102*(6), pp. 1067–96.

Cheal, David. "Strategies of Resource Management in Household Economies: Moral Economy or Political Economy?" in Richard R. Wilk, ed., *The Household Economy: Reconsidering the Domestic Mode of Production.* Boulder, CO: Westview Press, 1989.

———. "Poverty and Relative Income: Family Transactions and Social Policy," in David Cheal, Frances Woolley, and Meg Luxton, eds., *How Families Cope and Why Policymakers Need to Know.* CPRN Study No. F02. Ottawa: Renouf Publishing, 1998.

Chen, Zhiqi and Woolley, Frances. "A Cournot-Nash Model of Family Decision Making." Carleton University Working Paper, 1999.

Cherry, Robert. "Rational Choice and the Price of Marriage." *Feminist Economics,* 1998, *4*(1), pp. 27–50.

Chiappori, Pierre-Andre, Fortin, Bernard and Lacroix, Guy. "Household Labor Supply, Sharing Rule and the Marriage Market." University of Laval Working Paper 98–10, http://www.ecn.ulaval.ca/w3/recherche/cahiers/1998/9810.pdf, 1998.

Dobbelsteen, Simone and Kooreman, Peter. "Financial Management, Bargaining and Efficiency within the Household: An Empirical Analysis." *De Economist,* 1997, *145*(3), pp. 345–66.

Haddad, Lawrence, Hoddinott, John and Alderman, Harold. *Intrahousehold Resource Allocation in Developing Countries: Models, Methods and Policy.* Baltimore, MD, and London: Johns Hopkins University Press, 1997.

Grossbard-Shechtman, Shoshana. *On the Economics of Marriage: A Theory of Marriage, Labor and Divorce.* Boulder, CO: Westview Press, 1993.

Grossbard-Shechtman, Shoshana and Neuman, Shoshana. "Labor Supply and Marital Choice." *Journal of Political Economy,* 1988, *96*, pp. 1294–302.

Lundberg, Shelly and Pollak, Robert. "Separate Spheres Bargaining and the Marriage Market." *Journal of Political Economy,* 1993, *101*, pp. 988–1010.

Lundberg, Shelly, Pollak, Robert and Wales, Terence. "Do Husband and Wives Pool Their Resources? Evidence from the U.K. Child Benefit." *Journal of Human Resources,* 1997, *32*(3), pp. 463–80.

McElroy, Marjorie B. and Horney, Mary Jean. "Nash Bargained Household Decision-Making." *International Economic Review,* 1981, *22*, pp. 333–49.

Pahl, Jan. "The Allocation of Money and the Structuring of Inequality within Marriage." *Sociological Review,* 1983, *13*(2), pp. 237–62.

———. *Money and Marriage.* Basingstoke, Hampshire: MacMillan Education, 1989.

128   *Frances Woolley*

Papanek, Hanna and Schwede, Laurel. "Women Are Good with Money: Earning and Managing in an Indonesian City," in Daisy Dwyer and Judith Bruce, eds., *A Home Divided: Women and Income in the Third World.* Stanford, CA: Stanford University Press, 1988.

Phipps, Shelley and Burton, Peter. "Sharing within Families: Implications for the Measurement of Poverty among Individuals in Canada." *Canadian Journal of Economics*, 1995, *28*(1), pp. 177–204.

———. "What's Mine Is Yours? The Influence of Male and Female Incomes on Patterns of Household Expenditure." *Economica*, 1998, *65*, pp. 599–613.

Safilios-Rothschild, Christina. "A Macro and Micro-Examination of Family Power and Love." *Journal of Marriage and the Family*, 1976, *37*, pp. 355–62.

Sen, Amartya K. "Gender and Cooperative Conflicts," in Irene Tinker, ed., *Persistent Inequalities: Women and World Development.* New York: Oxford University Press, 1990, pp. 123–49.

Statistics Canada. *As Time Goes By . . . Time Use of Canadians.* Ottawa: Statistics Canada, Catalogue No. 89-544E, 1995.

Thomas, Duncan. "Intrahousehold Resource Allocation: An Inferential Approach." *Journal of Human Resources*, 1990, *25*(4), pp. 635–64.

Treas, Judith. "Money in the Bank: Transaction Costs and the Economic Organization of Marriage." *American Sociological Review*, 1993, *58*, pp. 723–36.

Wilson, Gail. "Money: Patterns of Responsibility and Irresponsibility in Marriage," in Julia Brannen and Gail Wilson, eds., *Give and Take in Families.* London: Allen and Unwin, 1987.

Woolley, Frances and Marshall, Judith. "Measuring Inequality within the Household." *Review of Income and Wealth*, 1994, *40*(4), pp. 415–31.

Woolley, Frances. "Family: Economics of," in Janice Peterson and Margaret Lewis, eds., *The Elgar Companion to Feminist Economics.* Cheltenham, UK: Edward Elgar, 1999.

Zelizer, Viviana A. *The Social Meaning of Money.* New York: Basic Books, 1994.

SIX

Marriage, Assets, and Savings

Joseph P. Lupton and James P. Smith

There has been considerable research documenting the economic consequences of differences among and transitions between alternative household arrangements (James P. Smith 1988). Invariably, these studies have
used some definition of income as the index of economic well-being.
While income is certainly critical, wealth is an important complementary
measure of a household's command over economic resources. Studies
using wealth also have the advantage of informing us about the impact
that alternative family arrangements have on individual and aggregate
savings, a subject about which we currently know relatively little.

One reason why existing research used income is that until recently,
household surveys have measured wealth either quite poorly or not at all
(Martin Browning and Annamaria Lusardi 1996). These data limitations
were so severe that they discouraged theoretical reasoning about the
impact of marriage on savings behavior. Fortunately, this situation has
been changing rapidly as a number of social science household surveys
now include well-designed wealth modules.

This paper explores the relationship between household type and asset
accumulation. Households are distinguished along standard demographic
lines – whether they marry, divorce, separate, or become widowed. We rely
on two household surveys with high-quality wealth modules. The first –
the Health and Retirement Survey (HRS) – is ideal for depicting wealth
disparities across households in a relatively narrow age range. Wealth is a

We greatly appreciate the excellent programming assistance of Iva Maclennan and
David Rumpel. We also appreciate the constructive comments of Shoshana Grossbard-
Shechtman. This research was supported by a grant from NICHD to RAND.

129

core HRS module, and considerable survey resources were spent on improving the quality of the asset information collected. The second survey is the Panel Study of Income Dynamics (PSID), which spans the full age span of households and included wealth modules in its 1984, 1989, and 1994 waves. The PSID allows us to model changes in wealth holdings of individuals living in different types of households across time. Furthermore, the PSID provides information regarding households' savings in various assets, including any capital gains that they had in a home, business, or the stock market.

This chapter first summarizes some theoretical reasons why different types of households may save at different rates. We then use the HRS to highlight the principal crosssectional wealth differences among alternative household arrangements and to describe household wealth changes associated with marital status transitions. The final section uses the three PSID wealth modules to model household savings behavior associated with alternative marital states.

THEORETICAL CONSIDERATIONS

Does marriage increase or decrease aggregate national savings? Will two people save more collectively as two unrelated individuals or will they have more assets as a married couple? Despite the simplicity of the question and the sharp secular changes taking place in the prevalence of marriage, very little theoretical or empirical research has addressed this issue. Family composition may affect savings in several ways. There is at least one good theoretical reason why marriage could depress savings. One motivation for savings is to insure against future risks, such as income or job loss or episodes of poor health (Jacob Mincer 1978). In part, marriage is a risk-reducing institution, as individual members insure each other against life's vagaries. To provide a simple example, one spouse may increase his or her labor supply to offset job problems faced by the other. Similarly, spouses may care for each other in times of poor health, lessening the necessity of accumulating a nest egg for future medical costs. For these reasons, precautionary savings may be higher for single households than for married ones.

Marriage may also be a wealth-enhancing institution, disproportionately altering total output and total consumption. Complementarities in production among the partners imply that the total product of the married couple is larger than the sum of outputs of each produced separately (Gary Becker 1981). In contrast, economies of scale in consumption suggest that they could achieve the same utility with less combined expenditure than the sum of their individual consumption if living apart. Indeed, these shared costs (housing, food preparation, and such) justify the widespread use of household equivalence scales. There are wealth and price effects associated with this effect of marriage (see Michael Hurd 1998). Of course, a couple might use all this additional wealth for additional consumption, leaving savings unaffected. However, if bequests are related to household wealth, the net implication of this more than proportionate expansion in output compared to consumption is that marriage should expand savings.

The price effects are due to scale economies of household consumption. Consider the extreme case with a single consumption pure public good. The best example is housing where two may well be able to live as cheaply as one. Two single people could live alone their entire lives, or they could marry for part of their lives and be single (divorced) thereafter. For the purpose of this argument, let incomes be unaffected by marriage and let divorce be exogenous. If demand for this consumption good (housing) is completely price inelastic, then the couple's combined utility from housing will be smoothed over the married and divorced states. But this smoothing implies lower consumption expenditures while married compared to the combined expenditures while single. Consequently, a household will save during the couple's married years to finance the additional combined housing expenditures when single.

This conclusion is tempered by the assumption of zero price elasticity. Economies of scale have made housing consumption cheaper during marriage, so a couple may respond by purchasing more housing (for example, a bigger house). Any additional housing consumption would reduce the savings-enhancing effects of marriage, and if the price elasticity exceeded one, total consumption expenditures could actually increase (and savings fall) while married. Barring this case, there is a presumption then that both the wealth and price effects due to economies of scale will produce higher savings rates during the married years.

A central distinction in economic models of savings is between permanent and transitory income shocks. With no uncertainty and perfect access to capital markets, the combination of current non-human wealth and human wealth (or permanent income) rather than current income is the determinant of household consumption (Angus Deaton 1992; Milton Friedman 1957). The household will consume increases in permanent income while saving temporary income increments. This rigid distinction between the influence of permanent and current income is weakened if we relax the two caveats on capital markets and uncertainty. Imperfect capital markets and incomplete foresight would both assign to current income an independent role in determining current consumption, a role that will likely depend on the life-cycle stage.

These distinctions should carry over to marital status transitions. If they see a transition into a separation or divorce as relatively transitory, disrupted families may try to maintain prior consumption levels and absorb more of their income loss through dissavings. This distinction between permanent and transitory income may vary across different household types. For example, divorced or separated families as well as those more recently married who have less collateral or assets would more likely absorb a current income decline by reducing consumption.

Several other effects of marriage may impact savings decisions. Several authors have argued that marriage is "protective" of health, thereby reducing mortality rates of spouses at older ages (Lee A. Lillard and Yoram Weiss 1996). This protective effect of marriage is larger for men than women, as women provide more care that enhances the health of their partner. Increases in life expectancy should encourage more wealth accumulation in order to store up funds for this longer lifetime of consumption. If the ages of retirement do not change, the married household should reduce its per period consumption flow somewhat, thereby accumulating more assets that it then depletes over a longer postretirement period.

Children are a primary reason for a family and may lead to variation in savings across family types. The rearing of children is a forward-looking activity. People may sort positively with an eye for the future advantages of longlasting marriage on children and may subsequently end up with larger families. Indeed, Irving Fisher (1930) in his classic work argued that children should enhance savings since they encourage time preference for the future. Similarly, a positive bequest motive should flatten consumption and wealth profiles especially at older ages (Hurd 1990), as families preserve some of their wealth to transfer to their heirs. Intergenerational bequests take the form of both human capital and financial transfers. With declining rates of return to human capital investments, families will initially specialize in these investments so that financial bequests will kick in only at higher income levels (Becker 1981). This argument suggests that significant asset accumulation for bequests may be operative only at high incomes.

The expected relationship between children and assets is complicated, because, in a life-cycle framework, the effect of childbearing on family savings flows through a number of additional channels. On the consumption side, children have two effects. Obviously, the needs of children must be met and the demands of commodities complementary with children will also increase. In addition, parents' consumption may change as they alter the allocation of their time to labor markets and home production. Whether the family as a whole consumes more or less depends, however, on whether market-purchased goods are net substitutes for or complements of children and household time.

Given the impact of children on total family consumption, their effect on savings and asset accumulation will depend on whether the reallocation of household members' time lowers family income more than family consumption. The dominant linkage on the income side is the reduction in family income resulting from the lower work effort of women induced by the presence of a young child. The impact of a child may depend on children's ages and their numbers. At older ages, parents may save to accumulate funds for such expenses as the costs of college. These arguments suggest that it may be necessary to disentangle these life-cycle factors before isolating any effect of children through bequests. The effect of children on savings may be negative early in the life cycle, when children tend to depress the labor supply significantly, but positive at older ages when college is on the horizon.

One difficulty precluding any simple causal interpretation of wealth differences across households is that the distribution of households across family types is non-random. Low-income families are the most likely to dissolve, either through widowhood, separation, or divorce, and are also less likely to remarry within any fixed time frame. Therefore, any association between wealth and family type could simply reflect selectivity. Crosssectional surveys are inherently incapable of distinguishing between selectivity and behavioral effects. To begin making these distinctions, we will use the PSID in the next section.

WEALTH DIFFERENCES ACROSS HOUSEHOLD TYPES

This section summarizes wealth disparities obtained from the baseline wave of the HRS, a nationally representative sample of 7,608 households with a member born between 1931 and 1941 (roughly 51–61 years old in 1992).[1] Given its focus on the preretirement years, HRS's principal objective is to monitor transitions in retirement, income, wealth, and health.

---

[1] For a more detailed description of the HRS design, see F. Thomas Juster and Richard Suzman 1995.

Table 6.1 *HRS Net Worth by Marital Status (Thousands of Dollars)*

	Means						
	Married	Partner	Separated	Divorced	Widowed	Never married	All
All	288.4	218.2	85.3	117.6	119.5	166.1	238.5
White	303.6	271.8	136.5	132.5	146.7	213.6	263.7
Black	120.4	44.0	18.8	45.7	36.3	23.2	71.6
Hispanic	106.6	64.6	8.6	36.9	50.2	31.1	79.7
	Medians						
	Married	Partner	Separated	Divorced	Widowed	Never married	All
All	132.2	56.5	7.6	33.7	47.3	35.0	99.5
White	141.1	91.0	30.3	38.7	65.2	52.3	115.0
Black	58.7	3.0	0.6	13.0	11.0	0.2	24.8
Hispanic	50.0	5.0	0.2	4.8	8.5	0.5	29.7

Source: Health and Retirement Survey. Calculations by the authors.

Because of their increasing importance in the policy debate, geographic areas with high-density black and Hispanic households were oversampled at a rate of two to one.

Table 6.1 highlights some salient characteristics of wealth disparities, with an emphasis on stratification by marital status.[2] Much more so than income, the distribution of wealth is severely skewed. Mean wealth is 2.4 times the median, indicating that wealth is concentrated among relatively few households. Second, race and ethnic disparities in wealth are enormous, far more than income differences. For every dollar of wealth that a middle-aged white household has, black (Hispanic) households have 27 (30) cents. Third, net worth varies significantly across marital categories. Not surprisingly, wealth is highest among married respondents. Somewhat distinct perceptions of the magnitude of disparities are obtained, depending on whether means or medians are used as the yardstick. With married couples as the reference group, median wealth disparities are considerably larger, a difference flowing from higher heterogeneity

---

[2] Household wealth in HRS consists of a number of categories. In addition to the value of the home and all mortgages, HRS separates assets into the following eleven categories: other real estate; vehicles; business equity; IRA or Keogh; stocks, trusts, or mutual funds; checking, saving, or money market funds; certificates of deposit, government savings bonds, or treasury bills; other bonds; other savings and assets; and other debt (see Smith 1995).

of asset holdings within all other groups. For example, mean wealth is almost five times the median among never married households, twice the multiplier that exists among married families. Many never-marrieds apparently possess considerable wealth while others have quite limited resources. This more extreme separation into haves and have-nots also characterizes the other not currently married samples. Because they better mimic the typical household in each group, medians will be used to describe wealth differences across marital groups.

Median assets of married households run at least three to four times larger than the other groups. Widows have approximately one-third the wealth of married families, while the divorced and never-married possess about one-fourth. By far the largest discrepancy exists among those who had separated. Median net worth of separated households is only 6 cents on the dollar of the wealth of married households. In all cases, married couples' net worth is far more than twice that in other household configurations, indicating that something more than a simple aggregation of individual savings behavior is taking place.

Marital disparities are much larger among blacks and Hispanics. Net worth is shockingly low among both separated or never-married minority households. Median wealth among blacks (Hispanic) separated households is only $594 ($150), trivial relative to separated white households. Similarly, among never-marrieds, Hispanic and blacks have very low assets, noteworthy since the study applies a very inclusive wealth concept (including housing equity). While they fare somewhat better, minority widowed and divorced households also score low in these asset comparisons.

These large disparities among alternative household structures may account for some of the overall racial wealth gap, given that blacks are far more likely than whites to reside in household arrangements that typically have low wealth. Forty-three percent of blacks live in married households, compared to more than 70 percent of whites. However, these large racial differences in prevalence rates "explain" only 10 percent of the racial wealth gap.[3]

Besides total assets, there are differences across families in the composition of assets. Table 6.2 displays a division of mean assets into tangible assets (business, real estate, and so on), financial assets, and equity held in the primary residence. With the exception of widowed and never-married

---

[3] This number was obtained by applying the white percents in alternative household types to the black means.

Table 6.2 *Composition of Wealth: Shares of Total Wealth*

	Married	Separated	Divorced	Widowed	Never married
Tangible	0.43	0.50	0.42	0.28	0.46
Financial	0.27	0.19	0.27	0.32	0.29
Primary Residence	0.26	0.28	0.30	0.38	0.22
TOTAL	1.00	1.00	1.00	1.00	1.00

Source: Health and Retirement Survey. Calculations by the authors.

households, home equity comprises a roughly similar proportion of net worth across family type. Widowed households hold a much higher fraction of their wealth in housing than single households do. Since both types of households have similar relative financial holdings, the offset occurs in the tangible investment category. Financial assets also vary significantly among these households. In absolute dollars, financial assets are lowest among separated or divorced families, suggesting that, as assets are lost with the end of a marriage, the first dollars to go are those held in financial forms. In contrast, these households may attempt to maintain their homes and other real investments.

Not only are there impressive crosssectional wealth differences by marital categories, quantitatively large disparities emerge by duration in a state. Median net worth among HRS couples married thirty-five years or more are 64 percent larger than the median wealth of couples married during the last five years. Since HRS respondents fall within a relatively narrow age span, age differences among them cannot explain these duration patterns. Equally pronounced duration effects exist in the divorced or separated state, but wealth is lower the longer the separation or divorce. This association is sharp among marriages that ended more than fifteen years ago. One possible explanation for this pattern follows from habit formation. If there are returns to scale that allow for higher levels of consumption in marriage, then divorce or separation combined with persistent habits in consumption would lead to a large reduction in saving and hence a wealth gap relative to married households that grows over time.

Wealth disparities across family types also vary by the gender of the household head. Sex differences in market earning power remain large, translating into very different capacities to save. Assets are dramatically lower in divorced, separated, or widowed households headed by women. Table 6.3 indicates that median assets in these female-headed households are two-thirds of those in similarly situated male-headed

Table 6.3 *Net Worth by Sex of Head (Thousands of Dollars)*

Marital status	Means			
	All	White	Black	Hispanic
Divorced or separated				
Male	162.0	192.1	35.0	32.0
Female	82.1	97.0	35.6	26.5
Widowed				
Male	170.5	220.7	50.6	49.4
Female	112.7	137.5	33.9	50.3
Never married				
Male	248.1	298.3	29.5	22.3
Female	92.4	124.3	19.7	37.3

Marital status	Medians			
	All	White	Black	Hispanic
Divorced or separated				
Male	35.0	52.0	3.0	3.0
Female	22.9	31.5	6.0	0.8
Widowed				
Male	43.6	95.8	15.0	1.8
Female	46.0	63.7	10.8	10.0
Never married				
Male	39.5	58.9	0.6	0.8
Female	30.8	50.6	0.2	0.5

Source: Health and Retirement Survey. Calculations by the authors.

families. This sex distinction, however, applies only to white households, and no systematic pattern of gender differences exists in minority households.

There are several possible reasons for such gender differences. Because children typically remain with their mother, the consumption requirements in female-headed families may be higher. Alimony and child support transfers from the father may not fully offset these higher consumption needs. Even if the assets built up during the earlier marriage were split evenly between the spouses, assets derived before or subsequent to that marriage are typically not joint property. The ability to accumulate these assets is in part tied to the differential earning power of each spouse. Moreover, savings are likely to be a highly non-linear function of wages, implying that these gender differences in wealth may emerge only at sufficiently high wages. Since sex differences in wages are

Table 6.4 *Total Wealth Distributions (Thousands of Dollars)*

		Means		
	Net worth	Pensions	Social security	Total
Total	238.5	103.6	120.8	465.9
Married	288.3	127.9	141.2	557.4
Separated	85.3	34.0	56.6	175.9
Divorced	117.6	58.2	73.7	249.5
Widowed	119.5	27.8	78.6	225.9
Never married	166.1	71.8	70.7	308.5
		Medians		
Total	99.5	41.0	115.4	320.9
Married	132.2	71.4	139.7	409.3
Separated	7.6	0.0	55.1	95.7
Divorced	33.7	2.0	73.7	153.8
Widowed	47.3	0.0	75.0	151.1
Never married	35.0	1.5	66.8	167.0

Source: Health and Retirement Survey. Calculations by the authors.

much smaller and wage levels are lower in black families, smaller gender wealth disparities may result.

Thus far, net worth is a conventional but narrow wealth concept ignoring some fundamental claims on future income flows. Fortunately, wealth measurement can be expanded in the HRS to include the two most prevalent of such claims: social security and pensions. These neglected and quantitatively large components are distributed quite differently across family types. Private and public sector social security are important sources of household wealth, particularly among the middle-aged Americans in the HRS sample.[4] Table 6.4 shows that in this age range net worth represents slightly more than half of total wealth while social security constitutes 26 percent and pensions 22 percent. The impact of this broadening is even greater on the median household. Of the three categories, personal net worth is the most unevenly distributed and social security by far the most equally distributed. The equalizing character of social security drives the differences that emerge between the conventional and comprehensive wealth concepts. Social security is especially important for the average household, because, for them, it dwarfs conventionally defined personal net wealth.

[4] See Smith (1995) for the details of these wealth computations.

Broadening the definition has a significant impact on wealth disparities across family types, especially for the average household. Most of these differences reflect the equalizing impact of social security. Evaluated at the medians, the typical married couple has more social security wealth than personal net worth. Social security is far more dominant in all other household types. The most extreme example occurs among separated households that have more than $7 of social security wealth for every dollar of personal net worth. While having a less extreme impact, social security wealth also looms large in other types of dissolved households, averaging about twice the net worth.

HOUSEHOLD STRUCTURE AND SAVINGS BEHAVIOR

Thus far, we have described only crosssectional differences in wealth by marital categories. However, models of asset accumulation require longitudinal data to test even the models' most basic implications. To model the dynamic process of household accumulation across the full life cycle, we used the 1984, 1989, and 1994 wealth modules of the PSID, a nationally representative sample of approximately five thousand families and thirty-five thousand individuals who live in those families who have been followed since 1968. Both spouses of a couple married in 1968 were interviewed following their divorce or separation. However, if the couple married after 1968, the study includes only that partner who was in the original 1968 sample.

The definition of personal net worth in the PSID closely parallels that used in the HRS: housing equity, other real estate, autos, farm, or business ownership; stocks, checking or savings accounts, certificates of deposits (CDs), savings bonds, and individual retirement accounts (IRAs); bonds, trusts, and life insurance; and other debts. The PSID made no attempt to measure social security or pension wealth.

We will use the PSID to examine changes in assets among the three wealth supplements. A distinction first must be made between families that maintained the same marital status between two successive wealth modules, and those families that changed it. Only the former families have asset growth that can be interpreted as partly mirroring their savings behavior. The changing asset position of families undergoing marital transitions largely results from the addition and subtraction of assets of incoming and outgoing family members. For example, a divorced 1984 family head who remarried by 1989 will exhibit a large expansion in assets that has little to do with savings behavior, as it merely reflects the combining of assets of the previously divorced household with those of

Table 6.5 *Net Worth by Type of Marital Transition*
(Thousands of Dollars)

	Means		Medians	
	1984	1989	1984	1989
Married in 1984				
Married–married[a]	220.9	280.2	95.2	118.9
Married–divorced[b]	95.7	66.5	40.8	36.2
Married–separated	121.9	111.2	35.2	11.3
Married–widowed	177.9	209.7	102.0	100.3
Divorced in 1984				
Divorced–divorced	57.9	67.8	18.0	24.8
Divorced–married	55.3	114.2	14.7	52.1
Separated in 1984				
Separated–separated	15.4	15.5	1.2	0.6
Separated–divorced	22.7	54.8	6.0	10.2
Separated–married	89.4	137.8	24.9	120.4
Widowed in 1984				
Widowed–widowed	108.0	102.6	62.3	50.3
Widowed–married	249.5	303.6	102.1	172.0
Never married in 1984				
Never married–never married	37.5	64.6	6.9	13.0
Never married–married	15.7	84.4	6.8	37.2

Notes:
[a] Married in 1984 and 1989.
[b] Married in 1984 and divorced in 1989. All other transitions in Tables 5 and 6 are interpreted in a similar manner.
Source: Panel Study of Income Dynamics. Calculations by the authors.

the person whom he or she married. Similar problems confound the interpretation of asset changes for 1984 married families that dissolved by 1989.

We use various subsets of the PSID in Tables 6.5 though 6.10 to control for these issues. Tables 6.5 and 6.6 restrict the original crosssection samples in 1984 and 1989 (6,915 and 7,111 households respectively) to those with the same head of household in both years, reducing the sample to 5,273 households. The analyses presented in Tables 6.7 through 6.9 further restrict the samples to control for changes in saving resulting from transitions into and out of marital states. The two samples (consisting of 4,408 and 4,416 households) examine the same head of household over the five-year period (1984 to 1989, and 1989 to 1994) where the marital state was unaltered over this period. Finally, Table 6.10 studies within-household

Table 6.6 *PSID Family Income by Type of Marital Transition (Thousands of Dollars)*

	Means		Medians	
	1984	1989	1984	1989
Married				
Married–married	63.0	66.8	52.6	53.4
Married–divorced	50.8	44.4	47.7	40.6
Married–separated	51.9	46.7	43.7	38.2
Married–widowed	37.4	42.7	32.2	23.3
Divorced				
Divorced–divorced	28.6	31.2	24.0	27.2
Divorced–married	51.4	69.7	40.5	55.9
Separated				
Separated–separated	19.3	22.3	14.0	15.5
Separated–divorced	26.4	30.7	21.8	26.2
Separated–married	47.1	68.0	38.7	61.9
Widowed				
Widowed–widowed	20.4	19.9	14.4	13.1
Widowed–married	45.2	45.4	46.5	36.9
Never married				
Never married–never married	27.7	32.6	24.1	25.4
Never married–married	39.0	66.7	32.1	60.2

variation and is restricted to the same head of household in each year from 1984 to 1994 (4,065 households). All values are presented in 1996 dollars.

Table 6.5 lists net worth for families stratified by their household status in 1984 and their subsequent transition by 1989 while Table 6.6 lists the changing family income between 1984 and 1989. Similar patterns exist if PSID wealth waves 1989 and 1994 are used instead. The initial 1984 asset levels have the same ranking as the crosssection – married, widowed, divorced, never married, and separated. Consider first households who were in the same marital situation in 1984 and 1989, as such families provide the only legitimate test of differential savings behavior across households. Among these families, there is evidence of a relationship between marriage and savings. Continuously married households enjoyed a large increase in mean assets of 4.7 percent per year, while asset growth for continuously divorced households was 3.2 percent per year, was essentially zero for separated families, and was negative among widowed families. Never-married households actually had the largest asset expansion, but this could largely result from their relatively young age. The non-control for confounding factors such as age argues against any strong savings interpretation of the data listed in Table 6.5. For example, the asset decline among the older widowed households may result more from their life-cycle position than from their marital status.

A comparison of Tables 6.5 and 6.6 indicates that wealth differences among those in the fixed-state sample are larger than the household income disparities. Median income of continuously married couples in 1984 exceeds that of divorced households by about two to one, while median wealth of these married families is four times higher than that of divorced households. Similarly, median incomes of continuously married families are almost four times larger than median incomes of separated families, while the wealth disparity is eighty to one. Income disparities among alternative household configurations alone cannot account for the vastly different household wealth positions.

Tables 6.5 and 6.6 demonstrate that selectivity is a central part of the association between marriage and savings. Table 6.6 shows that even among initially married households, families that subsequently dissolved have lower 1984 incomes. Similarly, divorced or separated families who remarried by 1989 have higher pre-1984 incomes than those families who remained unmarried. A marriage transition that can be characterized as economically downward (upward) ex-post is associated with lower (higher) ex-ante family income. Table 6.5 shows an even stronger selection on initial asset levels. Among 1984 married couples, those who subsequently divorced or separated have less than half the assets of those who remained married by 1989.

Finally, Table 6.5 summarizes the changing net worth position of households who did undergo a marital transition between 1984 and 1989. These asset changes largely reflect the addition or subtraction of household members associated with the union or split. A married head of household who divorced by 1984 suffered a 36 percent loss in net worth, while divorced heads who married doubled their wealth. In general, transitions into marriage are associated with large increases in household wealth while transitions out of marriage are correlated with large wealth declines. While important for the well-being of these families, wealth changes between marriage states do not inform us about the impact of marriage on household savings behavior.

A MULTIVARIATE MODEL OF HOUSEHOLD SAVINGS

We next present results obtained from multivariate models of household savings between successive waves of the PSID. Our principal interest is to examine marital differences in savings after controlling for other important factors. The first issue that arises concerns the computation of household savings. Panel surveys can measure savings as differences in household wealth, from one wave to the next, adjusted for any capital gains or losses and net transfers into the household. We computed total changes in household wealth between 1984, 1989, and 1994 using a sample of PSID households with the same household head in all three years. Net wealth transfers into the household were defined as the sum of money taken out of pensions, the value of new inheritances received, and assets brought in by new family members minus any assets that previous family members took with them when they left. The PSID includes a short transaction module that asks the amount of money put into real estate or business, as well as net transfers into stocks, bonds, and annuities, which enables us to separate so-called active saving from wealth accumulation that is a consequence of capital gains. Total capital gains were defined as the change in the total value of stocks, businesses, and real estate minus the net amount a household puts into these assets between waves. Active savings is defined as the change in total wealth minus the combination of net transfers into the household, inheritances received, and capital gains. Thus, these data provide two observations of active saving and capital gains for each household, from 1984 to 1989 and from 1989 to 1994.[5]

Some households are clearly savers while others are not. In light of this heterogeneity, in addition to the standard linear estimates of mean effects, we provide estimates of models at the twenty-fifth, fiftieth (median), and seventy-fifth percentiles.[6] These models tell us the effects of variables for the typical household located at the percentile. To examine the stability of coefficient estimates over time, we estimated separate models between the 1984 and 1989 PSID waves and between the 1989 and 1994 waves of the PSID. Finally, we restricted the sample to households whose marital states were unaltered over the two periods.

Table 6.7 summarizes models that include only simple demographic controls (age, race, whether the household was headed by a woman, and

[5] See Juster, Joseph Lupton, Smith, and Frank Stafford (1999) for a more detailed discussion of these issues.
[6] For all models except the mean, we computed boot-strapped estimates of standard errors added, since asset data are well known to be extremely "noisy."

Table 6.7 Baseline Models of Active Savings between PSID Waves ("T" Statistics in Parentheses)

	Median		25%		75%		Mean	
	84–9	89–94	84–9	89–94	84–9	89–94	84–9	89–94
Not married	−8,757	−8,251	−1,384	324	−22,802	−22,238	−10,711	−13,599
	(−6.44)	(−6.84)	(−2.09)	(0.31)	(−6.84)	(−5.49)	(−2.02)	(−1.29)
Black	−4,015	−6,213	1,604	1,929	−18,924	−17,455	−16,643	−19,339
	(−5.68)	(−7.78)	(2.41)	(2.61)	(−8.35)	(−6.73)	(−5.27)	(−2.77)
Female head	−705	773	−433	185	−4,534	−2,745	−11,323	−1,562
	(−0.78)	(1.10)	(−1.01)	(0.33)	(−1.96)	(−0.86)	(−2.00)	(−0.14)
Age	−75	−178	−154	−353	−44	−182	−277	−631
	(−3.06)	(−5.69)	(−5.18)	(−7.48)	(−1.24)	(−3.96)	(−3.04)	(−3.12)
Constant	16,048	20,819	3,303	7,106	49,908	55,327	45,662	63,017
	(11.28)	(15.51)	(2.76)	(3.68)	(24.20)	(22.45)	(10.51)	(6.48)

an indicator variable that the household was not married). In these specifications, asset growth declines with age, savings of black households were always less than those of other groups, and, most important, savings were significantly lower in unmarried households. Controlling for race and age, we find that on average, married couples saved about $11,000 to $14,000 more over a five-year period than non-married households saved (more than $2,000 per year). The size of these savings effects varies systematically across percentiles – quite small at the twenty-fifth percentile, about $8,500 at the median, and $22,000 at the seventy-fifth percentile. There do not appear to be large differences in marriage effects on savings estimated between the first and second or second and third PSID wealth modules.

When we allowed the impact of marriage to depend on the duration of time spent in the current marital state, the savings differences between married and not currently married households were largest in the earliest duration in marital states and steadily converged thereafter. This result is consistent with our prior speculation that dissavings are most common the shorter the duration in the non-marriage state, as households attempt to maintain their prior consumption levels.

These large savings differentials associated with marriage do not reveal the reasons why they emerged. Although economic status varies considerably across alternative household structures, no economic controls are included in Table 6.7. The augmented model listed in Table 6.8 includes base year quartiles of household labor income (households divided into four equal-sized groups ranked by their incomes), the head's education, changes in family income between PSID waves, the amount of net transfers and inheritances received between PSID waves, and variables measuring the number of children in the household in a set of age groups.

A common finding in the literature (Browning and Lusardi 1996) is that the impact of household income on savings is much higher at higher incomes. Using the model estimating mean effects, we find that the coefficient of labor income in the third quartile is more than twice that of the second quartile while the effect of the fourth quartile is more than thrice the third quartile. Larger impacts of household income are one reason that marriage affects savings, as dividing income between partners necessarily reduces total household income. Education of the head also exhibits similar non-linearities, with savings concentrated among college graduates. Families that received some inheritance between the waves apparently saved a significant fraction of it.

Table 6.8 Augmented Models of Active Savings between PSID Waves ("T" Statistics in Parentheses)

	Median		25%		75%		Mean	
	84–9	89–94	84–9	89–94	84–9	89–94	84–9	89–94
Age	−17.0	−82.2	−157.9	−362.7	10.8	−17.9	−222.0	−332.3
	(−1.29)	(−3.08)	(−3.16)	(−6.92)	(0.61)	(−0.44)	(−1.70)	(−1.16)
Not married	−5,996.3	−6,356.5	−4,883.9	−4,474.7	−9,118.2	−7,131.8	−15,019.9	−2,078.1
	(−4.58)	(−3.78)	(−2.61)	(−2.04)	(−3.76)	(−2.30)	(−2.16)	(−0.14)
Duration of marital status	−369.5	−282.7	−336.8	−246.8	−330.2	−231.0	−192.5	−20.48
	(−3.36)	(−2.97)	(−2.44)	(−1.87)	(−1.51)	(−1.54)	(−0.51)	(−0.03)
Duration not married	393.1	367.2	594.4	603.3	446.7	166.6	1229.8	392.4
	(4.07)	(3.54)	(5.53)	(3.39)	(2.34)	(0.76)	(2.24)	(0.39)
Black	−680.4	−732.9	1,655.3	1,727.9	−8,036.1	−3,982.7	−8,131.2	−5,710.6
	(−2.16)	(−1.01)	(2.42)	(1.26)	(−5.38)	(−2.38)	(−2.34)	(−0.74)
Female head	−3.41	1616.0	−952.3	786.6	586.7	1,168.0	−9,109.3	5,185.1
	(−0.01)	(2.08)	(−1.14)	(0.65)	(0.81)	(0.57)	(−1.50)	(0.41)
Household labor income in 2nd quartile	1,922.4	2,688.9	−1,415.1	−423.8	6,870.7	7,650.0	1,552.8	7,724.4
	(2.54)	(3.00)	(−1.50)	(−0.36)	(4.36)	(4.00)	(0.33)	(0.75)
Household labor income in 3rd quartile	9,687.2	9,232.0	−1,198.2	−1,572.1	19,547.7	22,150.4	−1,575.9	17,678.9
	((7.76)	(4.65)	(−0.81)	(−1.00)	(7.40)	(10.11)	(−0.28)	(1.48)
Household labor income in 4th quartile	25,178.3	23,787.4	3,309.7	1,366.7	50,470	65,880.0	17,655.5	57,932.6
	(12.58)	(7.70)	(1.15)	(0.41)	(10.14)	(11.0)	(2.87)	(4.39)
Change in household labor income	0.1372	.0913	0.0443	0.0394	0.1727	0.2106	.0530	0.6319
	(3.04)	(1.74)	(1.01)	(0.95)	(2.13)	(2.50)	(0.88)	(6.90)
Head education: high school degree	−.5876	−421.4	−1,069.1	−2281.4	1,373.6	2,885.4	698.5	−8,394.6
	(−0.00)	(−0.93)	(−1.56)	(−1.83)	(2.87)	(3.11)	(0.18)	(−0.97)

Head education: some college	1,938.6	2,177.7	−1,924.9	12.8	7,583.7	10,529.6	13,725.5	6,050.7
	(1.57)	(1.89)	(−2.06)	(0.01)	(2.49)	(4.97)	(2.80)	(0.59)
Head education: college or more	8,027.8	7,609.3	1,876.1	747.6	23,077.1	17,119.4	313,15.4	10,220.0
	(3.18)	(4.91)	(0.95)	(0.30)	(6.38)	(4.18)	(6.02)	(0.93)
Inheritance	0.2770	0.3711	0.0413	−.0416	0.5719	0.6439	0.2607	0.4697
	(1.69)	(2.03)	(0.28)	(−0.27)	(2.01)	(2.86)	(3.71)	(2.40)
Net transfer	0.0350	0.0225	0.0154	0.3080	.2212	−.0860	0.1185	−0.0778
	(0.24)	(0.13)	(0.14)	(2.15)	(1.40)	(−0.42)	(6.10)	(−0.44)
Number of kids age 1–13 in household	−96.2	−626.4	−99.7	−443.5	−396.63	−938.4	1.6932	208.9
	(−0.58)	(−2.99)	(−0.313)	(−1.15)	(−1.24)	(−1.59)	((0.00)	(0.06)
Number of kids age 14–17 in household	−34.6	−943.9	39.6	−720.5	344.4	−732.4	46.8	−5430.9
	(−0.09)	(−1.42)	(0.05)	(−0.76)	(0.32)	(−0.50)	(0.02)	(−0.75)
Number of kids age 18–20 in household	416.2	55.75	482.1	−243.3	1,587.7	1,043.3	8,897.6	−5965.2
	(1.39)	(0.06)	(0.65)	(−0.14)	(1.66)	(0.80)	(2.29)	(−0.58)
Number of kids age 21–29 in household	13.54	62.8	508.6	−941.2	−6.2	−490.0	−4254.9	−2047.1
	(0.05)	(0.08)	(1.02)	(−0.74)	(−0.01)	(−0.38)	(−1.16)	(−0.24)
Constant	6,998.6	9,198.1	6,540.9	11,365.2	16,471.6	14,057.1	26,932.9	17,741.5
	(4.55)	(4.03)	(2.85)	(3.72)	(5.04)	(3.92)	(3.21)	(0.95)

Since the effect of children on family savings may depend on their ages, we included the number of children in specific age groups. Young children may depress family savings since they simultaneously may increase family consumption and reduce family income (as women exit the labor force). In addition, children near the college-attending ages may encourage family saving to pay these bills, and more generally children may encourage families to save for future bequests. In spite of the plausibility of these arguments, we consistently find essentially no effect of children on family savings decisions.[7] Consequently, children do not appear to be the main reason that married families save more than other types of families.

If we compare Tables 6.7 and 6.8 for our most robust specification (the median model), these multivariate controls for household economic status explain little more than half of the asset accumulation differences among households by family type (as judged by the coefficient on the variable "not married"). Thus, while income selectivity into marriage is important, this suggests that the savings effect of marriage is not solely due to income differences across households.

Even after controlling for demographic and economic characteristics of the household, our analysis leaves much of savings behavior unexplained. If this unobserved heterogeneity is correlated with marital status, the estimated marriage effect will be biased. The most likely source of unobserved heterogeneity is that "prudent" individuals may be more likely to marry so that the impact of marriage could reflect the sorting of "prudent" people into marriage. With only two observations on saving per household, it is not yet possible to fully eliminate such selectivity. Instead, one would need to observe the same household's saving patterns in both states (married and not married) over a period in which a marriage transition did *not* take place. Otherwise, savings patterns would be dominated by the effect of the marital transition itself.

Nevertheless, we can control for other possible sources of heterogeneity by examining within-household variation in savings over the two five-year periods. Table 6.9 estimates the effects of all possible marital state combinations of the head in 1984, 1989, and 1994 on the change in household saving from the 1984–9 period to the 1989–94 period. The excluded reference group is that of households where the head was not married in 1984, 1989, and 1994. To distinguish between head of households that

---

[7] This finding is consistent with those reported by Hurd (1990), who reports that wealth accumulation by households was not related to the presence or number of children.

Table 6.9 *Within-Household Models of Change in Savings: PSID*

Variable	Change
Age	2,486
	(3.08)
Age squared	–24
	(–3.52)
mmn	–20785
	(–4.19)
mnm	6,814
	(0.85)
nmm	–6348
	(–1.13)
nnm	16,537
	(2.12)
nmn	–19533
	(–2.30)
mnn	19,275
	(3.39)
mmm	–5135
	(–2.17)
sss	–811
	(–0.23)
Net transfers	0.025
	(2.22)
Inheritances	0.464
	(6.69)
Income	0.085
	(1.82)
Capital gains, home	–.027
	(–1.05)
Capital gains, stock	–.170
	(–4.19)
Capital gains, business	0.019
	(0.82)
Constant	–48733
	(–2.20)

Note: m is for married, n is for not married, and s is for never married. For example, *mmn* means married in 1984 and 1989 but not married in 1994.

have never been married (single) and households that are simply not currently married, we include an indicator variable for single heads in 1984, 1989, and 1994.

The model in Table 6.9 also controls for certain household economic characteristics. Along with income and transfers into the household, the capital gains on various assets are included. As seen in Table 6.2, wealth in different assets varied by household type. This can lead to capital gains that also vary by household type, which can therefore bias the effects of marital status on savings. Table 6.9 indicates a household savings rate from household income of 8.5 percent (all else equal) while over half of all inheritances are consumed. Capital gains in stocks decrease saving by $0.17 to the dollar while gains in housing have a smaller effect ($0.03 to the dollar). Since the household is on both sides of the housing market (seller as well as buyer) and could also have inside information regarding gains in their own home, the small value for housing gains is not surprising.

Turning to the marital state variable in Table 6.9, the dominance of marital transitions is obvious. Households whose head was married in 1984 and 1989 but then unmarried by 1994 decreased saving by almost $21,000. On the other hand, households whose head was not married in 1984 and 1989 but then married by 1994 increased saving by $16,537. The only category that bypasses these transition issues is that of households whose marital state did not change: households whose head was married in all three years or never married in all three years.[8] These large effects estimated for marital transitions indicate that the PSID module was not completely successful in capturing the amount of assets that left or entered the household when a marital transition occurred.

Looking only at these fixed marital state groups, there is little difference between the never-married state and the not currently married state. However, the married state decreased the household's savings by $5,135 over the ten-year period relative to the never-married state. This is somewhat larger than the values estimated in Table 6.8. Consider the median regression in Table 6.8. Using the coefficient from the 1984 to 1989 period, a one-year increase in the duration of a household's marital state decreased the savings gap between married and not married by $386. This implies a decrease in the savings gap of $3,855 over the ten-year period.

---

[8] The reference group "not married" in all three years is also a valid "non-marital transition" group. Note that this is not completely accurate since it is possible for a transition out of and back into a marital state during the between period. However, these cases are less likely and do not impact the results in Table 6.9.

CONCLUSION

Our analyses suggest that married couples apparently save significantly more than other households, an effect not solely related to their higher incomes nor the simple aggregation of two individuals' wealth. If marriage is related to household savings, the sharp decline in the fraction of American households who are married may be one reason for the secular fall in U.S. private savings rates. Moreover, as the duration spent in each married state increases, the wealth gap between married and non-married households rises. However, comparing duration effects on *saving* (the change in wealth) of married households to *all* unmarried households, the gap in saving between these two marital states decreases with time.

Research on the relationship between demographic variables such as marriage and household savings is too new to consider these results established facts. More important, there is much we do not yet understand about the underlying theoretical reasons for the impact that marriage has on household savings. However, the strength of the relationship suggests that this may be an especially worthy subject for additional research.

REFERENCES

Abel, Andrew B. "Optimal Gift and Bequest Motives." *American Economic Review*, December 1987, 77(5), pp. 1037–47.

Becker, Gary S. *Treatise on the Family*. Cambridge, MA: Harvard University Press, 1981.

Bernheim, Douglas, Shleifer, Andrei and Summers, Lawrence. "The Strategic Bequest Motive." *Journal of Political Economy*, December 1985, 96(6), pp. 1045–76.

Browning, Martin and Lusardi, Annamaria. "Household Saving: Micro Theories and Micro Facts." *Journal of Economic Literature*, December 1996, 34, pp. 1797–1855.

Deaton, Angus. *Understanding Consumption*. Oxford, UK: Clarendon Press, 1992.

Fisher, Irving. *The Theory of Interest*. New York: MacMillan, 1930.

Friedman, Milton. *A Theory of the Consumption Function*. Princeton, NJ: Princeton University Press, 1957.

Hurd, Michael D. "Research on the Elderly: Economic Status, Retirement, and Consumption and Saving." *Journal of Economic Literature*, June 1990, 2, pp. 565–637.

_____. "Mortality Risk and Consumption of Couples." Unpublished paper, 1998.

Juster, F. Thomas and Suzman, Richard. "An Overview of the Health and Retirement Survey." *Journal of Human Resources*, Supplement, 1995, 30(5), pp. S7–S56.

Juster, F. Thomas, Lupton, Joseph, Smith, James P. and Stafford, Frank. "Savings and Wealth: Then and Now." Unpublished paper, October 1999.

Lillard, Lee A. and Weiss, Yoram. "Uncertain Health and Survival: Effect of End of Life Consumption." *Journal of Business and Economic Statistics*, 1996, *15*(2), pp. 254–68.

Mincer, Jacob. "Family Migration Decisions." *Journal of Political Economy*, 1978, *86*(5), pp. 749–73.

Smith, James P. "Assets and Labor Supply," in James P. Smith, ed., *Female Labor Supply: Theory and Estimation*. Princeton, NJ: Princeton University Press, 1980.

———. "Poverty and the Family," in Gary Sandefur and Marta Tienda, eds., *Divided Opportunities*. New York: Plenum Publishing Corporation, 1988.

———. "Racial and Ethnic Differences in Wealth," *Journal of Human Resources*, December 1995, *30*, pp. S158–S183.

SEVEN

The Economics of Child Support

Andrea H. Beller and John W. Graham

Economic interest in child support (that is, legally mandated payments from a non-custodial to custodial parent) has grown over time as the number of children living with only one parent has exploded. In 1970, fully 85 percent of children under the age of eighteen in the United States lived with two parents, while 12 percent lived with one parent. By 1995, just 69 percent lived with two parents, while 27 percent lived with one, most often their mother. Given high rates of divorce and out-of-wedlock births, demographers estimate that more than half of all children will spend part of their childhood with only one parent, while their other parent resides elsewhere (Larry L. Bumpass 1984; Irwin Garfinkel and Sara S. McLanahan 1986; McLanahan and Gary Sandefur 1994). Although the absent parent continues to have a legal and moral obligation to help provide financial support, in many cases establishing paternity (if the parents had never married), obtaining an adequate child support award, and collecting payments owed have proven to be difficult.

Concern for the well-being of children in child-support–eligible families stems from many sources. One source of concern is the below-average incomes and other resources (such as, parental time, school quality, and community services) available to many of them. In 1996 the median income of married-couple families with children was $51,894, compared to just $18,261 for mother-only families.[1] The regular receipt of child support

---

[1] The income differential narrows somewhat when taxes and cash transfers are also taken into account: $47,373 compared to $21,883. See Table F in U.S. Bureau of the Census, 1997.

We are grateful to Yunhee Chang for excellent research assistance and to the editor for helpful comments.

can make a difference: Custodial mothers receiving child support had incomes that averaged almost $8,000 higher than mothers without a child-support award.[2] Another source of concern is the high rates of poverty and welfare dependency of many mother-only families. In 1996, Congress abolished the traditional welfare entitlement program (known as AFDC), replacing it with Temporary Assistance to Needy Families (TANF), which places lifetime limits on welfare payments and requires most recipients to work. As a result of these changes, child support is likely to become an increasingly important source of income to many low-income families. And since in most states child support reduces welfare payments dollar for dollar, taxpayers too will benefit if more parents can be made to support their own children.

In this chapter, we examine determinants and consequences of child support payments for single parents and their children. We begin with an overview of the child support system, looking in detail at the latest national data on awards and receipts. We then go on to examine trends over time in these outcomes, assessing the roles played by demographic shifts, changes in economic conditions, and new child support laws, including guidelines in setting award amounts and wage withholding to collect support due. We pay particular attention to changes in paternity establishment and child support for never-married mothers, the fastest growing segment of custodial mothers. We also review recent evidence about the adequacy of award amounts and look at new policy initiatives to enhance the ability and willingness of low-income parents to pay support.

In the last part of the chapter, we examine some of the consequences of child support for parents and children. We show that child-support income is positively associated with a custodial mother's own employment and earnings, and does not appear to reduce her likelihood to marry or remarry. We also document a positive relationship between the amount of contact that non-custodial fathers have with their children and the amount of child support they pay. A substantial body of literature has established that growing up in a single-parent family is disadvantageous for children's educational attainment, but a number of recent studies have shown that receiving child support reduces the extent of the disadvantage. We discuss how child support benefits children, assess the magnitude of the relationship between child support and children's educational

---

[2] A small fraction of custodial mothers also receive alimony (a court-ordered interspousal transfer of money for some period after a divorce), but this support stops with remarriage and is not available to never-married women.

attainment, and address the issue of selection bias, which can confound this relationship.

AN OVERVIEW OF CHILD SUPPORT TODAY

Traditionally, laws about families and children, including those dealing with child support and alimony, child custody, and parental visitation, have been viewed as a state rather than a federal concern in the United States. In 1975, however, Congress passed Title IV-D, an amendment to the Social Security Act, which established the federal Office of Child Support Enforcement (OCSE), and mandated that each state establish a separate agency (dubbed the IV-D office) to handle the increasing number of complaints about nonsupport of children. Over time, Congress increased its mandates to states about establishing paternity, setting adequate award amounts, and enforcing support orders in laws passed in 1984, 1988, and most recently 1996, with the passage of welfare reform (Andrea H. Beller and John W. Graham 1993; Garfinkel, McLanahan, Daniel R. Meyer and Judith A. Seltzer 1998).

The best source of national data on child support is a supplemental questionnaire appended to the monthly Current Population Survey (CPS), about once every two years. Results from a recent survey are summarized in Table 7.1. In April 1996 the Census Bureau questioned a nationally representative sample (of persons fifteen years and older living with their own children under age twenty-one whose other parent was living elsewhere) about their child-support experiences during the previous year, 1995. According to the bureau's estimates, more than one in four children overall (or 22.8 million) lived with some 13.7 million custodial parents, of which 85 percent were mothers and 15 percent fathers. It should be noted that the term "custodial" simply refers to the parent with whom the child was living at the time of the survey, even though in a growing number of cases both parents may retain joint legal custody and/or share physical custody of the child. Most custodial parents have been married at some time, but nearly 30 percent of custodial mothers and 16 percent of custodial fathers have never been married. Among non-custodial parents, three out of four live in the same state as their children, and most have either visitation rights or joint custody, but nearly 24 percent of fathers have neither.

As shown in Table 7.1, just 58 percent of custodial parents had a child-support award as of April 1996, and only 35 percent reported receiving any payments in 1995. Among those parents with an award and due payment,

Table 7.1 *Child Support for Custodial Mothers and Fathers: 1995–6*

Characteristics	All custodial parents	Custodial mothers	Custodial fathers
Population (in millions)	13.739 (100%)	11.634 (84.7%)	2.105 (15.3%)
Percent:			
Awarded support	58.0%	61.2%	40.1%
Receiving support	34.7%	37.4%	19.8%
Never married	26.5%	28.4%	15.7%
Black	27.0%	28.6%	18.4%
Hispanic	12.7%	13.2%	10.2%
Poor	30.4%	33.3%	14.3%
Population due support	6.966 (100%)	6.233 (89.5%)	0.733 (10.5%)
Receipt rate (%)	68.5%	69.8%	56.8%
Mean amount due	$4,057	$4,126	$3,468
Mean amount received	$2,555	$2,631	$1,910
Population receiving support	4.769 (100%)	4.353 (91.3%)	0.416 (8.7%)
Mean amount received	$3,732	$3,767	$3,370
Mean expected payment	$1,295	$1,409	$667
Average total income if:			
Receiving child support	$22,543	$21,829	$30,030
Not receiving child support	$17,398	$16,093	$25,122
Not awarded child support	$18,927	$14,068	$36,312
Nonresident parent:			
Lives in same state	74.6%	74.7%	73.7%
No visitation nor joint custody	22.6%	23.9%	15.7%

Source: U.S. Bureau of the Census, 1999.

the mean amount due was $4,057, to support an average of 1.7 children, or about $200 per child per month. Unfortunately, not all support due is actually paid: These same parents actually received an average of $2,555 or about $125 per child per month. Child-support outcomes differ significantly by sex of the custodial parent: Mothers are more likely than fathers to have an award (61 compared to 40 percent) and more likely to receive some payment (37 compared to 20 percent). On average, custodial mothers were due 19 percent more support than fathers and received 38 percent more. Finally, we might define *expected* child-support payments to be the amount of child support that an average custodial parent is likely to receive, taking account of the overall likelihood of having an award and being due payment, the likelihood of receiving some, and the amount received. For mothers, expected payments were $1,409 in 1995, or about $70 per child per month; for fathers, they were $667, or $33 per child per month.

Are these expected payments adequate to pay the cost of raising children? Judged even by minimal standards, they would appear to be grossly inadequate. For 1995, the government estimates that a single parent earning the poverty level of income ($7,763) would need an additional $4,395 with two children in the household to escape poverty. Overall, 30 percent of custodial parents had incomes below the poverty line in 1995: Thirty-three percent of mothers and 14 percent of fathers were poor. Custodial mothers who receive child support have higher incomes than mothers who do not have an award, and the income differential between the two groups exceeds the average amount of child support received. This suggests that mothers who actually receive support are advantaged in other ways as well, as we will discuss in more detail later in this chapter. By contrast, custodial fathers without an award actually have higher incomes than fathers who receive support, suggesting that income alone may be an important reason why some fathers do not seek or are not granted an award in the first place.

TRENDS OVER TIME IN CHILD-SUPPORT PAYMENTS

Table 7.2 compares child-support outcomes for custodial mothers in three different years: 1979, 1986, and 1996. Custodial fathers are excluded from this analysis, because prior to 1992 the Census Bureau did not include them in its survey. Still, the 1996 data are not strictly comparable with the earlier two years. This is because the survey has changed over time in several important ways: After 1986, the minimum age of custodial mothers was reduced from eighteen to fifteen; and as of 1994, overdue payments (sometimes called "back support") were included in the amount of child support due. Nevertheless, the CPS remains the best instrument for tracking changes over time in child support.

There are several reasons why child-support award and receipt outcomes might be expected to have changed over time. First, there were some important demographic shifts in the overall child-support-eligible population, most especially a disproportionate increase in the number of never-married mothers, who tend to be disadvantaged at each stage of the child-support process. Second, changing economic conditions – especially inflation, unemployment, and the relative earnings of women

Table 7.2 *Child Support for Custodial Mothers: 1978–96*

Child-support outcome	1978–9	1985–6	1995–6
All custodial mothers (mil.)	7.094	8.808	11.634
Percent:			
White	71.7	72	68.5
Black	26.7	26.2	28.6
Hispanic	7.3	9.2	13.2
Never married	19.4	22.8	28.4
All custodial mothers			
Award rate (%)	59.1	61.3	61.2
Awarded and due (%)	48.3	49.7	53.6
Amount due (current $)	2,003	2,495	4,126
Amount due (1995 $)	4,682	3,534	4,126
Receipt rate (%)	71.7	74.0	69.8
Amount received (current $)	1,799	2,215	3,767
Amount received (1995 $)	4,205	3,137	3,767
Expected payment (current $)	623	814	1,409
Expected payment (1995 $)	1,456	1,153	1,409
Ever-married mothers			
Award rate (%)	70.8	74.0	68.0
Awarded and due (%)	58.0	59.9	60.3
Receipt rate (%)	71.4	73.8	73.0
Amount received (current $)	1,829	2,297	4,046
Amount received (1995 $)	4,275	3,253	4,046
Expected payment (current $)	757	1,015	1,781
Expected payment (1995 $)	1,769	1,437	1,781
Never-married mothers			
Award rate (%)	10.6	18.4	44.1
Awarded and due (%)	7.8	15.1	36.6
Receipt rate (%)	81.3	76.2	56.4
Amount received (current $)	976	1147	2,271
Amount received (1995 $)	2,281	1,625	2,271
Expected payment (current $)	62	132	469
Expected payment (1995 $)	145	187	469

Note: Award rate is as of April 1979, 1986, or 1996. All others figures are for the year 1978, 1985, or 1995. Expected payment equals (awarded and due) × (receipt rate) × (amount received).

Source: U.S. Bureau of the Census, 1981, 1989, and 1999.

to men – have an impact upon what is owed and how much is paid. Third, changes in federal and state laws play a role too. In 1984 and 1988, important new federal legislation required that states adopt child-support guidelines for setting award amounts and use several techniques to collect support, including automatic wage withholding.

Between 1979 and 1996, the population of custodial mothers eligible for child support increased 64 percent, from 7.1 to 11.6 million, and the number of children rose from about 13 to 20 million (not shown in Table 7.2). The composition of the population shifted as well: In 1979 less than one in five custodial mothers was never married; by 1996 more than one in four was never married. By race, the percentage of white mothers fell, while the percentage of black and Hispanic mothers rose, reflecting the greater incidence of minority mothers among the never married. Table 7.2 displays child-support outcomes for all custodial mothers and for ever-married and never-married mothers separately.

The first step in the child-support process is establishing an award. The percentage of mothers with an award (the "award rate") rose slightly over this period, from 59.1 percent in 1979 to 61.2 percent in 1996, with all of the increase coming by 1986. By marital status, the award rate of ever-married mothers actually declined after 1986, while the award rate of never-married mothers rose sharply throughout the period, from 10.6 percent in 1979 to 44.1 percent in 1996. Never-married mothers have always faced greater difficulty obtaining an award, for several reasons, including especially the added requirement of first having to establish paternity. New paternity laws and increased efforts to get fathers to acknowledge paternity (often in the hospital at the time of the child's birth) may be two important reasons why award rates of never-married mothers rose, but other factors may have contributed to the rise as well. For one, as the incidence of non-marital births has risen over time, the population of never-married mothers tends to include more and more women who (measured by their demographic characteristics) look and act like ever-married mothers, who have always had higher award rates.

How much child support are mothers due? Measured in current dollars, the mean amount due (in the year prior to the survey) more than doubled between 1978 and 1995. But when we take account of inflation, we find that the real value of support due (measured in 1995 constant dollars) actually declined overall. It fell 25 percent between 1978 and 1985, a period of unusually high inflation, and then rose again thereafter. Even so, by 1995 the average child-support award was worth 12 percent less than in 1978. Understanding why real award amounts fell remains controversial. One study attributed this decline to the increase over time in the earnings of women relative to men, which shifted the burden of supporting children more toward mothers (Philip Robins 1992). Another study found inflation to be a more important factor: Awards made in earlier years lost value since few were ever renegotiated and newly made awards were not rising as fast as prices due to money illusion and other institutional constraints (Graham 1995). Another contributing factor has been the demographic shift toward never-married mothers who have lower average awards. Several recent changes in laws and practices – the use of guidelines in setting new awards and more frequent review of older ones – may account for much of the increase since 1985 in the real value of child-support due, as discussed in more detail in the next section.

Not all child-support awards are paid or paid in full. We define the "receipt rate" as the percentage of mothers awarded and due support who actually received some in the year prior to the survey. Overall, the receipt rate has declined over time: Among ever-married mothers, it rose slightly; but among the never married it declined sharply from 81 percent in 1978 to 56 percent in 1995. In 1978 never-married mothers due support were actually more likely than ever-married mothers to receive some (81 compared to 71 percent); now they are far less likely to receive any (56 compared to 73 percent). Even among those never-married mothers who gave birth as recently as 1994–5, only 17 percent of the mothers of one-year-olds received any child support (Judi Bartfeld and Meyer 1999). And when the mothers refuse to cooperate with the IV-D agency in identifying fathers and establishing paternity for children born out of wedlock, the never-married fathers are much less likely to agree to a child-support award (Beller and Elizabeth Powers 2000). This suggests that while child-support advocates have been successful in raising award rates among the never married, they may be doing so by bringing into the system fathers who are increasingly reluctant to pay.

In general, about half of all mothers due support received the full amount due, one-quarter received partial payment, and one-quarter received nothing. Among those receiving some, the mean amount received more than doubled between 1978 and 1995, measured in current dollars. In constant 1995 dollars, receipts declined 10 percent overall, largely the result of the decline in the real value of support due. It appears, however, that this decline was confined to ever-married mothers: Among the never married, the real value of support received was nearly the same in both 1978 and 1995. So, although a declining percentage of the never married received any support, among those who did, child-support payments held constant.

As in the previous section, we define *expected* child-support payments as the average amount of child support received by the entire child-support-eligible population. This measure takes into account award rates, receipt rates, and amounts received all at the same time. Among all mothers and among ever-married mothers, the real value of expected payments held roughly constant: After declining from 1978 to 1985, they returned to their original value by 1995. Among the never married, real expected payments increased significantly, from $145 per year in 1978 to $469 in 1995. Even so, the typical never-married mother can expect to receive only one-fourth as much support as the average ever-married mother does.

CURRENT ISSUES IN IMPROVING CHILD-SUPPORT OUTCOMES

As we have seen, nonsupport of children has been and remains a widespread problem. Why do children, conceived in love and willingly supported when their parents live together, too often lose that support when parents live apart? Economists have offered several explanations why the state may have to compel parents to pay. One reason, of course, is that not all parents truly care about their children, especially if they lived with them for only a short time. (For this reason, never-married non-custodial parents are less likely to care about their children.) For the most part, however, economic models assume parents are altruistic – that is, they value their children's well-being. Even in this case, voluntary child support may not be forthcoming: Because child support cannot be given directly to children but must be transferred indirectly through the custodial parent (who might not spend all of it on them), the cost to the non-custodial parent of helping his children is increased and the likelihood of payment reduced (Yoram Weiss and Robert J. Willis 1985; Saul D. Hoffman 1990). When the custodial parent spends child support in ways the non-custodial parent does not approve, or when there is ongoing conflict between the parents, support may be even less likely. In some cases, parents use nonpayment of child support as a bargaining threat when there is conflict over child custody and visitation. Finally, when the non-custodial parent has an extremely low income or a second family to support, the custodial parent may not even bother to seek a support agreement in the first place, since the legal expenses can be considerable.

In this section, we focus on recent efforts by policy makers and child advocates to improve child-support outcomes. For never-married mothers, the first step to obtaining child support is establishing paternity. (Indeed, in April 1996, failure to establish paternity was one of the top reasons custodial mothers gave for not having a legal award.) The 1988 Family Support Act required states to meet new federal paternity standards, including the widespread use of genetic testing and the development of simple civil processes to establish paternity such as voluntary in-hospital acknowledgments. This latter program proved to be so successful that the Omnibus Budget Reconciliation Act of 1993 made it mandatory in all states. According to OCSE data, the total number of IV-D cases (that is, mothers receiving welfare, who are required to cooperate with the state in obtaining child support) in which paternity has been established has grown steadily, from 0.339 million in fiscal year (FY) 1989 to 1.459 million in FY 1998. In-hospital acknowledgments alone grew from 0.084 to 0.481 million between fiscal years 1994 and 1998 (U.S. Department of Health and Human Services 1995, 1998).

Higher rates of paternity establishment are a big reason why an increasing percentage of never-married mothers have a child-support award (Bartfeld and Meyer 1999). By contrast, award rates of ever-married mothers have not risen over time, and judging by some recent evidence, they are unlikely to rise, barring major new efforts by policy makers. In 1996, mothers without a *legal* award agreement were asked why they did not have one. The two reasons cited most frequently were: not needing one, because the father already provided what he could informally or because the child stayed with him sometimes (34 percent); and not wanting an award or not wanting the child to have to contact him (23 percent). Neither of these reasons would seem to indicate much scope for government action, except to the extent that non-contact with fathers stems from concerns over domestic violence. Only two of the reasons cited by mothers for nonsupport would suggest a direct role for government: her inability to locate the father (8 percent) and his inability to pay (14 percent).

Establishing adequate and equitable child-support orders, and maintaining them over time as prices rise, remain ongoing challenges. These problems were formally addressed by the 1988 Family Support Act, which mandated states to adopt presumptive guidelines in setting new award amounts and to review the adequacy of some existing awards (those established through the state's IV-D office) at least every three years. As we have seen, these provisions are starting to have some impact in reversing the real decline in support due that occurred through 1985 (Maureen A. Pirog, Marilyn E. Klotz, and Katherine V. Byers 1998). It is less clear whether they have resulted in establishing *adequate* award amounts. In most states, guidelines are based upon either a percentage of the noncustodial parent's income, or a share of both parents' income.

A recent analysis conducted for the American Bar Association's Section on Family Law shows that virtually no state guideline now in effect generates child-support orders that are as high as average expenditures made on children in intact two-parent families (Laura W. Morgan and

Mark C. Lino 1999). *Equity* also remains a problem, especially the treatment of low-income fathers: In many states, these men are being ordered to pay a higher percentage of their incomes than are men with higher incomes, particularly when support obligations are based upon potential rather than actual incomes, or when the state has a minimum requirement (Meyer, Maria Cancian, and Marygold S. Melli 1997).

Another provision of the 1988 Family Support Act, immediate wage withholding, has become the primary method by which states collect child support owed. Prior to 1988, wage withholding was used only to collect back support; today, all new and modified child-support orders (with a few exceptions) are required to be withheld from an obligated parent's pay immediately. According to OCSE data, wage-withholding collections rose from $26 million in FY 1985 to $6,733 million in FY 1996. Administering the wage-withholding program efficiently has proven to be a challenge in many states. One difficulty is ensuring that withholding is immediate for new hires – this requires that employers have timely access to state data on child-support orders. The 1996 Welfare Reform Act called for the creation of a national new hire reporting system to facilitate these information flows, both within and across state lines. It also required states to establish centralized state disbursement units, which proved difficult for many states (for example, Illinois).

Besides wage withholding, states use other techniques to collect support owed, including intercepting federal and state tax refunds and unemployment compensation. In recent years, many states have restricted access to state licenses (motor vehicle, professional, and others) to persons with overdue child support. Some states impose criminal penalties in which "deadbeat parents" are arrested and jailed – sometimes to great public fanfare – for their failure to pay support, and federal criminal penalties are now being imposed for failure to pay across state lines. It is difficult to assess the impact of each of these changes in enforcement separately, but one recent study attributes up to half of the overall gain in receipts to the adoption of six specific policies (Elaine Sorensen and Ariel Halpern 1999).

To repeat the question posed at the beginning of this section, why do many non-custodial parents fail to support their children voluntarily? New evidence is emerging from scholarly research on the characteristics, capabilities, and circumstances of non-custodial fathers, absent not only from their children's lives but also from most previous research. Do fathers fail to support their children due to low incomes, or perhaps because they have second families to support? According to one recent study, the answer to both questions appears to be a qualified no: The average income of nonpayers is only half that of fathers who pay, but still about three times the poverty threshold; and the incidence of fathers with second families to support (about one in three) is no higher among nonpayers than payers (Garfinkel, McLanahan, and Thomas L. Hanson 1998). Still, a sizable minority of nonpayers are poor (19–27 percent), substance abusers (9–12 percent), or in jail or homeless (7 percent).

While child-support enforcement is generally based upon penalties for non-compliance, several recent demonstration projects have begun to investigate the potential of the carrot rather than the stick. One is the Child Access Demonstration Project, funded by OCSE, which provides short-term counseling to resolve parental conflicts over visitation, custody, and child support. Another program, called Parent's Fair Share, is designed to increase a father's ability and willingness to pay support to children whose mothers are on welfare. It offers under- and unemployed fathers temporary reductions in their child-support obligations in exchange for their participation in employment and training services, along with peer support and group counseling programs known as the "Responsible Fatherhood" curriculum. While it may be too early to judge the effectiveness of these programs, it is already clear that they need to be long-term, innovative, and multidimensional, and, like comprehensive welfare reform, are certain to be expensive (Jessica Pearson and Nancy Thoennes 1998; Earl S. Johnson, Ann Levine, and Fred C. Doolittle 1999).

ECONOMIC CONSEQUENCES OF CHILD SUPPORT

It is now widely recognized that the economic consequences of divorce are almost always negative and prolonged for mothers and their children, while they are sometimes positive for fathers (Lenore J. Weitzman 1985; Hoffman and Greg J. Duncan 1988; Karen C. Holden and Pamela J. Smock 1991). Many single-parent households headed by women fall into poverty and have little choice but to resort to welfare (Beller and Graham 1993); the increasing incidence of such households over time led to the so-called "feminization of poverty." In this section, we look at some of the economic consequences of child support for custodial mothers who receive it and for non-custodial fathers who pay it.

Economic Well-Being of Custodial Mothers and Children

Child-support payments mitigate the strength of the relationship between living in a single-parent family and having low income for custodial parents and their children. They also affect poverty rates and the chances of needing to rely on welfare. In 1995, about 32 percent of custodial parents who did not receive support payments fell into poverty, whereas only 22 percent of the parents who received either some or all of their payment due fell into poverty.[3] Thus, it would appear that receiving child support cuts the poverty rate by about one-third. Child support may have an even bigger impact on welfare dependency: Twenty-four percent of custodial mothers who did not receive any child-support payments in 1995 received some AFDC payments, while only 14 percent of those who received any child support did (U.S. Bureau of the Census 1999).

On average, child-support payments account for about 17 percent of total family income among all mothers who receive any payment. Among never-married mothers who received child support during the 1990s, payments constituted 13 to 28 percent of income depending upon the age-cohort group considered (Bartfeld and Meyer 1999). For most mothers, child support is the largest source of income after personal earnings. A small fraction of ever-married mothers – less than 10 percent – also receive alimony from their ex-spouse; but averaged across all single mothers receiving child support, alimony represents only about 2 percent of total family income (Beller and Graham 1993). In addition, alimony rarely appears to be a substitute for child support – that is, mothers with little or no child support are unlikely to have alimony as an alternative source of support.

As noted previously, mothers who receive child support have higher incomes than mothers who do not, and their incomes are often higher by more than the amount of the child support received. Overall, in 1995, total family income averaged $21,829 among those receiving support, which is $5,736 (or 36 percent) more than the average income of $16,093 among those without child support (see Table 7.1). Given average receipts of $3,767, child support accounts for only 66 percent of the total income differential between the two groups. We can infer from previous work that the remainder of the differential, $1,969 (or 52 percent of the average amount of child support received), is largely a result of higher earnings of mothers who received child support.[4] According to Beller and Graham

---

[3] Analyses by Institute for Women's Policy Research (IWPR) (1999) based upon data from the U.S. Bureau of the Census' Survey of Income and Program Participation in 1990 and 1991 show that the poverty rate for mothers receiving child support would have increased to 46 percent had they not received their child support.

[4] Even mothers on AFDC had higher earnings if they had a child-support agreement than if they did not have one (IWPR 1999).

(1993), mothers with child support were more likely to work, and earned more if they worked. In 1995, 82 percent of mothers receiving child support worked, compared with just 76 percent of those due support who received none, and 69 percent of those without an award. Their higher earnings could be due to longer hours of work, higher hourly wage rate, or both. Some evidence that more of it is due to increased work effort is that, controlling for differences in work effort by focusing only on those custodial mothers who worked year-round full-time, the difference in income between those who received and those who did not receive child support of $4,925 is only $742 (or 18 percent) greater than the average amount of child support received, $4,183. The average income of those who received child-support payments was $29,672, and, of those who did not, $24,747.

Although we would like to conclude that receiving child support itself is responsible for pulling women and children out of poverty and off the welfare rolls, it may be wrong to do so. As we have seen, women who receive child support are more likely to work outside the home and to work longer hours than women who do not receive child support. The reason for this is not clear. One possibility is that child support per se causes women to work more, as will be discussed later in this chapter (and thus, if we could get child support paid to more women, we could expect to reduce poverty and welfare rates significantly). But it is also possible that the women who receive child support are simply different in some ways from those who do not. For example, they may have more education and may have been married to men with more education, higher earning power, or more dedication to their children. Due to positive assortative mating (see Gary S. Becker 1981 and Chapter 2 of this book by Michael J. Brien and Michelle E. Sheran), this is very likely to have been the case. If these types of men are more likely to pay child support, it would look like receiving child support had lifted these women out of poverty, whereas they might never have fallen into poverty in the first place. So, we need to examine what research says about the effect of child support on the behavior of women. This is what we turn to next.

The Mother's Behavior

Because child support is a form of unearned income, it can affect the recipient's work effort. Traditionally, due to what is known as the income effect, unearned income discourages work. The question we must ask is whether child-support income deters work effort as much as other sources of unearned income, such as welfare. Empirical research has shown that child support reduces work effort less than other forms of unearned income (Graham and Beller 1989). Based upon data from the early 1980s, a $1,000 increase in child support reduced hours of work by twenty-four per year, a reduction one-third the size of the reduction due to AFDC benefits or other non-wage income (Beller and Graham 1993). There are at least three possible explanations for this result. First, mothers may view child-support payments as income for the child, not for themselves. Indeed, in an expenditure study on divorced mothers, Daniela Del Boca and Christopher J. Flinn (1994) find that while 1.2 cents of every dollar of the mother's "own" income is spent on a broadly defined child-specific good, about 5.5 cents of every dollar of child-support income is. Second, this result may be explained in terms of the strategic behavior of mothers who work hard to encourage the non-custodial father to pay more child support. A third explanation that applies to low-income women is that child-support payments provide the income to pay for childcare, thus enabling the mother to go to work.

Child support may also affect a mother's chances of marrying or remarrying, and marriage is the surest way to increase the economic well-being of the single-mother family. To the extent that receiving child support deters marriage or remarriage, then policies aimed at increasing child support might not have as large a beneficial effect as at first glance. It is not obvious what the direction of the effect on marriage should be. Receiving child support reduces the urgency with which a mother would seek a new mate, but at the same time the higher income makes her a more attractive marriage partner, since the legal obligation to pay child support does not end with remarriage. We found that for mothers who remarry within five years of divorce, child-support payments have no impact on remarriage. For mothers who do not remarry that quickly, child support appears to have a very small deterrent effect upon eventual remarriage (Karen F. Folk, Graham, and Beller 1992). Thus, the immediate beneficial effect of child support is not likely to be diminished in the long run. Child support would be expected to have the same effect on first marriages among never-married mothers, but we were unable to study this because women in first marriages who had had a child out of wedlock were not interviewed in the data set used for our analyses.

The Father's Behavior

We know much less about the effects of child support on the economic well-being and behavior of non-custodial fathers, as these fathers have not been surveyed as much as custodial mothers. One reason for this is that they are not as easy to find. One large national survey that asked fathers about their children estimated that several million non-custodial fathers are missing: One-third of them are simply not in the survey because they are in the military or in jail; two-thirds are in the survey but fail to acknowledge paternity of children living elsewhere (Garfinkel, McLanahan, and Hanson 1998).

While the majority of non-custodial fathers can afford to pay child support, a large minority have a somewhat limited ability to pay. One study estimates that "between 9 and 19 percent of noncustodial fathers were poor in 1990 once the amount of child support paid that year was taken into account." By contrast, 29 percent of the custodial mothers were still poor once account was taken of the child support they received (Sorensen 1996). Another estimates that few fathers would have fallen into poverty even if they had paid everything owed, and few low-income fathers would be hurt by child-support guidelines unless they were based upon potential rather than actual income (Meyer 1998). However, a large minority of fathers could be defined as having low income after paying child support – at least 29 percent compared to 49 percent of the mothers after receiving support (Sorensen 1996).

As in the case of mothers, child-support payments may affect a father's decision about how much to work. Child-support awards may have both an income and a substitution effect on his hours of work. First, the obligation to pay child support acts like a lump-sum tax, and if leisure is a normal good, a child-support award will increase his labor supply (Marianne P. Bitler 1998). But because state guidelines usually specify child-support payments as a percentage of his income and he may have to give up, for example, 20 percent of his additional net income,[5] child-support obligations thus act like a tax on his marginal earnings, and thus according to the substitution effect support obligations may discourage work effort.[6] If this latter effect were to dominate the former, it could undermine efforts to increase child support through stronger enforcement. Fortunately, recent empirical results suggest a small positive effect of child-support obligations on non-custodial fathers' hours of work, and a somewhat larger effect of each additional dollar of child support paid (Bitler 1998). Other findings suggest that stronger

---

[5] This would be the case in Illinois if he has one child living elsewhere.

[6] We all hear stories about men who give up high-paying jobs to avoid paying large amounts of child support.

child-support enforcement is not likely to reduce male labor supply, and may even increase that of non-marital fathers (Richard B. Freeman and Jane Waldfogel 1998).

Child-support obligations will also affect a non-custodial father's ability to remarry and to have and support additional children. Having children to support can reduce a man's attractiveness as a potential marriage partner because it lowers the income he brings to the current marriage and it may divide his time between two families. This would also tend to reduce his ability to support additional children, especially since state child-support guidelines generally do not reduce child-support obligations to accommodate second families, whereas spending on existing children tends to fall when another child is added to an intact two-parent family. Recent empirical findings show that greater child-support enforcement reduces marriage and remarriage rates, especially among low-income fathers (David E. Bloom, Cecilia Conrad, and Cynthia Miller 1998).

Child-support enforcement can also affect the likelihood that marriages will dissolve and that children will be born out of wedlock in the first place. While no information is available on the former, a recent study finds that stronger enforcement of paternity establishment laws leads to moderately lower rates of non-marital fertility (Anne Case 1998).

A number of studies have found a strong positive link between visitation and child-support payments (for example, Seltzer et al. 1989). In turn, this finding is associated with better outcomes such as higher educational attainment for the children. According to data from the CPS, non-custodial parents with joint custody or with visitation arrangements were more likely to pay child support. Of the 6 million non-custodial parents with such arrangements in 1995, 74 percent paid child support, whereas of the 0.9 million without these arrangements, only 35 percent paid child support (U.S. Bureau of the Census 1999).

Contact with the non-custodial father tends to be beneficial for children, unless such contact results in greater conflict between the ex-spouses (Seltzer et al. 1998). Beyond the direct benefits of a father spending time with his children, greater contact tends to be associated with more child support being paid. At the same time, it is a legitimate concern that laws encouraging mothers to identify their child's father as a condition of eligibility for welfare may promote domestic abuse, if the father is prone to violence against his children and/or their mother (Vicki Turetsky and Susan Notar 2000).

CONSEQUENCES OF CHILD SUPPORT FOR CHILDREN

In the last decade, significant attention has been focused on the consequences of family structure for children's well-being and outcomes. The emerging literature shows that growing up in a single-parent family, usually headed by a woman, is disadvantageous for the children (see, for example, Sheila F. Krein and Beller 1988; McLanahan and Sandefur 1994). Single-parent families generally have fewer resources (of both time and money) to invest in their children than do two-parent families, and a direct link between these early home investments and the later socioeconomic attainments has been well established (for a review, see Robert Haveman and Barbara Wolfe 1995). The greatest number of studies focus on children's educational attainment, and find that children who spend time in a single-parent family attain less education, are less likely to graduate high school, and are less likely to go on to college (for example, Krein and Beller 1988). Receiving child support has been found to reduce the extent of this disadvantage (Beller and Seung Sin Chung 1988; Graham, Beller, and Pedro Hernandez 1994; Virginia W. Knox and Mary Jo Bane 1994). McLanahan and Sandefur (1994) document adverse outcomes not only on educational attainment, but also on the labor force attachment of young men and the risk that daughters become teen mothers, thereby putting them at risk for long-term poverty and welfare dependence.

We would expect child-support income to be at least as beneficial for children as other income. Would we expect it to be even more beneficial, and if so, why? Child-support income, like any other type of income, increases children's well-being directly by increasing the financial resources available to invest in children. But, as we have seen, unlike other sources of income, child support is often accompanied by increased contact with the non-custodial parent. If receiving child support also means that the child has more contact with the non-custodial parent, then the child will have greater parental inputs of time. In other words, time and money – when taken in combination – work to improve the outcomes of children more than when taken alone.

This naturally raises the question of whether policies strengthening child-support enforcement will lead to beneficial effects for children above and beyond those due to the added income per se. The answer to this question rests upon whether non-custodial fathers who pay child support are different in unobservable ways from those who do not in the absence of laws forcing them to pay. For example, fathers who pay child support (especially voluntarily) may have greater commitment to their children's education. If this were the case, then it might not be the payment of child support per se that causes the beneficial outcome, but rather some third unobserved factor that causes both fathers to pay and children to have better outcomes.

Empirical Findings

To date, most of the empirical studies on the consequences of child support have concentrated on educational outcomes. Controlling for the socioeconomic characteristics of the child and family, Laura M. Argys, H. Elizabeth Peters, Jeanne Brooks-Gunn, and Judith R. Smith (1998) find some evidence that the receipt of child support has a positive impact on children's cognitive test scores over and above its contribution to total income. Peters and Natalie C. Mullis (1997, p. 376) find that "black and white adolescents living in families that received child support had higher achievement test scores."

Beller and Chung (1988), the first study to examine the effect of child support on children's outcomes, found that child support increased educational attainment more than income from other sources. Subsequent studies confirmed this finding (e.g., Graham et al. 1994; Peters and Mullis 1997). Graham et al. showed that children who receive child support overcome about two-thirds of the disadvantage in years of school completed associated with their adverse family structure; they also found that child support reduces high school dropout rates and the percentage of students who fall behind their age cohort in high school, which can be interpreted as improved school performance.

However, these studies could not rule out the possibility that the effect of child support could be due to unobservable characteristics of non-custodial parents who pay support rather than to the effect of child-support income per se (Graham et al. 1994; Knox and Bane 1994). Hernandez, Beller, and Graham (1995, 1996) find evidence consistent with the hypothesis that as more reluctant payers were added to the system when child-support laws were strengthened during the 1980s, the magnitude of the beneficial effect on children's educational attainment declined.

The payment of child support can affect many socioeconomic outcomes of children and young adults. Another outcome that tends to be adversely affected by growing up in a single-parent family and to improve with higher family income is teenage non-marital childbearing. We have no direct evidence on whether child-support income is any more beneficial than other income, but welfare receipts appear to have the opposite impact and to increase teenage non-marital childbearing among daughters growing up in single parent families (Haveman and Wolfe 1995). Since receiving child support is associated with lower rates of welfare participation, child support is likely to have a particularly salutary effect on rates of teen non-marital childbearing.

Beyond the teenage years, how does having received child support as a child affect the outcomes of the young adult? The empirical evidence is mixed. Jeffrey Gray, Beller, and Graham (1997) found that child-support income increases the earnings of young adults, not only indirectly through its positive effect on educational attainment, but also directly. However, other studies (Krein 1986; Peters and Mullis 1997) found no direct effect on the labor market outcomes of earnings or work experience. Thus, it is still unclear whether the additional benefits from receiving child support extend beyond the immediate realm of education and into the young adult years of labor market entry.

SUMMARY AND CONCLUSIONS

In this chapter, we analyzed the economics of child support. This includes an analysis of child-support payments as an income source over time, the underlying economic behavior of custodial and non-custodial parents that determines whether and how much child support is paid, and the economic consequences of receiving child support for the parents and children. We have fairly reliable data on child support as an income source from Census data. Theory predicts the behavior of custodial parents, and we have convincing empirical evidence about custodial mother's behavior, but due to data limitations, only suggestive evidence about the behavior of non-custodial fathers. With respect to consequences, we have convincing evidence that child support benefits children, especially their educational attainment, above and beyond its role as income. We have some evidence that it is also beneficial for some of their other socioeconomic outcomes, but more research is still needed in this area. And finally, we have not yet sorted out the source of the beneficial effect of child support – whether it is the special quality of child-support income or whether it is the special quality of those fathers who pay child support without being coerced into it.

The challenges for child-support policy makers are many and difficult. The first is continuing to increase awards and receipts for never-married mothers, as non-marital fertility remains high. The second is finding new ways to encourage non-custodial parents to meet their support obligations, whether with the carrot or the stick. These are important goals for policy as welfare reform of the late 1990s makes child support an even more important component of the income package for single mothers, especially those with low income. And finally, adjustments should be made to child-support guidelines so that child-support payments can more closely approximate the true costs of raising a child. While these challenges appear difficult, the rewards from meeting them may be seen in the success of the next generation.

REFERENCES

Argys, Laura M., Peters, H. Elizabeth, Brooks-Gunn, Jeanne and Smith, Judith R. "The Impact of Child Support on Cognitive Outcomes of Young Children." *Demography*, 1998, *35*(2), pp. 159–73.

Bartfeld, Judi and Meyer, Daniel R. "The Changing Role of Child Support among Never-Married Mothers." Discussion Paper No. 1200–99, Institute for Research on Poverty, 1999.

Becker, Gary S. *A Treatise on the Family*. Cambridge and London: Harvard University Press, 1981.

Beller, Andrea H. and Chung, Seung Sin. "The Effect of Child Support Payments on the Educational Attainment of Children." Paper presented at the Population Association of America Annual Meetings, April 1988.

Beller, Andrea H. and Graham, John W. *Small Change: The Economics of Child Support*. New Haven, CT, and London: Yale University Press, 1993.

Beller, Andrea H. and Powers, Elizabeth. "Changes in Paternity Establishment and Child Support Enforcement under Welfare Reform: How Will Rural Residents Be Affected?" Paper presented at the Population Association of America Annual Meetings, March 2000.

Bitler, Marianne P. "The Effect of Child Support Enforcement on Non-Custodial Parents' Labor Supply." Unpublished paper, U.S. Federal Trade Commission, 1998.

Bloom, David E., Conrad, Cecilia and Miller, Cynthia. "Child Support and Fathers' Remarriage and Fertility," in Irving Garfinkel, Sara S. McLanahan, Daniel R. Meyer and Judith A. Seltzer, eds., *Fathers under Fire: The Revolution in Child Support Enforcement.* New York: Russell Sage Publications, 1998, pp. 128–56.

Bumpass, Larry L. "Children and Marital Disruption: A Replication and Update." *Demography,* 1984, *21*(1), pp. 71–82.

Case, Anne. "The Effects of Stronger Child Support Enforcement on Nonmarital Fertility," in Irving Garfinkel, Sara S. McLanahan, Daniel R. Meyer and Judith A. Seltzer, eds., *Fathers under Fire: The Revolution in Child Support Enforcement.* New York: Russell Sage Publications, 1998, pp. 191–215.

Del Boca, Daniela and Flinn, Christopher J. "Expenditure Decisions of Divorced Mothers and Income Composition." *Journal of Human Resources*, 1994, *29*(3), pp. 742–61.

Folk, Karen F., Graham, John W. and Beller, Andrea H. "Child Support and Remarriage: Implications for the Economic Well-Being of Children." *Journal of Family Issues*, 1992, *13*(2), pp. 142–57.

Freeman, Richard B. and Waldfogel, Jane. "Does Child Support Enforcement Policy Affect Male Labor Supply?" in Irving Garfinkel, Sara S. McLanahan, Daniel R. Meyer, and Judith A. Seltzer, eds., *Fathers under Fire: The Revolution in Child Support Enforcement*. New York: Russell Sage Publications, 1998, pp. 94–127.

Garfinkel, Irwin and McLanahan, Sara S. *Single Mothers and Their Children: A New American Dilemma*. Washington, DC: Urban Institute Press, 1986.

Garfinkel, Irwin, McLanahan, Sara S. and Hanson, Thomas L. "A Patchwork Portrait of Nonresident Fathers," in Irving Garfinkel, Sara S. McLanahan, Daniel R. Meyer, and Judith A. Seltzer, eds., *Fathers under Fire: The Revolution in Child Support Enforcement*. New York: Russell Sage Publications, 1998, pp. 31–60.

Garfinkel, Irwin, McLanahan, Sara S., Meyer, Daniel R. and Seltzer, Judith A. *Fathers under Fire: The Revolution in Child Support Enforcement*. New York: Russell Sage Publications, 1998.

Graham, John W. "A Comment on 'Why Did Child Support Award Levels Decline from 1978 to 1985?' by Philip K. Robins." *Journal of Human Resources*, 1995, *30*(3), pp. 622–32.

Graham, John W. and Beller, Andrea H. "The Effect of Child Support Payments on the Labor Supply of Female Family Heads." *Journal of Human Resources*, 1989, *24*(4), pp. 664–88.

Graham, John W., Beller, Andrea H. and Hernandez, Pedro. "The Effects of Child Support on Educational Attainment," in Irving Garfinkel, Sara S. McLanahan, and Philip K. Robins, eds., *Child Support and Child Well-Being*. Washington, DC: Urban Institute Press, 1994, pp. 317–54.

Gray, Jeffrey, Beller, Andrea H. and Graham, John W. "Childhood Family Structure, Child Support, and Socioeconomic Outcomes of Young Men." Paper presented at the Population Association of America Annual Meetings, Washington, DC, March 1997.

Haveman, Robert and Wolfe, Barbara. "The Determinants of Children's Attainments: A Review of Methods and Findings." *Journal of Economic Literature*, 1995, *33*(4), pp. 1829–78.

Hernandez, Pedro, Beller, Andrea H. and Graham, John W. "Changes in the Relationship between Child Support Payments and Educational Attainment of Offspring, 1979–1988." *Demography*, 1995, *32*(2), pp. 249–60.

_____. "The Child Support Enforcement Amendments of 1984 and Educational Attainment of Young Adults in the United States." *Review of Labour and Industrial Relations*, 1996, *10*(3), pp. 538–58.

Hoffman, Saul D. "An Economic Model of Child Support Payments." Unpublished paper, University of Delaware, 1990.

Hoffman, Saul D. and Duncan, Greg J. "What *Are* the Economic Consequences of Divorce?" *Demography*, 1988, *25*(4), pp. 641–5.

Holden, Karen C. and Smock, Pamela J. "The Economic Costs of Marital Dissolution: Why Do Women Bear a Disproportionate Cost?" *Annual Review of Sociology*, 1991, *17*, pp. 51–78.

Institute for Women's Policy Research. "How Much Can Child Support Provide? Welfare Family Income and Child Support," in *Research-in-Brief*, IWPR Publication # D435. Washington, DC: Institute for Women's Policy Research, 1999.

Johnson, Earl S., Levine, Ann and Doolittle, Fred C. *Fathers' Fair Share: Helping Poor Men Manage Child Support and Fatherhood*. New York: Russell Sage Publications, 1999.

Knox, Virginia W. and Bane, Mary Jo. "Child Support and Schooling," in Irving Garfinkel, Sara S. McLanahan and Philip K. Robins, eds., *Child Support and Child Well-Being*. Washington, DC: Urban Institute Press, 1994, pp. 285–316.

Krein, Sheila F. "Growing Up in a Single Parent Family: The Effect on Education and Earnings of Young Men." *Family Relations*, 1986, *35*, pp. 161–8.

Krein, Sheila F. and Beller, Andrea H. "Educational Attainment of Children from Single-Parent Families: Differences by Exposure, Gender, and Race." *Demography*, 1988, *25*(2), pp. 221–34.

McLanahan, Sara and Sandefur, Gary. *Growing Up with a Single Parent: What Hurts, What Helps*. Cambridge, MA, and London: Harvard University Press, 1994.

Meyer, Daniel R. "The Effect of Child Support on the Economic Status of Nonresident Fathers," in Irving Garfinkel, Sara S. McLanahan, Daniel R. Meyer, and Judith A. Seltzer, eds., *Fathers under Fire: The Revolution in Child Support Enforcement*. New York: Russell Sage Publications, 1998, pp. 67–93.

Meyer, Daniel R., Cancian, Maria and Melli, Marygold S. "Low-Income Fathers and Child Support Orders." Final Report to the Wisconsin Department of Workfare Development. Madison, WI: Institute for Research on Poverty, 1997.

Morgan, Laura W. and Lino, Mark C. "A Comparison of Child Support Awards Calculated under States' Child Support Guidelines with Expenditures on Children Calculated by the U.S. Department of Agriculture." *Family Law Quarterly*, 1999, *33*(1), pp. 191–218.

Pearson, Jessica and Thoennes, Nancy. "Programs to Increase Fathers' Access to Their Children," in Irving Garfinkel, Sara S. McLanahan, Daniel R. Meyer, and Judith A. Seltzer, eds., *Fathers under Fire: The Revolution in Child Support Enforcement*. New York: Russell Sage Publications, 1998, pp. 220–52.

Peters, H. Elizabeth and Mullis, Natalie C. "The Role of Family Income and Sources of Income in Adolescent Achievement," in Greg Duncan and Jeanne Brooks-Gunn, eds., *Consequences of Growing Up Poor*. New York: Russell Sage Publications, 1997, pp. 340–81.

Pirog, Maureen A., Klotz, Marilyn E. and Byers, Katherine V. "Interstate Comparisons of Child Support Orders Using State Guidelines." *Family Relations*, 1998, *47*(3), pp. 289–95.

Robins, Philip K. "Why Did Child Support Award Levels Decline from 1978 to 1985?" *Journal of Human Resources*, 1992, *27*(2), pp. 362–79.

Seltzer, Judith A., McLanahan, Sara S. and Hanson, Thomas L. "Will Child Support Enforcement Increase Father–Child Contact and Parental Conflict after Separation?" in Irving Garfinkel, Sara S. McLanahan, Daniel R. Meyer, and Judith A. Seltzer, eds., *Fathers under Fire: The Revolution in Child Support Enforcement.* New York: Russell Sage Foundation, 1998, pp. 157–90.

Seltzer, Judith A., Schaeffer, Nora C. and Charng, Hong-Wen. "Family Ties after Divorce: The Relationship between Visiting and Paying Child Support." *Journal of Marriage and the Family,* 1989, *51*, pp. 1013–31.

Sorensen, Elaine. "Low-Income Noncustodial Fathers: Who Are They and What Are States Doing to Assist Them in Their Efforts to Pay Child Support?" Washington, DC: Urban Institute, September 1996.

Sorensen, Elaine and Halpern, Ariel. "Child Support Enforcement Is Working Better Than We Think," in *New Federalism: Issues and Options for States,* Series A, No. A-31. Washington, DC: Urban Institute, 1999.

Turetsky, Vicki and Notar, Susan. "Models for Safe Child Support Enforcement." *American University Journal of Gender, Social Policy and Law*, 2000, *8*, pp. 657–716.

U.S. Bureau of the Census. *Current Population Reports*, Series P-23, No. 112, "Child Support and Alimony: 1978." Washington, DC: U.S. Government Printing Office, 1981.

———. *Current Population Reports*, Series P-23, No. 154, "Child Support and Alimony: 1985 (Supplemental Report)." Washington, DC: U.S. Government Printing Office, 1989.

———. *Current Population Reports*, Series P-60, No. 197, "Money Income in the United States: 1996." Washington, DC: U.S. Government Printing Office, 1997.

———. *Current Population Reports*, Series P-60, No. 196, "Child Support for Custodial Mothers and Fathers: 1995." Washington, DC: U.S. Government Printing Office, 1999.

U.S. Department of Health and Human Services. *Child Support Enforcement: Eighteenth Annual Report to Congress.* Washington, DC: U.S. Government Printing Office, 1995.

———. *Child Support Enforcement: FY 1997 Preliminary Data Report.* Washington, DC: U.S. Government Printing Office, 1998.

Weiss, Yoram and Willis, Robert J. "Children as Collective Goods and Divorce Settlements." *Journal of Labor Economics*, 1985, *3*(3), pp. 268–92.

Weitzman, Lenore J. *The Divorce Revolution: The Unexpected Social and Economic Consequences for Women and Children.* New York: Free Press, 1985.

EIGHT

Marriage Prospects and Welfare Use

John Fitzgerald

Over the last few decades, the decline in marriage rates and rise in childbearing among unmarried women have increased the number of women eligible for welfare. The consequent rise in caseloads has increased pressure on welfare programs. In 1996, one-third of unmarried mothers reported receiving Aid for Families with Dependent Children (AFDC), the primary cash welfare program in the United States (U.S. House Committee on Ways and Means, 1998). The AFDC program provided most of its aid to unmarried mothers. The AFDC eligibility criteria were quite restrictive in that aid was allowed to two-parent families only if the primary earner was unemployed or disabled (the AFDC-UP program). The AFDC program has recently been replaced by the Temporary Assistance to Needy Families (TANF). Although TANF has granted states greater leeway in eligibility rules, states have maintained marriage as a key determinant of eligibility, and the welfare caseload largely remains families headed by unmarried women. Since the quality and quantity of potential spouses affect marriage decisions that then interact with welfare use, spouse availability is expected to have an effect on welfare use.

This chapter begins by looking at the links between marriage and welfare use and develops the standard economic model of welfare use based on choice. I then briefly review literature on spouse availability and marriage rates and explore the resulting association between measures of spouse availability and welfare use by looking at crosssectional state data. This sets the stage for a multivariate model of welfare durations wherein we can control for confounding effects of personal characteristics, spouse availability, and labor market changes. I focus on results from one such multivariate study, Fitzgerald (1991). In that paper, I estimated a model of welfare durations that explicitly includes the conditions of the marriage market. I find evidence that spouse availability and quality affect exit rates from welfare, although the impact varies by race. Marriage market conditions matter for whites but not for blacks.

MARRIAGE AND WELFARE

Data on Welfare Entry and Exits

Spouse availability could affect welfare use in two ways: It could affect the rate of entry onto welfare programs and/or the rate of exit off welfare programs. Entry onto welfare is precipitated by earnings changes and by demographic changes – birth of a child to an unwed mother or divorce, for example. Table 8.1 shows tabulations of events leading to welfare use based on data from the Panel Study of Income Dynamics (PSID) (U.S. Department of Health and Human Services 1998). Spouse availability

Table 8.1 *Percentage of First AFDC Spell Beginnings Associated with Specific Events*

Event	Spell began 1973–9	Spell began 1980–5	Spell began 1986–91
First birth to an unmarried, non-cohabiting mother	27.9	20.9	22.2
First birth to a married and/or cohabiting mother	13.3	17.4	11.3
Second (or higher-order) birth	19.9	18.2	18.2
Divorce/separation	19.7	28.1	17.3
Mother's work hours decreased by more than 500 hours, but no change in family structure	26.3	18.8	26.2
Other adults' work hours decreased by more than 500 hours, and a change in family structure	4.7	7.9	11.4
Householder acquired work limitation	18.1	15.6	23.5
Other transfer income dropped by $1,000 or more (in 1996 $)	4.5	6.5	4.1
Changed state of residence	4.5	10.6	5.4

Note: Events are defined to be neither mutually exclusive nor exhaustive. Work limitation is defined as a self-reported physical or nervous condition that limits the type of work or the amount of work the respondent can do.

Source: Unpublished data from PSID, 1968–92. Reprinted from U.S. Department of Health and Human Services (1998).

Table 8.2 *Percentage of First AFDC Spell Endings Associated with Specific Events*

Event	Spell began 1973–9	Spell began 1980–5	Spell began 1986–91
Mother married or acquired cohabitor	16.1	17.1	21.7
Children under 18 no longer present	4.4	4.1	4.8
Mother's work hours increased by more than 500 hours, but no change in family structure	15.4	25.0	27.1
Other adults' work hours increased by more than 500 hours, but no change in family structure	21.8	16.8	16.7
Other adults' work hours increased by more than 500 hours, and a change in family structure	6.5	10.3	5.8
Householder no longer reports work limitation	13.0	19.2	15.8
Other transfer income increased by $1,000 or more (in 1996$)	5.0	5.5	5.8
Change state of residence	5.9	11.0	5.9

Note: Events are defined to be neither mutually exclusive nor exhaustive. Work limitation is defined as a self-reported physical or nervous condition that limits the type of work or the amount of work the respondent can do.

Source: Unpublished data from PSID, 1968–92. Reprinted from U.S. Department of Health and Human Services (1998).

potentially affects several of these events. It could affect the probability of having a child: Scott J. South and Kim M. Lloyd (1992) find that better marriage markets reduce non-marital fertility, although the effect is modest. Spouse availability could further affect the chance that a birth is made legitimate. The *Greenbook* reports that 68 percent of AFDC mothers were unmarried at the time of first birth whereas 27 percent of non-AFDC mothers were so (U.S. House Committee on Ways and Means 1998, Chart 7–6). Further, unwed mothers face reduced future marriage prospects (Daniel T. Lichter and Deborah Roempke Graefe 1999). All considered, favorable marriage markets should reduce the rate of entry onto welfare.

As for exits, past research has shown that marriage and earnings increases are primary routes off of AFDC. Table 8.2 shows tabulations of exits from welfare. Exits are classified by looking at events that occur at or near the end of a spell of welfare receipt, a technique originated by Mary

Jo Bane and David Ellwood (1983). Marriage is a key route off of welfare, and it has become more important over time. For welfare spells ending in the early 1980s, 17 percent ended in marriage or cohabitation, whereas of spells ending in 1986–91, 22 percent ended by marriage or cohabitation. Could this rise in marriage exits be the results of higher sex ratios for younger cohorts (see Chapter 10 by Shoshana Grossbard-Shechtman and Shoshana Neuman) or could improvements in the job market for men, and hence quality of potential spouses, be partly responsible? Data from the Survey of Income and Program Participation (SIPP) also show marriage to be an important route off of welfare. SIPP data are monthly and the panels are shorter than the PSID (SIPP panels are between twenty-four and forty months depending on the year, whereas PSID data have been gathered annually since 1968). The monthly SIPP data show earnings exits to be more important than marriage exits, with only 10 percent of welfare exits in the mid-1980s due to marriage (Fitzgerald 1995).

Different types of welfare exits may have different consequences. Kathleen Mullan Harris (1996) analyzes the speed of return to welfare following an exit, classified by exit type. She finds that work exits result in faster returns to welfare in the first six months than is the case for marriage exits, but marriage exits cumulate more returns to welfare through time. Marriage exits result in less future poverty and more education compared to earnings exits, but high marital separation rates also make marriage exits precarious.

If spouse availability and marital prospects are favorable, one would expect that women would leave welfare more quickly by marriage, all else equal. This should shorten spells on welfare. Differences in spouse availability across racial groups would then partly explain differences in lengths of welfare spells by race. The latter point deserves some emphasis. Higher rates of welfare use and longer stays on welfare by African American women have been ascribed to culture and expectations as well as local economic conditions. Differences in spouse availability offer a demographic explanation that reduces the role for unspecified "cultural differences" by race.

Conceptual Framework

The previous section suggested links between the marriage market and welfare use, and this section outlines the usual economic model of welfare use that underlies the links. Begin with the case of a woman currently on welfare and her decision to leave. The estimation of exit rates from AFDC is generally based on a model of choice: A woman on welfare chooses between the option of staying on or getting off welfare given her environment. Some studies further divide the choice of exiting welfare into marrying or getting a job. An early use of this framework in a static, crosssectional model is found in Sheldon Danziger et al. (1982). In these discrete choice models, a woman chooses to stay on welfare, take a job, or marry by choosing the option that delivers the highest present value of utility. To make this static equilibrium model explain the dynamics of exit and entry, one allows the availability of and returns on the various options or tastes to change over time and assumes that the woman reevaluates her options and possibly alters her behavior as the changes occur (see, for example, Rebecca Blank 1989). Information about options, especially marriage or job options, can be considered to be features of the environment that change over time.

Based on this discrete choice framework, the value of the welfare option relative to the option of work or marriage is usually viewed as depending on personal characteristics such as the mother's age and education, the number and ages of her children, and the availability of other income (non-transferred and non-earned). Policy parameters such as the level and type of AFDC benefits as well as characteristics of the environment such as job prospects and marriage prospects affect the relative value of the welfare option. Often we proxy jobs prospects with unemployment rates. As was done in Fitzgerald (1991), I proxy marriage prospects with measures of spouse availability and quality. Increased spouse availability should result in more marriage offers and thus speed exits off of AFDC.

The decision to enter welfare can be conceptualized similarly. A woman makes the choice based on expected future outcomes as outlined previously. An added complication is that the welfare entry decision may depend on the decision to have a child, with its many components – the decisions to become sexually active, to choose type of birth control, and to carry a pregnancy to term. This fertility decision is complex and beyond the scope of the current chapter (see Shelly Lundberg and Robert Plotnick 1995). My focus here is on the association between spouse availability and welfare use. This association relates to a broader literature on spouse availability and marriage.

Spouse Availability Affects Marriage Rates

The idea that the availability of potential spouses and more generally that the "marriage market" affects marriage-related behavior has been previously analyzed in the literature and is found in other chapters of this book. Marriage market conditions have been shown to influence the decision to marry (see Chapter 2 by Michael J. Brien and Michelle E. Sheran), individual consumption (Gary Becker 1981; Marjorie McLeroy and Mary Jean Horney 1981), and individual labor supply (Amyra Grossbard-Shechtman 1984; Chapter 10 by Grossbard-Shechtman and Neuman in this book).

Early work on marriage in economics modeled the search for potential spouses in the same way as the search for an acceptable job in the labor market. Sex ratios were used as an indicator of the arrival rate of marriage offers (see Michael Keeley 1977, 1979; Robert Hutchens 1979). Keeley found that sex ratio had a significant effect on marriage, but Hutchens did not. Both used crude sex ratios that were not disaggregated by race and included both married and unmarried men and women.

Early evidence from time series about the centrality of sex ratios for determining marriage rates or marriage timing generated mixed results. For example, David M. Heer and Grossbard-Shechtman (1981) and Marcia Guttentag and Paul Secord (1983) find support for the relationship, whereas Thomas J. Espenshade (1985a, 1985b), and Reynolds Farley and Susan M. Bianchi (1991) question it. One obvious problem with time-series analysis for questions of this type is that many other socioeconomic changes are simultaneously taking place.

Demographers have stressed that crude sex ratios are inadequate measures of spouse availability in the marriage market. Noreen Goldman, Charles Hammerslough, and Charles F. Westoff (1984) propose an improved measure of spouse availability that disaggregates by age group and race. They carefully calculate availability based on the age difference between spouses found in the population. These measures are shown to differ markedly from simple sex ratios. I later develop and use disaggregated measures of spouse availability along these lines.

More recent papers have investigated the impact of male employment ratios or male earnings as indicators of spouse quality. Aggregate data studies such as Lichter, Felicia B. LeClere, and Diane K. McLaughlin (1991) find that these measures of spouse quality have significant effects on local marriage rates. However, the use of aggregate county data may confound influences on marriage. Robert J. Wood (1995) uses a fixed-effect model with SMSA-level Census data on marriage market variables and marriage rates. He deals with the endogeneity of men's marriage and employment decisions and concludes that marriage market measures incorporating men's employment status do not predict historical changes in marriage rates for whites and predict only a small part of the decline in marriage rates for blacks.

Lichter et al. (1992) match marriage market characteristics into individual National Longitudinal Survey of Youth data. They find that spouse availability and men's earning capacity significantly affect the timing of marriage. Lichter, McLaughlin, and David C. Ribar (1997) use county-level data from the decennial census and find that sex ratio and male earnings measures are associated with less female headship.

Brien (1997) examines the timing of marriage using data from the high school class of 1972. These individual data are combined with a number of spouse availability and male employment measures derived from 1980 Census data. He finds that marriage market variables are significant predictors of marriage timing for blacks and for whites. Marriage market variables explain much but not all of differences in marriage rates by race. Further, he suggests that state-level marriage market variables may be the most appropriate. Smaller geographic disaggregations lead to significant measurement error and consequently may cause a lack of significance of local marriage market variables.

Policy concern over the availability of spouses stems from evidence on the low rate of family formation among blacks. Bane and Ellwood (1983), June O'Neill, Laurie Bassi, and Doug Wolf (1987), and Blank (1989) all report that black women have a much lower probability of leaving AFDC by marriage than whites. William J. Wilson and Katherine M. Neckerman (1986) and William A. Darity, Jr., and Samuel L. Meyers, Jr. (1983, 1986), argue that black women face a shrinking pool of "marriageable" employed black men. They suggest that the rise in black female–headed families over recent decades is more closely linked with this diminishing pool of marriage partners than with expansion of transfer programs. Several of the studies mentioned previously consequently focus on racial differences in marriage rates, especially Wood (1995) and Brien (1997).

We can conclude from the literature that measures of spouse availability and employment affect marriage rates, but do not fully explain time-series changes. Furthermore, appropriate measurement is important. Later in the chapter, I use geographically based sex ratios and male employment ratios to test a Wilson and Neckerman–style hypothesis that low availability of "marriageable" men increases the length of time that women remain on welfare.

STATE-LEVEL SPOUSE AVAILABILITY AND WELFARE USE

If spouse availability affects welfare use, we expect that geographic areas with low spouse availability would have above-average welfare use.

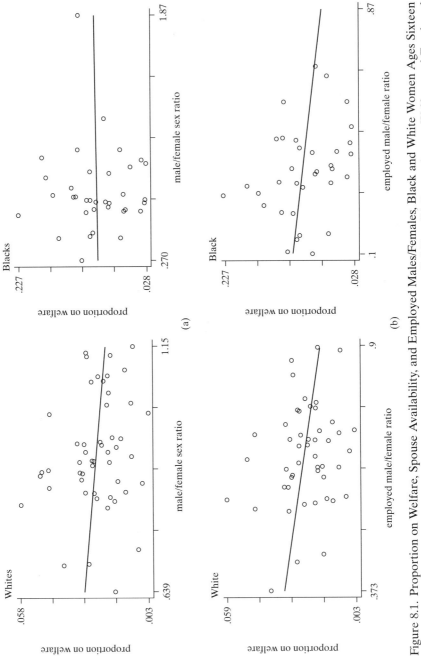

Figure 8.1. Proportion on Welfare, Spouse Availability, and Employed Males/Females, Black and White Women Ages Sixteen to Twenty-Five, State Means: (a) Proportion on Welfare and Spouse Availability; (b) Proportion on Welfare and Employed Males/Females. *Source:* Current Population Surveys, 1996–8

184

I begin by looking at the simple correlations in these measures across states. The choice of states as the geographic unit is arbitrary but convenient. As pointed out in Fitzgerald (1991) and Brien (1997), state areas are too big to serve accurately as the marriage market faced by a woman. But state aggregates are relevant and as demonstrated by Brien (1997), they may be the best compromise between small area accuracy and measurement error.

To construct state measures of welfare use and spouse availability, I pooled data from the March Current Population Survey (CPS) for 1996, 1997, and 1998. The pooling was done to get a large enough sample for each race/state cell. To simplify the presentation, I focused on young women. I constructed a state-level measure of welfare use by measuring the proportion of unmarried women age sixteen to twenty-five who receive any public assistance income as a proportion of unmarried women age sixteen to twenty-five.[1] This was done separately by race for blacks and whites, excluding other racial groups.

To measure spouse availability, I used a modified sex ratio. I divided the number of unmarried men age eighteen to twenty-seven by the number of unmarried women age sixteen to twenty-five, separately by race and state. As described more completely later in this chapter, this assumes that brides are of the same race and on average two years younger than their grooms, based on Goldman, Hammerslough, and Westoff (1984). The ten-year group allows for the fairly wide age range of most marriages and allows for adequate sample cell sizes of unmarried women.[2]

The overall means show the less favorable marriage market for young black women. The mean sex ratio across states is 0.92 for whites but only 0.74 for blacks. Black women also show much higher public assistance receipt, with 10 percent reporting receipt compared to 2.5 percent of young white women. This suggests that variation in spouse availability may explain part of the racial difference in welfare use.

Figure 8.1a shows scatterplots of welfare use and sex ratio separately by race. Each graph includes a regression line of the relationship using state means treating each state as one observation. Obviously there is great variation by state in both sex ratios and welfare use. Note that the

[1] The category *unmarried* includes never married, widowed, divorced, or separated. The sample is restricted to noninstitutionalized adults.
[2] I excluded any state–race group that had less than twenty persons to prevent small samples from producing outlier ratios, although measurement error remains a potential problem. This excluded fifteen states for blacks and none for whites.

scales differ for whites and blacks, with blacks showing much greater variation across states. There is a negative relation between welfare use and sex ratio for whites, but no relationship for blacks. Figure 8.1b shows the relation between the ratio of employed males to females for this age range. Employed males represent "better" potential spouses. The relation is negative for both races. The results hint at a welfare/spouse availability relation, but we need to condition on other variables to sort out the effect. The employed male ratio correlation with welfare use is stronger than that for sex ratio but it may be picking up labor market conditions.[3]

A MULTIVARIATE MODEL

Hazard Model

Correlations across states are suggestive, but not adequate to separate the various influences on welfare durations. One needs to control for other changes to separate the impacts of spouse availability from general trends or geographic variation in the labor market. At the same time, we want to control for personal characteristics. We accomplish this with a multivariate hazard model.

A hazard model works from spells or episodes of continuous welfare receipt. In any month of a spell, I estimate the probability of an exit from welfare conditional on the length of the spell to that point. This exit rate is the hazard.

Longitudinal data have advantages over retrospective data for determining the length of spells on welfare.[4] A spell of welfare is defined as the length of time in which the head of an AFDC unit continuously receives welfare. With longitudinal data, spells on welfare can be of three types: complete, left-censored, or right-censored. A complete spell occurs when I observe both the beginning and end in the sample period and thus know its exact length. A left-censored spell occurs when the recipient was receiving welfare at the beginning of the observation period; I do not observe the beginning of the spell and only have data for the part of the

---

[3] The multivariate model in the next section uses data from an earlier period, the mid-1980s. The relation shown here might have changed. To set up a comparison, I performed the same state-mean analysis using CPS data from 1984, 1985, and 1986, and obtained similar results, with negativity sloped regression lines in all cases.

[4] Retrospective data usually require longer recall, which may be subject to error. Further, the values of other relevant variables are not generally available over the recall period. This limits the use of time-varying covariates.

spell that occurs within the sample. A right-censored spell occurs when I observe the beginning of the spell during the sample period but not the end; I know that the spell was at least as long as observed.

As is common in this literature, the hazard model is estimated using complete and right-censored spells[5] with parameters of the model estimated by maximum likelihood.[6]

Modeling Welfare Durations

Before turning to the model's specification, we should establish the context for the duration model. The question of welfare dependency has a long history, but good data and methodology for studying this dependency are more recent. Hutchens (1979), Robert Plotnick (1983), Bane and Ellwood (1983), and the extension by Ellwood (1986), O'Neill, et al. (1987), and Blank (1989) provide us with early work about the determinants of exit rates from AFDC.

More relevant to this chapter, several of the studies previously discussed also include findings on exit rates from welfare disaggregated by type of exit. Three types of exit are considered: exit by marriage, exit by earnings increase, and the residual, that is, other exits. All studies conclude that marriage and earnings increases are the primary routes off of AFDC. Overall, the literature shows that blacks are less likely than whites to leave AFDC by marriage, yet the rate of exit by earnings increase is not significantly different for blacks and whites. These results imply that the lower overall rate of exit by blacks is due to their lower propensity to marry (Blank 1989). The studies do not attempt to measure the extent to which the lower marriage rates for black women are due to the poorer marriage prospects (that is, availability and income of potential spouses), as opposed to noneconomic cultural influences. Fitzgerald (1991) added marriage market variables to the standard welfare duration model.

---

[5] Use of left-censored spells requires strong assumptions and more complicated methods, e.g. Tony Lancaster (1990). The sample used only the first spell in cases with multiple spells.

[6] For those unfamiliar with hazard models, a hazard coefficient is analogous to a regression coefficient, showing the partial effect on the hazard function of variation in a covariate conditional on the linear effects of the other included variables. The particular hazard functional form used here is a complementary log-log with a flexible step-function hazard with seven steps. (See Fitzgerald 1991 for details or Paul D. Allison 1982 for general discussion of the method.)

Data from SIPP

Fitzgerald (1991) uses monthly data on AFDC receipt from the 1984 panel of the SIPP, a panel survey of approximately twenty thousand households that gathers monthly data by interviewing households every four months. The survey includes extensive information on income sources and government program use, which allows construction of spells of income receipt from these programs. These data are thus well suited for estimation of welfare durations. The 1984 panel begins in October 1983 and runs for thirty-two to thirty-six months. The sample is restricted to single female heads of AFDC units. The AFDC unit was defined as the family or sub-family of which the woman was the head with children under eighteen in the first month of receipt.[7] The sample was further restricted to those with an identifiable state of residence, and complete age and education data. I excluded races other than black and white to clarify interpretation of the race variable. These adjustments left 340 cases for the hazard models.

Variable Definitions

Much of the variation in variables of interest such as marriage market variables and unemployment comes from crossstate variation. The SIPP initially identifies state of residence for thirty-eight separate states; the rest are grouped or were not sampled. The measures of spouse availability, described in this section, are assumed to approximate the marriage market conditions faced by women in each state. To the extent that there is substantial variation within each state, this variable is not disaggregated enough. However, as noted previously, Brien (1997) concludes that state-level aggregations for marriage market variables are best because more local aggregations suffer from small cell sizes and hence measurement error.

I use two types of variables to measure conditions in the marriage market. The first, sex ratio, is the ratio of single males to single females of the same race and in a relevant age group by state of residence. The key assumption is that this ratio approximates the availability of a marriage partner for each woman in a particular state. Demographers Goldman, Westoff, and Hammerslough (1984) point out that sex ratios aggregated by age and race do not adequately represent the availability of potential

---

[7] This "family" definition may differ from the administrative AFDC unit when the family includes other relatives of the head but there is no subfamily. Some recoding was done, as described in Fitzgerald (1991).

spouses. The method in the next paragraph attempts to incorporate their ideas, but it is much rougher. The second measure is a male employment ratio, the ratio of employed single males to all single males, by age group, state, and race. This is in the spirit of Wilson and Neckerman's (1986) argument that the quality of potential spouses is important and is defined in terms of employment.

The sex ratio is calculated from the 1980 decennial Census by race, state, and age group. Goldman, Westoff, and Hammerslough (1984) present evidence that there is a fairly large variation in age differences at marriage, so I chose eleven-year age groups. I assume that grooms are on average two years older than their brides, also based on Goldman and her colleagues (1984). Thus, for a woman age thirty, I computed the number of unmarried men of age twenty-seven through thirty-seven and divided it by the number of unmarried women age twenty-five through thirty-five to get the sex ratio. This was done for each race, state, and woman's age from eighteen through fifty-four. I then associated these ratios with sample women by race, state, and age. I computed the male employment ratio from the 1980 Census, then updated to 1985 by adjusting to reflect changes in employment between 1980 and 1985.

The means in Table 8.3 further confirm the Wilson and Neckerman (1986) notion that the relative availability of employed single males is lower for blacks. Inspection of the ratios also reveals wide variation across states and within each race. Table 8.3 shows the definitions and means of the other explanatory variables, including a disaggregation by race. The additional covariates are necessary to separate the impact of the marriage market variables from personal characteristics and labor market changes. Some vary over the AFDC spell, and others do not. All dollar-denominated variables are adjusted to January 1984 dollars. State welfare benefits are measured by the AFDC benefit adjusted by family size. This variable is intended to capture the relevant components of a state's welfare package. Obviously, benefits may also pick up the effects of other unobserved state-specific attributes, as noted by Ellwood and Bane (1985). The variable for other income available includes property income and private transfers (alimony and child support). The unemployment rate is the monthly rate by state.

Results

The inclusion of marriage market variables improves the estimated model of welfare hazards. Table 8.5 in the appendix shows the model estimated

Table 8.3 *Means and Definitions of Explanatory Variables*

	Means		
Variable	All	Black	White
A. Median spell length in months			
(from estimated Survivor function)	20	>20	17
B. Fixed during the spell			
AGE (age at spell beginning)	27.3	27.2	27.4
RACE (0 = white, 1 = black)	0.438	–	–
SEXRATIO (ratio of single men to single women	0.916	0.852	0.966
of same race and age group, by state)			
EXPMALE (ratio of single employed men to	0.675	0.589	0.744
single men of same race and age group, by state)			
C. Vary during the spell			
EDUC (head's highest grade completed)	10.9	11.0	10.8
NKIDS (number of children younger			
than age 28 in the AFDC unit)	1.74	1.77	1.72
UKIDS (number of children younger			
than age 6 are in the AFDC unit)	0.98	0.97	0.99
AFDCMX (AFDC benefit maximum			
by family size, by state, in dollars)	300	280	317
OTHINC (private transfers and property			
income of female head, in dollars)	192	213	176
UNEMP (monthly state unemployment			
rate, in percentages)	7.85	7.67	8.01
D. Sample size	340	149	191

Notes: Mean values taken during the first month of the spell for first observed spells of female heads in SIPP. All dollar amounts in January 1984 dollars.

for both races combined as Model 2. Model 1 shows the results if the marriage market variables are omitted. In Model 2, the sex ratio has a statistically insignificant coefficient, but male employment ratio has a well-estimated positive coefficient. This suggests that availability of employed single males, a proxy for spouse quality, speeds exits from AFDC. The remaining coefficients vary little from those in Model 1, except that the coefficients on number of children, race, and unemployment decrease in size. The residual effect of race is quite small once the sex ratio and male employment ratio are added. This suggests that part of the difference in welfare usage by race is due to differences in marriage market conditions.

To better illustrate the magnitudes of the effects, Table 8.4 shows the proportions of the initial sample that would be expected to remain on welfare at the indicated spell length. These proportions are based on

Table 8.4 *Estimated Proportions Expected to Remain on Welfare at Various Durations*

	Proportion remaining at		
	6 months	12 months	24 months
A. Whites and blacks			
1. All persons (Model 2)	0.70	0.59	0.50
2. Education = 8	0.76	0.67	0.59
3. Education = 12	0.68	0.56	0.47
4. OTHPROP increased 10%	0.70	0.59	0.50
5. Age = 20	0.73	0.63	0.54
6. Age = 30	0.69	0.58	0.49
7. Race = 0 (White)	0.70	0.59	0.49
8. Race = 1 (Black)	0.70	0.60	0.50
9. YKID = YKID + 1	0.74	0.64	0.55
10. AFDC benefit increased 10%	0.71	0.60	0.51
11. Sex ratio increased 10%	0.70	0.59	0.50
12. Male employment ratio increased 10%	0.67	0.55	0.46
B. Whites (Model 3)			
1. Base case	0.66	0.56	0.46
2. AFDC benefit increased by 10%	0.68	0.57	0.48
3. Unemployment increased by 10%	0.64	0.54	0.43
4. Sex ratio increased by 10%	0.63	0.52	0.42
5. Male employment ratio increased by 10%	0.57	0.46	0.35
C. Blacks (Model 4)			
1. Base case	0.74	0.64	0.57
2. AFDC benefit increased by 10%	0.75	0.65	0.59
3. Unemployment increased by 10%	0.77	0.67	0.61
4. Sex ratio increased by 10%	0.76	0.65	0.59
5. Male employment ratio increased by 10%	0.74	0.63	0.57

Notes: Estimated proportions are means based on estimated hazard from the indicated model. Means are for 340 cases.

simulations of the survivor function using the coefficients from Model 2. For example, of all recipients, 50 percent are expected to have a welfare spell of at least twenty-four months.[8] The base case represents the average recipient. The other rows show changes from the base case. Based on the simulation, the sex ratio has negligible effects in this combined model.

---

[8] I computed the survivor function for each person based on the person's characteristics at the beginning of the spell, then averaged across persons at each month to produce a mean survivor function. Fitzgerald (1991) explains this in more detail.

The male employment ratio has a moderate impact. For example, raising the male employment ratio by 10 percent decreases the survivor function at twenty-four months by 8 percent (from 0.50 to 0.46). Young age and presence of children, both indirectly associated with lower marriage rates as well as employment, also lengthen time on welfare.

Separate Black and White Models

The lack of significance of race in the previous specifications does not imply that the hazards for the two groups are the same, because other coefficients may differ by race. Models 3 and 4 in the appendix's Table 8.5 explore this question by showing specifications separately for whites and blacks, and panels B and C of Table 8.4 show simulated proportions remaining on welfare for these specifications. The sample sizes for these models are relatively small: 191 whites of whom 77 have complete spells, and 149 blacks of whom 52 have complete spells. Given the large number of parameters and small samples, the separate race models are expected to have less precision.

For whites, the marriage market variables have positive, statistically significant effects on exit rates. The simulation shows that a 10 percent rise in the male employment ratio substantially lowers the proportion of those remaining on welfare at twenty-four months or more by one-fourth (from 0.46 to 0.35). A 10 percent rise in the sex ratio lowers the proportion of survivors by 9 percent. For blacks, these variables have nearly negligible, statistically insignificant effects. For blacks, lower unemployment rates hasten exits, but not for whites. One interpretation consistent with these results and other studies (Blank 1989; Bane and Ellwood 1983) is that marriage markets may be more important for whites, but that the labor market is more important for blacks.[9]

Another difference between the black and white hazard models is that education and other income are significant for blacks, but not whites. Education by itself or as a proxy for wages has an ambiguous effect on marriage probabilities (education increases one's attractiveness as a partner but may cause one to be choosier[10]), but likely has a positive effect

---

[9] The findings that the participation of black women in AFDC does not depend on male incomes, number of children, or sex ratio is consistent with the theoretical model of Grossbard-Shechtman (1995). She models the ways in which marriage market conditions affect labor supply, marriage, and welfare use.

[10] Further, very high education levels may reduce marriageability. See Chapter 2 by Brien and Sheran in this book or Grossbard-Shechtman (1993).

on the returns to a job. Perhaps education has more impact for blacks because labor markets are more important in explaining exit rates.

CONCLUSION

This chapter presents evidence that spouse availability affects welfare usage. Using state-level aggregates, it showed that measures of favorable spouse availability correlate with lower welfare caseloads. But this could be due to other factors related to both spouse availability and welfare usage, such as labor market conditions. The chapter then describes a narrower test: Does spouse availability affect the length of time that individual women stay on welfare? Based on a multivariate model for exit rates from AFDC, I conclude that it does.

Further work using a competing-risk framework, which distinguishes exits from AFDC by marriage and earnings, could help clarify the role of spouse availability. But when the competing risks are not independent, as seems likely here, identification of a model becomes problematic.[11] To better sort out the impacts of marriage and labor markets, future studies will benefit from new approaches to defining individual marriage markets. Further detailed geographic information on both labor markets and marriage markets will help but may not be adequate to overcome measurement error in small geographic areas. Additional work on how spouse availability affects the decision to enter welfare also remains to be done.

Past literature has questioned the extent to which racial differences in welfare use is due to different environments (schools, labor markets) or to different attitudes toward single motherhood or welfare dependency. This chapter concludes that part of the observed difference in welfare use is due to marriage market differences – lower availability of employed black males per female. From a policy perspective, this suggests that we focus on the economic and demographic constraints faced by African American mothers on welfare rather than on possible differences in tastes, attitudes, or culture of dependency. The results further show that for African American women, labor market conditions are more important than marriage market conditions.

A second implication is that improved labor market conditions are important in two ways: They reduce welfare rolls directly by increasing earnings exits and indirectly by increasing marriage exits. Employment

---

[11] Fitzgerald (1995) uses a competing risk model but finds no significant effect of a simple sex ratio on marriage exits. The crudeness of the sex ratio and the small samples of marriage exits may account for lack of significance.

policies focused on men will have an impact on welfare rates. Recent improvements in both labor markets and marriage markets (see Chapter 10 by Grossbard-Shechtman and Neuman) should shorten welfare spells, and this explains part of the recently observed decrease in welfare use. The high employment labor market of the 1990s has reduced welfare rolls both through jobs for welfare recipients and by improving marriage prospects for welfare mothers.

APPENDIX

Table 8.5 *AFDC Exit Rate Hazard Models*

	Both races		Whites	Blacks
	Model 1	Model 2	Model 3	Model 4
Education	0.109***	0.0965**	0.0490	0.265**
	(.00409)	(0.0417)	(0.0525)	(0.0905)
Other income ($100s)	0.163***	0.142**	0.0302	0.279***
	(0.0610)	(0.0678)	(0.113)	(0.0943)
Number of kids < 18	0.177*	0.127	0.123	0.0712
	(0.108)	(0.110)	(0.141)	(0.192)
Number of kids < 6	–0.243*	–0.182	–0.298*	0.113
	(0.133)	(0.136)	(0.174)	(0.240)
Age	0.0166	0.0169	0.0292	0.0215
	(0.0121)	(0.0140)	(0.0221)	(0.0218)
Race (black = 1)	–0.317	–0.0267	–	–
	(0.194)	(0.284)		
Unemployment rate (%)	–0.0750	–0.0441	0.0881	–0.213***
	(0.0482)	(0.0529)	(0.0753)	(0.0785)
AFDC benefit ($100s,	–0.148*	–0.153*	–0.179*	–0.202
by family size)	(0.795)	(0.0813)	(0.102)	(0.157)
Sex ratio	–	0.0993	1.15*	–0.900
	–	(0.463)	(0.685)	(0.699)
Males employment ratio	–	1.95*	4.22**	0.191
	–	(0.982)	(1.90)	(1.25)
Log of likelihood	–504.0	–502.2	–291.0	–201.1
Sample size				
Persons months	3,170	3,170	1,681	1,489
Persons	340	340	191	149

Notes: Standard errors are in parentheses. Sample consists of first observed spells by female-headed households with children. Models 1 and 2 include a constant and seven time dummies for spell duration to that month. Models 3 and 4 include a constant and six time dummies.
 * Statistically significant at the 10 percent level.
 ** Statistically significant at the 5 percent level.
 *** Statistically significant at the 1 percent level.

REFERENCES

Allison, Paul D. "Discrete-Time Methods for the Analysis of Event Histories," in Samuel Leinhart, ed., *Sociological Methodology*. San Francisco: Jossey-Bass, 1982.

Bane, Mary Jo and Ellwood, David. *The Dynamics of Dependence: The Route to Self Sufficiency*. Report prepared for U.S. Department of Health and Human Services: Urban Systems Research and Engineering, Inc., 1983.

Becker, Gary. *A Treatise on the Family*. Cambridge, MA: Harvard University Press, 1981.

Blank, Rebecca. "Analyzing the Length of Welfare Spells." *Journal of Public Economics*, 1989, *39*, pp. 245–74.

Brien, Michael. "Racial Differences in Marriage and the Role of Marriage Markets." *Journal of Human Resources*, 1997, *32*(4), pp. 741–78.

Danziger, Sheldon, Jakubson, George, Schwartz, Saul and Smolensky, Eugene. "Work and Welfare as Determinants of Female Poverty and Household Headship." *Quarterly Journal of Economics*, 1982, *97*(3), pp. 519–34.

Darity, William A., Jr. and Myers, Samuel L., Jr. "Changes in Black Family Structure: Implications for Welfare Dependency." *American Economic Review*, 1983, *73*(2), pp. 59–64.

———. "The Marginalization of Black Males and the Rise of Female Headed Families." Chapel Hill, NC: University of North Carolina Department of Economics, 1986.

Ellwood, David. *Targeting "Would Be" Long-Term Recipients of AFDC*. Report prepared for U.S. Department of Health and Human Services. Princeton, NJ: Mathematica Policy Research, 1986.

Ellwood, David and Bane, Mary Jo. "The Impact of AFDC on Family Structure and Living Arrangements," in Ronald Ehrenberg, ed., *Research in Labor Economics*, Vol. 7. Greenwich, CT: JAI Press, 1985.

Espenshade, Thomas J. "Marriage Trends in America: Estimates, Implications, and Underlying Causes." *Population and Development Review*, 1985a, *11*, pp. 193–245.

———. "The Recent Decline of American Marriage: Blacks and Whites in Comparative Perspective," in Kingsley Davis and Amyra Grossbard-Shechtman, eds., *Contemporary Marriage: Comparative Perspectives on a Changing Institution*. New York: Russell Sage Publications, 1985b, pp. 53–90.

Farley, Reynolds and Bianchi, Suzanne M. "The Growing Racial Difference in Marriage and Family Patterns," in Robert Staples, ed., *The Black Family: Essays and Studies*. 4th ed. Belmont, CA: Wadsworth Publishing Co., 1991, pp. 5–22.

Fitzgerald, John M. "Welfare Durations and the Marriage Market: Evidence from SIPP." *Journal of Human Resources*, 1991, *26*, pp. 545–61.

———. "Local Labor Markets and Local Area Effects on Welfare Duration." *Journal of Policy Analysis and Management*, 1995, *14*(1), pp. 43–67.

Goldman, Noreen, Hammerslough, Charles and Westoff, Charles F. "Demography of the Marriage Market in the United States." *Population Index*, 1984, *50*, pp. 5–25.

Grossbard-Shechtman, Amyra. "A Theory of the Allocation of Time in Markets for Labor and Marriage." *Economics Journal*, 1984, *94*, pp. 863–82.

———. *On the Economics of Marriage*. Boulder, CO: Westview Press, 1993.

———. "Marriage Markets and Black/White Differences in Labor, Marriage, and Welfare." Mimeo, San Diego State University and University of California, San Diego, 1995.

Guttentag, Marcia and Secord, Paul. *Too Many Women? The Sex Ratio Question*. Beverly Hills, CA: Russell Sage Publications, 1983.

Heer, David M. and Grossbard-Shechtman, Amyra. "The Impact of the Female Marriage Squeeze and the Contraceptive Revolution on Sex Roles and the Women's Liberation Movement in the United States, 1960–1975." *Journal of Marriage and the Family*, 1981, *43*(1), pp. 49–65.

Hutchens, Robert M. "Welfare, Remarriage, and Marital Search." *American Economic Review*, 1979, *69*, pp. 369–79.

Keeley, Michael C. "The Economics of Family Formation." *Economic Inquiry*, 1977, *15*, pp. 238–50.

———. "An Analysis of the Age Pattern of First Marriage." *International Economic Review*, 1979, *20*, pp. 527–44.

Lancaster, Tony. *The Economic Analysis of Transition Data*. Cambridge, UK: Cambridge University Press, 1990.

Lichter, Daniel T. and Graefe, Deborah Roempke. "Finding a Mate? The Post-Birth Marital and Cohabitation Histories of Unwed Mothers." Mimeo, Population Research Institute, Pennsylvania State University, 1999.

Lichter, Daniel T., LeClere, Felicia B. and McLaughlin, Diane K. "Local Marriage Markets and the Marital Behavior of Black and White Women." *American Journal of Sociology*, 1991, *96*(4), pp. 843–67.

Lichter, Daniel T., McLaughlin, Diane K., Kephart, George and Landry, David J. "Race and the Retreat from Marriage: A Shortage of Marriageable Men?" *American Sociological Review*, 1992, *57*(6), pp. 781–99.

Lichter, Daniel T., McLaughin, Diane K. and Ribar, David C. "Welfare and the Rise of Female Headed Families." *American Journal of Sociology*, 1997, *103*(1), pp. 112–43.

Lundberg, Shelly and Plotnick, Robert D. "Adolescent Premarital Childbearing: So Economic Incentives Matter?" *Journal of Labor Economics*, 1995, *13*(2), pp. 177–200.

McElroy, Marjorie and Horney, Mary Jean. "Nash-Bargained Household Decisions: Toward a Generalization of the Theory of Demand." *International Economic Review*, 1981, *22*(2), pp. 333–49.

Mullan Harris, Kathleen. "Life after Welfare: Women, Work, and Repeat Dependency." *American Sociological Review*, 1996, *61*, pp. 407–26.

O'Neill, June, Bassi, Laurie and Wolf, Doug. "The Duration of Welfare Spells." *Review of Economics and Statistics*, 1987, *69*(2), pp. 241–8.

Plotnick, Robert. "Turnover in the AFDC Population: An Event History Analysis." *Journal of Human Resources*, 1983, *18*, pp. 65–81.

South, Scott J. and Lloyd, Kim M. "Marriage Markets and Nonmarital Fertility in the United States." *Demography*, 1992, *29*(2), pp. 247–64.

U.S. Department of Health and Human Services. *Indicators of Welfare Dependence*. Annual Report to Congress, Washington, DC, 1998.

U.S. House Committee on Ways and Means. *Greenbook*. Online at http://www.hhes, 1998.

Wilson, William J. and Neckerman, Katherine M. "Poverty and Family Structure: The Widening Gap between Evidence and Public Policy Issues," in Sheldon Danziger and Daniel Weinberg, eds., *Fighting Poverty: What Works and What Doesn't*. Cambridge, MA: Harvard University Press, 1986, pp. 232–59.

Wood, Robert J. "Marriage Rates and Marriageable Men: A Test of the Wilson Hypothesis." *Journal of Human Resources*, 1995, *30*(1), pp. 163–93.

PART III

EFFECTS OF MARRIAGE ON TIME USES

NINE

Marriage, Household Production, and Earnings

Joni Hersch

Survey data and time diaries indicate that employed married women spend two to three times as much time on housework as their husbands. This chapter deals with two important sets of implications associated with time spent on home production: labor market outcomes and legal issues involving home production.

First, time in home production affect labor market opportunities and outcomes, via lower job skill acquisition, more limited professional opportunities, and lower wages. Second, home production has important implications in a litigation context. In the case of wrongful death litigation, the economic loss will be the sum of the value of lost earnings and the value of lost home services. In many cases, the economic loss of a wife's home services exceeds her earnings loss. This is due to the large amount of time that wives spend on home production, as well as to the lower market earnings that result from this time allocation. Similarly, in many divorce cases, the main claim of wives to the assets accumulated during marriage is their contribution to home production.

This chapter discusses economic theories that lead to the division of home production time along observed gender lines, evidence on the allocation of home production time between spouses, and the economic consequences of this division. To demonstrate the salient legal issues, I discuss the *Wendt v. Wendt* divorce case, in which Lorna Wendt argued that her role as a corporate wife was essential to her husband's career success,

I acknowledge with gratitude the research assistance of Jessica Pishko and excellent comments from the editor.

entitling her to a larger share of the marital assets than conventionally awarded under Connecticut law.

WHO DOES THE HOUSEWORK: THEORY

Does marriage itself, or expectations of marriage, lead to women earning less than men? Under certain assumptions, economic analysis predicts precisely this outcome. Leaving aside the determination of who marries and who marries whom, let's consider a married household with two adults. Goods consumed at home can either be purchased in the market or produced at home in combination with purchased goods. Theories of specialization and exchange imply that it is optimal for one spouse to specialize in home production and for the other spouse to specialize in labor market work (Gary Becker 1991). In doing so, the household maximizes its utility and generates greater output to be shared among the household than the sum of the individual outputs. Households produce private goods, consumed only by individuals, as well as public goods that are shared by all members of the household, without reducing any individual's consumption. For example, if a wife washes her husband's laundry, this is a private good that directly benefits only him (although see the *Wendt* case discussed later for an example of investing in the husband as an investment in family human capital). Raising nice children is an example of a household public good that both parents can enjoy.

The spouse who specializes in home production will optimally invest less in labor market skills, such as education and job training. Economic theory, supported by a vast number of empirical studies, predicts higher earnings for individuals with greater amounts of labor market–oriented human capital.

While theories of specialization and exchange predict that members of households will specialize in either labor market work or in home production, these theories alone do not predict which spouse will specialize in which activity. The observed gender-based division of labor within the household can be explained by theories of comparative advantage, and market and bargaining models of marriage, discussed in this section.

According to the theory of comparative advantage, it is optimal for the spouse with the lower opportunity cost to specialize in home production, where the opportunity cost is given by the value of the best alternative use of the time. In this context, the opportunity cost is the wage rate the individual would earn in the market. Since women on average earn less than men do, their opportunity cost is lower on average. Of course, the lower expected earnings of women may result from a self-fulfilling cycle: Women anticipate earning less (perhaps due to discrimination or due to preferences about the lifetime allocation of time to market work), which lowers their optimal investment, which lowers their wage, and so on.

Even if there are no differences by gender in market wage, if there are innate gender differences in home production skills, then it will be optimal for the spouse with the comparative advantage to specialize in home production. By observing the labor market, it seems unlikely that there are innate gender differences in housecleaning skill, cooking, or laundry, since we observe male and female janitors, cooks and chefs, and laundry workers. However, only women are able to bear children, and in the past many women interrupted their labor market careers for child rearing. This time away from the labor market reduces the time available for a woman's investment in labor market skills and possibly depreciates her existing stock of market-related human capital. This pattern would have led to women developing a comparative advantage in home production, leading to the observed gender-based division of labor within the household. Of course, as women spend less time away from the labor market, and as the gap in entry-level wages by gender continues to shrink, this argument has less merit as a rationale for a gender-based division of labor within the home.

The bargaining models of Marilyn Manser and Murray Brown (1980) and Marjorie B. McElroy and Mary Jean Horney (1981), and the market models of marriage of Becker (1973) and Amyra Grossbard-Shechtman (1984) predict that the partner who will be relatively better off if divorced has greater bargaining power. If housework is considered undesirable, the spouse with the weaker bargaining position will perform a greater share of the household responsibilities. Since on average the husband has higher earnings, he is better able to purchase market substitutes for home-produced goods possibly provided by his wife and thus has a relatively stronger bargaining position.

The separate spheres bargaining model of Shelly Lundberg and Robert Pollak (1993) implies that specializing along gender lines is a means of reducing the costs of coordinating behavior in producing household public goods. Under this model, rather than using divorce as the threat, spouses can maximize household welfare with minimal interaction. For instance, the main public good of a household is children, and defaulting to stereotypical gender roles in raising children reduces spouses' needs to discuss and coordinate behavior.

WHO DOES THE HOUSEWORK: EVIDENCE

As we saw previously, several different economic theories predict that wives will perform a greater share of housework than their husbands will. In this section, we examine the empirical evidence on time spent on home production.

Time allocation is one of the fundamental issues addressed by economists and, accordingly, substantial work has been done in this area. Much of the theoretical analysis stems from Jacob Mincer (1963) and Becker (1965). Becker provides a general model in which individuals act to maximize their utility by allocating their time between labor market employment and a wide variety of household production activities. Time spent on household production is combined with purchased goods to produce utility-generating consumption goods, thus emphasizing the productive nature of household time.

Reuben Gronau (1977) simplifies the Becker model to allow three uses of time: production in firms, home production, and leisure. Home production is best defined as those activities that can be done by paying a third party. Leisure is an activity that can be enjoyed only if done by oneself, such as reading a book or riding a bike. However, no data source elicits time use in this fashion, and so our information on home production time is imperfect.

Table 9.1 summarizes time on home production reported in representative studies.[1] The statistics in this table are derived from two types of studies. The most reliable method of gathering time use data is from time diaries. Using this method, respondents report in chronological order and in their own words what they were doing at each moment of the previous twenty-four-hour period.

The second source of information on time allocation is provided by surveys that ask respondents to simply report the total time spent on labor market hours and household activities. National data sets that report estimated time spent on housework in addition to a wide array of information on labor market activity and demographics include the Quality of Employment Surveys (QES), Panel Study of Income Dynamics (PSID),

---

[1] F. Thomas Juster and Frank P. Stafford (1991), Beth Anne Shelton (1992), and John Robinson and Geoffrey Godbey (1997) are excellent sources of information on time use. Juster and Stafford provide a survey of the time allocation literature, from both a national and an international perspective. The focus in Shelton is on time use differences by gender. Robinson and Godbey report trends in time use from the Americans' Use of Time Project for the years 1965, 1975, and 1985.

Table 9.1 *Summary of Housework Time Reported in Representative Studies*

Author (year)	Data source, year, method	Sample	Activities included	Female mean	Male mean
Robinson & Godbey (1997)	Study of Time Use 1965 – diary	Urban, household member in labor force	Housework, childcare, shopping	All 40.2 Employed 26.1 Not empl. 51.5	All 11.5 Employed 11.1 Not empl. 15.2
Robinson & Godbey (1997)	Study of Time Use 1975 – diary	Representative sample of U.S. population	Housework, childcare, shopping	All 32.9 Employed 23.7 Not empl. 42.0	All 12.2 Employed 10.7 Not empl. 16.1
Robinson & Godbey (1997)	Study of Time Use 1985 – diary	Representative sample of U.S. population	Housework, childcare, shopping	All 30.9 Employed 25.6 Not empl. 39.0	All 15.7 Employed 14.5 Not empl. 20.3
Hill (1983)	Study of Time Use 1975 – diary	Married subset of representative sample of U.S. population	Housework, childcare, shopping	All 34.85 Work FT 24.58 Work PT 33.43 Not empl. 40.90	All 14.25 Work FT 12.70 Work PT 17.60 Not empl. 20.01
Juster and Stafford (1991)	Study of Time Use 1981 – diary	Representative sample of U.S. population	Housework	30.5	13.8
Coverman (1983)	Quality of Employment Survey 1977 – estimate	White, married, employed ≥ 20 hours/week	Housework and childcare	47.12	25.09
Hersch and Stratton (1994)	Panel Study of Income Dynamics 1979–87 – estimate	White, married, both spouses employed/ both spouses employed full-time	Housework	19.66 Full time 17.32	7.36 Full time 7.37
Presser (1994)	National Survey of Families and Households 1987–8 – estimate	Married, both spouses employed	Housework	33.4	17.6

and the National Survey of Families and Households (NSFH). While the wording varies among these surveys, respondents are usually asked to report how much time they spend during the week on activities such as cleaning, cooking, and laundry.

The two methods typically give rather divergent values. By design of time diaries, the total time spent on all activities must sum to the 1,440 minutes of the day. In contrast, surveys frequently indicate estimates of time use that are unrealistically high or even exceed the total available time in the relevant period (for example, 168 hours in a week).

Since time diaries record all activities, the analyst can identify those activities that represent home production, and sum over the relevant activities to get measures as aggregated or detailed as desired. On the other hand, survey estimates are highly influenced by how the respondent interprets the question. For instance, since the PSID does not separately request information on time spent shopping or paying bills, it is unclear whether respondents implicitly include these activities in reported housework time. Neither the PSID nor the NSFH ask specifically about time spent in childcare, although much of time spent on childcare is doubtlessly included in the reported time spent on household activities in general.

Both methods present challenges in distinguishing between home production time and other time uses. Recall that home production is best conceptualized as those activities that can be done by paying a third party. Are gardening or playing with one's children home production, or are they leisure activities? The interpretation of both time diary information and survey estimates is further complicated by the joint production nature of many household activities. It is common to fold laundry or cook while on the phone or while watching television, and time spent caring for children is often combined with other productive activities, especially while the child sleeps or watches television.[2]

As noted in Table 9.1, it is clear that women average far more time than men on home production, regardless of the method utilized to measure housework time. To give some idea of the magnitudes and the trends, using time diary information, Robinson and Godbey (1997) report that in 1985 men spent on average 15.7 hours per week on housework, up from an average of 11.5 hours per week in 1965. Women, by contrast, have experienced a large drop in their average housework time over this period, from 40.2 hours per week in 1965 to 30.9 hours per week in 1985. Using time

---

[2] Respondents who complete time diaries report secondary as well as primary activities, but home production time reported in Table 9.1 is calculated from time spent on primary activities.

diary data for 1975, Martha S. Hill (1985) reports that married women who are employed full-time average almost twenty-five hours in home-oriented work. In contrast, married men employed full-time average only half that amount, at 12.7 hours per week.

THE EFFECT OF HOUSEWORK TIME ON EARNINGS

Whether she is a full-time homemaker or works both in the labor market and at home, a wife's home production affects her own earnings by lowering her stock of labor market–related human capital. In addition, as reported in this section, time spent on home production also directly reduces earnings for women. At the same time, a wife's home production enhances her family's well-being. Her contributions may also allow her spouse to be more successful in his education and career, as Lorna Wendt claims in her divorce case, discussed later in this chapter.

Estimates from wage equations that include time spent on housework provide quite consistent evidence of a negative relation between housework and wages, particularly for women. This negative impact for women has been found using a variety of data sets: by Shelley Coverman (1983) using the 1977 QES; Joni Hersch (1985) using data collected in 1980 from piece rate workers; Beth Anne Shelton and Juanita Firestone (1989) using data from the 1981 Time Use Survey; Hersch (1991a) using data collected from wage and salary workers in Oregon in 1986; Hersch (1991b) and Hersch and Leslie S. Stratton (1997) using data from the PSID for the years 1979–87; and Hersch and Stratton (2002) using data from the NSFH. The evidence for men generally does not indicate that housework influences wages; the exceptions are Coverman (1983) and Hersch and Stratton (1997), both of whom restrict their analyses to married men and women.

While the studies by Coverman (1983), Hersch (1985), and Shelton and Firestone (1989) estimated wage equations controlling only for standard human capital characteristics, the negative relation between housework and wages persists after further analysis. Hersch (1991a) finds such an effect for women after controlling for working conditions as well as for human capital characteristics, number of children, and marital status. Estimates based on more sophisticated statistical techniques yield similar results.[3] The inverse wage-housework effect appears to be real.

---

[3] Hersch (1991b) estimates a simultaneous wage-housework system, which recognizes that housework time is jointly determined with wage. Hersch and Stratton (1997) provide

Why does housework affect wages, beyond the effect of housework on human capital accumulation? There are a number of possible explanations for this inverse relation, although empirical evidence on any causal mechanism is limited. Housework may reduce earnings by reducing the amount of energy and effort available for labor market work. Or, while housework may not affect labor market time directly on a regular basis, there may be intermittent disruptions to labor market work caused by the need to attend to unpredictable home-related chores such as emergency home repairs or childcare, which may reduce the labor market productivity of the household member primarily responsible for home production. A related possibility is that the spouse primarily responsible for home production might be less able to work late to complete projects under deadlines, which may likewise reduce labor market productivity.

THE EFFECT OF HOUSEWORK SPECIALIZATION ON THE HUSBAND'S EARNINGS

A large number of empirical studies find a marriage premium for men of at least 10 percent.[4] That is, controlling for human capital and other characteristics, married men earn more than single men with the same characteristics. A leading explanation for this marriage premium is that specialization within the household results in genuine labor-market productivity differences between married men who have the opportunity to specialize in labor market work and unmarried men who lack this option.

To examine this hypothesis, some researchers have included indicators of the wife's employment status as a proxy for specialization (Eng Seng Loh 1996; Jeffrey Gray 1997). The argument is that if marriage enhances labor market productivity by allowing men to specialize, then married men whose wives do not work in the labor market (or who work fewer hours) will have higher wages than either unmarried men or men with employed wives. The conclusions drawn from these studies are mixed. Loh finds that married men whose wives work in the labor market while

---

instrumental variables estimates that correct for the endogeneity of housework, and fixed-effects estimates that correct for unobserved individual specific characteristics that may be correlated with housework. Note that fixed-effects estimation mitigates the possibility that the wage-housework effect is spurious and caused by the negative correlation between productivity in the labor market and time on housework.

[4] See Chapter 10 by Shoshana Grossbard-Shechtman and Shoshana Neuman for an excellent survey of the empirical literature on the marriage premium.

married earn a *larger* premium, which suggests that productivity differences due to specialization do not explain the marital wage premium. Gray finds an inverse relation between the husband's wage and his wife's labor market hours, and attributes the observed decline in the marital wage premium over the 1980s to a decrease in the amount of specialization within marriage, despite an increase in the return to specialization.

The mixed evidence is not surprising based both on theoretical grounds and on evidence about time spent on home production. The effect of the wife's employment status on her husband's housework time could go either way, as there are competing income and substitution effects. Men with employed wives may spend less time on housework than men whose wives are not employed because household income is greater (income effect), or they may spend more time because the value of their spouse's time may be greater (substitution effect). The net effect will depend on the relative magnitude of these two components.[5] In terms of empirical support, Scott J. South and Glenna Spitze (1994) report that although married women who are employed spend significantly less time on home production activities than married women who are not employed, their husbands' time allocation is virtually invariant.

Hersch and Stratton (2000) examine whether specialization explains the male marriage premium by directly including time spent on home production in wage equations. This avoids the ambiguity associated with using wife's employment status as a proxy for specialization. We consider the effect on wages of total housework time performed by the man as well as housework time broken down into different types (for example, cooking and cleaning, which are done almost daily, versus car repair and yard work, which are done infrequently and can often be postponed). Further, we consider the direct effect of the wife's housework time on her husband's wage. The evidence suggests that the male marriage premium is *not* due to specialization within the household.

HOUSEWORK, TAXATION, AND EMPLOYEE BENEFITS

Although productive, housework is not taxed. This differential tax status of labor market work and home production may have an impact on work

---

[5] Grossbard-Shechtman (1999) extends the basic labor market framework to incorporate a spousal labor market. In her framework, for instance, an increase in wife's labor market income will increase her demand for her husband's spousal labor due to both an income and substitution effect. However, as in the basic labor market model, the net effect of a wife's employment on her husband's housework time cannot be predicted from theory.

incentives. In effect, housework is subsidized relative to market work. In a static situation, in order for labor market participation to be optimal, the after-tax hourly wage must exceed the costs of day care and the extra cost of purchasing replacements for home production, such as take-out meals. Edward McCaffery (1997) provides examples in which the family income is actually lower when a mother works in the labor market than when she doesn't.[6]

Home production may be subsidized, but it does not provide some of the advantages that participation in the labor market confers. In addition to receiving wages, labor market workers have access to social security, disability, Medicare, and unemployment compensation benefits. Working conditions are subject to Occupational Safety and Health Administration (OSHA) standards, and most jobs are covered under National Labor Relations Act regulations (which mandate, for example, time and one-half pay for overtime hours and the right to organize). In contrast, spouses who work only on home production do not receive social security benefits accruing from their own labor, but instead receive social security tied to their spouses' earnings.[7]

Individuals who work only in home production are not eligible for disability benefits. The closest concept to unemployment compensation is alimony (now usually called maintenance). In contrast to unemployment compensation in which the benefit is tied to wages at the former job, the amount of maintenance is determined by need. While OSHA regulates job safety, private homes are not regulated. Homes involve much work with household chemicals, potential fire and burn hazards from stoves and irons, sharp instruments such as kitchen knives, and activities such as standing on ladders changing light bulbs. There are more unintentional disabling injuries in the home than in the workplace and in motor vehicle crashes combined (National Safety Council 1999).

Many feminist scholars consider housework demeaning and generally harmful to women by relegating them to an inferior status, making them

---

[6] Note, however, that working at a temporarily lower (even negative) net wage may be perfectly optimal over the long run, as time in the labor market is an investment in the entire future stream of earnings. In this sense, employment in the labor market while paying for childcare corresponds to the years of internship and residency undertaken by physicians or the years spent in graduate school.

[7] Benefit payments are based on earnings and time in social security jobs. A career as a homemaker, or a mixed career, results in social security benefits from husbands' job, since wives get the greater of their own benefit from their covered work or half of their husband's benefit if they were married at the time that social security benefits are paid, or, if divorced, if they were married at least ten years.

dependent on their spouses for financial support. Under this view, gender equality means equality in the labor market. To this end, scholars have recommended changes in tax law that eliminate the subsidy of housework relative to labor market work and thereby increase women's labor market activity. For instance, McCaffery (1997) recommends lowering married women's tax rates. Nancy Staudt (1996) proposes an alternative that preserves the notion that housework is valuable and should not be assumed to be inferior to labor market work. Her suggestion is to tax the imputed value of housework and allow home workers access to benefits tied to the labor market, including social security and disability benefits.

THE VALUE OF HOUSEWORK IN DIVORCE OR DEATH

Despite the exclusion of housework from measures of gross domestic product (GDP), economists recognize that housework is productive work. As Katharine Silbaugh (1996) describes, the U.S. legal system does not share this view. Instead, U.S. laws regard housework largely as a marital obligation and an expression of affection. State laws explicitly note that marriage is not merely a private contract. A contract stating that the wife will perform housework for payment is not enforceable.[8] The underlying rationale employed by the courts is that marriage requires spouses to support and provide services to one another. One could not contract for payment for household services since one cannot be paid for something the individual is already legally obligated to perform. Silbaugh cites a number of cases in which courts refused to enforce agreements between spouses in which one spouse would pay the other for personal care through

---

[8] Most state courts have refused to support contracts between spouses under the theory that a marriage is not a commercial relationship. The underlying philosophy is eloquently expressed in *Graham v. Graham*, 33 F. Supp. 936 at 938 (D.C. Mich. 1940):

Under the law, marriage is not merely a private contract between the parties, but creates a status in which the state is vitally interested and under which certain rights and duties incident to the relationship come into being, irrespective of the wishes of the parties. As a result of the marriage contract, for example, the husband has a duty to support and to live with his wife and the wife must contribute her services and society to the husband and follow him in his choice of domicile. The law is well settled that a private agreement between persons married or about to be married which attempts to change the essential obligations of the marriage contract as defined by the law is contrary to public policy and unenforceable.

The only exceptions courts have made are for antenuptual agreements relating to the disposition of property and maintenance. See, e.g., *Edwardson v. Edwardson*, 798 S.E. 2d 941 (Ken. 1990).

provisions in the will. The courts' rationale in refusing to enforce such agreements is that such payments are degrading and commodify marriage. Instead, services within marriage should arise from love and affection between spouses.

How, then, is a wife who specializes in home production compensated in the event of divorce? There is no direct connection between the wife's home production contribution to her family and the financial aspects of divorce. For instance, the Uniform Marriage and Divorce Act (adopted by many states) tells courts to consider in the division of property "the contribution of a spouse as a homemaker or to the family unit." But this is only one of many factors. Other factors specifically noted are duration of the marriage, age, health, occupation, amounts and sources of income, vocational skills, employability, estate liabilities, needs, custodial provisions, opportunities for future acquisition of assets and income, and so on. Since there are no weights given to the array of factors, courts are left with a great degree of discretion over the weight given to the contribution of home production.

Maintenance is awarded for need, not in recognition of housework as a contribution to family wealth. Courts generally divide assets equally. But most couples have limited assets so the main asset is human capital investments. Wives who defer or limit their labor market investments during marriage are rarely given a supplement in recognition of their reduced employment prospects postdivorce.

The one area in which the legal system values housework is torts. In the event of wrongful death or injury to the spouse, one spouse may sue the injurer for the lost services formerly provided by the spouse. As Silbaugh (1996, p. 34) notes, these "loss of consortium damages may be owed to one spouse when the other is injured on the theory that the first spouse had a legal right to services the injurer has taken away." However, whether the court will allow testimony on these economic damages varies by jurisdiction. When allowed, the plaintiff presents evidence on lost earnings as well as the value of lost home production. The next section describes how to value such lost home production.

VALUING HOME PRODUCTION

In litigation, housework is usually valued at either the replacement cost or the opportunity cost.[9] The replacement cost method values household

---

[9] For further discussion of these issues, see Hersch (1997).

production by assigning the market cost of replacing the lost home production. A number of issues arise in valuing time using replacement cost. As noted in discussing measures of time use, much household activity involves joint production. Joint production makes it hard to separate out market equivalents.

For instance, a typical evening for a mother might include cooking dinner, cleaning the house, doing laundry, driving a child to a friend's home, and supervising her children's homework. Assume that we can identify and assign a time to each household activity. Now we need to assign a monetary value to this time. The replacement cost for these five activities can be evaluated at the wage rates of specialists (such as cooks, janitors, laundry workers, taxi drivers, and tutors or teachers), or it can be evaluated using the wage rate of a generalist, such as a paid housekeeper. Even the replacement cost for something as well defined as cooking dinner can vary from a chef's salary rate to that of a short-order cook. Further, the transactions costs involved with hiring substitutes for each of these activities can be high, requiring transportation, directing the activity, supervising, and monitoring, and usually involve a minimum charge regardless of the actual amount of time required. For instance, a tutor will charge a minimum rate whether the child needs ten minutes of help or a full hour. Thus, the replacement cost method allows for a wide range of values of home production.

The opportunity cost method is based on the assumption that rational individuals will choose the best among the set of alternative options. If we observe that an individual chooses to do housework, then time spent on housework must be at least as valuable as time spent in the next-best alternative activities, in particular labor market work. The opportunity cost method therefore values the time spent on home production at the wage rate if an individual is employed in the labor market, and the predicted wage rate based on personal characteristics if the individual is not employed. Since those not in the labor market will acquire a different set of characteristics than those who are, this method will lead to a lower estimate of opportunity cost. In addition, even for those who are in the labor market, the direct effect of housework on earnings noted earlier will lead to a lower wage than for those doing less housework.[10]

---

[10] Some issues that arise in valuing home production in litigation include whether to use before or after tax earnings, and whether to deduct work-related expenses. If courts deduct work-related expenses, further issues arise on what the courts should consider a work-related expense. Direct commuting expenses are clearly work-related, but should

In most cases, the replacement cost method will result in a higher value of a homemaker's time than the opportunity cost method. In part, it is easier to inflate the time spent on home production and the value of this production than it is to argue for higher-than-average lost earnings for someone with specific skills and education. Therefore, in litigation, plaintiff attorneys will usually evaluate a homemaker's time at replacement costs, while the defense attorneys will prefer opportunity costs. In litigation proceedings, defense attorneys rarely provide damage estimates out of concern that this concedes liability or provides a floor on damage values, thus replacement costs are the most widely used measure in litigation.[11] However, plaintiff attorneys will use the opportunity cost method in cases such as wrongful death or injury to children in which there is no history of contributions to home production.

THE LORNA WENDT AND GARY WENDT DIVORCE CASE

A highly public and precedent-setting recent divorce case tested how to value the contributions of a wife. The plaintiff, Lorna Wendt, maintains that her specialization within the home enabled her husband, GE Capital Services (GECS) CEO Gary Wendt, to succeed in the labor market, thus entitling her to half of the $52–100 million estate. Lorna Wendt was awarded $20 million in January 1998, instead of the $8 million plus alimony offered by her husband.[12]

Most divorce settlements are private, and this case provides a rare and instructive opportunity to look at the specifics of the valuation of housework as marital property. Although the amount of money involved is unusually large, the issues are common to all divorce cases. As background, Lorna Jorgenson and Gary Wendt met in high school and married after graduation from college in 1965.[13] Gary Wendt attended Harvard

---

day care be considered work-related, and if so, should this be deducted for women only?

[11] Charles C. Fischer (1994) discusses valuing home production in litigation and presents results from a survey of forensic economists on the methods that they use to value housework in litigation. The survey reveals that forensic economists tend to use conservative estimates of the value of housework.

[12] This case received wide coverage in the press, including cover stories in *Business Week* and *Fortune* magazines, and first page stories in the *Wall Street Journal*. Lorna Wendt appealed, continuing to seek 50 percent of the assets, but the original ruling was affirmed by the Connecticut Supreme Court in December 2000. See *Wendt v. Wendt*, 255 Conn. 918, 763 A.2d 1044 (Conn. 2000).

[13] *Lorna J. Wendt v. Gary C. Wendt*. D.N.FA 96 014 95 62 S. Superior Court of Connecticut, Judicial District of Stamford-Norwalk. Judge Kevin Tierney's decision, March 31,

Business School, with tuition paid by his parents, and both Lorna Wendt and Gary Wendt had income from jobs during his schooling. Mrs. Wendt worked as a public school music teacher until shortly after the birth of the couple's first child. From that point on, she was never formally employed, but gave private music lessons through 1988. Over the course of their marriage, Gary Wendt rose to the position of CEO of GECS. By the time of their separation in December 1995, the family's assets exceeded $50 million.

Throughout their thirty-one-year marriage, Lorna Wendt raised the couple's two daughters, was a homemaker, and entertained business associates in her unpaid role as a corporate wife. The witnesses testified that she was an exemplary wife and mother, and supported her husband's rise through the ranks of GECS by accompanying her husband on vacation and other trips paid for by GE and hosting an annual Christmas party for business associates.

The financial decisions at divorce involve providing for custodial children, alimony, and division of property. State laws regarding the division of property vary. Connecticut is an equitable distribution state, which does not require equal division of assets. In equitable distribution states, courts have a great deal of discretion over the division of property. Among the many factors to be considered in allocating property are the non-monetary contributions of the non-wage earning spouse.[14] Courts usually divide assets equally in most long-term marriages. However, in cases of large assets (usually considered to be over $10 million), the non-earning spouse has typically received less than half. Gary Wendt's settlement offer was $8 million in property and annual alimony of $250,000.

Lorna Wendt's position was that a less than 50 percent division was unfair to her and that "a woman's worth has value, a corporate wife has value." She maintained that her specialization within the home enabled her husband to succeed in the labor market, thus entitling her to half of the $52–100 million estate. Professor Myra Strober, at the time a Stanford University professor of education, testified on behalf of Lorna Wendt. She proposed three methods of valuing Mrs. Wendt's non-monetary contributions: market value replacement, opportunity cost, and human capital.

1998. The full text is available at http://ct-divorce.com/wendt.htm. The details of the case discussed here are reported in Judge Tierney's decision.

[14] See, e.g., *O'Neill v. O'Neill*, 13 Conn. App. 300, 308, 536 A.2d 978, cert. denied, 207 Conn. 806, 540 A.2d 374 (1988). In this case, the court held that non-monetary contributions are considered in distribution of property in divorce.

Using the replacement value approach, Strober broke down Lorna Wendt's home production into three categories: childcare, cooking, and housecleaning. Strober then assumed that each of these activities would be performed by a worker who would work a separate eight-hour day, every day of the year, at $10.00 per hour. Evaluated at twenty-four hours per day, 365 days per year, for thirty-one years, she estimated the replacement value of Lorna Wendt's time in home production at $2,715,600, unadjusted for price changes over time, discounting, or income tax ramifications. Although arguably inflated on a number of grounds, including the request for compensation for thirty-one years of childcare, this estimate was well below Gary Wendt's settlement offer.

Although Lorna Wendt's only training and employment had been as a public school music teacher, Strober indicated that she considered the opportunity cost method unreliable since Lorna Wendt could have been a highly paid opera singer.[15] The opportunity cost method would have resulted in a lower value of Lorna Wendt's contributions than the replacement cost method, even if the earnings of an opera singer were included with the appropriate weight.

Strober testified that the "human capital" method is the most accurate. Under a human capital theory of marriage as described by Elisabeth M. Landes (1978), both spouses invest in family-specific human capital that is not transferable beyond the marriage. If the husband specializes in the labor market while the wife specializes in home production, divorcing spouses end marriages with very different opportunities. A related situation occurs when couples invest in the human capital of one spouse in anticipation of jointly enjoying the anticipated increased earnings. The stereotypical example is that of a wife who financially supports the family while her husband pursues a graduate degree in medicine, law, or business. Indeed, at the graduation ceremony where Gary Wendt received his MBA, all of the wives received a PHT ("putting hubby through"). In such cases, although both spouses invest in the professional degree, the resultant human capital is not family-specific, but instead accrues to only one individual.[16]

---

[15] The opportunity cost method is widely used in litigation to value a life or lost earnings that involve far more speculation than in the Wendt case – for instance, cases involving the wrongful death of children.

[16] For the most part, courts have held that a professional degree does not constitute divisible marital property, and the supporting spouse is not entitled to a claim on the enhanced earnings of the spouse who earned the degree. An important exception is New York, where enhanced earnings are considered divisible property. In *O'Brien v. O'Brien*, 489

The family human capital premise underlying an equal division of assets at divorce is that if the spouses had invested equally during marriage, then each spouse is entitled to half the assets if divorced. Indeed, one can argue that the wife is entitled to more than half of the assets because of her reduced professional opportunities postmarriage.

Strober did not rely on this interpretation of Lorna Wendt's human capital contributions to the marriage. Instead Strober attempted to demonstrate that Gary Wendt would not have succeeded in his career without Lorna Wendt's contributions to his "two-person career." Using the human capital approach, Strober claimed that it would be difficult to provide a dollar value for the non-monetary contributions made by Lorna Wendt during the marriage. Strober argued that Gary Wendt's corporate career required two people to perform the functions necessary for his success, and that this two-person career was one of "equal effort and equal sacrifice." Her opinion is that the contributions should be valued equally regardless of whether the contributions were monetary or non-monetary, and the division of all assets and earnings should likewise be equal.

In cross-examination, Strober was unable to provide support for the claim that Gary Wendt would not have been successful without Lorna Wendt's contributions. She also acknowledged that single and divorced men and single parents had similarly successful corporate careers. Numerous witnesses testified to the limited role Lorna Wendt played in her husband's career, and in her testimony Lorna Wendt demonstrated only casual knowledge of her husband's business activities.

The judge ultimately did not base his decision on any of these economic arguments in awarding Lorna Wendt $20 million. His decision to award Lorna Wendt more than Gary Wendt's initial settlement offer was based on the greater financial needs of someone in her position.[17] Of course,

---

NE 2d 712 (N.Y. 1985), the court held that the medical degree earned by the husband is marital property subject to division, and the wife received 40 percent of his estimated increased earnings.

[17] The judge also noted that the human capital approach involved problems of measurement and did not account for the role of numerous factors, including hard work and talent. Further, the judge noted that marriage should not be commercialized, and "the attempt to value investments in human capital pushes the institution of marriage from a relationship based on love and obligation toward one based on self interest." Although the economic arguments were rejected in this case, the judge also provided examples, such as Claudia Sanders, the widow of the founder of Kentucky Fried Chicken, and Leona Helmsley, in which the spouses' role in their family's financial success appeared equal to their husband's. Neither of these examples involved divorce, leaving one to wonder whether a

the more conventional methods proposed – replacement cost and opportunity cost – led to a division of assets well below Gary Wendt's offer.
Only the human capital approach would argue for an equal division of
property.

We can draw at least four lessons from the Wendt divorce case. First,
it is very hard to sell the argument that someone such as Gary Wendt
would not have been successful without his wife's contributions. Indeed,
as noted earlier, the evidence in Hersch and Stratton (2000) indicates
that household specialization does not enhance married men's earnings.
Second, where you live matters, as state law on the division of assets
varies considerably. Had the Wendts lived in New York rather than in
Connecticut, Lorna Wendt would have been more likely to receive half
of the assets.[18] Third, a prenuptial agreement detailing how assets will be
divided, updated as circumstances change, would be valuable by clarify-
ing the expectations of each spouse and perhaps avoid protracted and
emotional battles over assets in divorce cases. Fourth, stock options exer-
cisable after a period of service and other forms of deferred compensation
represent a large share of compensation among high-level executives such
as Gary Wendt. These forms of compensation are often intended as incentives to motivate and retain executives. To the extent these are considered
divisible marital property, their value as an incentive will be diluted, and
firms might turn to compensation schemes that are less efficient or less
visible.[19]

SUMMARY AND CONCLUDING REMARKS

As this chapter discusses, whether employed in the labor market or not,
married women on average spend considerably more time on home production than their husbands do. This gender-based allocation of labor is

stronger case for equal division could be made in a case where the evidence of the wife's
contributions to her husband's success was more compelling than that of Lorna Wendt.

[18] See, e.g., *Traut v. Traut*, 181 A.D. 2d 671, 580 N.Y.S.2d 792 (N.Y.A.D. 1992), where the
court increased the wife's share of marital assets from 40 percent to 50 percent.

[19] In most states, unvested stock options are generally considered divisible marital property,
but it varies between jobs and courts. See, e.g., *Garcia v. Mayer*, 122 N.M. 57, 920 P. 2d 522
(N.M.App. 1996). (The court held that unvested stock options were divisible property in
divorce proceeding.) In the Wendt case, the court discussed the divisibility of unvested
stock options as "contingent" resources based on a "mere expectancy" of profit; yet, the
court held that such stock options, like contract rights, were divisible property. The court,
however, specifically refrained from creating a bright-line rule about the divisibility of
stock options in general.

consistent with economic theories of marriage and bargaining within the household. However, wives' contribution to family welfare comes at a personal cost: Time spent on housework has a direct substantial negative impact on own wages. Further, if labor market human capital investments are curtailed by time spent in home production, wives' labor market opportunities may be reduced over their lifetimes. In contrast, there is little evidence that men's earnings are affected by their time on home production, nor is there evidence that the widely observed male marriage premium is due to specialization within the household.

Although largely ignored until recently, issues involving balancing a family with labor market activity have gained prominence. For example, in 1991 the *Wall Street Journal* introduced Sue Shellenbarger's weekly column on "Work & Family," which attests to a widespread interest in attaining a balance between personal life and career. Men have likewise increased their time on home production. More research is needed on the consequences of these trends for both the labor market and the home.

Specifically, more information is needed on the causal mechanism underlying the inverse effect of housework on women's wages and the absence of such an effect for men. Identifying this mechanism is necessary to understand how changes in the labor market can allow all employees, not only women, to establish a better balance between personal life and labor market activity. Does this trend toward increased integration of market work and family life lead to greater productivity and job satisfaction? Given the negative impact of housework on women's earnings, will men's earnings similarly be affected if their home production activities continue to increase?

Although productive, housework is not taxed and is therefore subsidized relative to labor market work. In theory, this relative subsidy of housework may create a disincentive to labor force participation for women, although there is no empirical evidence on this issue. In contrast to work in the labor market, work in the home does not confer social security, disability, Medicare, or unemployment benefits. For these reasons, some legal scholars have proposed reducing the income tax rate applicable to women or taxing housework directly and providing benefits similar to those provided in the labor market. Research is needed to provide evidence on the consequences of such policies. Other fruitful areas for research include how housework should be valued in the division of assets in divorce, particularly in situations in which one spouse's specialization in home production permitted greater labor market success for the spouse specializing in the labor market.

REFERENCES

Becker, Gary S. "A Theory of the Allocation of Time." *Economic Journal,* September 1965, *75*(299), pp. 493–517.

———. "A Theory of Marriage: Part I." *Journal of Political Economy,* August 1973, *81*(4), pp. 813–46.

———. *A Treatise on the Family.* Cambridge, MA: Harvard University Press, enlarged edition, 1991.

Coverman, Shelley. "Gender, Domestic Labor Time, and Wage Inequality." *American Sociological Review,* October 1983, *48*(5), pp. 623–37.

Fischer, Charles C. "The Valuation of Household Production: Divorce, Wrongful Injury and Death Litigation." *American Journal of Economics and Sociology,* April 1994, *53*(2), pp. 187–201.

Gray, Jeffrey S. "The Fall in Men's Return to Marriage: Declining Productivity Effects or Changing Selection?" *Journal of Human Resources,* Summer 1997, *32*(3), pp. 481–504.

Gronau, Reuben. "Leisure, Home Production, and Work – the Theory of the Allocation of Time Revisited." *Journal of Political Economy,* December 1977, *85*(6), pp. 1099–123.

Grossbard-Shechtman, Amyra. "A Theory of Allocation of Time in Markets for Labor and Marriage." *Economic Journal,* December 1984, *94*(376), pp. 863–82.

Grossbard-Shechtman, Shoshana. "Why Women May Be Charged More at the Cleaners: A Consumer Theory with Competitive Marriage Markets." Working Paper 99–01, Center for Public Economics, San Diego State University, 1999.

Hersch, Joni. "The Effect of Housework on Earnings of Husbands and Wives." *Social Science Quarterly,* March 1985, *66*(1), pp. 210–17.

———. "Male–Female Differences in Hourly Wages: The Role of Human Capital, Working Conditions, and Housework." *Industrial and Labor Relations Review,* July 1991a, *44*(4), pp. 746–59.

———. "The Impact of Non-Market Work on Market Wages." *American Economic Review Papers and Proceedings,* May 1991b, *81*(2), pp. 157–60.

———. "The Economics of Home Production." *Southern California Review of Law and Women's Studies,* Spring 1997, *6*(2), pp. 421–40.

Hersch, Joni and Stratton, Leslie S. "Housework, Fixed Effects, and Wages of Married Workers." *Journal of Human Resources,* Spring 1997, *32*(2), pp. 285–307.

Hersch, Joni and Stratton, Leslie S. "Household Specialization and the Male Marriage Wage Premium." *Industrial and Labor Relations Review,* October 2000, *54*(1), pp. 78–94.

Hersch, Joni and Stratton, Leslie S. "Housework and Wages." *Journal of Human Resources,* Spring 2002, *37*(1), pp. 217–29.

Hill, Martha S. "Patterns of Time Use," in F. T. Juster and F. P. Stafford, eds., *Time, Goods, and Well Being.* Ann Arbor, MI: Survey Research Center, Institute for Social Research, University of Michigan, 1985.

Juster, F. Thomas and Stafford, Frank P. "The Allocation of Time: Empirical Findings, Behavioral Models, and Problems of Measurement." *Journal of Economic Literature,* June 1991, *29*(2), pp. 471–522.

Landes, Elisabeth M. "Economics of Alimony." *Journal of Legal Studies*, January 1978, *7*(1), pp. 33–63.

Loh, Eng Seng. "Productivity Differences and the Marriage Wage Premium for White Males." *Journal of Human Resources*, Summer 1996, *31*(3), pp. 566–89.

Lundberg, Shelly and Pollak, Robert A. "Separate Spheres Bargaining and the Marriage Market." *Journal of Political Economy*, December 1993, *101*(6), pp. 988–1110.

Manser, Marilyn and Brown, Murray. "Marriage and Household Decision-Making: A Bargaining Analysis." *International Economic Review*, February 1980, *21*(1), pp. 31–44.

McCaffery, Edward. *Taxing Women*. Chicago, IL: University of Chicago Press, 1997.

McElroy, Marjorie B. and Horney, Mary Jean. "Nash-Bargained Household Decisions: Toward a Generalization of the Theory of Demand." *International Economic Review*, June 1981, *22*(2), pp. 333–49.

Mincer, Jacob. "Market Prices, Opportunity Costs, and Income Effects," in Carl F. Christ, ed., *Measurement in Economics*. Stanford, CA: Stanford University Press, 1963.

National Safety Council. *Injury Facts, 1999 Edition*. Itasca, IL: National Safety Council, 1999.

Presser, Harriet B. "Employment Schedules among Dual-Earner Spouses and the Division of Household Labor by Gender." *American Sociological Review*, June 1994, *59*(3), pp. 348–64.

Robinson, John P. and Godbey, Geoffrey. *Time for Life: The Surprising Ways Americans Use Their Time*. University Park, PA: Pennsylvania State University Press, 1997.

Shelton, Beth Anne. *Women, Men, and Time: Gender Differences in Paid Work, Housework, and Leisure*. New York: Greenwood Press, 1992.

Shelton, Beth Anne and Firestone, Juanita. "Household Labor Time and the Gender Gap in Earnings." *Gender and Society*, March 1989, *3*(1), pp. 105–12.

Silbaugh, Katharine. "Turning Labor into Love: Housework and the Law." *Northwestern University Law Review*, 1996, *91*(1), pp. 1–86.

South, Scott J. and Spitze, Glenna. "Housework in Marital and Nonmarital Households." *American Sociological Review*, June 1994, *59*(3), pp. 327–47.

Staudt, Nancy. "Taxing Housework." *Georgetown Law Review*, May 1996, *84*(5), pp. 1571–1647.

TEN

Marriage and Work for Pay

Shoshana Grossbard-Shechtman and Shoshana Neuman

This chapter reports some differences between married and unmarried people – marital differentials – with respect to the following characteristics of paid employment: labor force participation, labor force attachment, and wages.[1] Most of the evidence that we report is for the United States, although we also report patterns for some other parts of the world. We also explore some ethnic variations in marital differentials, and some changes over time.

Observed relationships between paid employment and marriage may have three possible causes: Marriage may affect labor market experience, labor market experience may affect marriage, or the relationship between marriage and labor market experience may be explained by third factors influencing both marriage and paid employment. Any explanation of marital differentials in paid employment has to start by recognizing these two facts: Marriage is an institution that organizes household production, and work in household production is a major alternative to paid employment.

Gender differences in labor supply and earnings have been well documented, and we look at women and men separately. These gender differences could be related to gender differences in household production (see Chapter 9 by Joni Hersch). At least since Jacob Mincer (1962), it has been postulated that for women household production and paid employment are inversely related.

---

[1] Our analysis is not necessarily about formal marriage; many of our statements apply to both marriage and cohabitation.

We very much appreciate the help of Catalina Amuedo-Dorantes, Evelyn Lehrer, and Jeff Woerner. Bisakha Sen contributed helpful comments.

We then present econometric models that attempt to disentangle causal relationships. We also present marriage market models that lead to the inclusion of marriage-related variables that are usually overlooked in labor supply models, including a number of individual characteristics (such as age, ethnicity, and religion) and aggregate characteristics (such as sex ratios and government policies) that are expected to affect opportunities in marriage and labor markets.

SOME STYLIZED FACTS

We first look at employment rates in the United States, using two measures of employment: participation in the labor force and labor force attachment (defined as full-time year-round labor force participation).

Employment Rates

In 2000, 94 percent of all men ages thirty-two to thirty-six and 76 percent of all women ages thirty to thirty-four were active in the labor force. As far as full-time year-round employment was concerned (labor force attachment), the rates were 81 percent for men and 49 percent for women. These are ages when a majority of the population is married (64 percent were married in 2000) and have young children.[2] Table 10.1 reports some labor force patterns for married and unmarried men and women in the United States in 1990, 1995, and 2000. The comparisons were made for women ages thirty to thirty-four and men ages thirty-two to thirty-six, using March Current Population Surveys (CPS).

Women. Table 10.1 indicates that in 2000 the labor force participation (LFP) rate for married women ages thirty to thirty-four stood at 71 percent, whereas for unmarried women in this age group it was 84 percent, indicating a negative marital differential of 13 percent.[3]

The more employment requires a time commitment, the more it is likely to interfere with household production. It is therefore not surprising that U.S. women also experienced a large negative marital differential in labor force attachment. Labor force (LF) attachment was 43 percent

---

[2] More precisely 63.8 percent of men ages thirty-two to thirty-six and 64.4 percent of women ages thirty to thirty-four were married. This age difference between men and women is close to the average difference in age at marriage in the United States.

[3] Based on calculations using the March Current Population Survey. This is also the source of the other 2000 statistics reported in this chapter.

Table 10.1 *Labor Force Participation and Attachment, by Married Status[a]: Women Ages Thirty to Thirty-Four and Men Ages Thirty-Two to Thirty-Six, 1990 to 2000*

	Women			Men		
	1990	1995	2000	1990	1995	2000
% in labor force, By marital status:						
% in labor force, married	69.3	73.0	70.8	97.0	96.5	96.6
% in labor force, unmarried	79.5	78.5	84.0	90.3	87.2	89.7
Marital differential in LFP	–10.2	–5.5	–13.2	6.7	9.3	6.9
% attached to the LF, By marital status						
% attached to LF, married[b]	37.4	42.4	42.8	81.4	82.3	85.9
% attached to LF, unmarried	53.1	54.2	61.3	66.1	63.3	71.7
Marital differential in LF attachment	–15.7	–11.8	–18.5	15.3	19.0	14.2

[a] Married status is defined as married, spouse present. If not married and a spouse is not present, the person is categorized as unmarried.
[b] Attached to labor force (LF) is defined as working full-time (i.e., thirty-five hours a week or more) and year-round (i.e. forty weeks a year or more)
Source: Current Population Survey, March 1990, 1995, 2000.

among married women and 61 percent among unmarried women, implying a negative marital differential in labor force attachment of 18 percent. For women in this age group, the marital differential in LF attachment thus exceeded the marital differential in LFP.

It is well known that the presence of young children tends to be negatively correlated to women's paid employment, as women – especially married women – often are the primary caretakers of young children. Given that most children are born in wedlock, the presence of children in marriage is expected to be a major factor associated with marital differentials in employment. However, studies of individual women's paid employment reveal that the "effect" of marriage on employment decreases but does not disappear after control for number and age of children.

Marital differentials in women's employment may also vary with husband's income, as many studies based on individual data indicate that married women's labor force participation is often negatively correlated with husband's income. Mincer (1962) and many other studies have interpreted this finding as a discouraging effect of married men's income on married women's employment (see, for example, Mark R. Killingsworth and James J. Heckman 1986). In the case of both number of children and husband's income, it is not so clear what affects what. Are these effects of marriage, children, and husband's income on employment in the

LF, or effects of employment on these other variables? With respect to a husband's income, it could be that women who intended to engage in more homemaking were more likely to marry rich husbands than women who intended to engage in a demanding career outside the home. Whether causality originates with men wanting women to perform homemaking tasks or with women wanting to engage in such tasks, a negative correlation between a husband's income and wife's LFP implies a negative correlation between traditional gender roles and a wife's LFP, and a positive correlation between preference for traditional gender roles and marital differentials in women's paid employment. Marital differentials in women's employment have to be examined in conjunction with marital differentials in men's employment.

Men. Table 10.1 indicates that in 2000, men's paid employment also varied with marital status in the United States. For men ages thirty-two to thirty-six, these differentials were positive: Ninety-seven percent of married men and 90 percent of unmarried men were in the labor force, a positive marital differential in LFP of 7 percent. The marital differential in men's labor force attachment was about double that in men's labor force participation: Eighty-six percent of married men and only 72 percent of unmarried men were year-round full-time workers, that is, a marital differential of 14 percent. Similar differentials were found for other age groups as well.

Changes over Time: The Effect of Welfare. Table 10.1 also indicates trends in marital differentials in employment. The most dramatic change is the increase in marital differentials in women's employment from 1995 to 2000, which is in part the result of a drastic reduction in welfare benefits to unmarried mothers when welfare reform passed in 1996.[4] As a result, both the LFP and labor force attachment of unmarried women increased dramatically. For instance, LFP increased from 81 percent to 86 percent for white women, and from 70 percent to 79 percent for black women. It can be seen that the reduction in welfare benefits also led to substantial increases in the employment of unmarried men. The increase in this group's attachment to the labor force was particularly dramatic: from 63 percent attached to the labor force in 1995, to 72 percent attached in 2000.

---

[4] Aid for Families with Dependent Children (AFDC) was replaced by Temporary Assistance for Needy Families (TANF). The expansion of Earned Income Tax Credits (EITC) also played a role. More on choices between welfare, employment, and marriage can be found in Chapter 8 by John Fitzgerald and in Grossbard-Shechtman (1995a).

Earlier, the increased popularity of Aid for Families with Dependent Children (AFDC) in the 1970s and 1980s helped explain decreases in marital differentials in the LFP and attachment of young mothers. In 1966, only about 4 percent of all families with children under eighteen were on AFDC (David O'Neill and June O'Neill 1997). That year, married women with children under three had a labor force participation (LFP) rate of 21 percent while similar women who had been married and were currently not married had an LFP rate of 39 percent, which is a substantial negative marital differential (Francine D. Blau, Marianne A. Ferber, and Anne E. Winkler 1998; Chapter 4). By 1994, about 13 percent of all families with children were on AFDC, more than a tripling of the incidence of AFDC, and the negative marital differential had disappeared among mothers of young children. CPS data for all women ages thirty to thirty-four in 1970 indicate negative marital differentials of 19 percent and 17 percent in LFP and LF attachment respectively. By 1990 the marital differential in LFP had shrunk to a negative 10 percent. The differential in LF attachment was not much lower in 1990: It stood at 16 percent. That more blacks received AFDC benefits helps explain why increases in LF participation and attachment of women ages thirty to thirty-four from 1995 to 2000 were larger for black unmarried women than for white unmarried women (and the same is true for women younger than that).

Changes over Time: The Effect of Sex Ratios. In contrast to recent trends for unmarried women, young married women's labor force participation underwent a 2 percent decrease from 1995 to 2000, causing a dramatic increase in marital differentials in LFP (more than doubling from 5.5 percent to 13 percent).[5] In parallel, from 1995 to 2000 there was an increase in the LF attachment of married men (from 82 percent to 86 percent). Even though a 2 percent decrease in married women's LFP does not seem dramatic, it is significant as it stands in contrast to a secular trend toward increasing LFP by married women, especially mothers of young children. This decrease is particularly noteworthy as it is the first decrease over a five-year period since 1950. As shown for example in Blau, Ferber, and Winkler (1998), both women's labor force participation and their attachment have grown continuously over the period 1950–94.

---

[5] Note that the decrease in married women's labor force participation ages thirty to thirty-four was limited to white women, who went from a LFP rate of 73.4 percent in 1995 to a rate of 70.2 percent in 2000. In contrast, during this period, the LFP rate of married black women ages thirty to thirty-four rose from 77.6 percent to 82.1 percent.

Prior growth in the LFP of married women has been explained in terms of wage effects (see, for example, Mincer 1962; Sherwin Rosen 1992), reduced fertility (for example, Arleen Leibowitz and Jacob A. Klerman 1995), and increased popularity of marriages based on an egalitarian division of labor (for example, Myra H. Strober and Agnes Miling Kaneko Chan 1998).

Time trends in women's LFP indicate that (1) the late 1960s and 1970s were a period of particularly rapid increases in married women's labor force participation (see David M. Heer and Amyra Grossbard-Shechtman 1981; Grossbard-Shechtman and Clive W. J. Granger 1998), and (2) the decrease in the labor force participation of married women ages thirty to thirty-four documented in Table 10.1 is part of significant slowdown in married women's LFP (see Grossbard-Shechtman 2000).

Time trends in LFP may reflect differences in the behavior of various cohorts, and cohorts may differ due to differences in cohorts' marriage market conditions, which in turn are a function of variations in sex ratio. Women who expect unfavorable marriage prospects due to excess supply of women in marriage markets are less likely to be married and more likely to enter non-traditional lifestyles. These marriage markets can possibly be interpreted as markets for Work-in-Marriage (WIM) (see Chapter 1). One way of measuring marriage prospects is by calculating sex ratios, that is, ratios of marriageable men to marriageable women. It was argued in Chapter 1 that a higher sex ratio in a marriage market where women engage in Work-in-Marriage more than men implies that women interested in supplying Work-in-Marriage are more likely to be compensated for engaging in such work. This implies that women in a marriage market with high sex ratios – that is, a relatively large number of men competing for women – will be less likely to participate in the labor force and more likely to engage in homemaking than where sex ratios are low. This hypothesis is particularly applicable to married women, who tend to engage in more household production than unmarried women, and to women who do not particularly enjoy going to work.[6] As argued later in this section, this hypothesis also helps account for individual variation in labor supply.

---

[6] This hypothesis applies separately to married women as a subcategory, and therefore differs from Marianne A. Ferber and Helen M. Berg's (1991) sex ratio hypothesis stating that the higher the sex ratio, the more women get married and therefore the less women (regardless of marital status) are likely to participate in the labor force.

Sex ratios vary across cohorts as a result of a combination of two things: (1) cohort size varies, and (2) the average age at marriage of men exceeds that of women over the whole period that we are considering.[7] As a result, women born at the beginning of a baby boom face a lower sex ratio in marriage markets than women born during a period of stable or decreasing births, a baby boom being simply defined as an increase in the number of births. In the United States a baby boom started in 1937, when the number of births started to increase as an effect of New Deal policies.

A number of studies indicate cohort effects on labor force participation of women. According to the pooled time series analysis for five age groups of U.S. women over the period 1965–90 reported in Grossbard-Shechtman and Granger (1998), the generations of women born in the years 1941 to 1950 experienced faster increases in labor force participation than women born in earlier or later generations. John Pencavel (1998) reported a similar finding. Cohort differences can possibly be interpreted as evidence of a sex ratio effect on women's LFP: The women born in the years 1941 to 1945 (during World War II) and from 1946 to 1950 (right after World War II), who on average married men born in 1938–48, are precisely the women faced with the lowest sex ratios of the twentieth century! As can be seen in Table 10.2, the sex ratio for the World War II generation was 90.7 men (born in 1939–43) per 100 women (born in 1941–5). It was even worse for the post–World War II generation of women born in 1946–50: 87.4 men (born in 1944–8) per 100 women.[8] Increases in LFP and LF attachment over time would then be explained in part by decreases in sex ratio, other explanations for the increases in LFP being secular increases in women's wages, decreased fertility, and increased taste for egalitarianism, as suggested in the literature cited previously.

Using U.S. data for 1965–99, Grossbard-Shechtman (2000) replaced cohort dummies with estimated sex ratios for each cohort and found that changes in women's labor force participation were substantially correlated with the rate of growth in the nationwide sex ratio.[9] The sex

---

[7] There have been limited fluctuations in differences in age at marriage over the last fifty years.

[8] The number of births increased from 1937 to 1960. A temporary dip in births during the years 1943–5, when large numbers of American men were at war, had little impact on the way Grossbard-Shechtman and Granger (1998) calculated sex ratios for five-year age groups.

[9] These models control for trends, autocorrelation, male and female wages, national product, fertility, and education.

Table 10.2 *Sex Ratios for Thirteen Generations*
(United States)

Women's year of birth[a]	Generation name	Sex ratio[b]
1916–20	World War I	0.95
1921–25	Early 1990s	0.93
1926–30	Pre-Depression	0.98
1931–5	Depression	1.00
1936–40	New Deal	0.95
1941–5	World War II	0.91
1946–50	Post–WW II	0.87
1951–5	Korean War	0.95
1956–60	Sputnik	0.97
1961–5	Kennedy	1.03
1966–70	Moon	1.06
1971–5	*Roe*	1.07
1976–80	First Echo	1.01

[a] Men are two years older.
[b] Ratio of men age twenty-two to twenty-six to women age twenty to twenty-four or men age twenty-seven to thirty-one to women age twenty-five to twenty-nine calculated based on Census data from 1940 to 2000. The age group depends on the Census year.
Source: Grossbard-Shechtman and Catalina Amuedo-Dorantes (2002).

ratio effect captured not only large increases in the labor force partici-pation of baby-boom women, but also less than average increases in the labor force participation of women born at the height of the baby bust: the Moon generation of women born in the years 1966–70, and the Roe generation, born around the passage of *Roe v. Wade* (ratio of men born in 1969–73 to women born in 1971–5).[10] Sex ratios for these two baby-bust generations were respectively 1.06 and 1.07. In other words, for the *Roe* generation of men born in the years 1969–73, there are seven missing women for every one hundred men. The earlier Kennedy generation of women, born in the years 1961–5, has a sex ratio of 1.03. As young mar-ried women of the Moon generation were replacing those of the Kennedy generation, the sex ratio went up and, as expected from marriage market analysis, the LFP of married women went down: Labor force participation rates for married women of the Moon generation (who were ages thirty to thirty-four in 2000) stood at 71 percent, which was lower than the 73 percent LFP rate of the Kennedy generation of women who were in

[10] *Roe v. Wade* is the Supreme Court ruling that legitimized abortions in 1973.

that age group in 1995. This drop in the participation of married women occurred for white women only. As young married women of the *Roe* generation were replacing those of the Moon generation, the sex ratio went up even higher, and the LFP of married women kept going down: Recently, the LFP of young married women decreased (74 percent of the labor force in 1998 to 70 percent in 2000), possibly the result of women ages twenty-five to twenty-nine becoming increasingly part of the *Roe* generation rather than the Moon generation.[11]

Black/White Differences A macrolevel marriage market analysis helps explain not only time trends in women's employment, but also black/white differences in employment. In the United States, marital differentials in black women's employment are positive rather than negative. In part this racial difference results from the existence of some degree of black/white segregation in marriage markets and the fact that marriage market conditions for black women are less favorable than for white women.[12] Less favorable marriage market conditions for black women help explain why there is much less of a negative marital differential in women's LFP and LF attachment among blacks than among whites.

According to marriage markets analysis, the logic for the lower-paid employment of married women has to do with a choice between two forms of paid work: work in the LF and WIM. Given less favorable marriage market conditions, it is expected that black women who get married do not get paid much for their WIM. It is even possible that they do not get paid at all, and have to pay in order to get married (see Robert Cherry 1998). As a result, marriage is not likely to entail much reduction in black women's paid employment, whereas such reduction occurs for white women for whom marriage often entails a positive quasiwage for supplying WIM.[13]

In 2000, the labor force participation rate of married white women ages thirty to thirty-four stood at 70 percent, which was substantially lower than

---

[11] By 2000 this age group included women born in 1974 and 1975, after the ruling of *Roe v. Wade*.

[12] Evidence and explanations for the lower sex ratio among blacks in the United States can be found, for example, in Graham B. Spanier and Paul C. Glick (1980), W. Julius Wilson (1987), Grossbard-Shechtman (1993), and in Chapter 8 by John Fitzgerald in this book. One of the factors contributing to the black/white difference in sex ratio is that interracial marriages involving a black groom and a white bride were at least twice as frequent as interracial marriages involving a black bride and a white groom (see Grossbard-Shechtman 1995a).

[13] Some cohabitants may also supply WIM and be categorized as unmarried.

that of unmarried white women (85 percent), implying a negative marital differential of 15 percent. In contrast, married black women participated more in the labor force than unmarried black women (82 percent in the LF compared to 79 percent in the LF), a positive marital differential of 3 percent. This ethnic difference in marital differentials in women's LFP is found for other age groups and earlier periods as well. As for labor force attachment, ethnic differences in marital differentials are even starker: in 2000, for women ages thirty to thirty-four in the United States, the marital differential was a negative 21 percent for white women and a positive 5 percent for black women. The larger gap between black and white married women's behavior in the case of LF attachment relative to LFP reflects the fact that LF attachment is more likely to reflect marriage market conditions than is the case with LFP.

The statistics discussed in this chapter are mostly for Americans in their early thirties. The same data indicate that there were marital differentials in LFP for all five-year age groups of women between the ages of twenty and forty-nine.[14] For white women, there were large negative marital differentials at all ages and over the entire period 1965–2000. For black women, marital differentials in LFP were small and not always of the same sign. For instance, in 2000 the differentials were negative for women ages twenty to twenty-nine, nonexistent for women ages thirty-five to thirty-nine, and positive for women ages forty to forty-nine. This may reflect an improvement in the marriage market position of young black women, relative to earlier generations of black women.

Black/white differences in marriage market conditions may also help explain other black/white differences in the labor supply of women, such as a different husband's income effect (see Grossbard-Shechtman 1995a) and different propensities to work from home while engaging in paid employment (see Chapter 12).

These differences in the marriage market conditions of blacks and whites in the United States may also help explain black/white differences in married *men*'s employment. One expects less need for men interested in a serious relationship with a black woman to excel in breadwinning than for men who are interested in a serious relationship with a white woman.[15]

---

[14] Marital differentials have also been found for women in other age categories.

[15] It could also be that black men's earnings are low for reasons unrelated to marriage market conditions, and that such low earnings help account for black women's higher labor force participation (see Grossbard-Shechtman 1995a). However, Evelyn M. Lehrer (1992) has shown that black/white differences in men's incomes do not account for the entire black/white difference in marital differentials in women's employment, supporting

Given that most marriages and serious relationships are endogamous, black men will need less income in order to marry than is the case with white men. In fact, the LFP rates of black and white married men ages thirty-two to thirty-six in 2000 were very similar: 95 percent and 97 percent respectively. LF attachment rates were respectively 83 percent and 86 percent for black and white men. Positive marital differentials in labor force participation were substantially larger for black men (12 percent) than for white men (6 percent), due principally to the lower participation rate of unmarried black men relative to unmarried white men. In turn, this black/white difference is related to black/white differences in incarceration rates of unmarried men. Some of these ethnic differences may be related to differences in the incidence of marriage: In 2000 only 37.5 percent of black women ages thirty to thirty-four were married (in contrast to 75 percent of white women). Black/white differences in sex ratio can also help explain some of the black/white differences in marriage formation described in Chapter 2 by Michael J. Brien and Michelle E. Sheran.

In light of a marriage market model, changes in labor force participation and attachment can also be the result of institutional change (such as changes in laws, policies, or cultural prescriptions) affecting marriage markets. It has been argued that no-fault divorce laws are associated with lower protection for marital production workers, and therefore these laws, introduced in most of the United States between 1970 and 1980, may have caused growth in women's labor force participation (see Elizabeth H. Peters 1986; Allen Parkman 1992, 1998). No study has attempted to separate this explanation from a sex ratio explanation of variations in women's labor force participation over time. The same disadvantageous marriage market conditions faced by early baby-boom women may simultaneously explain why no-fault divorce laws passed (Grossbard-Shechtman 1995b) and why women experienced rapid increases in labor force participation. Gray (1998) shows that the effect of unilateral divorce laws interacted with the effect of property laws. In states where community property prevails, unilateral divorce laws may have benefited women as divorce, and no-fault divorce led married women to experience higher labor force participation, more leisure, and fewer hours of household production. In common law states, unilateral divorce led married women to experience lower labor force participation and more

an interpretation whereby different sex ratios cause different gender roles for men and women.

household production, but had no impact on leisure (see also Chapter 4 in this book).

Crosscountry Differences. Negative marital differentials in women's paid employment have been observed in many parts of the world. The importance of culturally prescribed gender roles in explaining marital differentials in women's paid employment is evident from large observed crosscultural variations in marital differentials in employment. In some societies, such as Sweden, egalitarian gender roles prevail more than in others. Undoubtedly, such egalitarian preferences help account for the fact that in Sweden the labor force participation rate of women closely approximates that of men: In 1992 women comprised 45 percent of the Swedish paid labor force (Blau, Ferber, and Winkler 1998, Chapter 11). However, in Sweden differentials in the labor force attachment of married men and women remain substantial. Relative to Swedish married men, married women are more likely to work part-time and to take family leaves (Christina Jonung and Inga Persson 1993).

In contrast to Sweden, in that same year, women comprised 41 percent of the workforce in the United States, 27 percent in Mexico, 19 percent in Iran, and 8 percent in Saudi Arabia. It is hard to imagine that all these differences could be attributed to technological and economic factors. Cultural differences in ideas about gender roles – regarding work, childcare, how husbands and wives treat each other – seem to be important. While women's involvement in marital household production exceeds that of men everywhere in the world, the degree of this excess involvement varies crossculturally. The countries most likely to discourage women's employment in the paid labor force also tend to encourage traditional roles in marriage. International comparisons in degree of traditionalism in marriage are not so easy to measure as LFP or percentage of the labor force consisting of women. Traditional gender roles are expected to influence men's work patterns as well as women's.

The degree to which individuals are free to compete in marriage markets can help explain paid employment patterns. Alternatively, coercion may be used to force them into certain roles. Given that men typically yield more political power than women, and have often used this power to coerce women into certain forms of time allocation, competitive marriage markets tend to benefit women more than men. For instance, if a country sets low punishments for rapists or encourages marriages between rapists and their victims, as is the case in many Latin American countries, women, who tend to be rape victims rather than perpetrators, are likely to suffer. Ceteris paribus, such a situation is likely to discourage women from preparing themselves for a career in homemaking and to encourage them to establish a career outside the home. Laws like these may help explain why today's young women in Latin America appear more eager to obtain an education than their male counterparts. In the Middle East, competitive marriage market mechanisms may be operating more frequently among Christians and Jews than among Moslems, which helps explain why husband's income had more impact on the labor force participation of non-Moslem married women than on that of Moslem women (see Grossbard-Shechtman and Neuman 1998). Marriage institutions – such as age at marriage, polygamy, the legitimization of cohabitation and dowry – are also expected to influence LFP, LF attachment, or earnings.

Some policies related to marriage directly affect paid employment. For instance, as pointed out by Claudia Goldin (1990), prior to 1940, the United States had marriage bars that discouraged married women's labor force participation by excluding married women from certain forms of employment. Marriage bars still exist in some other countries, such as Japan. In contrast, countries may encourage the labor force participation of married women by introducing tax schedules favorable to two-earner couples, family leaves available to both parents, and subsidized day care (see Chapter 11 by Rachel Connelly and Jean Kimmel). For instance, in the United States, a 1986 reduction in the marginal tax rate affecting married couples encouraged married women's labor force participation and their hours of work (Nada Eissa 1995).[16]

Earnings

Not only are married men more likely to work in the labor force than unmarried men, but they generally earn more than unmarried men. The economic literature on marital differentials in earnings has dealt mostly with men's earnings and has often called these differentials "marital wage premiums." Positive marital differentials in men's earnings were found for instance, by Lee Benham (1974) and Lawrence Kenny (1983) for the United States, by Gerald Scully (1979) for Iran, by Grossbard-Shechtman and Neuman (1991) for Israel, by Yue-Chim Wong (1986) for Hong Kong, and by Robert F. Schoeni (1995) for industrialized countries included in

---

[16] See Chapter 4 by Leslie Whittington and James Alm for a discussion of the effects of such policies on marriage and divorce.

the Luxembourg Income Study. Marital differentials in earnings are rarely found for women, and if they are found, they are considerably smaller than those for men, and their sign varies (see Kermit Daniel 1995).

The literature provides at least four explanations for marital differentials in men's earnings (see Grossbard-Shechtman 1993). First, according to Mincer and Solomon Polachek (1974), married men are more likely to specialize in paid employment and therefore become more productive. This is the *specialization* explanation. Second, it is possible that a spouse's household production enables a worker to be more productive at the workplace not only because the worker spends more time at work, but because the spouse invests in the worker's human capital and prepares the worker better for the workplace (the *Work-in-Marriage* explanation).[17] For instance, a spouse can contribute directly to a worker's productivity by preparing a nutritious meal, a form of Work-in-Marriage. Direct contributions can also take the form of performance of actual tasks that are part of a job description (see Grossbard-Shechtman 1993, Chapter 12). Together, these two explanations are about productivity-enhancing effects of marriage.

Third, it is possible that men who earn more are more likely to be married. This is a *selectivity* explanation. If this explanation holds and selection into marriage does not vary with men's earnings potential (the *pure selectivity* version of this explanation), marriage does not explain marital differentials in men's earnings. However, there also is a *breadwinner* version of this selectivity explanation, and it is hard to disentangle these two versions of a selectivity explanation empirically. According to the breadwinner explanation, women who engage in household production that benefits men expect to get paid for it, that is, they look for breadwinners in the marriage market. Competition in the marriage market then leads men to seek better pay in order to be better breadwinners and better afford a traditional marital lifestyle. In all but the random selectivity explanation, preferences for traditional marital roles of men/breadwinners and women/homemakers help explain marital differentials in men's earnings. These explanations also help account for the absence of positive marital differentials in women's earnings. We now interpret a number of findings from the economic literature in light of some of these explanations.

According to a breadwinner explanation, married male workers might be willing to trade favorable job amenities (such as flexible hours or a

---

[17] More on Work-in-Marriage can be found in Chapter 1.

pleasant work environment) for higher wages (Robert Reed and Kathleen Hartford 1989), more than is the case with single men. Employers' policies may reinforce this "breadwinner" factor by using it as a reason for discriminating in favor of married male workers. Claudia Goldin (1990) brings U.S. evidence suggesting that employers promoted married office workers more frequently during the Depression era.

This breadwinner explanation is based on a presumed preference that men have for marriage and possibly for children. A positive effect of children on wages is reported in Christopher Cornwell and Peter Rupert (1987). From this study, it appears that young men with children are in more urgent need for high wages and are favored by the employer and/or compensated for trading pleasant job characteristics for greater wage compensation. However, the presence of children does not explain most of the marital differentials in men's earnings (see Greg Duncan and Bertil Holmund 1983; Hersch 1991).

The specialization and Work-in-Marriage explanations are related. The specialization explanation entails that by performing household chores or taking responsibility for childcare, a spouse could augment a worker's productivity indirectly by allowing the worker more time to work and/or to get more or better sleep. A comprehensive survey of research on medical incidents, auto and truck accidents, and errors in industrial and technical operations concluded that inadequate sleep can greatly exaggerate the tendency for errors (Daniel 1995).

Benham (1974) and Daniel (1995) found that men married to more educated women receive a higher marriage premium. Benham (1974) divided the total number of years of schooling of a male worker's wife into two: years of education accumulated prior to marriage, and years of schooling acquired after marriage. He entered each of the two as an independent variable in the wage equation and found similar effects for both. This finding can be interpreted as an indication that a Work-in-Marriage effect depends on education, no matter when it was acquired. This finding seems to be incompatible with an explanation based on education-based selectivity in marriage. If men married to more educated wives earn more because their higher earnings led them to marry more educated women, one expects a positive effect of education before marriage and a non-significant effect of schooling acquired after marriage.

Grossbard-Shechtman and Neuman (1991) report two other findings that were interpreted as supporting a Work-in-Marriage explanation: (1) A wife's social and human capital accumulated during longer residence in the country has a positive effect on married men's earnings; and

(2) the duration of marriage is positively related to men's wages.[18] Sanders Korenman and David Neumark (1991) also report that the positive relationship between marriage and wages increases with the number of years a man is married.[19] If marital differentials in earnings arise when two people coordinate their actions and have the opportunity to augment each other's productivity, this could explain why Wong (1986) finds that productivity-augmentation effects are stronger in families where the spouses work together as business entrepreneurs.

One expects reduced opportunities for reciprocity within marriage as divorce approaches, so it seems reasonable to expect that even couples still living together will spend less time augmenting productivity as divorce nears. Therefore, it follows from a Work-in-Marriage explanation that there will be less productivity augmentation among couples near the date of divorce, leading to a decline in marital differentials in earnings as divorce nears. Daniel (1995) finds that the marriage premium declines as divorce nears.

Living with a heterosexual partner indicates the desire and opportunity to engage in joint behavior, so the marriage premium should not be limited to those in a formal marriage, nor should it always arise whenever couples are formally married. A couple living together outside formal marriage reveals a desire and ability to coordinate activities, as evidenced by the fact that spells of cohabitation often end in formal marriage. There should therefore be a marriage premium for cohabitants too. Daniel (1995) finds that both black and white men who are cohabiting receive a wage premium, but Gary Gates et al. (2000) find that cohabiting men do not earn a wage premium compared to married men. Cohabitation differentials seem to be limited to heterosexual unions: using the 1990 Census, Gates et al. (2000) found that gay men living with a partner did not earn more than men living alone. This contrast between heterosexual and gay men reinforces the view that marital differentials in earnings are related to traditional gender roles, and that these roles are possibly more prevalent in heterosexual cohabitation than among cohabiting gay men.

That marital differentials are often negative for women possibly indicates that women's productivity at the workplace does not benefit from

---

[18] In a study employing Israeli census data from 1983, Grossbard-Shechtman and Neuman (1991) find a parabolic relationship between duration of marriage and male earnings, with a peak after twenty-five to forty-five years of marriage (varying by the ethnicity of the worker and his wife).

[19] This is indicated by the faster wage growth for married men as compared to non-married men observed using the 1976, 1978, and 1980 U.S. longitudinal survey data.

wives' husband's marital production, and/or that hours of housework lead women to be less productive (see Chapter 9 by Hersch). Wives tend to help their husbands' careers more than husbands help their wives' careers (Arlie Hochschild 1989). However, in an analysis of Israeli managers, female managers reported that their career benefited from their husbands' help more than male managers reported such spousal help (Grossbard-Shechtman, Dafna Izraeli, and Neuman 1994). This may reflect traditional gender roles leading women to consider men's household production as help with their career, whereas husbands take for granted women's household production and do not recognize such production as career help.

Very few empirical studies have explored correlates of marital differentials in women's wages. An exception is Daniel (1995), who divided his National Longitudinal Survey Youth (NLSY) sample by gender and ethnicity. He found that for white women, a net effect of marriage (controlling for children) appears after a few years of marriage and is small but positive. Black women earn a significant positive marriage premium of about 3 percent, which the negative effect of children does not offset.

Even though Goldin (1990, p. 102) suggests that, historically, male marriage differentials have been "virtually unchanged" in the United States since the nineteenth century, recent empirical studies find evidence that marital differentials in men's earnings have changed over time. McKinley Blackburn and Korenman (1991) use annual crosssection data for 1967–88 and show that over these two decades the returns to years married increased. At the same time, they found that the marriage premium decreased because men married later and were thus married for shorter periods of time. Using U.S. data from the National Longitudinal Surveys (NLS), Gray (1997) confirmed this result, providing evidence of a decline of more than 40 percent in marital differentials in men's earnings during the 1980s.

ECONOMETRIC MODELS

Among the econometric models that economists have used to shed light on marital differentials in paid employment are fixed-effects models using panel data and econometric models based on marriage market analysis.

Fixed-Effects Models Based on Panel Data

To explain marital differentials in paid employment, it is desirable to separate effects of marriage on paid employment from effects of paid employment on marriage. Fixed-effects models using panel data help us separate changes over time for the same individuals from variation across individuals. This allows us to disentangle causal links in the relationship between labor supply, marriage, and divorce (for example, Michael C. Keeley 1980; William R. Johnson and Jonathan Skinner 1986; Wilbert Van der Klaauw 1996; Goldin 1997). One of the questions that this literature addresses is whether women are working more because they are not married, or are they not married because they work more. Both decisions are expected to be related to how traditional a woman is. Are traditionally minded women more likely to work part-time or not at all after they marry, or are women who are initially less interested in a career outside homemaking more likely to be married? By controlling for fixed effects, many unmeasured variables are controlled for, including preferences for traditional roles.

Johnson and Skinner (1986) find that expectations of divorce had a positive effect on married women's labor force participation, but that their labor force participation did not affect their probability of divorce. Bishakha Sen (2000) finds that divorce had a much larger impact on the labor supply of women born in the years 1944–54 than on those born in the years 1957–64. From Sen (forthcoming), it appears that for women born in the years 1957–64, working in the paid labor force might have led to a decrease in the probability of divorce. Even if it can be established from a fixed-effects model that a woman's career success or labor force participation affects her marital status, it could be that her (unmeasured) initial expectations about marriage or divorce influenced both her career in paid employment and her probability of divorce, and that the effect of paid employment is not a causal effect.

Similarly, economists have used panel data and fixed-effects models to separate whether marriage enhances men's productivity from whether more productive men are more likely to be married. Using a U.S. longitudinal data set, the NLS from 1976 to 1980, Korenman and Neumark (1991) conclude that less than half of the marriage wage premium is attributable to selection effects; the remainder of the marriage wage premium is due to productivity-enhancing effects of marriage, which include what we call the Work-in-Marriage explanation and the specialization explanation. Daniel (1995) uses NLSY data from 1979 and 1987 and attributes a larger fraction of the marriage wage premium to selection effects than Korenman and Neumark, though he still finds significant productivity effects associated with marriage.

Using the NLS for Young Men (for the years 1971, 1976, 1978, and 1980) and a fixed-effects model, Cornwell and Rupert (1987) show that much of the premium normally attributed to marriage is associated with unobservable individual effects that are correlated with both marital status and wages. They estimate marital differentials net of selectivity at no more than 5 percent to 7 percent. Likewise, Shelly J. Lundberg and Elaina Rose (2000) first estimated the effect of marriage on men's wages to be 10 percent in a model without fixed effects, thus including selectivity processes. Using a fixed-effects model, they estimate the effect of marriage on men's wages to be 6 percent. They also found that introduction of fixed effects also reduced marital differentials in hours of work, from a marital differential of about 200 hours a year without fixed effects to a marital differential of 116 hours with fixed effects.

What such fixed-effects models tell us is what part of the marital differentials are due to selectivity into marriage and what part are productivity-enhancing effects of marriage. However, as mentioned earlier, the selectivity effect could be a breadwinner effect: It could be that an unmeasured motivation to marry had led men to enhance their labor market productivity and earnings, knowing that this would increase their chances of getting married. So identifying a sequence running from productivity to marriage does not prove that it is not marriage that makes men more productive. If selectivity effects are breadwinner effects, it is the prospect of marriage that makes men more productive.

Marriage Market Econometric Models

Economic analyses of the interaction between labor and marriage via marriage markets can help us design more comprehensive econometric models of paid employment. Marriage market models shed new light on how previously considered variables, such as income, are related to paid employment and marriage.[20] Such models also lead to new variables that help explain paid employment patterns. Two categories of additional variables are discussed: individual characteristics that matter in marriage and that are usually overlooked by labor economists, such as differences between wife's age and husband's age, and macrolevel variables influencing marriage markets, including sex ratios and divorce laws.

Reconsidering Income Effects. It follows from marriage market models that each spouse's income is likely to affect labor supply separately,

---

[20] Marriage market models are related to bargaining models such as Marilyn Manser and Murray Brown (1980). See Chapter 1 for a detailed comparison between various marriage market models, see Grossbard-Shechtman (1999).

and that one should not pool all household income when estimating income effects on individual labor supplies (see Grossbard-Shechtman 1984; Marjorie B. McElroy 1990, Daniela Del Boca 1997; Grossbard-Shechtman and Matthew Neideffer 1997).

Additional Variables: Individual Characteristics. Some individual characteristics, such as loyalty, energy, and emotional intelligence, are unobservable.[21] These characteristics may affect productivity and success in paid employment as well as marriage and divorce probabilities via effects on success in the marriage market, as in the case of intelligence that is appreciated both at the workplace and at home. Marriage market analyses can help us capture effects of some unobservable variables to the extent that observable marriage-related behavior is associated with unmeasurable characteristics related to decisions about paid employment. For instance, individual preferences for traditionalism in household production (such as a traditional gender-based distinction between the homemaker and breadwinner roles) may be unobservable, but the fact that a couple involves a younger woman married to a much older man may reveal that this couple has more traditional preferences for a traditional lifestyle than a comparable couple with little age difference.

Accordingly, relative to an identical woman who is married to an otherwise identical man who is closer to her own age, a woman married to a man much older than herself is more likely to be a traditional homemaker and her husband is more likely to be a traditional breadwinner. To the extent that the husband shares more of his income with his wife, a woman married to an older husband is receiving a higher quasiwage for her Work-in-Marriage (WIM) than a comparable woman married to a husband her own age, where quasiwage for Work-in-Marriage is defined as in Chapter 1. Consequently, she will have less need to participate in the labor force participation and to be attached to the labor force. Alternatively, her own traditional preferences may keep her away from the labor force.

An analysis of competitive markets for WIM takes account of both demand and supply for WIM. Even if a particular couple observed in a study is totally committed to an egalitarian lifestyle and has no trace of traditionalism, we may observe *compensating differentials* in their marriage, reflecting marriage market valuation of youth and/or willingness to follow traditional gender roles (see Grossbard-Shechtman 1984, 1993).

---

[21] More on emotional intelligence can be found in Daniel Goleman (1995).

The relative scarcity of younger women interested in marrying older men will lead to high quasiwages for the WIM supplied by young women who are willing to marry older men.[22] Competition in WIM markets will cause these quasiwages to be paid even to individual market participants who do not personally adhere to traditional gender preferences.

A marriage markets model using Israeli data confirmed this prediction. When Grossbard-Shechtman and Neuman (1988) included a husband/wife age difference variable in regressions of women's labor supply, they found that Israeli women married to men substantially older than themselves were less likely to participate in the labor force than otherwise identical women married to identical men who are closer in age. A similar finding regarding women's LFP in Hawaii is reported by Grossbard-Shechtman and Xuanning Fu (2001). Frances Woolley finds that husband/wife age differences at marriage also help explain another correlate of quasiwages for WIM: who controls the money in marriage (see Chapter 5).

Ethnicity differences between husband and wife can also be associated with compensating differentials in marriage, and can therefore help explain paid employment. Grossbard-Shechtman and Neuman (1988) found that Israeli Jewish women married to a spouse belonging to a lower-status ethnic group had a lower tendency to be part of the paid labor force. Using Hawaiian data, Grossbard-Shechtman and Fu (2001) found lower labor force participation among white women married to men belonging to other ethnic groups considered less prestigious than whites, relative to the LFP of white women who married white men. Opposite results were found for Hawaiian women, Hawaiians being rated low on the ethnic prestige scale of most Hawaiians. These findings can be explained if individuals belonging to certain ethnic or racial groups can obtain higher value in marriage markets relative to other ethnicities. Women whose ethnic group is considered less prestigious will be less in demand and consequently be paid lower quasiwages, leading to lower transfers of income from husband to wife. Competition in marriage markets will lead to compensating differentials even if the particular people observed are totally neutral with respect to ethnicity or race. Lower quasiwages create more of a need for women to go to work for pay.

Econometric models including sex ratio measures in addition to the variables that are usually included in such models show that this variable helps explain intercity variations in the labor force participation

---

[22] More on WIM quasiwages can be found in Chapter 1.

and hours of work of married women in the United States (Grossbard-Shechtman and Neideffer 1997) and Canada (Pierre-Andre Chiappori, Bernard Fortin, and Guy Lacroix 1998).

CONCLUSIONS

Substantial differences in paid employment are associated with marital status. A simple recognititon of traditional gender roles in marriage helps us explain most of these marital differentials. However, to obtain a fuller understanding of these differentials, it helps to use economic models. Some of these models help us disentangle causalities and rely on the availability of panel data. Marriage market models justify inclusion of additional explanatory variables in models of labor supply. Marriage market models lead to novel insights from natural experiments such as the coming of age of baby boomers or baby busters. Faster-than-average increases in LF participation and attachment characterized baby-boom women, faced with low sex ratios, whereas slower-than-average increases (and some decreases) in the LF participation and attachment of baby-bust women are likely to be related to the high sex ratios faced by women born in the late 1960s and early 1970s. Marriage market analysis also helps account for some striking black/white differences in young women's LF participation and attachment.

We also discussed interesting insights about possible compensating differentials in intramarriage transfers that could help explain variation in women's labor force behavior. Various interpretations of marital differentials in men's earnings were also offered.

More research is needed on marital differentials in men's LFP and LF attachment. These differentials are substantial, and we have very few insights on that topic. We also need a better understanding of what marriage accomplishes, leading to these sizeable differentials. In particular, we could gain from a better understanding of joint household production by husbands and wives, of the processes by which spouses add to each other's productivity in paid labor and at home,[23] of the degree to which differentials in both spouses' productivity at home and the workplace are influenced by one of the spouses' paid employment being based at home, and of men's changing roles in household production. Psychologists have shown recently that married men who are more involved in household

---

[23] See Chapter 9 by Hersch. We have explored these topics in Grossbard-Shechtman, Izraeli, and Neuman (1994) and in Chapter 15 in Grossbard-Shechtman (1993).

production considerably increase their chances of staying married. For instance, in John M. Gottman and Nan Silver's (1999) study of newly-wed couples, marriages where men were actively involved in housework were 81 percent less likely to end in divorce than other marriages. We need more studies of traditional marriages, non-traditional marriages, and paid employment patterns.

REFERENCES

Benham, Lee. "Benefits of Women's Education within Marriage," in Theodore W. Schultz, ed., *Economics of the Family*. Chicago, IL: University of Chicago Press, 1974.

Blackburn, McKinley and Korenman, Sanders. "Changes over Time in Earnings Differentials by Marital Status." Unpublished manuscript, University of South Carolina, 1991.

Blau, Francine D., Ferber, Marianne A. and Winkler, Anne E. *The Economics of Women, Men, and Work*, 3rd ed. Englewood Cliffs, NJ: Prentice Hall, 1998.

Cherry, Robert. "Rational Choice and the Price of Marriage." *Feminist Economics*, 1998, *4*, pp. 27–49.

Chiappori, Pierre-Andre, Fortin, Bernard and Lacroix, Guy. "Household Labor Supply, Sharing Rule and the Marriage Market." University of Laval Working Paper 98-10, 1998, http://www.ecn.ulaval.ca/w3/recherche/cahiers/1998/9810.pdf.

Cornwell, Christopher and Rupert, Peter. "Unobservable Individual Effects, Marriage and Earnings of Young Men." *Economic Inquiry,* 1987, *35*(2), pp. 285–99.

Daniel, Kermit. "The Marriage Premium," in Mariano Tommasi and Kathryn Ierulli, eds., *The New Economics of Human Behavior*. Cambridge, UK: Cambridge University Press, 1995.

Del Boca, Daniela. "Intrahousehold Distribution of Resources and Labor Market Participation Decisions," in Inga Persson and Christina Jonung, eds., *Economics of the Family and Family Policies*. London: Routledge, 1997.

Duncan, Greg and Holmund, Bertil. "Was Adam Smith Right After All? Another Test of the Theory of Compensating Wage Differentials." *Journal of Labor Economics*, 1983, *1*(4), pp. 366–79.

Eissa, Nada. "Taxation and Labor Supply of Married Women: The Tax Reform Act of 1986 as a Natural Experiment." NBER Working Paper #5023, 1995.

Ferber, Marianne A. and Berg, Helen M. "Labor Force Participation of Women and the Sex Ratio: A Cross-Country Analysis." *Review of Social Economics*, 1991, *49*, pp. 1–14.

Gates, Gary, Black, Dan, Sanders, Seth and Taylor, Lowell. "The Effects of Sexual Orientation on the Wages of Gay Men." Paper presented at the Population Association of America, March 2000.

Goldin, Claudia. *Understanding the Gender Gap*. Cambridge, UK: Oxford University Press, 1990.

———. "College Women across the Twentieth Century," in Francine Blau and Ronald Ehrenberg, eds., *Gender and Family Issues in the Workplace*. New York: Russell Sage Foundation, 1997.

Goleman, Daniel. *Emotional Intelligence*. New York: Bantam, 1995.

Gottman, John M. and Silver, Nan. *The Seven Principles for Making Marriage Work*. New York: Crown Publishers, 1999.

Gray, Jeffrey S. "The Fall in Men's Return to Marriage-Declining Productivity Effects of Changing Selection." *Journal of Human Resources*, 1997, *32*(3), pp. 481–504.

———. "Divorce-Law Changes, Household Bargaining, and Married Women's Labor Supply." *American Economic Review*, June 1998, *88*(3), pp. 628–42.

Grossbard-Shechtman, Amyra. "A Theory of Allocation of Time in Markets for Labor and Marriage." *Economic Journal*, 1984, *94*, pp. 863–82.

Grossbard-Shechtman, Shoshana Amyra. *On the Economics of Marriage: A Theory of Marriage, Labor, and Divorce*. Boulder, CO: Westview Press, 1993.

———. "Marriage Markets and Black/White Differences in Labor, Marriage and Welfare." Paper presented at the conference on Economics and Sociology in Honor of Gary Becker and James Coleman, San Diego, July 1995a.

———. "Marriage Market Models," in Mariano Tommasi and Kathryn Ierulli, eds., *The New Economics of Human Behavior*. Cambridge, UK: Cambridge University Press, 1995b.

———. "Why Women May Be Charged More at the Cleaners: A Consumer Theory with Competitive Marriage Markets," Working Paper 99–01, Center for Public Economics, San Diego State University, 1999.

———. "Marriage Market Imbalances and the Changing Economic Roles of Women." Paper presented at the Journees d'Economie Appliquee, Quebec City, June 2000.

Grossbard-Shechtman, Shoshana and Amuedo Dorantes Catalina. "Marriage Market Imbalances and Labor Supply of Women: A Model with Competitive Markets for Wife-Services and Application to U.S. Regions." Paper presented at the University of Amsterdam, October 2002.

Grossbard-Shechtman, Shoshana and Fu, Xuanning. "Women's Labor Force Participation and Status Exchange in Intermarriage: A Model and Evidence for Hawaii." Paper presented at the Population Association of America, March 2001.

Grossbard-Shechtman, Shoshana and Granger, Clive W. J. "Women's Jobs and Marriage – From Baby-Boom to Baby-Bust." *Population*, 1998, *53*, pp. 731–52 (in French).

Grossbard-Shechtman, Shoshana A., Izraeli, Dafna N. and Neuman, Shoshana. "When Do Spouses Support a Career? A Human Capital Analysis of Israeli Managers and Their Spouses." *Journal of Socio-Economics*, 1994, *23*, pp. 149–67.

Grossbard-Shechtman, Shoshana and Neideffer, Matthew. "Women's Hours of Work and Marriage Market Imbalances," in Inga Persson and Christina Jonung, eds., *Economics of the Family and Family Policies*. London: Routledge, 1997.

Grossbard-Shechtman, Shoshana A. and Neuman, Shoshana. "Labor Supply and Marital Choice." *Journal of Political Economy*, 1988, *96*, pp. 1294–1302.

————. "Cross Productivity Effects of Education and Origin on Earnings: Are They Really Reflecting Productivity?" in Roge Frantz, Harinder Singh, and James Gerber, eds., *Handbook of Behavioral Economics*, Vol. 2A, Greenwich, CT: JAI Press, 1991, pp. 125–45.

————. "The Extra Burden of Moslem Wives – Insights from Israeli Women's Labour Supply." *Economic Development and Cultural Change*, December 1998, *46*, pp. 491–517.

Heer, David M. and Grossbard-Shechtman, Amyra. "The Impact of the Female Marriage Squeeze and the Contraceptive Revolution on Sex Roles and the Women's Liberation Movement in the United States, 1960 to 1975." *Journal of Marriage and the Family*, 1981, *43*, pp. 49–65.

Hersch, Joni. "Male–Female Differences in Hourly Wages: The Role of Human Capital, Working Conditions, and Housework." *Industrial and Labor Relations Review*, 1991, *44*, pp. 746–59.

Hochschild, Arlie. *The Second Shift*. New York: Viking, 1989.

Johnson, William R. and Skinner, Jonathan. "Labor Supply and Marital Separation." *American Economic Review*, 1986, *76*, pp. 455–69.

Jonung, Christina and Persson, Inga. "Women and Market Work: The Misleading Tale of Participation Rates in International Comparisons." *Work, Employment and Society*, 1993, *7*(2), pp. 259–74.

Keeley, Michael C. "A Simultaneous Model of Marital Stability and Labor Supply Response to an NIT." Unpublished manuscript, Stanford Research Institute International, 1980.

Kenny, Lawrence. "The Accumulation of Human Capital during Marriage by Males. " *Economic Inquiry,* 1983, *21*, pp. 223–31.

Killingsworth, Mark R. and Heckman, James J. "Female Labor Supply: A Survey," in Orly Ashenfelter and Richard Layard, eds., *Handbook of Labor Economics*, Vol. I. Rotterdam: North-Holland, 1986, pp. 103–204.

Korenman, Sanders and Neumark, David. "Does Marriage Really Make Men More Productive?" *Journal of Human Resources*, 1991, *26*, pp. 282–307.

Lehrer, Evelyn M. "The Impact of Children on Married Women's Labor Supply. Black–White Differentials Revisited." *Journal of Human Resources*, 1992, *27*, pp. 422–44.

Leibowitz, Arleen and Klerman, Jacob A. "Explaining Changes in Married Mothers' Employment Over Time." *Demography*, August 1995, *32*, pp. 365–70.

Lundberg, Shelly J. and Rose, Elaina "The Effects of Sons and Daughters on Men's Labor Supply and Wages." Paper presented at the Population Association of America, March 2000.

Manser, Marilyn and Brown, Murray. "Marriage and Household Decision Making: A Bargaining Analysis. " *International Economic Review*, 1980, *21*, pp. 31–44.

McElroy, Marjorie B. "The Empirical Content of Nash-Bargained Household Behavior." *Journal of Human Resources*, 1990, *25*, pp. 559–83.

Mincer, Jacob. "Labor Force Participation of Married Women: A Study of Labor Supply," in Harry Gregg Lewis, ed., *Aspects of Labor Economics*. Princeton, NJ: Princeton University Press, 1962.

Mincer, Jacob and Polachek, Solomon. "Family Investments in Human Capital: Earnings of Women." *Journal of Political Economy*, March/April 1974, *82*, pp. S76–S108.

O'Neill, Dave M. and O'Neill, June E. *Lessons for Welfare Reform: An Analysis of the AFDC Caseload and Past Welfare to Work Programs*. Kalamazoo, MI: W. E. Upjohn Institute for Employment and Research, 1997.

Parkman, Allen M. *No-Fault Divorce: What Went Wrong?* Boulder, CO: Westview Press, 1992.

———. "Why Are Married Women Working So Hard?" *International Review of Law and Economics*, 1998, *18*, pp. 41–9.

Pencavel, John. "The Market Work Behavior and Wages of Women: 1975–94." Paper presented at the Meetings of the Society of Labor Economics, San Francisco, May 1998.

Peters, Elizabeth H. "Marriage and Divorce: Informational Constraints and Private Contracting," *American Economic Review*, 1986, *76*, pp. 437–54.

Reed, Robert and Hartford, Kathleen. "The Marriage Premium and Compensating Wage Differentials." *Journal of Population Economics*, 1989, *2*, pp. 237–65.

Rosen, Sherwin. "Mincering Labor Economics." *Journal of Economic Perspectives*, Spring 1992, *6*, 157–70.

Schoeni, Robert F. "Marital Status and Earnings in Developed Countries." *Journal of Population Economics*, 1995, *8*, pp. 351–9.

Scully, Gerald W. "Mullahs, Muslims and Marital Sorting." *Journal of Political Economy,* 1979, *87*, pp. 1139–43.

Sen, Bishakha. "How Important Is Anticipation of Divorce in Married Women's Labor Supply Decisions?" *Economic Letters*, 2000, *67*(2), pp. 209–16.

———. "Does Married Women's Market Work Affect Marital Stability Adversely? An Intercohort Analysis Using NLS Data." Forthcoming in *Review of Social Economy*.

Spanier, Graham B. and Glick, Paul C. "Mate Selection Differentials between Whites and Blacks in the United States." *Social Forces,* 1980, *58*, pp. 707–25.

Strober, Myra H. and Chan, Agnes Miling Kaneko. "Husbands, Wives, and Housework: Graduates of Stanford and Tokyo Universities." *Feminist Economics*, Fall 1998, *4*(3), pp. 97–128.

Van der Klaauw, Wilbert. "Female Labour Supply and Marital Status Decisions: A Life-Cycle Model." *Review of Economic Studies,* 1996, *63*, pp. 199–235.

Wilson, W. Julius. *The Truly Disadvantaged*. Chicago, IL: University of Chicago Press, 1987.

Wong, Yue-Chim. "Entrepreneurship, Marriage, and Earnings," *Review of Economics and Statistics*, November 1986, *68*, pp. 603–99.

ELEVEN

Marriage, Work for Pay, and Childcare

Rachel Connelly and Jean Kimmel

On the most superficial level, the relationship between childcare and marriage is clear. Because married people are more likely to have young children than unmarried people, the former confront childcare issues more often than the latter. Furthermore, single parents typically do not have available a partner's income to permit stay-at-home parenting. Childcare choices for married versus unmarried individuals also vary in less tautological ways. In this chapter, we limit our analysis to a comparison of the childcare choices of married couples and unmarried women with young children, two populations differing in marital status and facing comparable childcare choices. The mere presence of young children in a household creates the need to make a set of decisions – including the use of parental versus non-parental childcare and paid versus unpaid childcare – as well as related decisions concerning employment.

A substantial literature exists on the economics of childcare, though most of the studies are quite recent. The first economic analysis explicitly on childcare was James J. Heckman's 1974 study. He and many authors since then took the importance of marital status for granted to the extent that they only considered the childcare choices of married women. For example, see Evelyn Lehrer (1983); David M. Blau and Philip K. Robins (1988); Rachel Connelly (1992a); David Ribar (1992, 1995); Susan H. Averett et al. (1997); Lisa Powell (1997, 1998, 2002); Charles Michalopoulos and Robins (2000a). The papers that have included single mothers have done so in a variety of ways. In a few papers, the analysis was performed separately for married and single mothers (Patricia Anderson and Phillip Levine 1999; Connelly 1990; Connelly and Jean Kimmel forthcoming; Wen-Jui Han and Jane Waldfogel 1999; Kimmel 1998; Michalopoulos, Robins, and Irwin Garfinkel 1992). Alternatively, a full sample has been used that combines both married and unmarried mothers with marital status controlled with a dummy variable (see Lehrer 1989; Arleen Leibowitz, Jacob A. Klerman, and Linda J. Waite 1992; Karen Fox Folk and Andrea Beller 1993; GAO 1994; Paul Fronstin and Douglas A. Wissoker 1994; Joseph V. Hotz and M. Rebecca Kilburn 1994; Blau and Alison P. Hagy 1998; and Duncan Chaplin et al. 1996). Sandra L. Hofferth and Wissoker (1992) adjust for the number of choices of childcare modes available to married and unmarried women (unmarried women don't have the option of husband care), but assume that "the relative probabilities of choice among available types of care are the same for married and unmarried women" (p. 94). Finally, Mark Berger and Dan Black (1992), Kimmel (1995), and Michalopoulos and Robins (2000b) limit their analyses to single mothers. In this chapter, we add to this literature by considering explicitly the reasons married and single mothers may make distinct choices about hours of employment, the amount they pay for childcare, and the mode of childcare used. We also analyze how differences in the price of childcare affect single versus married mothers in their decisions concerning labor force participation and mode of care choice.

The topic of the "economics of childcare" is central to any discussion of marriage and the economy. Children are a major motivation for marriage (Gary S. Becker 1974), and childcare is a major aspect of home production. The presence of children also acts as a deterrent to divorce (Becker et al. 1997; Elizabeth Peters 1986). This understanding strengthens our resolve to include marital status in any analysis of childcare but also introduces the problem of the interconnectedness of marriage and childbearing. To some extent, the marital status we observe may be the result of the mother or the father's desire to have children and their preferences over alternative childcare arrangements. Our empirical analysis ignores this potential endogeneity, taking marital status as given.

We begin our analysis with a discussion of the economic decisions surrounding childcare choices, including a discussion of how marital status might affect this decision making. Following this, we look at data showing the choices about childcare made by American families and discuss the research that has been done concerning differences between married and unmarried women's childcare choices.

EXPLANATIONS

Modeling Childcare/Work for Pay Choices of All Parents

Whether explicitly or implicitly, all parents must make decisions about childcare options. Even though in this chapter we do not present a detailed model of childcare choices, we build our arguments and tests on existing models and explanations. The standard economic model of childcare choice presents the parents as the decision makers who take into account, among other things, their children's current and future well-being, including the children's preferences. The parents also take into account their own needs or preferences, such as the need or preference to have one or two incomes, the need or preference to be at work at the same time of day as one's spouse (for married mothers), and the convenience and dependability of the childcare arrangement(s). The children's current needs include the need to be kept out of danger, to be loved and nurtured, to be fed and changed, and so on. The children's future needs include a supportive environment for normal child development and a foundation for education. Both current and future child well-being are often lumped together as parental concern for "child quality."[1] Full models explain family time allocation in a framework where the parent or parents make decisions about employment and childcare while considering constraints related to family income, time budgeting, and investments in child quality.[2] Given our emphasis on marital status, we are also guided by models that assume that skills involved in home childcare are transferable and that individuals participate in competitive marriage markets.[3]

Let's consider the childcare choices available to the mother and father of a preschool child. In general, the parents of a young child face the following options: (1) Neither parent works in the labor force, leaving both available for parental childcare; (2) one parent is employed in the labor market while the other parent serves as primary caregiver for their child; (3) both parents are employed in the labor market but at separate times of the day, using split shifts so that there is always a parent at home to care for the young child; and (4) both parents work at approximately the same times and rely on any one of a variety of non-parental childcare

---

[1] See, for example, Heckman (1974). For a more recent update of the discussion of the role of childcare in early investments in child quality, see Heckman (1999).

[2] For an example of a formal model of childcare demand and employment, see Connelly (1992a) or Ribar (1992, 1995).

[3] See, for example, Grossbard-Shechtman (1999, 2001).

options for their child.[4] Looking at a sample of Americans with a young child, we find some parents in each one of these categories, but categories two and four are much more common than others. We know that the vast majority of prime-aged men are in the labor force – approximately 94.8 percent of men age twenty-five to fifty-four are in the labor force. Thus, the majority of American parents do not choose the option of having both parents withdraw from the labor force and care for the child. Nor do they often choose the option of having the mother work full-time in the labor market and the father care full-time for the child.

Sociologist Harriet Presser (1986) has led the way in the study of split shifts and non-standard work schedules. Recent data from the Survey of Income and Program Participation (SIPP) show that 10 percent of children with employed mothers are cared for by their fathers while their mothers are at work (Lynn Casper 1997). When the mother works full-time during the day, 5 percent are cared for by their fathers, whereas 9.3 percent are cared for by their father when their mother is employed part-time during the daytime hours. However, when the mother's labor market employment involves a non-day schedule, 13.9 percent of children of mothers employed full-time and 18.8 percent of the children of mothers employed part-time are cared for by their fathers. In most cases, the father is also employed full-time in the labor market, thereby implying that the total workload of the mother and father combined has increased. The total workload increases precisely because time in the labor force does not reduce time spent working with children. Parents undertake this type of childcare arrangement either because they strongly value parental childcare over third-party childcare or because they cannot afford third-party childcare. However egalitarian splitting the childcare may be, we must remember that it may not be the preferred strategy for most parents given the increased total workload and the reduced time the two parents have available for themselves. Thus, we expect the probability that the use of this strategy diminishes as income increases.

Since father care represents a relatively small percent of care arrangements, the bulk of studies examining parents' childcare choices collapse the options listed earlier into a model of mother's work for pay jointly determined with the family's childcare option. When young children are present the mother's work-for-pay decision takes into account the net effect on child quality of mother care versus non-mother care, the income

---

[4] We do not consider self-care because it is typically not an option for young children. See, for example, Hofferth et al. (1990).

she would earn if she were employed, the cost of the non-maternal child-care, the quality of the "mothering" as influenced by the number of hours spent on the task as primary care provider, as well as consumption preferences and the other income available (including unearned income, government transfers, and husband's income, if married).

Up to this point, we have discussed labor market employment as if it were an on/off switch. However, a substantial proportion of women work part-time. Mothers' part-time employment can ease the labor force work/childcare conflict, in part because fathers who are not available for full-time childcare may be available for part-time care. Part-time work can occur at a different time than the father's full-time work with less stress than if both parents were working full-time on separate shifts. In addition, there may be other relatives willing to provide part-time childcare. Or, parents may consider relative care to be an acceptable option for a few hours each week but not for full-time care. Finally, because people may enjoy certain nonpecuniary aspects of their jobs, including the social interactions and the mental or physical challenges, part-time employment may be desired even if the childcare costs nearly equal the earnings of the mother and/or even if there is a substantial hourly wage penalty for part-time work.

Modeling the Type of Third-Party Childcare Chosen

In addition to the decision-making process outlined in the preceding section, there is also interest in the choices parents make among the types of third-party childcare that are available to them if they choose non-parental care. Third-party childcare can be categorized by the location at which it takes place (the child's own home, another person's home, a day care center or school); or it can be categorized by the type of provider (the child's grandparent, other relative or a non-relative). Most often these two criteria are combined into a taxonomy that includes the child's relative in a home setting (either at the child's own or the relative's home), a non-relative in a home setting, or a day care center. There is some evidence that parents see these three types of care as qualitatively different (see Waite, Arleen Leibowitz, and Christine Witsberger 1991). In addition, these options often have different price tags since relative care may be provided without a monetary exchange, and non-relative home care can be performed in conjunction with housework or caring for one's own children, thereby lowering the opportunity cost of home care (that is, the value of the caregiver's time had she not provided this service;

see Connelly 1992b). The child's relative may get pleasure out of watching the child or being helpful to the young parents, or may receive some in-kind transfer in return for his or her childcare efforts either now or in the future.

Besides differing in location and provider, childcare arrangements also differ in quality. Child development experts characterize high-quality childcare as providing a more stimulating environment, more educational content, or more attention per child. Several studies have tried to measure differences in quality with quality so defined (see Blau and Hagy 1998, for example). Since higher-quality care so defined requires lower child/staff ratios and higher levels of teacher training, it tends to be more expensive. Parents generally do care about the quality of care that their children receive and the level of educational content, as evidenced by the number of children with a stay-at-home parent who are enrolled in preschools. However, parents also are concerned with the convenience, dependability, commonality of values, and the cost of alternative modes of care (Freya Sonenstein 1991; Hofferth and Chaplin 1998). Given the high cost of quality care relative to family income and the time constraints facing most families, it is not surprising that location and price often win out over quality in the choice of third-party childcare providers.[5]

Differences in Childcare/Employment Choices between Married and Single Parents

Having explored the scope of childcare decision making for all parents with a young child, we now consider how the choices of a single parent of a young child might differ from those of married parents. Two big differences affecting their choices are that (1) single parents (mothers particularly) usually lack substantial income from the child's other parent, and (2) single parents tend to receive less help with childcare from relatives, including the child's father. In addition, differences between married and

---

[5] Affordability is a problem for both married and single parents. However, it is particularly a concern for single mothers, because childcare costs are substantial, especially when considered as a percentage of expected earned income. (See Table 11.3 later in this chapter for further detail.) On average, single women enjoy limited earning power but face relatively high childcare costs, making it difficult for the mother's employment to offer a way out of abject poverty. For example, a single mother who has one young child and is working full-time year-round at the minimum wage would spend approximately 30 percent of her income on childcare expenses were she to utilize an average-cost childcare option. At the average wage for single mothers, they still must devote approximately 18 percent of earned income to childcare expenses.

single parents' childcare and work-for-pay decisions may be the result of the differential effects of government programs by marital status.

Lack of Income from the Child's Other Parent. Some single parents receive child support or may co-reside with a partner, but the income available from these sources alone is usually insufficient to enable the custodial parent to stay out of the labor market. The single parent's choices can be characterized simply as (1) withdrawing from the labor market and caring for her child by herself, or (2) working in the labor market and using childcare by others. The income available to a single parent if the first option is chosen would be child-support payments (if any) and government transfers, most notably state welfare payments, Medicaid, and Food Stamps.

Income support programs such as AFDC in the past and now Temporary Assistance for Needy Families (TANF), while theoretically available to both married and single parents, are much more likely to be used by single parents. Several federal programs are designed to reduce the cost of childcare to working parents, including the Child and Dependent Care Tax Credit, the Exclusion of Employer Contributions for Child Care Expenses, and the Child Care and Development Block Grant (CCDBG). Of these, the first two are income tax–based and have their largest impact on middle-income families. Thus, married couples are much more likely to benefit from these tax-based programs than single parents. The Child Care and Development Block Grant is targeted at the low-income population and thus more likely to be utilized by single parents. In addition, some childcare subsidies are available through efforts to reduce welfare dependency, with eligibility defined as having recently received means-tested transfer income.

The additional income typically available to married mothers often has strings attached to it. Chapter 10 by Grossbard-Shechtman and Shoshana Neuman in this book argues that married women are often working within marriage (what they call Work-in-Marriage) – that is, tending to the needs of a husband and receiving "pay" for this labor in the form of access to husband's earnings. One can certainly think of caring for the husband's children from a previous marriage as Work-in-Marriage, but some home-produced childcare of joint children may also be considered as Work-in-Marriage. To the extent that married mothers are compensated for their labor, they can consume additional goods, and this income will affect their demand for paid childcare.

As a result of these income differences by marital status, childcare costs represent a higher portion of the family income of single mothers than of married mothers. (We show later that for single mothers, market-priced childcare can easily represent one-quarter of their income.) This larger share of expenses is important in our comparison of the effects of the price of childcare between married and single mothers.

Fewer Relatives to Help with Childcare But Perhaps More Help from Some Relatives. One way to avoid the high cost of childcare is to use relative care, which is often provided at little or no monetary cost. As listed previously, another important difference between single parents and married couples is that single parents may have less access to relative care than married couples, especially in the case of never-married parents. Although unmarried mothers often can get some childcare assistance from their own family members (as do married mothers), they are less likely to receive help from the child's father or his relatives.

A related difference between single and married parents lies in the frequency that they co-reside with an adult other than the co-parent. Many single parents co-reside with another adult, but married couples seldom choose this option. Cohabitation with another adult implies a loss of privacy and autonomy. The cost of reduced privacy and co-residence are higher for a couple than for an unattached adult. As a result, Connelly and Kimmel (forthcoming) found that whereas 8 percent of married mothers with children under age six lived with another adult besides their spouses, 47 percent of single mothers lived with another adult. Often, these cohabiting arrangements are undertaken for the explicit purpose of providing childcare and other support to facilitate the single parent's employment efforts or to provide income support to facilitate the single parent's care for his or her own child. Thus, in the United States, the living arrangements of single parents appear to be more interrelated to labor market and childcare choices than the living arrangements of married parents.

Government Childcare Policies Differentials by Marital Status. The federal Dependent Care Tax Credit is largely a middle-class subsidy that is more likely to benefit dual-parent families than single-parent families. This nonrefundable credit provides no benefit to the poor or near poor since they do not have tax obligations. Some states supplement this credit with their own small credits, but still the poor are not subject to sufficient state income taxation to benefit from the credit. On the other hand, the federally funded CCDBG targets the welfare-to-work and at-risk populations and so benefits mostly single-mother families. While the maximum income eligibility cutoff was set by the Personal Responsibility and Work Opportunity Reconciliation Act (PRWORA) of 1996, the more recent federal welfare reform legislation has led the actual eligibility limits to vary across states. In 1999, only five states had set their limits up to the federal maximum limit. Nationwide, only about 15 percent of those families that would be eligible based on the federal standard received this childcare assistance in 1997 (Schumacher and Greenberg 1999). With the lower than federally allowed levels in most states, it is clear that most of the CCDBG funds will go to poor single mothers. The welfare reform, which has block-granted federal childcare dollars to the states, also results in much more variation across states in the way that the CCDBG funds can be used. State-based programs will affect the choices available to subsidy recipients in terms of the relative cost of various types of childcare.

Resulting Differences in Paid Childcare Use from Changing the Price of Childcare

These differences by marital status are expected to influence the effect of childcare costs on both paid childcare utilization and employment. Regarding paid childcare for the purpose of employment, married mothers are expected to have a more elastic demand for paid care since they have access to more substitutes for paid childcare. But, as shown in Grossbard-Shechtman (1999), the price elasticity of demand for a service that has home-produced substitutes includes a number of substitution effects and a real income effect. While the substitution effect, which we have just described, is expected to be larger for married mothers than for single mothers, the opposite is true for the real income effect since married mothers typically have access to more sources of income. If the real income effects differ much by marital status, the elasticity (or responsiveness) of demand for childcare with respect to the price of childcare may be larger for single mothers, whose real income is so much lower than that of married mothers.[6] Which difference by marital status will dominate will be determined by empirical work, some of which is reported in the next section.

---

[6] See Grossbard-Shechtman (1999) for a full treatment of real income effects and substitution effects in comparing elasticities for consumer goods related to household production, such as childcare.

Resulting Difference in Employment from Changing the Price of Childcare

Married parents determine employment and childcare jointly. Single parents determine welfare recipiency, employment, and childcare jointly.[7] Welfare work rules can affect the choice of number of hours of labor market employment, which thus may differ between single and married mothers. The choice of part-time employment may also differ by marital status for other reasons. Part-time employment may be a parent's first choice or it may result from a lack of full-time employment opportunities. Married and single parents may differ in their individual preferences for part-time employment. One of the goods that some married women are more likely to "consume" given their access to their husband's income is an interesting part-time job that brings in little income beyond childcare expenses but provides stimulation and adult contact. Single mothers do not have access to husbands' earnings and thus are less likely to "consume" such part-time jobs. In addition, Rebecca Blank (1988) showed that female household heads face significant fixed costs of work for relatively few hours per week. We suspect that childcare needs account for most of those fixed costs both due to higher hourly costs of care of part-time childcare and to the time and effort required to transport children to and from childcare arrangements.[8] Thus, a small number of hours worked is less likely to reflect the preferred choice of a single mother than of a married mother. This is important because one might expect that individuals whose preference is for part-time employment would be less sensitive to the price of childcare than those whose part-time employment status is the result of the unavailability of full-time employment.

We also expect that the price of childcare will have less impact on all employment – part-time and full-time – decisions of married mothers than on that of single mothers. This can be explained in terms of the wider set of earnings opportunities available to married women, who can also earn access to their husband's income via the supply of Work-in-Marriage. If employment is modeled as a three-way choice between leisure, work, and in-marriage home production, following Grossbard-Shechtman (2001), it follows that a change in real wage is more likely to affect single women than married women who do not have a husband who pays them for

---

[7] See Kimmel (1995) for issues of childcare and low-income single mothers.

[8] See Table 11.2 for differences in hourly childcare prices by part-time/full-time labor market employment status. Table 11.2 also shows that single mothers are more likely to pay relatives for part-time childcare than married mothers.

producing goods in home production. More expensive childcare is the equivalent of a lower net wage for paid work. Therefore, an increase in paid childcare is expected to reduce employment outside the home more than work in marital production, including Work-in-Marriage, and the paid employment of single mothers who do not engage in Work-in-Marriage is more likely to respond to changes in real (net) wage than that of married mothers.

Resulting Differences in the Type of Third-Party Childcare Used

The choices that parents make regarding the type of third-party childcare used are also expected to differ by marital status. Since we expect single parents to face greater financial constraints, we expect price to weigh more heavily in their decision making. Also dependability, hours, and location may be more important choice criteria to single parents since they lack a spouse to serve as backup care or to assist in transporting the children to and from day care. Finally, government subsidy programs of third-party childcare may favor one type of childcare arrangement over another, adding another reason why married and single parents may differ in their choices of type of childcare arrangement

AN EMPIRICAL LOOK AT CHILDCARE CHOICES
BY MARITAL STATUS

In the preceding section, we argued that married and single mothers can be expected to differ from one another in their choices of whether to be employed and use non-maternal childcare, in their choice of full-time versus part-time labor market work status, in their expenditures on childcare, in the type of non-maternal care chosen, and in the share of income that childcare expenses represent. In this section, we provide statistical evidence of those differences.

Differences in Employment Status

Table 11.1 compares selected employment characteristics of the married and single mothers with children under age six.[9] This is the key population

---

[9] The data come from the overlapping panels of SIPP, panels of respondents from whom data were first collected in 1992 and 1993. The specific data we use were collected during the second half of 1994 and records the childcare arrangements of American women who were employed in the month before the survey questions were collected. Our samples include 4,241 married women and 1,523 single women with at least one child under the

Table 11.1 *Differences in Employment Status, Wages, and Hours Worked by Marital Status and Full-Time/Part-Time Employment* [a]

	1	2	3	4	5	6
	Married mothers			Single mothers		
Variables	All	Employed full-time	Employed part-time	All	Employed full-time	Employed part-time
Age	31.46	31.43	31.69	28.01	29.06	26.98
	(5.88)	(5.50)	(5.76)	(6.82)	(6.48)	(6.85)
Years of	13.31	13.77	13.77	11.82	12.64	12.12
schooling	(2.67)	(2.51)	(2.48)	(2.12)	(1.92)	(2.02)
# of children 0–2	0.64	0.60	0.65	0.59	0.48	0.56
	(0.61)	(0.58)	(0.61)	(0.59)	(0.54)	(0.53)
# of children 3–5	0.75	0.67	0.71	0.72	0.67	0.60
	(0.63)	(0.58)	(0.60)	(0.63)	(0.55)	(0.58)
% nonwhite	0.12	0.16	0.07	0.39	0.37	0.30
	(0.32)	(0.36)	(0.26)	(0.49)	(0.48)	(0.46)
% in poverty	0.11	0.02	0.06	0.55	0.16	0.50
	(0.32)	(0.16)	(0.23)	(0.50)	(0.37)	(0.50)
% receiving	0.02	0.002	0.01	0.43	0.07	0.24
welfare	(0.13)	(0.04)	(0.08)	(0.49)	(0.25)	(0.43)
% employed	0.55	–	–	0.47	–	–
	(0.50)			(0.50)		
% part-time of	0.33	–	–	0.27	–	–
those employed	(0.47)			(0.45)		
Weekly work	–	41.47	21.02	–	40.69	22.14
hours		(5.37)	(7.64)		(5.04)	(7.19)
Hourly wage	–	11.73	11.21	–	8.79	6.81
		(7.07)	(9.32)		(5.71)	(4.31)
Monthly	–	2,039.31	970.27	–	1,470.79	605.30
earnings		(1,286.19)	(828.04)		(1,006.57)	(490.77)
Number of	4,241	1,568	782	1,523	534	204
observations						

Note:
[a] Data from 1992 and 1993 panels of SIPP. These means and standard deviations are weighted to obtain population averages using the topical module weights supplied by SIPP. Standard deviations are shown in parentheses.

of interest since at least one of their children is in need of continual supervisory care from an adult and is below the age of public education.

age of six. As we argued previously, prime-age American men overwhelmingly are in the labor force, the mothers of young children make most employment/childcare decisions. Due to data constraints, unmarried mothers cohabiting with partners, perhaps even the child's father, are included in the single-mother sample.

Single mothers have a lower probability of being employed than married mothers – 47 percent compared to 55 percent for married mothers. However, of those single mothers who are employed, more are likely to be employed full-time: Of the married mothers who are employed, 67 percent are employed full-time compared to 73 percent of the single mothers. The hourly wage at which married and single women work is substantially different: The average hourly wage for employed married mothers of young children is $11.73 for full-time employment and $11.21 for part-time employment, compared to $8.79 and $6.81 for comparable groups of single women. Note that the part-time employed single mothers have significantly lower average wages than the full-timers, which may reflect differences in the women's characteristics or differences in the market wage for full-time versus part-time employment. We did not observe this large a difference in wages between the married mothers. Monthly earnings follow the same pattern as wages, with higher earnings for married women in each category. Finally, welfare recipiency shows a large percent of single mothers receiving welfare payments, 43 percent, compared to 2 percent of married women.[10] Welfare recipiency is not confined to non-employed single mothers; 24 percent of those who are employed part-time are receiving welfare payments, compared with seven percent of the full-time employed single mothers.

As mentioned previously, some of the differences shown in Table 11.1 come from differences in demographic characteristics between single and married mothers. For example, single mothers are slightly younger, twenty-eight years on average, versus 31.5; they are also less educated, 11.8 years of school completed on average versus 13.3 years. They differ substantially in the income available to them from sources other than their own labor market employment (non-self LF income), since this category includes husband's income in the case of the married women.[11] As might be expected, single mothers have fewer children than married mothers, though the difference in each category is small and is not significantly different in the case of the oldest children. Single mothers are more likely to be nonwhite, and much more likely to be living below the poverty line. In fact, 80 percent of single mothers have family income that is below 200 percent of the poverty line, compared to 33 percent of married

---

[10] This also related to eligibility rules based on marital status under AFDC.

[11] Non-self LF income is defined from savings, child-support payments, and husband's income and/or the income of other household members. Income from welfare is excluded because such payments are tied to the mother's paid work effort.

mothers. Single mothers who are employed have a lower incidence of poverty, but still, 26 percent of employed single mothers live below the poverty line compared to 4 percent of employed married mothers. However, controlling for all these characteristics, married mothers of young children are more likely to be employed, both full-time and part-time, than single mothers. Married mothers also have significantly higher wages than single mothers after controlling for other demographic characteristics (Connelly and Kimmel forthcoming).

Differences in Use of Non-Maternal Childcare

Table 11.2 contains childcare expenditure information, including the percentage paying for care, differentiating between married and single mothers, between full-time and part-time, and in addition, distinguishing type of childcare arrangement used for the youngest child.[12] For the full-timers, modal choice is split fairly evenly between relative care and center-based care, and at similar percentages across marital status (37.2 percent to 41.8 percent). However, part-timers rely much more on care by relatives: Over half of married and single mothers working part-time rely on relative care. Comparing married and single mothers, we find the percentage paying for care similar. Among full-timers, 62 percent of married mothers pay for childcare compared to 59 percent of single mothers. For the part-timers, the comparable numbers are 37 percent for married mothers and 39 percent for single mothers. However, single and married mothers do differ substantially in the percentage paying for a particular mode of childcare. For example, single mothers are more likely to pay for relative care than married mothers: Of the single mothers employed full-time using relative care, 32.5 percent pay for that care, compared to 21.0 percent of the married mothers employed full-time using relative care. For those single women employed part-time who use relative care, 17.5 percent pay for that care compared to only 8.3 percent of the married women employed part-time and using relative care. Thus, single mothers thinking about part-time employment facilitated by a relative caring for the child

---

[12] We have no information in our data about childcare usage by unemployed mothers, a significant data gap given that 45 percent of married mothers with young children and 53 percent of single mothers of young children are not employed and so have chosen maternal care for all or most of their children's care. But many unemployed mothers do utilize some non-maternal childcare. Hotz and Kilburn (1994) showed that there is a fundamental difference between employment-related and non-employment-related childcare.

Table 11.2 *Childcare Mode Choice and Weekly Expenditures by Mode of Care for Employed Mothers*[a]

	Married		Single	
	Employed full-time	Employed part-time	Employed full-time	Employed part-time
Percentage using each childcare mode:				
Relative care	37.2	59.2	41.8	52.5
Home-based care	23.4	15.5	17.9	16.1
Center-based care	39.4	25.4	40.3	31.4
% Paying for care	62.4	37.1	58.6	39.1
Percentage paying for each mode of care:				
Relative care	21.0	8.3	32.5	17.5
Home-based care	97.6	89.7	91.5	87.6
Center-based care	80.5	72.1	70.8	50.2
Of those paying for care:				
# of observations	990	292	312	83
Weekly cost (total)	85.44	72.73	62.76	53.83
Weekly cost (youngest child)	80.27	67.75	59.37	50.51
Hourly cost (all children)	2.15	3.44	1.64	2.62
Hourly cost (youngest child)	1.96	3.20	1.47	2.40
Weekly expenditure on childcare for each mode:				
Relative care	$64.83	$51.75	$49.35	$43.01
Home-based care	$87.85	$70.71	$61.10	$53.65
Center-based care	$88.79	$79.91	$70.05	$60.32
Percentage using each mode of care:				
Relative care	12.5	13.3	23.2	23.6
Home-based care	36.6	37.4	27.9	36.4
Center-based care	50.9	49.3	48.9	40.3

Note:

[a] These means are weighted to obtain population averages using the topical module weights supplied by SIPP. All numbers relate to care arrangements for each employed mother's youngest child except for weekly expenditure figures or where indicated otherwise.

face a substantially higher cost of employment than married women. This may be related to lower income of the single mother's relatives or to the unavailability of the child's father and relatives of the father.

As was the case with relative care, the percentage paying for center care differs between the married and the single mothers: 80.5 percent and 72.1 percent pay for center care among full-timers and part-timers who are married, versus 70.8 percent and 50.2 percent among full-timers and part-timers who are single. These distinctions indicate that childcare subsidies such as Head Start or welfare-related subsidies are available to single mothers more than to married mothers. Overall, the percentage paying for care varies substantially by mode of care used, with relatives the least likely to be paid and home-based care the most likely to be paid.

Looking only at those who pay for care, single mothers pay less than married mothers in each expenditure category and in each type of childcare arrangement. This is true for both full-timers and part-timers, and holds whether one considers weekly or hourly expenditures on childcare. For both married and single mothers, those employed full-time pay more per week but less per hour than those employed part-time. We believe that higher hourly cost of part-time care is one reason for Blank's (1988) finding of high fixed cost of part-time employment. However, fixed cost of part-time employment is reduced by the high probability of not paying for childcare that is linked to part-time employment.

The differences in percent paying and in the expenditure amounts between the married and single mothers show the complexity of thinking about a single price of childcare: A substantial proportion pay nothing, and some portion of the differences in expenditures represent parental choices of quality or convenience. However, a clear pattern of differential expenditures by marital status emerges from this table for those paying for care: For all types of paid care, single mothers pay substantially less than married women. Overall, Table 11.2 shows substantial differentials in both type and cost of childcare across marital status and full-time/part-time employment status, indicating the importance of considering marital status when studying employment/childcare decision making.

Differences in Percentage of Family Income Spent on Childcare

Childcare as a percentage of family income also varies substantially between married and single mothers. Table 11.3 shows the distribution of childcare costs as a percentage of family income, broken down by marital status, full-time/part-time work status, and childcare mode. In every category, single mothers devote a higher percentage of their family income to childcare. For example, married mothers working full-time spend 8.8 percent of family income on childcare whereas single mothers working full-time spend 14.8 percent. For those working part-time, the comparison is 9.6 percent versus 36.3 percent. The percentage of family income that single mothers who work part-time devote to childcare is shockingly high, and stems in part from their reliance on relatively expensive center and non-relative care and in part from their low wages for part-time employment. Looking only at families with incomes less than twice the poverty level, married and single mothers working full-time

Table 11.3 *Percentage of Family Income Spent on Childcare[a]*

	Married			Single		
Variables	All	Employed full-time	Employed part-time	All	Employed full-time	Employed part-time
All income levels	8.97	8.97	9.60	19.14	14.79	36.34
Mothers living below 2 times poverty	18.58	16.66	22.99	24.64	17.63	47.19
Percentage of family income spent on childcare by mode						
All income levels						
Relative care	9.72	8.24	14.59	13.20	11.75	18.87
Non-relative care	7.86	8.19	6.72	19.20	14.48	33.48
Formal care	8.47	8.58	8.08	19.33	15.00	40.20
Mothers living below 2 times poverty						
Relative care	23.49	18.75	31.70	16.64	14.47	24.52
Non-relative care	13.27	13.60	12.34	23.70	16.30	44.00
Formal care	16.73	17.22	15.63	26.21	18.89	51.16

Note:
[a] All numbers relate to total childcare expenditures for all preschool children. Calculating these percentages using only the youngest child yields nearly identical results.

spend comparable percentages of their incomes on childcare. But even for this poor subgroup, single mothers who work part-time devote a substantially larger percentage of earned income to childcare than their married counterparts.

Differences in the Responsiveness of Childcare Use and Employment to Changes in the Price of Childcare: Results from Multivariate Data Analyses

The statistical portrait in the preceding sections involved comparisons of one trait at a time. A more thorough analysis requires a multivariate approach in which the effect of each relevant determinant of the employment/childcare decision or the mode of care decision is measured holding all the other effects constant. Several studies of this type have been undertaken recently, each comparing married mothers with their unmarried counterparts (Anderson and Levine 1999; Connelly and Kimmel forthcoming; Han and Waldfogel 1999). Each paper uses the SIPP data to estimate the effect of childcare prices on the probability of being employed.[13] Each study shows that the employment decisions of mothers

[13] The statistical model requires a measure of childcare price for each mother, even those who do not pay for care. (SIPP data do not contain childcare data for mothers not in

of children under the age of six are affected significantly by the price of childcare.[14] Each of the studies has also found that single mothers' employment responds to changes in childcare costs more than married mothers' employment – that is, that the estimated single mothers' elasticity of employment with respect to the price of childcare is greater than the elasticity for married mothers.[15] The implication of the findings is that programs designed to lower the price of childcare for poor families are expected to have a larger effect on the employment of single parents than of married parents.

This greater sensitivity to the price of childcare can be interpreted with help of the choice-based framework outlined in the previous section. There we argued that single mothers' employment is likely to be more sensitive to childcare costs than that of married mothers. Connelly and Kimmel (forthcoming) explored whether this finding is related to married women's more frequent choice of part-time employment by estimating the elasticities of full-time and part-time employment with respect to the estimated price of childcare separately for married and single mothers. For both married and single mothers, the elasticity of full-time employment with respect to the predicted hourly price of childcare is much larger than the elasticity of part-time employment, but the employment of single mothers is more elastic with respect to the price of childcare for both full-time and part-time employment than is the employment of married mothers. The elasticity of married women's part-time employment with respect to the price of childcare is –0.082, essentially zero, whereas the elasticity of single mothers' part-time employment is –0.372; the elasticity of married women's full-time employment with respect to the price of childcare is –0.709, whereas the elasticity of single mothers' full-time employment is –1.221.[16] Thus, the pattern of single mothers' employment

---

the labor force, even if they did pay for care.) Han and Waldfogel (1999) run these preliminary equations using the SIPP data, but then estimate the employment equation with Current Population Survey. This gives them the advantage of larger sample sizes but limits somewhat the information that can be used to estimate the hourly price of childcare.

[14] Anderson and Levine (1999) conducted their analysis for a sample of mothers with children under the age of thirteen and samples limited to mothers of children under the age of six. We are reporting on their results for the latter sample since it matches more closely the analysis in the other two papers.

[15] The elasticity tells the percentage response in the probability of being employed arising from a 1 percentage change in childcare price.

[16] Powell (1998) estimated a similar model of full-time/part-time employment determinants, including an estimated price of childcare for married mothers, using only Canadian

being more responsive (as exhibited by a larger but negative elasticity) with respect to childcare costs is maintained across employment states, and the pattern of part-time employment, being more responsive with respect to childcare costs than full-time employment, is maintained across marital states.

A number of multivariate studies that have examined choice of childcare arrangement have included marital status as a control variable (for example, see Folk and Beller 1993; Chaplin et al. 1996). In these studies, married mothers are shown to be more likely to use maternal care than single mothers. Chaplin et al. also found that married mothers were more likely to use relative care than center care, holding everything else constant, while Folk and Beller found no difference between married and single women in choice between relative and center care. Connelly and Kimmel (forthcoming) also studied the choice of childcare arrangements, completely dividing the analysis of choice of childcare mode by the mother's marital status and allowing all effects to differ between the two groups. Their analysis is limited to employed mothers, so maternal care is not listed as one of the care options. For both married and single mothers of young children, many of the variables included in their analysis have a consistent effect on the mode of care chosen, indicating that parents see relative care, home-based care, and center-care as systematically different from one another. For both married and single employed mothers, increases in the price of center-based care cause a decrease in the probability of using center-based care and an increase in the probability of using relative care, while increases in the price of home-based care increase the probability of using center-based care. As was the case with employment, single mothers' choices of childcare type are substantially more sensitive to mode price than married mothers' choices. For example, the price elasticity of center-based care is –4.021 for single mothers and –2.297 for married mothers. These large elasticities signal a high level of substitution among types of care. In light of the discussion in the previous section, these findings suggest that the price elasticity of demand for childcare contains a large real income effect.

Among married mothers, higher non-self LF income (essentially higher husband's income) was also shown to increase the probability of using

---

data. Her findings are similar to those of Connelly and Kimmel forthcoming in that she finds evidence of greater elasticity of full-time employment versus part-time employment for married women. Powell's elasticity estimates in regard to price of childcare are –0.2 for part-time and –0.7 for full-time.

either home-based care or center-based care and to reduce the probability of using relative care. One explanation for this finding is that as income rises, families are less likely to use father care as their choice for non-maternal care since the total workload of the family is increased when the father provides childcare instead of a third-party provider. Families may also be less likely to use other relatives such as the children's grandparents, as the grandparents may also have high opportunity costs of time. For single mothers, no effect of higher non-self LF income is seen. Finally, for both married and single women, being more likely to be employed full-time affects the families' choice of childcare arrangements: Those who are more likely to work full-time are more likely to use center-based care and less likely to use relative care.

CONCLUSIONS

We have presented a framework for understanding the choices made by parents of young children with regard to childcare and employment. While marital status may be interrelated to these choices, we have treated marital status as given throughout the chapter and have analyzed how marital status is correlated with differences in employment and childcare decisions of parents of young children. Choices of living arrangements and welfare recipiency can also be thought of as interrelated, especially for single mothers. Important differences across marital status emerge in the propensity to use relative care, in the probability of working part-time, in the amount paid for childcare, and in the sensitivity of employment to changes in the cost of childcare. These differences are consistent with the economic framework of choice constrained by potential income, the value of time, and the availability of others to serve as childcare providers.

The policy implications of these findings are that welfare policy makers must be very careful in their assumptions concerning childcare utilization patterns of single mothers, for it is clear that the patterns of childcare use for single mothers will change as their participation in full-time employment grows. Also, because of the high expenses of childcare costs relative to family income, childcare subsidies to the employed poor (both married and single) should be more readily available. It is shortsighted for policy makers to leave a portion of the overall federal TANF block grant money unspent when it can be used to supplement the childcare funds available to the at-risk population by assisting them in purchasing reliable, quality childcare. When subsidies are available, they seem to have the desired impact, increasing the probability of employment more for single mothers than for married mothers. Finally, the lower spending on childcare by single mothers in every mode of care raises questions about the relative quality of childcare available to children of single mothers versus children of married couples.

REFERENCES

Anderson, Patricia M. and Levine, Phillip B. "Child Care and Mothers' Employment Decisions," in David E. Card and Rebecca M. Blank, eds., *Finding Jobs: Work and Welfare Reform*. New York: Russell Sage Publications, 2000, pp. 420–62.

Averett, Susan, Peters, H. Elizabeth and Waldman, Donald M. "Tax Credits, Labor Supply, and Child Care." *Review of Economics and Statistics*, 1997, *79*(1), pp. 125–35.

Becker, Gary S. "A Theory of Marriage," in T. W. Schultz, ed., *Economics of the Family*. Chicago, IL: University of Chicago Press, 1974, pp. 293–344.

Becker, Gary S., Landes, Elizabeth M. and Michael, Robert T. "An Economic Analysis of Marital Instability." *Journal of Political Economy*, 1997, *6*(4), pp. 1141–87.

Berger Mark C. and Black, Dan A. "Child Care Subsidies, Quality of Care, and the Labor Supply of Low-Income, Single Mothers. *Review of Economics and Statistic*, 1992, *74*, pp. 635–42.

Blank, Rebecca. "Simultaneously Modeling the Supply of Weeks and Hours of Work among Female Household Heads." *Journal of Labor Economics,* 1988, *6*(2), pp. 177–204.

Blau, David M. and Robins, Philip K. "Child Care Costs and Family Labor Supply." *Review of Economics and Statistics,* 1988, *70*(3), pp. 374–81.

Blau, David M. and Hagy, Alison P. "The Demand for Quality in Child Care." *Journal of Political Economy*, 1998, *106*(1), pp. 104–46.

Casper, Lynn. "My Daddy Takes Care of Me! Fathers as Care Providers." *Current Population Report*. U.S. Census Bureau P70-54, September 1997.

Chaplin, Duncan, Robins, Philip, Hofferth, Sandra, Wissoker, Douglas and Fronstin, Paul. *The Price Elasticity of Child Care Demand: A Sensitivity Analysis*. Unpublished manuscript, Urban Institute, 1996.

Connelly, Rachel. "The Cost of Child Care for Single Mothers – Its Effect on Labor Force Participation and AFDC Participation." Institute for Research on Poverty Discussion Paper, DP920-90, 1990.

———. "The Effects of Child Care Costs on Married Women's Labor Force Participation." *Review of Economics and Statistics*, 1992a, *74*(1), pp. 83–90.

———. "Self-Employment and Providing Child Care; Employment Strategies for Women with Young Children." *Demography*, April 1992b, *29*, pp. 17–29.

Connelly, Rachel and Kimmel, Jean. "Marital Status and Full-Time/Part-Time Work Status in Child Care Choices." *Applied Economics*, forthcoming.

Council of Economic Advisers. "The Economics of Child Care." December 1999.

Folk, Karen Fox and Beller, Andrea. "Part-Time Work and Child Care Choices for Mothers of Preschool Children." *Journal of Marriage and the Family*, 1993, *55*, pp. 146–57.

Fronstein, Paul, and Douglas A. Wissoker. "The Effects of the Availability of Low-Cost Child Care on the Labor Supply of Low-Income Women." Unpublished manuscript, 1994.

GAO. "Child Care Subsidies Increase Likelihood That Low-Income Mothers Will Work." United States General Accounting Office, report for the Congressional Caucus for Women's Issues, House of Representatives. GAO-HEHS: 94–20, 1994.

Grossbard-Shechtman, Shoshana. "Why Women May Be Charged More at the Cleaners: A Consumer Theory with Competitive Marriage Markets." Working Paper 99–01, Center for Public Economics, San Diego State University, 1999.

———. "A Model of Labor Supply and Marriage." Paper presented at the meetings of the American Economic Association, January 2001.

Han, Wenjui and Waldfogel, Jane. "Child Care Costs and Women's Employment. A Comparison of Single and Married Mothers with Pre-School Age Children." *Social Science Quarterly*, 2001, *82*(3): pp. 552–68.

Heckman, James J. "Effects of Child-Care Programs on Women's Work Effort." *Journal of Political Economy*, 1974, Part II (March/April), *82*(2), pp. S136–S163.

———. "Policies to Foster Human Capital," NBER Working Paper 7288, August 1999.

Hofferth, Sandra L., Brayfield, April, Deich, Sharon and Holcomb, Pamela. *National Child Care Survey 1990*. National Association for the Education of Young Children (NAEYC) Study, Urban Institute Report 91–5, 1991.

Hofferth, Sandra L. and Chaplin, Duncan D. "State Regulations and Child Care Choice." *Population Research and Policy Review*, 1998, *17*(1), pp. 111–40.

Hofferth, Sandra L. and Wissoker, Douglas A. "Price, Quality, and Income in Child Care Choice." *Journal of Human Resources,* 1992, *27*(1), pp. 70–111.

Hotz, Joseph V. and Kilburn, M. Rebecca. "Regulating Child Care: The Effects of State Regulations on Child Care Demand and Cost." Unpublished manuscript, School of Public Policy, University of Chicago, 1994.

Kimmel, Jean. "The Effectiveness of Child Care Subsidies in the Welfare to Work Transition of Low-Income Single Mothers." *American Economic Review*, 1995, *85*(2), pp. 271–5.

———. "Child Care as a Barrier to Employment for Married and Single Mothers." *Review of Economics and Statistics*, 1998, *80*(2), pp. 287–99.

Lehrer, Evelyn L. "Determinants of Child Care Modal Choice: An Economic Perspective." *Social Science Research,* 1989, *12*, pp. 69–80.

Leibowitz, Arlene, Klerman, Jacob A. and Waite, Linda J. "Employment of New Mothers and Child Care Choice." *Journal of Human Resources,* 1992, *27*(1), pp. 112–33.

Michalopoulos, Charles and Robins, Philip K. "Employment and Child-Care Choices in Canada and the United States." *Canadian Journal of Economics*, May 2000a, *33*(2), pp. 435–70.

———. "Child Care and the Supply of Labor in Canada and the United States," in William T. Alpert and Stephen A. Woodbury, eds., *Employer Benefits and*

Labor Markets in Canada and the United States. Kalamazoo MI: W. E. Upjohn Institute, 2000b.

———. "Employment and Child-Care Choices of Single-Parent Families in Canada and the United States." Unpublished manuscript, 2000b.

Michalopoulos, Charles, Robins, Philip K. and Garfinkel, Irwin. "A Structural Model of Labor Supply and Child Care Demand." *Journal of Human Resources,* 1992, *27*(1), pp. 166–203.

Moffitt, Robert. "Incentive Effects of the U.S. Welfare System: A Review." *Journal of Economic Literature*, 1992, *30*(1), pp. 1–61.

Peters, Elizabeth. "Marriage and Divorce: Informational Constraints and Private Contracting." *American Economic Review*, 1986, *76*(3), pp. 437–54.

Powell, Lisa M. "The Impact of Child Care Costs on the Labour Supply of Married Mothers: Evidence from Canada." *Canadian Journal of Economics,* 1997, *30*(3), pp. 577–94.

———. "Part-Time versus Full-Time Work and Child Care Costs: Evidence for Married Mothers." *Applied Economics*, 1998, *30*, pp. 503–11.

———. "Joint Labor Supply and Child Care Choice Decisions of Married Mothers." *Journal of Human Resources*, 2002, *37*(1), pp. 106–28.

Presser, Harriet. "Shift Work among American Women and Child Care." *Journal of Marriage and the Family*, 1986, August, pp. 551–64.

Presser, Harriet and Cox, Amy. "The Work Schedules of Low-Educated American Women and Welfare Reform." *Monthly Labor Review*, 1997, April, pp. 25–34.

Ribar, David. "Child Care and the Labor Supply of Married Women: Reduced Form Evidence." *Journal of Human Resources,* 1992, *28*(1), pp. 134–65.

Ribar, David. "A Structural Model of Child Care and the Labor Supply of Married Women." *Journal of Labor Economics,* 1995, *13*(3), pp. 558–97.

Schumacher, Rachel and Mark Greenberg. "Child Care after Leaving Welfare: Early Evidence from State Studies." Center for Law and Social Policy, October 1999.

Sonenstein, Freya. "The Child Care Preferences of Parents with Young Children," in Janet Hyse and Marilyn Essex, eds., *Parental Leave and Child Care: Setting a Research and Policy Agenda*. Philadelphia, PA: Temple University Press, 1991.

U.S. Department of Health and Human Services. "Temporary Assistance for Needy Families (TANF) Program." Second Annual Report to Congress, August 1999.

Waite, Linda, Leibowitz, Arlene and Witsberger, Christina. "What Parents Pay For: Child Care Characteristics, Quality, and Costs." *Journal of Social Issues*, 1991, *47*(2), pp. 33–48.

TWELVE

Marriage and Home-Based Paid Employment

Elizabeth Field-Hendrey and Linda N. Edwards

In recent years, the growing labor force participation of married women, coupled with their continuing household responsibilities, has led to an increased demand for a host of flexible work arrangements such as part-time work, contingent work, and work with variable scheduling. Another work arrangement that offers this flexibility, and may in addition reduce the costs of work, is home-based paid employment.[1] In this chapter, we examine the relationship between a woman's marital status and her likelihood of choosing to be a home-based worker.

Past decades have seen a steady rise in the labor force participation rates of women, from 45.9 percent in March 1975 to 59.8 percent in September 1999 (Howard Hayghe 1997; U.S. Department of Labor, Bureau of Labor Statistics 1998). The increase has been particularly noteworthy for married women, especially those with small children. Although the recession of the early 1990s led to a slowdown in the growth in women's participation rates, since 1994 women's labor force participation has once again begun to grow steadily. The biggest increase has been among women with young children, of whom the vast majority are married with a spouse present. From 1975 to 1996, the participation rate for mothers whose youngest child was in school rose 22 percent, and the rate for mothers of preschoolers rose 24 percent (Hayghe 1997).

---

[1] Throughout this chapter, we will use the term "home-based work" to mean work at home for pay, either as an employee or as a self-employed worker, as opposed to unpaid household production.

Funding for this research was provided in part by the National Science Foundation, Grant No. SBR-9320820. We thank Andrew Beveridge, Susan Weber, and Wonchan Lee for their assistance in preparing and analyzing the Public Use Microdata Sample (PUMS) data.

Despite this growth in labor force participation, women remain largely responsible for the care of family and home. This "second shift" adds about twenty hours to the total weekly work hours of women who are in the labor force, in contrast to just seven hours for comparable men (Joni Hersch and Leslie S. Stratton 1994). The multiple responsibilities of employed women translate into a need for greater flexibility in all aspects of the employment arrangement. For example, in a recent survey of employees concerning their child and elder care responsibilities, work flexibility was a factor that significantly reduced the stress associated with performing their dual roles of earner and caretaker (Margaret B. Neal et al. 1993).

One way in which married women can achieve this flexibility is through home-based paid employment. The number of people doing home-based work (people whose primary workplace is the home rather than an office or other place of business), while small, has been growing, and in 1990 comprised 3.4 million people (U.S. Bureau of the Census 1993, Table 12.18).[2] Recent evidence suggests that this number is likely to be substantially larger in the next Census. Data from a May 1997 supplement to the Current Population Survey indicate that more than 4.1 million of the nonagricultural self-employed reported that they were working in home-based businesses. This number is greater than *all* home-based workers in 1990, self-employed and employees combined (U.S. Department of Labor, Bureau of Labor Statistics 1998).[3]

These developments are particularly important for women, and especially for married women.[4] In 1990, women comprised 59 percent of all home-based workers, but accounted for just 46 percent of "on-site" workers (people who worked at an establishment away from home). Furthermore, female home-based workers were much more likely to be married than were on-site workers: Among home-based women workers, 80.4 percent were married, whereas for on-site workers, this percentage

[2] Data from the U.S. Censuses of Population show that the declining trend in the number of home-based workers from 1960 to 1980 was reversed in 1990, from 4.7 million in 1960 to 2.2 million in 1980, to 3.4 million in 1990. (The data for 1960 and 1980 come from Hillary Silver 1989, and the data for 1990 come from U.S. Bureau of the Census 1993, Table 18.)

[3] Moreover, the number of people who take any of their work home is much greater. Again referring to the May 1997 supplement to the Current Population Survey, 17.8 percent of all nonagricultural workers did some job-related work at home for their primary job, and for self-employed workers this proportion is 30.1 percent.

[4] We use the term "married" to denote women who are married with a spouse present (MSP) and "unmarried" to include women who are unmarried (whether never married or divorced) and those who are married but not living with their spouse.

was 63.5. Clearly, there is something that makes the home-based work arrangement attractive to married women. In contrast, home-based work and marriage do not appear to be related for men: Male home-based workers showed the same probability of being married as male on-site workers, 69 percent.

Why do married women choose home-based work for pay more often than unmarried women do? We suggest that not only does marriage per se make home-based work more attractive, but that married women are more likely to have characteristics that predispose them to home-based work, such as having small children or living in a rural area. These characteristics, we argue, are associated with high "fixed costs" of employment on-site. These fixed costs include the time and out-of-pocket costs associated with getting to a job (commuting time and costs, for example), the cost of childcare while getting to and from the work site, and clothing costs. Furthermore, married women, who are constrained by their husband's work location, may have higher costs of on-site work because they have less discretion over their place of residence than unmarried women. That is, if the husband's work tends to dominate the family's decision concerning the location of the family home, either because of the traditional male role of breadwinner or because men continue to earn more than women, married women may experience a more lengthy (and costly) commute to an on-site work location. The latter difference may partly explain why married men, in contrast to married women, are no more likely than unmarried men to be home-based.

BACKGROUND

Home-based work for pay has long been a controversial form of work organization, and, for much of the postwar period, was subject to restrictive legislation. For example, from the early 1940s until January 1989, industrial homework was banned in seven industries: women's apparel, jewelry manufacturing, knitted outerwear, gloves and mittens, button and buckle manufacturing, handkerchief manufacturing, and embroidery. These bans were established in response to evidence that in these industries both minimum wage and child labor laws were being routinely violated for home-based wage workers (*Federal Register* 1988). The only exceptions permitted were for workers who were disabled or too old to get to a place of business, or workers who had to care for the disabled. In these exceptional cases, special certificates had to be obtained from the Department of Labor (Regulation 29 CFR Part 530).

These bans remained virtually unchanged until the early 1980s, when the Reagan administration initiated actions that led to their removal. Effective January 9, 1989, the bans were lifted in all seven industries except women's apparel and "unsafe" jewelry production (the ban on homework in knitted outerwear had been lifted effective December 5, 1984).[5] Paradoxically, at the same time that existing bans on industrial homework were being dismantled, the Service Employees International Union (SEIU) was calling for the introduction of a new ban – this time on clerical rather than industrial homework, and especially when it involved the use of home computers.[6] Even into the early 1990s, unions continued to resist the growth of home-based work (*Wall Street Journal* 1992).

Despite past controversy, however, home-based work for pay and a host of other nonstandard work arrangements are becoming more accepted. More now than in the past, workers are seeking – and employers are providing – work arrangements that permit flexibility in many dimensions. The new language both of the labor market and of human resource management reflects the variety of these arrangements: flextime, contingent work, the alternative workplace, compressed work schedules, job sharing, and flexplace.[7] A recent annual research volume of the Industrial Relations Research Association, entitled *Nonstandard Work: The Nature and Challenges of Changing Employment Arrangements* (2000), focuses on documenting and explaining the emergence of these alternative arrangements and the decline of more traditional work. Even the *Harvard Business Review* has devoted an article to new forms of work organization, entitled "The Alternative Workplace: Changing Where and How People Work" (Mahlon Apgar IV 1998). Further, recent increases in the employment-to-population ratio suggest that the growth in the

---

[5] The revised Regulation 29 CFR Parts 516 and 530 appear in *Federal Register* (1988). Also included in this publication is a detailed review of all of the proposed rule changes beginning with that of May 11, 1981, and a precis of all of the comments received at the various hearings conducted up until the promulgation of the 1989 rule.

[6] See the letter submitted for the record by Jackie Ruft, executive director of District 925 of SEIU, in U.S. House of Representatives (1986). At present we are aware of just one union contract covering home-based workers. It is between Local 2412 of the Wisconsin State Employees Union and the University of Wisconsin's Hospital and Clinics in Madison, Wisconsin (Kathleen E. Christensen 1990).

[7] For example, the Dun and Bradstreet *17th Survey of American Small Business* surveys firms on their use of such alternative arrangements. It defines flexplace as an arrangement that "enables employees to work from a different location – such as from home" (Appendix I).

acceptability of nonstandard work arrangements may be drawing into the labor force new demographic groups – such as married women with small children – who would be less likely to participate if they were to be restricted to conventional work environments. And the tightness of the labor market in the late 1990s, with the unemployment rate falling to a twenty-five-year low, undoubtedly made firms ever more willing to accommodate workers' desires for more flexibility.

The specific nonstandard work arrangement that we focus on, home-based work, sometimes termed "telecommuting" or "telework," is clearly on the increase. In acknowledgment of the importance of this work arrangement, the U.S. Department of Labor held a conference in October 2000 entitled *Telework: The New Workplace of the 21ˢᵗ Century,* the proceedings of which were published in 2000 in a conference volume of the same name. The conference brought together the nation's experts in telework from academia, government, and business. Because all of these experts did not use the same definition of what is meant by telework, the range of their estimates of the number of teleworkers in the United States was broad, from 13 to almost 20 million in 1999 (p. 11). What was very clear, however, no matter what definition or data set was used, is that the number of such workers, however defined, has been growing dramatically over the past decade.

The three basic themes addressed by the papers in the conference were telework's potential (1) to help employers cope with a skills shortage, (2) to help workers meet family obligations, and (3) to help society achieve greater workplace diversity (p. vi). This chapter ties in with the first two of those themes by investigating how home-based work facilitates the entry of married women into the paid labor force while still enabling them to meet family obligations. In fact, many of the speakers at the *Telework* conference, in their discussion of individuals' motivation to telework, pointed to the opportunities for a "work-life" balance (p. 84) and the importance of "gender and family life cycle stage" (p. 75) in identifying the reasons that people choose telework. One speaker, Naomi Gerstel, raised not only the issue of how the "experiences of men and women working for pay at home [were] different," but noted that "women working at home for pay typically do not receive employer-provided workplace benefits" (p. 120). Her comment highlights yet another reason why home-based work may be an especially viable alternative for married women: Unlike unmarried women, they are in a position to access fringe benefits provided through their spouses' employment. Despite the wide variety of issues discussed in the *Telework* conference, evidence about the determinants of the decision to engage in home-based work was largely qualitative and descriptive. No systematic quantitative analysis of the workplace decision was presented and none of the papers specifically focused on married women, as we do in this chapter.

AN ECONOMIC MODEL OF CHOICE OF WORK SITE

In order to understand the relationship between a woman's marital status and her choice of work site, we make use of a model of work site choice that we developed in earlier research (Linda N. Edwards and Elizabeth Field-Hendrey 2002). This model takes as a starting point the study by John F. Cogan (1981), which shows that the existence of fixed costs, in time and money, of working raise the reservation wage (defined as the minimum wage at which a person is willing to enter the labor market) compared to what it would be in the absence of these costs. Since the fixed money and time costs of paid employment are lower for home-based work than for on-site work, Cogan's model leads directly to the conclusion that individuals will have a lower threshold wage for choosing to enter the labor market as a home-based worker than as an on-site worker.

Our model generalizes Cogan's simple framework by (1) explicitly permitting women a choice between home-based and on-site work, and (2) allowing for the possibility of a different, most likely lower, wage in home-based work than on-site work.[8] In addition, we incorporate the possibility of joint production (or production complementarities) between labor-market output of a home-based worker and her household work, such as child or elder care, by specifying that there is some level of household production per hour of home-based work.

---

[8] We expect the wage that a woman with a given set of skills can expect to earn in home-based work to be lower than what she would earn in on-site work because it is likely that the demand for home-based wage workers is low relative to the demand for on-site workers and relative to the supply of people who would like to do home-based work. There are four reasons why we expect the demand for home-based workers to be relatively low. First, home-based jobs may simply not be available in certain types of industries, such as those that require large amounts of fixed capital or require workers to be on-site to interact with customers. Heavy manufacturing, retail trade, and elementary and secondary schooling are examples. Second, a worker's marginal product may be lower in home-based work because of synergies among workers. Third, a worker's marginal product may be lower at home because of the lack of monitoring or supervision. Finally, employers may simply hold a belief (or suspicion) that a worker's marginal product is lower when she is at home than when she is on-site, possibly because of the difficulty in monitoring home-based employees.

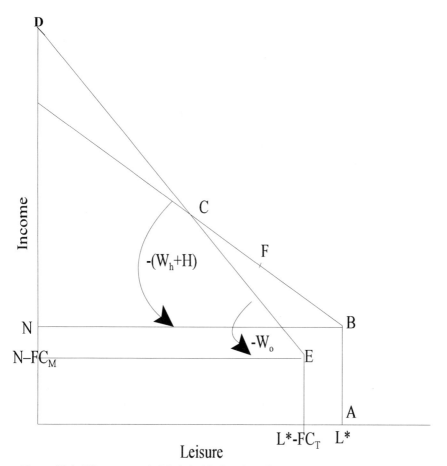

Figure 12.1. Diagrammatic Model of Labor Supply by Work Site

Our model is illustrated in Figure 12.1. In this figure, N represents unearned income, L^* represents the total time available, FC_M represents the monetary fixed cost of working on-site (such as commuting costs), FC_T represents the time costs of working on-site (such as commuting time), W_h and W_o represent the hourly earnings a woman can expect for home-based and on-site work, respectively, and H represents the monetary value of household production per hour of home-based paid employment.[9] We assume for the purposes of the diagram that $W_h + H < W_o$,[10] and that the

---

[9] We assume in the diagram that H is zero for on-site work, although the econometric model allows for the possibility of nonzero values.

[10] It is possible that for some individuals that $W_h + H > W_o$, in which case home-based work would dominate on-site work for these individuals, and if they chose to be in the labor force, it would only be as a home-based worker.

monetary and time fixed costs of home-based work are zero. The budget constraint is ABFCD. Depending on the woman's indifference map, she may locate at point B and be out of the labor force, she may locate on the segment BC and be a home-based worker, or she may locate on the segment CD and be an on-site worker. In this model, the reservation wage and reservation hours (the minimum number of hours that a person is willing to work and remain in the labor force) will be lower for home-based work than for on-site work.[11] This lower reservation wage for home-based work translates into an increased likelihood that a woman actually participates in the labor force. Put differently, the figure illustrates that the presence of the home-based work option leads some women who would have chosen to be out of the labor force to enter as a home-based worker.

We can also use this figure to make clear the role of varying fixed costs on the choice between home-based and on-site work for pay, as follows. The larger the fixed costs, the further to the left will be the on-site segment of the budget constraint (CD), the less likely a person with a given indifference map will find it optimal to be on the on-site segment, and the more likely she will either be a home-based worker or out of the labor force. Therefore, if married women are more likely to have high fixed costs of working on-site, our model implies that there will be a higher rate of home-based work for pay among such women.

The role in labor force choices of the value of joint household production (H) while engaged in paid work at home can also be illustrated using Figure 12.1. The higher H, the lower the woman's reservation wage for home-based work (the reservation wage is the absolute value of the slope of the indifference curve at point B less the value H). Thus, a higher H will increase the probability that a woman enters the labor force as a home-based worker. H may be higher for married women, for two reasons: (1) Home productivity may be higher and/or (2) the value that a household places on home production may be higher. Since we expect that married women both will have more scope for household productivity and will place a higher value on home production as compared to unmarried women,[12] we again predict that a larger proportion of married women than unmarried women will be home-based workers in the labor force.

---

[11] See Edwards and Field-Hendrey (2002) for a full discussion of these propositions.

[12] In the context of the model of marriage markets developed by Shoshana Grossbard-Shechtman, the value that a household places on home productivity is a "quasiwage" y, for home production time paid by a spouse or other household member. See, for example, Grossbard-Shechtman (forthcoming). One could argue that it is likely that $y_{married} > y_{unmarried}$, making H higher for married women.

WHAT DO THE DATA SHOW?

To investigate the relationship between marital status and home-based work for pay, we use data from the 5 percent Public Use Microdata Sample (PUMS) of housing units from the 1990 Census of population of the United States.[13] Included in our analysis are all women aged twenty-five to fifty-five years who were either employed or out of the labor force, who did not live in group quarters, who were not in the armed forces, and who were not in school.[14] Identification of home-based workers is derived from answers to the journey to work question (No. 23A), which asked, "How did this person usually get to work last week?"[15] Persons who responded to this question that they "worked at home" are defined for the purposes of this study as home-based workers. Thus, our sample of home-based workers includes only those who worked primarily at home and excludes those who worked mainly on-site but did some work at home. Note that our sample includes both employees and the self-employed. We focus on women in the prime working years, twenty-five to fifty-five, so as not to confuse the work site decision with decisions regarding schooling and retirement.[16]

The distribution of women across the three work states that we consider is shown in Table 12.1, compared to the same distribution for men. Consistent with the preceding discussion, Table 12.1 documents that married women are indeed more likely than unmarried women to be home-based workers. In fact, they are twice as likely as unmarried women to choose this work arrangement (2.4 percent versus 1.2 percent). For men, in contrast, the proportion of home-based workers is about the same regardless of their marital status. Notice also that married women are more likely

---

[13] The data and sampling procedure are fully described in U.S. Bureau of the Census (1992).

[14] We exclude unemployed women from the analysis because we have no way of determining their desired work site. In addition, we exclude those women whose class of worker information is not consistent with their reported earnings – for example, someone who reports herself as self-employed in 1990, yet reports wage and salary income for 1989.

[15] Persons who used more than one mode of transportation were requested to identify the one used for most of the distance.

[16] To obtain approximately equal sample sizes for the three groups in the sample (on-site workers, home-based workers, and women out of the labor force), we use all observations of home-based workers from the 5 percent PUMS, while for women who are on-site workers or who are out of the labor force, we take a .04 subsample of the 5 percent PUMS, yielding a 0.2 percent sample of the population of on-site workers and women out of the labor force.

Table 12.1 *Percentage of Individuals Age
Twenty-Five to Fifty-Five in Each Labor Force
Class, by Sex and Marital Status*

	Out of labor force	On-site	Home-based
Female			
Married	32.2	65.4	2.4
Unmarried	21.1	77.7	1.2
Male			
Married	5.2	93.2	1.6
Unmarried	13.6	84.9	1.5

than married men (or unmarried men) to be home-based workers. Thus, these data indicate that home-based work for pay is a relatively more attractive work alternative for married women than for unmarried women or for married or unmarried men.

The model illustrated in Figure 12.1 demonstrates that the attractiveness of home-based work for married women results from the much lower (perhaps even zero) fixed costs that they incur when they engage in home-based work as compared to on-site work, and their greater opportunity for engaging in joint household production while working at home for pay. Our next step, then, is to examine a set of variables that proxy these factors to see whether, in fact, they do differ between married and unmarried women.

To proxy the fixed costs of working on-site, we select variables that reflect the care-giving responsibilities of women and the costs of traveling to work. To capture the care-giving responsibilities of women, we include three variables: whether a woman has preschool children under six years of age; whether she has school-age children six to seventeen; and whether there is a person over age sixty-five living in the household.[17] To capture the costs of traveling to work, we include variables that represent

---

[17] Two of these characteristics, having children age six to seventeen and having someone in the household over sixty-five, may not be unambiguously associated with an increase in fixed costs. If older children and elderly relatives function as low-cost babysitters when parents are away from home, these characteristics may be associated with a *reduction* rather than an increase in fixed costs. Alternatively, older children or elderly family members might act as unpaid family workers, making home-based work more lucrative and therefore relatively more attractive than on-site work. In sum, the relationship between these two characteristics and the probabilities of being in the various labor force states cannot be unambiguously predicted.

whether a woman lives in a rural area[18] and whether she has a physical disability. We also include a variable indicating whether a woman lives on a farm, since persons living on farms have a prime opportunity to engage in farming, the oldest form of home-based work. In addition, marriage itself may be associated with higher costs of working. Unlike unmarried women, married women must consider the work location of a spouse as well as their own work site, and therefore may be less able to coordinate the location of their residence and their work site in a way that reduces commuting costs.

Some of the same characteristics used to proxy fixed costs of working on-site also reflect a woman's joint household productivity while she is doing paid work at home: whether there are children in either age group or someone over sixty-five in the household and whether the woman is married. These measures reflect the family's potential demand for caretaking and other services in the home, services that a woman may be able to perform at the same time she is doing paid work at home. For example, a woman may be able to respond to the occasional needs of a school-age child or an elderly relative while engaged in home-based work, whereas doing so would be much more difficult if she were away from home. Similarly, a married home-based worker might find it worthwhile to prepare food at home in a way that requires intermittent, but not constant attention, whereas a single woman or a married couple who both work outside the home might opt to purchase such meal-preparation services.

Everything else equal, these joint productivity/fixed-cost characteristics are expected to be more prevalent among married women than unmarried women. In addition, we examine demographic factors that may affect the value that a household places on home production: race and ethnicity. Shoshana Grossbard-Shechtman (1995) argues that because the marriage market is not as favorable for black women as for white women, black women might obtain fewer benefits from engaging in marital home production.[19] If so, home-based work will be a less attractive option for

---

[18] One might expect wage offers to be lower in rural areas, at least for on-site work. In addition, living in a rural area may be related to the cost of running a home-based business, because zoning laws regarding home-based businesses are likely to be less restrictive in rural areas, and real estate values lower. These factors, along with increased commuting costs, will raise the probability of home-based work for rural residents.

[19] If black women face a poorer marriage market, they might have a weaker bargaining position with respect to the division of labor within the household, and hence what Grossbard-Shechtman terms their "quasiwage" for home production might be lower than that earned by white women, even after controlling for income.

Table 12.2 *Percentages of Women Age Twenty-Five to Fifty-Five Exhibiting Fixed-Cost/Joint Productivity and Personal Characteristics, by Marital Status*

Characteristic	Unmarried	Married	Difference
Presence of children under 6*	10.73	29.02	18.29
Presence of children 6–17*	26.61	48.60	21.39
Disabled*	10.44	4.95	–5.49
Urban residence*	84.54	71.01	–13.53
Rural residence, non-farm*	14.93	27.23	12.30
Rural residence, farm*	0.53	1.76	1.23
Presence of person over 65*	9.84	3.40	–6.44
White, non-Hispanic*	66.93	82.25	15.32
Black, non-Hispanic*	21.27	6.74	–14.53
Hispanic*	8.53	6.99	–1.54
Other race*	3.27	4.02	0.75

Note: For those characteristics marked with an asterisk (*), differences in the proportions of married and unmarried women exhibiting these characteristics are statistically significant at a 1 percent significance level.

black married women than for white married women. We also investigated this marriage market hypothesis for Hispanic women, and women of other race and ethnicity (not white, black or Hispanic).

Table 12.2 shows the proportion of married and of unmarried women with the characteristics previously discussed. If our speculations are correct, we expect that the proportions of married women with children, with elderly people in the household, who are living in rural and rural farm areas, and who are disabled to be greater than the corresponding proportions for unmarried women. If the marriage market hypothesis is correct, we expect the proportion of blacks and Hispanics to be lower among married than unmarried women.

These characteristics, of course, are not indicators just of fixed costs, the value of joint household and labor market productivity, or marriage market opportunities, but may themselves affect the likelihood that a woman is married. The simple univariate analysis in Table 12.2, however, provides us with a starting point to investigate whether married women do indeed have characteristics that make home-based work a relatively more attractive work option.

On the whole, the statistics in Table 12.2 are supportive of our hypotheses. We find that, overall, married women are more likely to exhibit characteristics that reflect higher fixed costs of work, greater scope for joint household/labor-market productivity, and superior marriage market opportunities. Married women are more likely than unmarried women to have preschool children (29.02 percent versus 10.73 percent); to have school-age children (48.60 percent versus 26.61 percent); and to live in rural areas (27.23 percent versus 14.93 percent) or farm areas (1.76 percent versus 0.53 percent). We also find that racial and ethnic differences between the married and unmarried are consistent with our hypothesis that black non-Hispanic and Hispanic women have poorer marriage market opportunities than white women and therefore may find home-based work less attractive.

Two of the proxy measures we examine, however, being disabled and having someone over sixty-five in the household, are significantly more prevalent among unmarried women than among married women. A plausible explanation is that these two measures are not just indicators of higher fixed costs of working and greater potential for joint household/labor market productivity, but are themselves important determinants of the likelihood of being married. For example, disabled women may have fewer opportunities in the marriage market and therefore be less likely to be represented in the population of married women (though once married, they may find home-based work a desirable labor force alternative for the reasons that we have outlined). Similarly, women who have someone over sixty-five in the household may include a disproportionate number of women who chose never to marry and have remained with their parents.

Given the interrelationships between the fixed-cost/home productivity variables and marital status, the next step in our analysis is to use multivariate techniques to examine the impact of these variables on the probability that married and unmarried women choose home-based work. In particular, we compute separate estimates for married and unmarried women of the effects of each of these variables on the probability of being a home-based worker. The analysis is carried out in a multivariate context in order to isolate the effects of each variable. We use a multinomial logit model, which is an econometric technique that takes account of the fact that the choice variable (whether to be a home-based or on-site worker) is categorical rather than continuous. We estimate the probability that a woman will choose one of three work states – being out of the labor force, working on-site, and working at home for pay – as a function of the woman's characteristics. This approach allows us to examine the direct effect of each of the characteristics in Table 12.2 while holding constant all

Table 12.3 *Predicted Probability of Home-Based Work for Pay by Marital Status*

Characteristic	Unmarried	Married	Effect of marriage
Base probability of being a home-based worker	1.87	2.12	+0.25
Effect of having children under 6	+0.30	+1.30	+1.00
Effect of having children 6–17	−0.30	+0.55	+0.85
Effect of disability	−0.52	+0.21	+0.73
Difference, rural, non-farm – urban	+0.56	+0.18	−0.38
Difference, farm – rural, non-farm	+5.08	+6.16	+1.08
Difference, farm – urban	+5.64	+6.34	+0.70
Effect of having person(s) over 65	+0.09	+0.04	−0.05
Difference, black, N-H – white, N-H	−1.05	−1.79	−0.74
Difference, Hispanic – white, N-H	+0.96	−1.16	−2.12
Difference, other race – white, N-H	+0.31	−1.04	−1.35

Note: Probabilities are computed using the logit coefficients presented in Appendix Table 12.4.

of the remaining characteristics, as well as a host of other socioeconomic and demographic factors that affect labor force and marriage decisions.

The resulting estimates appear in Table 12.3. The entries in Table 12.3 are predicted probabilities of home-based work associated with the characteristics listed in Table 12.2 for unmarried women (in the first column) and married women (in the second column) and the marital differential in these characteristics, that is, the differential effect of those characteristics for married and unmarried women (in the third column). The probabilities are predicted for an archetypal "average" woman; that is, in the computations that generate these estimates for each characteristic, the values of all other characteristics are set at their sample averages. Base probabilities of being a home-based worker for the archetypal married and unmarried woman (computed at a common set of sample means) appear in the first row of the table.[20]

The estimates in Table 12.3 confirm many of our predictions. Factors associated with higher fixed costs of on-site paid work and joint household/labor-market productivity do have a larger positive impact

---

[20] The probabilities are derived from the multinomial logit coefficients in Appendix Table 12.4. For a detailed explanation of how the probabilities are derived, see Edwards and Field-Hendrey 2002.

on the probability of home-based work for married women than for unmarried women. First, notice that marital status in and of itself raises the probability of home-based work from 1.87 percent to 2.12 percent. That is, everything else equal, a married woman is 13 percent (0.25/1.87) more likely than an unmarried woman to be a home-based worker.[21] Next, the presence of children has a higher impact on the probability of home-based work for married women than for unmarried women, and this marital differential is statistically significant.[22] The increase in the probability of being a home-based worker associated with having preschool children is more than four times greater for married women than for unmarried women (1.30 percentage points versus 0.3 percentage points). Similarly, having school-age children is associated with a larger increase in the probability of home-based work for married women than for not-married women (0.55 percentage points versus –0.30 percentage points). Having a disability also has a differential impact by marital status: It is associated with a reduced probability of home-based work for unmarried women and an increased probability for married women, the net effect being that married women have a 0.73 percentage point higher probability of being home-based workers (and this marital differential is statistically significant).[23]

[21] There are several explanations for this difference between married and unmarried women. First, married women are more likely to have access to spousal fringe benefits. Home-based workers, who are mostly self-employed, are not likely to get these fringe benefits. This suggests that married women with children may be able to choose to work at home, without having to sacrifice health benefits for their children, for example, because they can get them through their spouse. Second, married women have access to additional income through their spouse. They may, for example, be able to finance the startup costs of a home-based business, and thereby be able to be home with their children while still working for pay. Or they may simply be better able to afford to trade off the lower earnings in home-based work for the opportunity to combine work for pay with time spent with their children. This is consistent with our findings concerning the effect of unearned income (family income less the woman's earnings) on home-based work. We find that for an average woman, whether married or unmarried, an increase in income raises the probability of home-based work and lowers the probability of on-site work.

[22] Because the logit coefficient of the variable representing the interaction of marital status and the presence of children is statistically significant for the home-based work category, we infer that the difference in probabilities computed in Table 12.3 is also statistically significant. We draw a similar conclusion for any other variables with a statistically significant interaction coefficient.

[23] Contrast this result with the results in Table 12.2, where we found that married women were less likely to be disabled than unmarried women, rather than vice versa. We speculated that the reason for the finding in Table 12.2 was that the marriage market for

The relationship between the other variables in Table 12.3 and the labor force participation/work site decision also differs by marital status, but the marital differentials are not always statistically significant or in the direction we predicted. Living in a rural area raises the probability of home-based wage work more for unmarried women than for married women, so that the net effect of marriage in this case is negative rather than positive, although the difference is not statistically significant. For women living on a farm, however, marriage has a positive impact on the probability of being a home-based worker, but here too the difference by marital status is not statistically significant. In the case of having a person over sixty-five in the household, the effect of marriage is again negative rather than positive, but here too the difference by marital status is not statistically significant. One possible explanation for the latter finding is that this variable is an ambiguous measure of fixed costs of working; the older person in the household, instead of needing care, may serve as a caretaker, facilitating on-site work.

Racial and ethnic characteristics do affect the probability that a woman will choose to work at home for pay, and the effects of those characteristics differ by marital status, much in the way suggested by Grossbard-Shechtman's (1995) marriage market theory. For both married and unmarried women, being black non-Hispanic lowers the probability of home-based work, compared to white non-Hispanics, but the impact is much larger for married women (–1.79 versus –1.05), and this difference is statistically significant. Being Hispanic raises the probability of home-based work relative to whites for unmarried women, but lowers the probability of home-based work relative to whites for married women. As with blacks, the marital differential is negative and significant. For nonwhite women of other ethnicities, the results are similar to those for Hispanic women, but the differences by marital status are not statistically significant.

CONCLUSIONS

Home-based work for pay is a work arrangement that offers flexibility to working women with many responsibilities. It lowers the time and

---

disabled women was likely to be poorer. Looking at the effects of disability and marital status jointly, as we do with this multivariate analysis, allows us to observe the independent effects of disability on the probability of home-based work within the married and unmarried subsets of women.

money costs of working and provides a richer set of options to coordinate work and family responsibilities. It is not surprising, therefore, that married women are more likely than unmarried women to choose home-based wage work. Marriage in and of itself may explain some of these differences. Married women typically have greater home responsibilities and more scope for combining the needs of the home and family with home-based work. But we also find that married women tend to have personal characteristics that we believe are associated with high costs of working – small children, living in a rural area, living on a farm – that also contribute to the probability that they would choose to work at home. In the case of preschool or school-age children, the effect is reinforced because not only are married women more likely to have children, but having children has a stronger effect on the probability of home-based work for these women. In contrast, for some racial and ethnic groups, marriage does not raise the probability of home-based work, perhaps because minority women face a less advantageous marriage market and consequently view the possibility of joint market and household production as less valuable. Grossbard-Shechtman (1995) uses the same reasoning to explain why black women's labor force participation responds less to changes in their husband's income than is the case with white women.

Our results from the Census of Population demonstrate at the macro level what has been revealed in detailed interviews with home-based wage workers. A survey of twenty-four professional and clerical women in the New York City area who use some type of computer technology in their home-based work cited the following advantages of their work arrangement: the flexibility and autonomy in structuring their work and the financial benefits associated with not going to an office (Christensen 1985). Not surprisingly, many mothers with young children said that they would not be in the labor force at all if they could not work at home for pay.

We foresee that home-based work for pay will be increasingly attractive as technology continues to make it ever more feasible and as changes in the population and the economy increase the number of women workers. And home-based work will be especially appealing to married women, who will continue to opt for a work arrangement that enables them to juggle their many responsibilities. Our results further suggest that home-based employment may also become more common among married men as they begin to take on more child-rearing and other responsibilities related to home production.

Table 12.4 *(Appendix): Multinomial Logit Coefficients*

Variable	On-site workers	Home-based workers
Constant	−3.35**	−9.05**
Age	0.20**	0.32**
Age squared	−0.002**	−0.004**
Years of education	0.01	−0.20**
Years of education squared	0.02**	0.02**
Age* education	−0.003**	−0.0004
Unearned income	−0.01**	0.005**
Presence of children under 6 (CU6)	−1.19**	−0.76**
Presence of children 6–17 (C617)	−0.42**	−0.51**
Disabled	−2.67**	−1.91**
Rural residence	−0.23**	0.10
Farm residence	−0.34	0.97**
Presence of person over 65	−0.12	−0.05
Spouse disabled	−0.26**	−0.52**
Black, non-Hispanic	−0.64**	−1.29**
Hispanic	−0.56**	−0.45
Other race	−0.71**	−0.41**
Married, spouse present (MSP)	2.49**	2.60**
Age* MSP	−0.09**	−0.18**
(Age squared)* MSP	0.0003	0.002**
Education* MSP	−0.05	0.31**
(Education squared)* MSP	−0.009**	−0.02**
Age*education* MSP	0.004**	0.007
Unearned income* MSP	−0.002	−0.009**
CU6* MSP	−0.07	0.46**
C617* MSP	0.12*	0.54**
Disabled* MSP	0.87**	0.99**
Rural* MSP	0.16**	−0.06
Farm* MSP	0.11	0.26
Person over 65* MSP	0.03	−0.004
Black, non-Hispanic* MSP	1.07**	0.41**
Hispanic* MSP	0.45**	−0.65**
Other Race* MSP	0.56**	−0.23

Notes: All logit coefficients refer to the odds of being in the specified labor force category versus being out of the labor force. Estimates are weighted to adjust for choice-based sampling and the non-random nature of the 1990 PUMS.

  * denotes significance at the 5 percent level in a two-tailed test.

 ** denotes significance at the 1 percent level in a two-tailed test.

REFERENCES

Apgar, Mahlon, IV. "The Alternative Workplace: Changing Where and How People Work." *Harvard Business Review*, May–June 1998, *76*(3), pp. 121–36.

Christensen, Kathleen E. "Impacts of Computer–Mediated Home-Based Work on Women and Their Families." Mimeo, CUNY Graduate Center, June 1985.

————. "Re-evaluating Union Policy toward Home-Based Work." Mimeo, CUNY Graduate Center, 1990.

Cogan, John F. "Fixed Costs and Labor Supply." *Econometrica*, July 1981, *49*(4), pp. 945–63.

Dun and Bradstreet. *17th Survey of American Small Business.* Murray Hill, NJ, 1998.

Edwards, Linda N. and Field-Hendrey, Elizabeth. "Home-Based Work and Women's Labor Force Decisions." *Journal of Labor Economics*, January 2002, *20*(1), pp. 170–200.

Federal Register, November 10, 1988, *53*(213), pp. 45706–27 (reprint, incorporates corrections printed in *Federal Register* on November 17, 1988).

Grossbard-Shechtman, Shoshana. "Marriage Markets and Black/White Differences in Labor, Marriage, and Welfare." Unpublished paper, San Diego State University and University of California, San Diego, 1995.

————. "Why Women May Be Charged More at the Cleaners: A Consumer Theory with Competitive Markets for Work in Marriage." *Journal of Socio-Economics*, forthcoming.

Hayghe, Howard. "Developments in Women's Labor Force Participation." *Monthly Labor Review*, September 1997, *120*(9), pp. 41–6.

Hersch, Joni and Stratton, Leslie S. "Wages and the Division of Housework Time for Employed Spouses." *American Economic Review, Papers and Proceedings*, 1994, *84*, pp. 118–25.

Hutchens, Robert, Jakubson, George and Schwartz, Saul. "AFDC and the Formation of Subfamilies." *Journal of Human Resources.* Fall 1989, *24*, pp. 599-628.

Industrial Relations Research Association. *Nonstandard Work: The Nature and Challenges of Changing Employment Arrangements*. Champaign, IL: Industrial Relations Research Association, 2000.

Neal, Margaret B., Chapman, Nancy J., Ingersoll-Dayton, Berit and Emlen, Arthur C. *Balancing Work and Caregiving for Children, Adults, and Elders.* Newbury Park, CA: Sage Publications, 1993.

Silver, Hillary. "The Demand for Homework: Evidence from the U.S. Census," in Eileen Boris and Cynthia R. Daniels, eds., *Homework: Historical and Contemporary Perspectives on Paid Labor at Home*. Urbana IL: University of Illinois Press, 1989.

U.S. Bureau of Labor Statistics. "Labor Force Statistics from the Current Population Survey." cpsinfo@bls.gov, accessed October 20, 1999.

U.S. Bureau of the Census. *1990 Census of Population and Housing: Public Use Microdata Samples U.S. Technical Documentation*. Washington, DC: Bureau of the Census, 1992.

U.S. Bureau of the Census. *1990 Census of Population: Social and Economic Characteristics: United States.* Washington, DC: USGPO, 1993.

U.S. Department of Labor. *Telework: The New Workplace of the 21ˢᵗ Century*. Washington, DC: USGPO, 2000.

U.S. Department of Labor, Bureau of Labor Statistics. "Work at Home in 1997." News Release USDL 98-93, March 11, 1998.

U.S. House of Representatives, Subcommittee of the Committee on Government Operations, Hearing, "Pros and Cons of Home-Based Clerical Work," February 26, 1986. Washington, DC: USGPO, 1986.

Wall Street Journal. "Union Resistance Could Slow the Growth of 'Telecommuting.'" September 22, 1992, p. A1, col. 5.

PART IV

MARRIAGE AND THE MACROECONOMY

THIRTEEN

Married Households and Gross Household Product

Duncan Ironmonger and Faye Soupourmas

The measurement of household production is an exciting new field for empirical economic research and analysis. There is growing interest in research on macroeconomic importance of the value added by households using their own unpaid labor and their own capital. Governments in many countries (such as Australia, Canada, Finland, Germany, Italy, New Zealand, and Norway) have been providing millions of dollars for their national statistical offices to collect regular data on household time use. These data then help provide estimates of Gross Household Product (GHP), the value added by unpaid labor and household capital (Duncan S. Ironmonger 1996a, 2001).

This chapter provides estimates of the value of GHP contributed by married households. The estimates could be called "Married Households GHP." The chapter also provides estimates of the GHP produced by unmarried households. The GHP estimates are for Australia for the twelve months to June 30, 1994, and are probably the first estimates for any country of the contribution of married households to household production. In macroeconomic terms, while married households were 63 percent of all households, they contained 74 percent of the adult population and produced 75 percent of GHP.

The structure and detail of this chapter owe a great deal to the suggestions by the editor of this volume, Shoshana Grossbard-Shechtman. Any remaining imperfections are due to the authors.

293

MARRIED AND UNMARRIED HOUSEHOLDS DEFINED

The criteria for distinguishing married households from unmarried households need to be determined before the household production accounts can be prepared. What definition of marriage should be adopted – legal or de facto? In keeping with the broad definition of marriage adopted by this book, married households include all households containing adult couples who state they are married, either legally or de facto.

All one-adult households are excluded, even if that adult is married. Thus single-adult households, with or without children present, are defined as unmarried households. However the married households definition obviously does not include all multi-adult households. Although the majority of multi-adult households consist of or contain married or cohabiting couples, some do not. For example, a proportion of two-adult households will be a parent and an adult offspring; some will be two brothers, two sisters or brother and sister. Some will be two unrelated adults. However, the majority of two-adult households consists of, or contains, married or cohabiting couples.

For example, in Australia in 1994, 84 percent of the reference heads of all two-adult households said they were married (registered or de facto). This proportion ranges from 64 percent in younger households without children and 89 percent in older households without children, to 94 percent in households with children. For this analysis, a child has been defined as a person age zero to fourteen years. Consequently adults are those age fifteen years and older. Alternative ages (for example, eighteen years) or definitions (for example, based on dependency or attending educational institutions) of what is a child could be used and would give a slightly different allocation of households between types.

Similarly the majority of households with three or more adults contain a married couple. Again using the Australian data for 1994, 84 percent of these households were "married." The percentage married was 92 percent of households containing children, 92 percent of older households without children, but only 75 percent of younger households of three or more adults without children.

For the purpose of the analysis in this chapter, married households are defined as comprising multi-adult households without children where the reference heads stated they were legally or de facto married. In summary, 62.6 percent of Australian households in 1994 were married and 37.4 percent were unmarried (25.4 percent had one adult, and 11.9 percent were multi-adult households).

THE RISE OF ONE-ADULT HOUSEHOLDS AND THE DECLINE OF HOUSEHOLDS WITH CHILDREN

During the twentieth century, the developed industrial countries have seen a large rise in the number of one-adult households, not only of sole person households where an adult lives alone, but also of sole parent households where an adult lives with one or more young children. In recent decades, these two types of households have been among the fastest growing. One-adult households without children are now more than one-quarter of all households in countries such as Australia, Britain, France, Japan, and the United States. In Austria, Germany, the Netherlands, and Switzerland, more than one-third of all households are now one-adult, while in the Scandinavian countries the proportion has now reached more than 40 percent.

The converse of this growth in one-adult (unmarried) households has been the relative, if not absolute, decline in the number of multi-adult (mostly married) households. In Australia the proportion of multi-adult households has fallen to less than 75 percent. Fifty years earlier, more than 90 percent of all households were multi-adult. Going back beyond another half century, perhaps almost all households were multi-adult and married. The rise in one-adult households has been driven largely by growth in older households, particularly by the number of older women living alone, widowed, divorced, or separated.

Also accompanying the decline in the proportion of multi-adult households has been a large decline in the proportion of households with children. This decline has taken place within multi-adult households, as few children live in one-adult households. For example, in Australia in the first half of the twentieth century, the number of multi-adult households with children far exceeded the number of multi-adult households without children. However, the proportion of multi-adult households with children declined and by 1975 there were as many multi-adult households without children as multi-adult households with children. By 1998 only 36 percent of multi-adult households contained a child. Again, an aging population, with an increasing number of older "empty-nest" households, has driven this relative decline.

LIFE STAGE HOUSEHOLDS

Figure 13.1 shows an array of fifteen types of households, covering all possible households and arranged according to four stages of life. The six

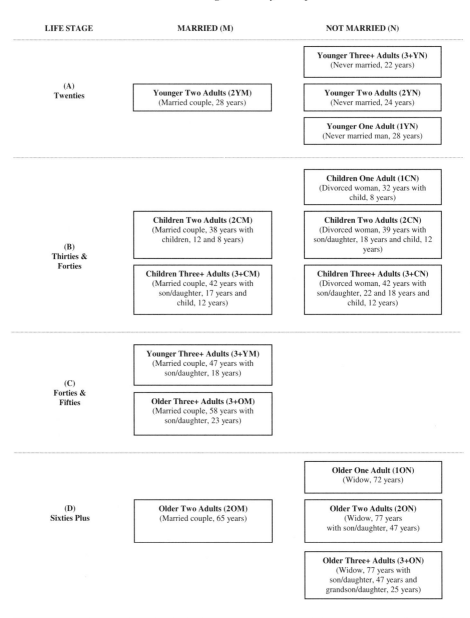

| LIFE STAGE | MARRIED (M) | NOT MARRIED (N) |

(A) Twenties

Younger Two Adults (2YM)
(Married couple, 28 years)

Younger Three+ Adults (3+YN)
(Never married, 22 years)

Younger Two Adults (2YN)
(Never married, 24 years)

Younger One Adult (1YN)
(Never married man, 28 years)

(B) Thirties & Forties

Children Two Adults (2CM)
(Married couple, 38 years with children, 12 and 8 years)

Children Three+ Adults (3+CM)
(Married couple, 42 years with son/daughter, 17 years and child, 12 years)

Children One Adult (1CN)
(Divorced woman, 32 years with child, 8 years)

Children Two Adults (2CN)
(Divorced woman, 39 years with son/daughter, 18 years and child, 12 years)

Children Three+ Adults (3+CN)
(Divorced woman, 42 years with son/daughter, 22 and 18 years and child, 12 years)

(C) Forties & Fifties

Younger Three+ Adults (3+YM)
(Married couple, 47 years with son/daughter, 18 years)

Older Three+ Adults (3+OM)
(Married couple, 58 years with son/daughter, 23 years)

(D) Sixties Plus

Older Two Adults (2OM)
(Married couple, 65 years)

Older One Adult (1ON)
(Widow, 72 years)

Older Two Adults (2ON)
(Widow, 77 years with son/daughter, 47 years)

Older Three+ Adults (3+ON)
(Widow, 77 years with son/daughter, 47 years and grandson/daughter, 25 years)

Figure 13.1. Types of Married and Not Married Households, Australia 1993–4 (Typical Marital Status, Gender, and Age Structure)

types of married households contain at least one legally married or de facto married couple. The mean age of all adults in the household, rather than, for example, the age of the youngest or of the oldest adult, is used to classify younger and older households without children. Older adult-only households are those with a mean age of forty-five years or older. The boxes in Figure 13.1 show the typical marital status, gender, and age structure of each household type.

The younger never-married or young couple households, typically aged in their twenties, are at the beginning in Life Stage A. At the middle of the array in Life Stage B are the five types of households that contain children, two married and three not married. The adults in these households typically are aged in their thirties or forties. The not-married households with children are usually headed by a divorced or separated woman.

Life Stage C comprises two types of larger households with three or more adults and no children. Typically they comprise a married couple in their late forties or fifties with one or more adult sons and/or daughters still living at home. The classification separates the younger households with mean age less than forty-five years from the older ones.

The final Life Stage, D, covers the remaining older households, typically a married couple age sixty to seventy years or a widow age seventy to eighty years. Some of the households headed by widows also include a younger divorced daughter with perhaps an adult grandson or granddaughter.

MOVEMENT THROUGH LIFE STAGE HOUSEHOLDS

Recognizing that there are exceptions, during an adult's life the main sequence of movement through different types of households is progressively down the household types shown in Figure 13.1.

A young adult perhaps starts a separate household in the first instance in Life Stage A by leaving home at age twenty-two and living in a "group" household with two others of the same age. Subsequently, two young adults could form a partnership and live together as a young de facto married couple household. If the couple goes to the next demographic life stage and has one or more children, the couple becomes a children household in Life Stage B.

If the children continue to stay at home, and also depending on the age gaps between parents and children, the household will become a younger married household of adults only with a mean age less than forty-five years. If the household continues with these residents, eventually it would become an older married household of adults only with a mean age greater than forty-five years. These are the younger and older households of Life Stage C.

After the offspring have left home, the original couple becomes an older couple household and finally, when one partner dies, an older household of one widowed adult. Some of these older widows combine with other younger adults for help and support in larger older households in Life Stage D.

Naturally, there are many other ways in which individuals and couples could move through the life stage households in the course of a lifetime. The right-hand, not-married, side branch of a sole parent household can be visited for a time, before returning to the main married household sequence after remarriage.

Table 13.1 shows the distribution of the 6.6 million Australian households in 1993–4 according to the various life stage categories of married and unmarried households. Almost two-thirds (62.6 percent) of Australian households in 1993–4 were married households.

Among the 4.1 million married households in Australia in 1993–4, only 15 percent were younger married couple households without children in Life Stage A. The majority (58 percent) were married couple households living with children or with grown-up offspring in Life Stages B and C. The remaining 27 percent were older married couple households without children (Life Stage D).

Of the 2.5 million not-married households, two-fifths (41 percent) were "never-married" young adult households in Life Stage A. The older "widowed" households in Life Stage D were 45 percent of the not-married households, whereas the single parent households in Life Stage B were only 14 percent of the not-married households. Thus the married households are concentrated in the middle stages of life, and the not-married in the early and late stages.

Of the 13.6 million adults in Australia in 1993–4, 10.0 million (74 percent) were living in the married households and only 3.6 million adults (26 percent) were living in unmarried households. There were 1.7 million adults (12 percent of the adult population) living either alone or as a sole-parent household. Women are the majority in these one-adult households.

Of the 4.1 million children in Australia in 1993–4, 3.6 million (88 percent) were living in married or unmarried (multi-adult) households, and only 490,000 (12 percent) were living in sole parent households.

Table 13.1 Australian Households, 1993–4, Distribution of 6,616,800 Households

Life Stage	Age*	Number of households			Percent		
		Married	Not married	Total	Married	Not married	Total
(A)							
Younger three+ adults	22	–	181,100	181,100	–	2.7	2.7
Younger two adults	28/24	605,500	343,300	948,800	9.2	5.2	14.3
Younger one adult	28	–	480,100	480,100	–	7.3	7.3
(B)							
Children one adult	32	–	237,400	237,400	–	3.6	3.6
Children two adults	38/39	1,175,300	74,100	1,249,400	17.8	1.1	18.9
Children three+ adults	42/42	389,000	34,200	423,300	5.9	0.5	6.4
(C)							
Younger three+ adults	47	535,000	–	535,000	8.1	–	8.1
Older three+ adults	58	328,000	–	328,000	5.0	–	5.0
(D)							
Older one adult	72	–	962,000	962,000	–	14.5	14.5
Older two adults	65/77	1,109,600	135,300	1,244,800	16.8	2.0	18.8
Older three+ adults	77	–	26,900	26,900	–	0.4	0.4
ALL HOUSEHOLDS		4,142,300	2,474,500	6,616,800	62.6	37.4	100.0
Of which:							
Life Stage A	20s	605,500	1,004,500	1,609,900	9.2	15.2	24.3
Life Stage B	30s–40s	1,564,300	345,800	1,910,100	23.6	5.2	28.9
Life Stage C	40s–50s	863,000	–	863,000	13.0	–	13.0
Life Stage D	60s–70s	1,109,600	1,124,200	2,233,800	16.8	17.0	33.8

Note:
* Age of typical household reference person.

COMPARATIVE CONTRIBUTIONS OF WOMEN AND MEN
OVER LIFE STAGE HOUSEHOLDS

It is well established that women, collectively and on average, contribute more time to unpaid work in household production than do men. For example, in twelve Organization for Economic Cooperation and Development (OECD) countries in the late 1980s, women worked on average 34.4 hours per week in unpaid work, twice the average for men of 17.2 hours per week (Ironmonger 1996a, p. 45). These data are taken from a report for the United Nations Human Development Report Office (Luisella·Goldschmidt-Clermont and Elisabetta Pagnossin-Aligisakis 1995). On the other hand, it is also well established that men do more paid work than women; data from the same United Nations report show that men's average paid work in OECD countries was 31.3 hours per week (hpw) compared to 17.2 hours for women. Total work, both paid and unpaid, in the developed industrial countries of the OECD, is thus comparatively equal but with women doing on average three hours per week more total work than men, 51.6 hours compared to 48.5 hours.

The first comprehensive Australian time use data were obtained in 1974 from a relatively small sample of 1,500 diary days in just two cities, Melbourne and Albury-Wodonga. Subsequently the Australian Bureau of Statistics (ABS) conducted a survey in May 1987 in Sydney, with two consecutive diary days from all adults in 750 households (3,300 days in all). In 1992 and 1997, the ABS conducted nationwide time use surveys across four seasons of the year and with samples of more than three thousand households in each year. These later surveys provide more reliable data on household time use, each survey providing more than fourteen thousand diary days.[1]

Data from the 1992 and 1997 Australian national time use surveys have been combined to form estimates of time use by Australian men and women for the year ended June 30, 1994. These estimates have then been combined with data from the 1993–4 ABS household expenditure survey to provide a set of satellite accounts of the Australian household economy.

The hours of total work by women in Australian households in 1993–4 were slightly more than those by men. However, in married two-adult households with children men worked 71.6 hpw, a little more than the

---

[1] Additional information on the use of different kinds of household surveys can be found in Chapter 9 by Joni Hersch.

70.2 hours worked by women. The statistics show men in these households combining 41.3 hours of market work with 30.3 hours of household production work, while women combined 10.8 hours of market work with 59.4 hours of household production work. These are of course average figures; individual households would have a range of time use patterns.

EFFECTS OF LIFE STAGE, NUMBER OF ADULTS,
AND MARRIAGE ON WORK

Figure 13.2 shows comparative data in graphical form for the hours of household production work and market production done by the fifteen types of households, arranged according to the four stages of life. Separate details are shown according to the number of adults in the household and whether the households are "married" or "not married."

Panel A shows the data for the four types of younger households in Life Stage A (twenties) and panel B for the five types of children households in Life Stage B (thirties and forties). The two types of larger adult-only households in Life Stage C (forties and fifties) are shown in panel C, and panel D shows data for the four types of older households in Life Stage D (sixties plus).

In each panel, the horizontal axis shows the average hours per week of market production work per adult and the vertical axis the average hours of household production work per adult. The diagonal 45-degree line divides each panel into the upper area where household work exceeds market work and the lower area where market work exceeds household work.

Work in Younger Households without Children: Life Stage A, Twenties

In contrast to all other households, younger households in their twenties do much less household production work and they do more market work. Figure 13.2 shows that all four types of younger households, one married and three not married, lie close to or below the 45-degree line of equality of household production and market work. Moreover, there is hardly any variation in the amount of household work per head. The younger three-person group household, typically aged only twenty-two years, does a little more household work (30 hpw); the others, whether one or two, married

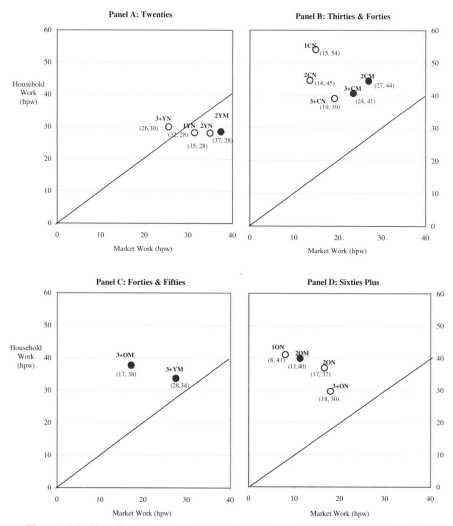

Figure 13.2. Time Spent on Household Production and Market Work, Australia, 1993–4, Hours per Adult per Week.

Notes: Not married = O, Married = ●. For definitions of the categories, see Figure 13.1. Numbers in parentheses indicate average hours of work per adult per week (market work, household work). Hpw = hours per adult per week.

or not married, all do only 28 hpw of household production. However the married couple, typically age twenty-eight years, do the most paid work, 37 hpw each. The younger never-married two-adult household, typically age twenty-four years, do somewhat less paid work, 35 hpw each.

Thus marriage in younger households appears to increase the hours of market work but have little or no effect on household production. However, the married households are typically four years older and hence more advanced in their career development; this may be the main explanation of the greater hours of market work.

Average total work hours by women and men in younger households without children are almost identical at very close to 63.5 hpw. Typically the members of these households are in their twenties or early thirties, and although the average hours of paid work for men exceed those for women, there are only small differences between married and the unmarried.

Work by Adults in Children Households: Life Stage B, Thirties and Forties

Typically the one-adult children household consists of a divorced woman age thirty-three years, with one child. Panel B of Figure 13.2 clearly shows that this household does the maximum amount of household production work per adult (54 hpw) of any of the fifteen household types at any stage of life. This is almost twice the household work in younger one-adult households (28 hpw) and nine or ten hours per week more than the household production work in two-adult married and unmarried households with children (44 and 45 hpw respectively).

The typical two adult *married* household with children comprises a married couple aged about thirty-five years with two children. Whereas the typical two-adult *unmarried* household comprises a divorced or separated parent age thirty-eight, with an eighteen-year-old non-dependent young adult and only one child under the age of fifteen years.

The larger three plus adult households with children, also shown in Panel B, do less household work again (39 hpw unmarried and 41 hpw married). As with the younger households, the weekly amount of market work is more for married households than for unmarried. This is particularly demonstrated by the two-adult households with children, shown in Panel B, where married households do an average of 27 hpw of paid work and unmarried only 14 hpw.

For women in children households, paid work is very much less than that for women in younger households – only 11 hpw for women in two-adult households with children and 10 hpw for the single-adult children household. In comparison, women do more than 30 hpw of paid work in the one- or two-adult younger households. Paid work for men in a two-adult household with children is 41 hpw, only slightly more than the man in a younger no-children couple household (40 hpw). The unmarried single male parent does only 20 hpw of paid work. However, he does more than 50 hpw of unpaid (household) work, almost as much as the single mother, 57 hpw.

Women in the couple household with children do 59 hpw of unpaid work, 2 hpw more than the single mother does. In multi-adult households, the amount of unpaid household work done by men seems to show little variation: around 30 hpw regardless of the number of adults in the household or whether the household has children or not.

Adults in children households do rather more total work than adults in younger households and significantly more than those living in older households. Children obviously increase the total amount of work required; the increases apply both to men and to women and in both married and unmarried households.

For households with children, although the scale of the household (the number of adults and the number of children) has a major effect on the amount of household production work done per adult in Australia, marriage itself has little effect on household work. It does appear to have a positive effect on market work. However, the observed marriage effect is compounded by the different age and gender structures of the married and not-married households.

For example, the typical married two-adult children household comprises a couple age thirty-eight years with two children age twelve and eight. The not-married children household of two adults comprises a divorced woman age thirty-nine, her eighteen-year-old son or daughter and one child age twelve, virtually a sole parent with two dependent children. Thus it is not surprising that the average market work of 14 hpw each in the not-married household is virtually only half of that in the married couple household, 27 hpw each. Both households do around 44 to 45 hpw per adult of household production.

The comparison between the larger three or more adult married and unmarried households also shows an apparent effect of marriage to increase market work – 24 hpw for married households and 19 hpw for not-married households. Again there is an age and gender effect compounding the comparison. The typical married household comprises a man age forty-two, a woman age forty-two, and a son or daughter age seventeen, whereas the typical unmarried household comprises a woman age forty-two with sons and/or daughters age twenty-two and eighteen.

Work by Larger Married Households without Children:
Life Stage C, Forties and Fifties

The younger married households with three or more adults are a little older than the smaller one- or two-adult households with a mean age of thirty-four years. Typically these households comprise a married couple of forty-seven years of age with one eighteen- to twenty-two-year-old adult offspring.

The older married households without children with three or more adults have a mean age of fifty-two years. Typically these households comprise a married couple of sixty-two years of age with a third adult around thirty years. The average total work of the men in these larger older households without children (55.2 hpw) is almost identical to that of the women in these households (55.5 hpw). Again, the average paid work of the men (22.2 hpw) is almost ten hours more than that of the women in these households (12.6 hpw). Consequently, to balance the total, the unpaid work of women (42.9 hpw) is almost ten hours more than that of the men (33.0 hpw).

Panel C of Figure 13.2 shows the average market and household production work in these households. The main difference is in the volume of market work, an average of 28 hpw in the younger households and only 17 hpw in the older ones. This difference is entirely an age or cohort effect as there is no marriage or gender difference between the structures of these households. As the older members of these households move into retirement, there is a large reduction in paid work with a small increase in household work.

Work by Older Households without Children:
Life Stage D, Sixties Plus

The older one-adult households do the least amount of total work – 49 hpw with 41 hpw of household production and only 8 hpw of paid work. Typically the men and women in these households are around seventy years of age. The amount of paid market work is small, 4 hours a week for women and 15 hours for men. However, as men are usually a few years older than their wives and they die at an earlier age, the majority of these households are women, typically a widow age seventy-two years.

The typical older married couple household is somewhat younger, around sixty-five years of age, but has slightly more hours of total work,

51 hpw. Being a little younger, the members of these households do a little more paid work than their single counterparts, 11 hpw. Nevertheless, household production work hours are similar (40 and 41 hpw). The typical older unmarried two adult household comprises a widow age seventy-seven years living with a son or daughter forty-seven years.

The remaining two older household types for which data are shown in Panel D are both unmarried households. Typically both these types are headed by a widow age seventy-seven years and with a divorced daughter aged in her forties. In the larger household of three or more adults, there is typically a grandson or granddaughter age twenty-five years. As can be seen from Panel D of Figure 13.2, these households do rather more market work (17 and 18 hpw), with contributions from the younger members still in their twenties, thirties, or forties.

Economies of scale and absence of any children bring down to 30 hpw the average household production work in the larger older household. This is identical with 30 hpw of household production work in the younger three plus "group" household of twenty-two-year-olds at the start of the life stage sequence shown in Panel A.

Summary of Effects

We can conclude from this discussion that marriage makes for only small differences in total work independent of life stage and the number of adults. The apparent positive effect of marital status on market production work can be explained by age and gender structural differences between married and unmarried households.

The differences between men and women in paid work are balanced by compensating differences in unpaid work. Women's market work is high in younger households, but very low in children and older households. Men's market work is high in both younger and children households, with the exception of male single-parent households. Women's household production work is lowest in younger households in their twenties and highest in children households. In contrast, men's household production work is relatively low, again, except for the male single parents.

NATIONAL ACCOUNTS OF HOUSEHOLD PRODUCTION

The statistical data on the use of time have been combined with detailed statistics on the number and age and gender structure of households, and use of capital and other inputs of energy, materials, and services to produce fully articulated national accounts of household production. These accounts show estimates (in monetary terms and for a whole accounting period) of the value of the labor, capital, and intermediate inputs used by all the households of a country to provide shelter, nutrition, clothing, and personal care to the children and adults living within those households. These accounts of the unmonetized household economy, also called Household Input-Output Tables, have become known as "satellite" accounts as they complement the core national accounts of the monetized market economy. Official statistical offices produce national accounts on a quarterly or annual basis as part of the worldwide System of National Accounts (SNA). Universally used national statistics, such as Gross National Product (GNP), are estimated according to the rules and conventions laid down in the SNA established in 1953. The most recent revision of the structure of this system was completed in 1993 (United Nations 1993).

Much of the original pioneering work on the development of household accounts has occurred in Australia using survey data on the uses of time and money by Australian households. The first satellite accounts were published in 1987 using data from the Cities Commission 1974 time use survey and the Australian Bureau of Statistics 1975–6 household expenditure survey (Ironmonger and Evelyn Sonius 1987). An important feature of household accounts is that they have been produced for different types of households. The 1975–6 accounts of the Australian household economy were disaggregated into separate accounts for the 1.7 million households with children (aged zero to fourteen years) and the 2.4 million households without children. The different requirements for, and resources available to, these two types of households were compared and contrasted through these economic statements.

The major differences of course relate to the need for the care of children, particularly the time needed to provide direct care of very young children. A one-week-old baby requires and receives (and is recorded in time use surveys as receiving) 168 hours per week of childcare – twenty-four hours per day. The Australian 1992 time use survey shows that a child aged less than two years received 115 hpw of care. This reduces to 77 hpw for a child age two to four years, 66 hpw at age five to nine years, and only 30 hpw at age ten to fourteen years (Ironmonger 1996c, p. 37). In terms of macro hours, total childcare time in Australia in 1992 amounted to 203 million hpw. This compares with 330 million hpw for all other unpaid work besides childcare and 272 million hpw for paid work in the monetized economy (Ironmonger 1996a, pp. 44, 56). In 1993, hours of paid childcare in Australia were less than 10 million hpw (Ironmonger 1996c, p. 32; Australian Bureau of Statistics 1994a).

Rather than just provide accounts for households with and without children, as was done for the initial 1975–6 Australian household accounts, the 1993–4 accounts were prepared for nine life stage households (Ironmonger and Faye Soupourmass 1999).

These accounts have been recalculated for each of the fifteen life course household types discussed earlier in this chapter. For presentation of the accounts, the six types of married households have been combined as three types – younger, children, and older – and the nine types of not married households have been combined as six types: younger, children, and older households, separately for the one-adult and the multi-adult cases.

NEW ESTIMATES OF AUSTRALIAN HOUSEHOLD PRODUCTION

Estimates of the value of Gross Household Product (GHP) have been published for several countries using the household input-output methodology pioneered in Australia. These include Canada, Finland, Norway, Sweden, and the United States. For Australia, GHP in 1992 was estimated to be $A 341 billion ($U.S. 245 billion)[2] (Ironmonger 1996a, p. 52). This compares with an estimate of $A 362 billion ($U.S. 261 billion) for Gross Market Product (GMP), the output from the Australian monetized economy. This latter estimate is $33 billion less than the official Gross Domestic Product (GDP) estimate of $395 billion because the imputed contribution to value added by owner-occupied housing has been included with GHP rather than in GDP. According to these estimates, the household economy in Australia in 1992 was just 5.8 percent smaller than the adjusted estimate of the monetized economy.

New estimates for Australian GHP have been prepared by the Households Research Unit of the Department of Economics, University of Melbourne. These estimates are based on the official surveys by the Australian Bureau of Statistics on household expenditure in 1993–4 and of time use in 1992 and 1997 (Australian Bureau of Statistics 1996, 1994b, 1999). The GHP estimates were first presented to the meeting of the International Association for Time Use Research at the University of Essex in October 1999 (Ironmonger and Soupourmas 1999).

Total GHP in Australia in 1993–4 (the financial year to June 30, 1994) is estimated at $488 billion. This compares with the GDP estimate for

---

[2] In 1992 and 1994, Australian dollars were exchanged at just over 70c U.S. dollars.

1993–4 of $450 billion. Adjusted for the value added by owner-occupied dwellings, the GMP estimate for 1993–4 is $414 billion. Hence these later estimates show GHP to be 18 percent more than GMP rather than 6 percent less.

There are two reasons for this large increase in the ratio of GHP to GMP, as shown by the 1992 estimate (published in 1996) and the 1993–4 estimate (published in 1999). The first reason is the decision to include the time spent by adults in self-education as part of household production. Although this activity does not fall within the "third-person" criterion for unpaid work, in that it cannot usefully be done by hiring a third person to undertake the study required, it is a productive activity leading to the increase in human capital. Arguments in favor of including self-education have been made in the recent report by the International Institute for Training and Research for the Advancement of Women (INSTRAW) (1995).

The second reason for the change in the measurement of GHP is the decision to include the time and resources that adults spend caring for themselves, not just the time and resources adults devote to caring for children and other adults. This is a somewhat radical decision. However, the basis for this decision is that this time – the time spent in self-care – is legitimately within the general boundary of production defined by the "third-person" criterion. Other people can be, and often are, paid to do the work of shaving, hairdressing, bathing, and dressing of adults, particularly the very young, the very old, and those unwell or disabled. Increasingly, with an aging population, these personal care activities will be undertaken on both a paid and an unpaid basis by a third person. Accordingly, it was decided to include as part of household production all time and resources spent in care whether it is for others or for oneself.

Throughout the new 1993–4 household accounts, the average national accounts figure of $15.00 per hour for wages, salaries, and supplements has been used to value unpaid household labor time. To bring the earlier estimates for Australian GHP in 1992 on to a basis comparable to the 1993–4 estimates, it is necessary to include the value of the time and resources spent in self-education and in other personal and health care. At the average market wage of $14.25 per hour in 1992, the inclusion of these activities would boost the 1992 GHP estimate by $101.4 billion to $442 billion, 22 percent more than GMP in 1992.

Thus, on a comparable basis for estimation, the unmonetized household economy in Australia in the early 1990s was producing about 20 percent more valuable economic output than the monetized market economy – 22 percent more in 1992 and 18 percent more in 1993–4. The higher percentage in 1992 is perhaps mainly a cyclical effect due to the recession in the monetized economy in 1991–2 that was followed by an economic recovery in 1993–4. The household economy appears to take up a large proportion of the cyclical slack in the measured economy in a countercyclical way. Ironmonger (1996b, p. 151) hypothesized that the countercyclical trade-off coefficient between the two economies is less than 1.0 – perhaps a coefficient of 0.8. This means that, on average, a $100 million cyclical rise (fall) in GMP is balanced by a $80 million countercyclical fall (rise) in GHP.

CONTRIBUTION OF MARRIED HOUSEHOLDS
TO HOUSEHOLD PRODUCTION

Table 13.2 shows the GHP estimates both in aggregate billions of dollars per year for all households (the macro numbers) and as average dollar values per adult household member (the micro numbers).

Married households were 63 percent of all households, contained 74 percent of the adult population, and produced 75 percent of GHP. On average, adults in unmarried households produced $34,700 of GHP, while those in married households produced $36,400 of GHP, about 5 percent more. Note the very large contribution of GHP from the single parent households of $53,200 a year. Married households with children also made a large contribution of $41,100 per adult member.

The need to provide accommodation, care, meals, and clothing for children obviously has great impact on the labor and capital used in households with children. For older unmarried households living alone, the diseconomies of scale impact the amount of labor and capital used in household production. Accordingly, this household life stage also requires a relatively large GHP per adult of $37,900 a year.

Economic value added, whether from household production or from market production, includes contributions from both human and non-human capital. Some $91 billion of GHP in Australia in 1993–4 was attributed to the capital cost of household vehicles, equipment, land, and dwellings. Household production is comparatively labor-intensive compared to market production. Despite the substantial and growing contribution from tangible non-human capital, 81 percent of GHP ($397 billion) is attributable to labor time. In the monetized market economy, the contribution of non-human capital is proportionately higher so that labor contributes somewhat less than 60 percent of GMP.

Table 13.2 Gross Household Product, Australia, 1993–4

Life Stage	Age[a]	In billions of dollars			Dollars per adult[b]		
		Married	Not married	Total	Married	Not married	Total
(A)							
Younger three+ adults	22	–	16.5	16.5	–	28,900	28,900
Younger two adults	28/24	40.6	19.9	60.5	33,500	29,000	31,900
Younger one adult	28	–	16.4	16.4	–	34,200	34,200
(B)							
Children one adult	32	–	12.6	12.6	–	53,200	53,200
Children two adults	38/39	101.2	5.9	107.2	43,100	40,100	42,900
Children three+ adults	42/42	48.8	3.8	52.6	37,600	35,400	37,500
(C)							
Younger three+ adults	47	59.9	–	59.9	31,600	–	31,600
Older three+ adults	58	35.7	–	35.7	33,600	–	33,600
(D)							
Older one adult	72	–	36.5	36.5	–	37,900	37,900
Older two adults	65/77	79.2	8.9	88.0	35,700	32,800	35,400
Older three+ adults	77	–	2.3	2.3	–	27,100	27,100
ALL HOUSEHOLDS		365.4	122.9	488.3	36,400	34,700	36,000
		74.8%	25.2%				
Of which:							
Life Stage A	20s	40.6	52.9	93.5	33,500	30,400	31,700
Life Stage B	30s–40s	150.0	22.4	172.4	41,100	45,400	41,600
Life Stage C	40s–50s	95.6	–	95.6	32,400	–	32,400
Life Stage D	60s–70s	79.2	47.7	126.8	35,700	36,200	35,900

Note:
[a] Age of typical household reference person.
[b] Rounded to the nearest $100 per annum.

311

Table 13.3 shows the contribution to GHP of both human and non-human capital according to various types of households in Australia. The data shown are in dollars per adult per year.

In aggregate, 18.6 percent of GHP was contributed by non-human capital – 18.2 percent for married households and 19.9 percent for unmarried households. However, at the extremes were the older married couple households with only 12.9 percent capital share of GHP (87.1 percent from the couple's own unpaid labor) and the younger unmarried households living alone with 35.9 percent of GHP from capital (64.1 percent from the household's own labor). These are quite large differences and indicate the relative abilities of these two types of household to afford to use capital instead of labor in household productive activities.

HOUSEHOLD PRODUCTION INCOME AND EXTENDED INCOME

Although GHP is often considered only as economic "production," it is also economic "income" and could also be called Household Production Income (HPI). This income is instantly distributed to, and consumed by, household members as it is produced. An imputed dollar of HPI is as valuable as a dollar of income from the monetized economy because the amount involved is a substitute for the money that would be required to purchase equivalent goods and services from the market. Thus the relative importance of household production as a source of income can be seen by calculating the contribution of HPI to "extended income," the total money and non-money income.

For the present estimates of extended income, it has not been possible to take account of monetary income from all sources. However, it has been possible to include estimates of the income from paid work, the gross money income before income tax deductions. These estimates use the same $15.00 per hour wage rate used in imputing value to unpaid work for the estimates of GHP. The total extended income is $732 billion. This includes $244 billion from paid work, somewhat more than the $212 billion estimate of compensation of employees in the official national accounts estimates for 1993–4. This is largely because the estimates in Table 13.4 include compensation not only for employees but also for self-employed labor. Hence, HPI of $488 billion contributed exactly two-thirds (66.7 percent) of extended income. Table 13.4 shows the contribution of HPI to extended income for the various types of households.

Although the HPI contribution for married households (66.3 percent) is only marginally less than for unmarried households (67.8 percent), for

Table 13.3 *Household Production Labor and Equipment and Housing, Australia, 1993–4, Dollars Per Adult Per Year*[a]

Life Stage	Age[b]	Household production labor			Household production equipment & housing		
		Married	Not married	Total	Married	Not married	Total
(A)							
Younger three+ adults	22	–	23,300	23,300	–	5,600	5,600
Younger two adults	28/24	22,100	21,900	22,100	11,400	7,100	9,800
Younger one adult	28	–	21,900	21,900	–	12,300	12,300
(B)							
Children one adult	32	–	44,000	44,000	–	9,200	9,200
Children two adults	38/39	34,600	34,800	34,600	8,400	5,300	8,200
Children three+ adults	42/42	31,700	30,500	31,600	5,900	4,900	5,800
(C)							
Younger three+ adults	47	26,300	–	26,300	5,300	–	5,300
Older three+ adults	58	29,400	–	29,400	4,200	–	4,200
(D)							
Older one adult	72	–	32,400	32,400	–	5,600	5,600
Older two adults	65/77	31,100	28,800	30,800	4,600	4,000	4,500
Older three+ adults	77	–	23,100	23,100	–	4,000	4,000
ALL HOUSEHOLDS		29,800	27,800	29,300	6,600	6,900	6,700
Of which:							
Life Stage A	20s	22,100	22,400	22,300	11,400	8,100	9,400
Life Stage B	30s–40s	33,600	38,300	34,200	7,500	7,100	7,500
Life Stage C	40s–50s	27,400	–	27,400	4,900	–	4,900
Life Stage D	60s–70s	31,100	31,000	31,100	4,600	5,200	4,800

Note:
[a] Age of typical household reference person.
[b] Rounded to the nearest $100 per annum.

313

Table 13.4 Contribution of HPI to Extended Income, Australia 1993–4, Billions of Dollars and Percent Contribution

Life Stage	Age[a]	Extended income (billions of dollars)			Contribution of HPI (percent)		
		Married	Not married	Total	Married	Not married	Total
(A)							
Younger three+ adults	22	–	28.0	28.0	–	58.9	58.9
Younger two adults	28/24	76.3	37.0	113.3	53.2	53.9	53.4
Younger one adult	28	–	30.2	30.2	–	54.4	54.4
(B)							
Children one adult	32	–	14.6	14.6	–	86.6	86.6
Children two adults	38/39	151.5	7.5	159.0	66.8	78.9	67.4
Children three+ adults	42/42	72.8	5.4	78.2	67.1	70.1	67.3
(C)							
Younger three+ adults	47	101.2	–	101.2	59.2	–	59.2
Older three+ adults	58	50.2	–	50.2	71.1	–	71.1
(D)							
Older one adult	72	–	42.6	42.6	–	85.8	85.8
Older two adults	65/77	98.9	12.4	111.3	80.0	71.5	79.1
Older three+ adults	77	–	3.5	3.5	–	65.8	65.8
ALL HOUSEHOLDS		550.9	181.2	732.1	66.3	67.8	66.7
Of which:							
Life Stage A	20s	76.3	95.2	171.5	53.2	55.5	54.5
Life Stage B	30s–40s	224.2	27.5	251.8	66.9	81.2	68.5
Life Stage C	40s–50s	151.4	–	151.4	63.2	–	63.2
Life Stage D	60s–70s	98.9	58.4	157.4	80.0	81.6	80.6

Note:
[a] Age of typical household reference person.

younger married couple households in their twenties, without children the contribution is only 53 percent. For older married couple households in their sixties, without children the contribution is 80 percent. The total extended income used here does not include other sources of income, such as pensions, superannuation, or returns from investments. For older households, particularly retired households, these sources of income are likely to be much more significant than income from paid work. If these incomes were to be included, the apparent importance of HPI would be less.

A more suitable indicator of the relative importance of income from household production would be the contribution of HPI to a concept of Extended Disposable Household Income (EDHI). This would include after-tax income from paid work, from social security benefits, and from investments – the economist's usual concept of disposable income, extended to include the imputed income from household production. HPI would be included as a gross value, what households would have to pay someone (including the hire of the capital equipment and housing involved) to produce the outputs from household production. The HPI used would be a gross value because logically it should include a payment large enough for the third persons involved to pay their own income taxes. A still better calculation of HPI would be based on actual market prices for the household production outputs less the market cost of the intermediate goods and services purchased to produce these outputs.

In Australia in 1993–4, EHDI was about $775 billion, comprising Household Disposable Income (HDI) of $290 billion (37 percent) and HPI of $488 billion (63 percent). More research is needed to estimate the HPI contributions for the various types of married and unmarried households.

SUMMARY AND CONCLUSION

Research into the measurement of household production still has a way to go before it will be possible to provide a continuous assessment of the importance of household production in the welfare of households, both married and unmarried, across a range of countries. In Australia, in the early 1990s, household production (GHP) was about 20 percent more than the output from the monetized market economy (GMP). The imputed income resulting from these activities (HPI) was 67 percent more than Household Disposable Income (HDI), the income after taxes from paid work, from social security benefits, and from investments.

During the twentieth century, the sustained growth in the number of one-adult households had led to a relative decline in the number of multi-adult households. In Australia the proportion of multi-adult households is now less than 75 percent, and only 84 percent of these contain married or de facto couples. However, the married households, 63 percent of all households, produce 75 percent of GHP.

Gradually, as the new satellite accounts of household production are developed and the data they will provide become better known, the perceptions and understanding of the fundamental economic importance of households as producers of value will gradually be appreciated. Proper recognition of the household economy will have arrived when national household accounts are published each quarter alongside national accounts for the monetized economy. These data will enable greater scientific research on the organization of household production, the interactions with the monetized economy, the role of households in building human capital, and the effects of marital status, household technology, and alternative social and economic policies on gender divisions of labor and family welfare.

REFERENCES

Australian Bureau of Statistics. *Child Care, Australia June 1993.* Canberra: Australian Bureau of Statistics, 1994a.

———. *How Australians Use Their Time 1992.* Canberra: Australian Bureau of Statistics, 1994b.

———. *Household Characteristics, Household Expenditure Survey, Australia 1993–94.* Canberra: Australian Bureau of Statistics, 1996.

———. *How Australians Use Their Time 1997.* Canberra: Australian Bureau of Statistics, 1999.

Goldschmidt-Clermont, Luisella and Pagnossin-Aligisakis, Elisabetta *Measures of Unrecorded Economic Activities in Fourteen Countries.* New York: U.N. Human Development Report Office, 1995.

International Research and Training Institute for the Advancement of Women (INSTRAW). *Measurement and Valuation of Unpaid Contribution: Accounting through Time and Output.* Santo Domingo: INSTRAW, 1995.

Ironmonger, Duncan S. "Counting Outputs, Capital Inputs and Caring Labor: Estimating Gross Household Product." *Feminist Economics,* 1996a, 2(3), pp. 37–64.

———. "Priorities for Research on Nonmarket Work." *Feminist Economics,* 1996b, 2(3), pp. 149–52.

———. "Bringing Up Betty and Bobby: The Macro Time Dimensions of Investment in the Care and Nurture of Children," in Nicholas J. Taylor and Anne B. Smith, eds., *Investing in Children,* Proceedings of the Children's Issues Centre

Inaugural Child and Family Policy Conference, July 1996c. Dunedin: University of Otago, pp. 27–42.

———. "Household Production." *International Encyclopedia of the Social & Behavioral Sciences.* Oxford, UK: Elselvier Science, 2001.

Ironmonger, Duncan S. and Sonius, Evelyn. *Household Productive Activities.* Research Discussion Paper No. 2, Centre for Applied Research on the Future. Melbourne: University of Melbourne, 1987. (Subsequently published as "Household Productive Activities," in Duncan Ironmonger, ed., *Households Work*. Sydney: Allen & Unwin, 1989, pp. 18–32.)

Ironmonger, Duncan S. and Soupourmas, Faye. "Life Stages of the Household Economy: How Do Spending Time and Money Change through Life?" *International Association for Time Use Research Conference*, October 1999, Colchester, UK: University of Essex.

United Nations, Inter-Secretariat Working Group on National Accounts. *System of National Accounts 1993*. Brussels/Luxembourg, New York, Paris, Washington: Commissions of the European Communities–Eurostat, International Monetary Fund, Organization for Economic Co-operation and Development, United Nations, World Bank, 1993.

FOURTEEN

Marriage, Parental Investment, and the Macroeconomy

Shirley Burggraf

> Parents' investments in children are a far more important source of an
> economy's capital stock than are bequests or the life-cycle accumulation of
> physical capital.
>
> Gary S. Becker, Presidential Address to the American Economic
> Association, 1988

Family functions usually aren't considered to be an important concern
of macroeconomics, but Becker's forceful statement has many implications for macroeconomic theory and policy that are interesting to contem-
plate. What if institutions concerned with economic performance, such as
the Council of Economic Advisors and the Federal Reserve Board, paid
the same attention to the "parental-investment climate" as they do to the
business-investment climate? What if agencies concerned with economic
organization and market efficiency, such as the Federal Trade Commission and the Securities and Exchange Commission, were as concerned
about family structure as about industrial structure and financial structure? What if macroeconomic modelers focused as much on family investment as on business investment?

This chapter is an argument for taking the investment role of parental
partnership very seriously and for adopting policies that support marriage

The concepts discussed here are summaries and extensions of ideas developed by the
author in several publications: *The Feminine Economy and Economic Man: Reviving the
Role of Family in the Postindustrial Age* (Reading, MA: Perseus Books, 1999); "Valuing
the Family Economy," in Helen Wilkinson, ed., *Family Business* (London: Demos, 2000,
pp. 33–9); "How Should the Costs of Child Rearing Be Distributed: The Buck Has to
Stop Somewhere," *Challenge*, September–October 1993, pp. 48–55.

commensurately with its contribution to economic performance. First, the financial dimensions of parental investment are outlined in a way that illustrates Becker's point that the family is in fact our major investment institution. The outline highlights an enormous gap that exists between the economic value of parental investment at the macro level versus private return to parents at the micro level, a disconnection between social value and private experience that probably accounts for the general perception of parental investment as having little economic significance.

Next, the chapter discusses the role of marriage in facilitating parental investment and sketches some thoughts about where marital partnership fits into macroeconomic theory and policy. In terms of the organization of this book, marriage is conceptualized as the major facilitating institution for investment of both time and money in the economy's stock of human capital. The conclusion is that attending to the needs of marital partners for legal protection, property rights, and infrastructure in a manner consistent with the institutional requirements of economic growth and development should be a major priority of economic policy. Such policies, it is argued, need to go beyond the transfer programs of a welfare state and find ways of providing the more substantive forms of support and protection to parental partnerships that are given to other wealth-producing institutions.

THE PARENTAL INVESTMENT ENTERPRISE

A Rhetorical Problem

Inevitably, it is somewhat distasteful to think of parents as investors with all that the term "investment" implies. Talking seriously about the macroeconomic consequences of marriage and the investment role of parents is something that most societies have never had to do because family structure and family functions could be taken for granted in most countries and in most cultures for most of human history. Prior to the 1960s, an almost universal social system ensured that people would mate, women would bear and rear children, men would support their families, and the young and the elderly would be cared for within the family. Women had few choices for working outside of a marital relationship, and men required the services of a wife in order to survive.

The family has been held together historically by very strong social and economic ties. In today's advanced economies, however, much of the social infrastructure that has dictated family roles throughout history has disintegrated, leaving the family institution much more dependent on love and altruism among its members. Reduction of social and economic constraints on sexual behavior and family roles may seem in some ways like a blissful state, but it constitutes a momentous change in human history.

While the social pressures to assume family roles have been reduced, the costs of rearing children have increased enormously. Instead of being important assets in a family, children in modern economies have become an exceedingly expensive project for their parents with little expectation of economic return. Yet, as Becker notes, the family is the major wealth-producing institution in an economy. Surely, much of the frustration surrounding public discussion of family issues is a result of disconnection between the value of family investment at the social/macro level versus family returns at the individual/micro level and the difficulty of talking about a problem that has seldom been discussed in any realistic way. A necessary step toward "getting real" is to be as clear as possible about what parents actually do in economic terms.

The Family Business

What are the dimensions of parental investment? In order for parental partnership and parental investment to be substantively incorporated into macroeconomic thinking, it is necessary to pay as much attention to the details of family business as analysts pay to other investment institutions such as banks and stock markets. A very blunt but useful way of looking at parental investment is to conceptualize a family profit-and-loss (P & L) statement that lists costs and returns to parental partners of investing in re-production. Although there are many intangible aspects of parenting such as love, risk taking, and parental cooperation that are virtually impossible to cost out, provision costs are tangible and time costs can be estimated. Table 14.1 is a partial, hypothetical P & L statement for rearing one child to age eighteen in a middle-income family in the United States in 1999.

The numbers in Table 14.1 are derived as follows.[1]

Provisions. Average provision expenditures by husband–wife families for a first child to age seventeen are computed by the Family Research Group of the U.S. Department of Agriculture, which uses the 1990–2

---

[1] For more detailed explanations of the numbers in Tables 14.1 and 14.2, see Chapter 5 in Burggraf 1999, pp. 51–66.

Table 14.1 *Profit-and-Loss Statement, Medium-
Income Family ($36,800–$61,900,
Average = $ 49,000)*

(1) Revenues	(2) Expenses	
Personal	Provisions	
Love, pride	Housing	$67,729
Parental instinct	Food	35,948
	Transportation	29,562
	Clothing	13,888
	Health care	14,310
	Educ. & childcare	19,983
	Misc.	23,622
	Total	$204,482
Family labor?		
	Time	$684,000
Old-age insurance?	Education	?
	Total	$888,482

Consumer Expenditure Survey (updated to 1999 prices) administered by the Bureau of Labor Statistics (USDA 1999). The USDA estimates that for a middle-income family, provision costs for a second child are 19.4 percent less than for the first, and that a third child costs 23 percent less than the second. The numbers in Table 14.1 have been extrapolated from the USDA data to extend through age eighteen. Excluded from the estimates are all costs prior to birth and all costs after age eighteen.

Time. The USDA estimates are only for the direct costs of provisions for one child through high school; they make no allowance for the cost of parental time, which is likely to be by far the higher cost. With economic development, child-rearing becomes an increasingly expensive undertaking as the period of childhood dependency lengthens, as children's needs for parental attention and guidance in a more complex world increase, and as the opportunity costs of parental time increase (Wanda Minge-Klevana 1980). Given that people tend to marry those of similar educational backgrounds and aspirations (sociologists call it *assortative mating*), differentials in spousal incomes can be attributed primarily to the costs that one spouse incurs from being the more flexible partner in the job market for the sake of family responsibilities.

Time cost in Table 14.1 is derived from assumptions about labor market participation by a family's primary caretaker; specifically, in a middle-
income family with an average lifetime income of $49,000, if the primary
breadwinner averages $32,100 per year by working full-time continuously
while the primary caretaker averages $16,900 by working part- time and/or
intermittently, the cost of being the flexible parent over a forty-five-year
working life would be $15,200 × 45 = $684,000. Time costs vary considerably, of course, among individuals according to personal circumstances,
but several empirical studies confirm the likely costs of being a flexible
parent who has primary responsibility for children (see, for example,
Sanders Korenman and David Neumark 1992; Heather Joshi 1992).

Education. The USDA figures in Table 14.1 for Education and Child Care
are for parental expenditures (private-school tuition, books and supplies,
tutors, Standard Achievement Test prep, and so on) to age eighteen. In
the substantial portion of the U.S. education system that is publicly fi-
nanced, costs are shared by parents and nonparents. Parents who buy
larger houses to accommodate children or houses in neighborhoods with
better schools pay additional property taxes for having children. Although
the USDA counts the property taxes paid by parents as housing costs
and thus lists them under "Provisions," much of what parents pay in
property taxes is actually expenditure for education.

Total Costs. The total cost figure in Table 14.1 must be regarded as incomplete and hypothetical, but it is probably an understatement for most
families. In a March 3, 1998, cover story, *U.S. News and World Report*
added on prenatal costs, college tuition, and various likely "extras" and
estimated the lifetime parental costs of producing one middle-class child
at $1.43 million in 1997 dollars. For the lower third of families (with income
of $36,800 or less, averaging $23,000), adding provision costs to time
costs results in an estimated cost of $445,180 for rearing one child to
age eighteen in 1999 dollars. For families in the upper third of the income
distribution (with income of $61,900 or more, averaging $92,700), the cost
is similarly estimated at $1,630,752.

Revenues. Because family labor by children has become an insignificant
item for most families and because Social Security has transferred a major part of old-age insurance out of the family, almost the only return
remaining on the revenue side of a modern family's accounting statement is parental love and altruism for children. No attempt is made here

to put a price on parental love, but that in no sense discounts its value in the family equation. To the contrary, in the context of such accounting, parental love appears as an extremely valuable asset given that modern parents incur such enormous costs for so little financial return. This is another way of saying what many people, from fundamentalist conservatives to evolutionary biologists, assert that parental love is an extremely precious thing.

The Family's "Profit Squeeze." Table 14.1 highlights the economic pressure points on the modern family. Parental investment has been squeezed from both the cost and the revenue sides of the family-investment equation. As the value of family labor by children and of children's support of parents in old age has disappeared from family accounts, as child-rearing costs have escalated with increasing length of dependency and need for parental guidance in a complex economy, and as the opportunity costs of caretakers' time have soared with increased job opportunities in the labor market, especially for women, parental investment has become an economically heroic undertaking. Parents have in effect been disinherited from the value of family while the costs have risen enormously. Understanding the modern family's "profit squeeze" goes a long way toward explaining why "family values" and family dysfunction have become such contentious social issues. From an economic standpoint, parents are being asked to do more and more with less and less.

Family Business versus Public Business. When a market system works efficiently, costs to a producer also represent the costs to society of the resources consumed, and revenues to producers measure the benefit of the producer's output to society. "Market failure" occurs when producers' costs and/or revenues are out of line with social costs and/or benefits respectively and therefore give misleading signals about where society wants resources to go. In a practical sense, the essence of the "family values" problem is a kind of market failure – an economic system that sends one message to the economy about the value of workers in the labor force and a very different message to parents about the value of parental investment in the future labor force. Table 14.2 is an extension of Table 14.1 with columns added on the left and right sides to compare the private benefits and costs of rearing children with their social counterparts.

Private Costs/Social Costs. In Table 14.2 there is little difference between private costs (column 3) and social costs (column 4). The message that a

Table 14.2 *Social Profit-and-Loss Statement, Medium-Income Family*
($36,800–$61,900, Average = $49,000)

(1) Social benefits	(2) Private revenues	(3) Private expenses		(4) Social costs
Workers (human capital)	Personal	Provisions		
$1,444,500	Love, pride	Housing	$ 67,729	$ 67,729
	Parental instinct	Food	35,948	35,948
		Transportation	29,562	29,562
		Clothing	13,888	13,888
		Health & care	14,310	14,310
		Educ. & childcare	19,983	19,083
		Misc.	23,622	23,622
		Total	$204,482	$204,482
	Family labor?			
		Time	$684,000	$684,000
$221,008	Old-age insurance	Education	?	$97,500
		Total	$888,482	$985,982

market economy sends to parents about the social costs of rearing children
is basically accurate in terms of signaling the costs of resources expended
and their alternative value to society. Except for the portion of school
taxes paid by nonparents, families outside the welfare system typically
incur most of the social costs of bearing and rearing their children.

If half of public school taxes are paid by parents, families such as the
one illustrated in Table 14.2 pay about 90 percent of the total cost of rearing a child to age eighteen. Given that econometric studies consistently
estimate that more than two-thirds of economic output is attributable to
labor, producers of the labor force (that is, parents) generate more than
half (90 percent of two-thirds) of the productive wealth in an economy,
which constitutes the dominant contribution to capital stock by parents
that Becker asserted in his presidential address. Parental investment is
literally the major wealth-producing institution in our economy.

Social Benefits/Private Revenues. It's on the output/revenue side of the
family accounts that the major disconnection between social and private
values occurs. Economic productivity of parental investment is represented by the value of human capital in column 1 of Table 14.2. This
value is estimated as the lifetime earnings of a worker who replicates the

lifetime earning capacity of his or her parents ($32,100 × 45). The value of old-age insurance from children, which has been transferred out of the family in most industrial countries, is estimated in column 1 as the 15.3 percent of earnings that U.S. workers pay for retirement, disability, and medical insurance to the Social Security and Medicare systems.

When a producer in a market economy succeeds in producing something that society values, the economic values of column 1 generally are matched by returns to producers in the private accounts of column 2. For example, if a wheat farmer produces a bushel of wheat that sells for $2.00, $2.00 appears in both the social and private accounts – society gets $2.00 worth of wheat and the farmer gets $2.00 of revenue. The social value of parental investment in column 1 of a family's account, however, has no matching private return in column 2 for the family that has produced a worker. The financial hole in column 2 of a family's P & L statement is the essence of society's "family values" problem from an economic perspective – an almost total disconnection between the social and private values of parental investment.

FAMILY STRUCTURE AND ECONOMIC PRODUCTIVITY, OR WHAT DOES MARRIAGE HAVE TO DO WITH IT?

The Role of Parental Cooperation

To the extent that marriage is a partnership for joint investment in reproduction and human capital investments in children, the "profit squeeze" on family investment outlined in the preceding sections is a squeeze on returns to marital partnership. It can hardly be accidental that an economic squeeze of such proportions has coincided with a declining tendency for people to marry and to stay married to the mothers and fathers of their children. Becker's statement about where the majority of capital stock originates implies, however, that family structure may be at least as important as industrial structure in determining economic productivity and efficiency.

A unique aspect of family organization is that it inevitably involves sexual partnership. Although modern economies have degendered many jobs and roles that once were considered men's work or women's work, parenting still fundamentally requires cooperation between male and female, starting at the level of sperm and egg. The human child requires an enormous amount of care and attention in order to become a healthy, responsible, and productive citizen, a degree of care and attention that depends on the kind of cooperative environment traditionally provided by married couples. Author Erica Jong describes the basic need for families as a cooperative institution:[2]

> One thing has always been true of us big-brained, slow developing mammals: it takes us two decades to reach maturity. This is both the glory and the curse of the human race. We cannot survive without thinking of ourselves as tribal, communal animals, without promoting cooperation among the generations and between the sexes.

Jong goes on to say that the cooperative family relationships necessary for human development are being stretched to the breaking point:

> In our time cooperation among the generations and between the sexes has diminished almost to the breaking point where it can barely sustain life. We have gone from the three-generation family, to the two-parent family, to the single-parent family in less than a century. Relationships between men and women have never been more problematic. Nor has there ever been less consensus about what constitutes civilized sexual behavior or sound child-rearing.

Social workers and family therapists reinforce Jong's conclusions about the importance of family organization for effective family functioning (for example, Maggie Scarf 1995). Family investment requires both intergeneration and intrageneration cooperation among family members. Intergeneration cooperation between parents and children forms the long warp threads of the family fabric that tie generations together over time. Intrageneration cooperation between parental partners forms the woof cross threads that hold a family together within a generation. There are many indications that the woof of family structure matters considerably in determining household productivity in parental investment.

While single mothers and fatherless children can survive more easily in modern societies than they could in earlier times and while various non-traditional family forms and lifestyles can work for some people, there is still a premium on extensive, day-to-day cooperation between mothers and fathers in the project of rearing their children. The expense of provisioning and caretaking outlined in Table 14.1 is a heavy load for two parents to shoulder jointly, let alone for one. For many reasons, stable family situations with two heads, two hearts, two pairs of hands, two sets of grandparents, friends, and relatives, and frequently two paychecks have a better chance of covering the parental bases than one parent trying to do it all alone without an extensive network of support.

---

[2] Quoted in "Pro-Life or Pro-Death?" *New York Times*, January 26, 1989.

The disproportionate number of men in prisons who come from fatherless families is evidence that children reared in two-parent families have better chances of being productive citizens.[3] Girls living without active, nurturing fathers are reportedly 2.5 times more likely to get pregnant before marriage and 53 percent more likely to commit suicide (U.S. Department of Human Services 1999). Strong statistical linkages between single parenthood and poverty and between poverty and school performance make the same point. Single-parent families are six times as likely to be poor as two-parent families,[4] and the socioeconomic status of families correlates very highly with student success in school.[5]

Much is written these days about the demise of the traditional family and the redefinition of what a family is. It is still the case, however, that alternative arrangements for rearing children such as child support by a non-custodial parent or families consisting of parents and stepparents tend to have problems that married, cohabiting parents don't encounter. Child support is frequently hard to collect from absent parents, predictably so because of the additional cost of maintaining two households and because the non-custodial parent gets a smaller return from parental investment by not being present in the household (Andrea H. Beller and John W. Graham 1993, Chapter 7 in this book; Casey B. Mulligan 1997). Studies also indicate that stepparents are often no better and sometimes worse for children's welfare than absent parents.[6] It isn't an exaggeration to say that marital cooperation between mothers and fathers in rearing their children is as important for family investment

---

[3] "Some 60 percent of the nation's rapists, 72 percent of adolescent murderers, and 70 percent of long-term prison inmates came from homes where the father wasn't present." "Family Values Gain Ground," *Wall Street Journal*, December 28, 1995, p. A6.

[4] Reported in David Popenoe, "The Controversial Truth: Two-Parent Families Are Better," *New York Times*, December 26, 1992, p. A19.

[5] A statement of this proposition was presented by James S. Coleman in his report, "Equality of Educational Opportunity," undertaken under Section 402 of the Civil Rights Act of 1964 to establish a basis for equalizing educational opportunities. Coleman found that socioeconomic characteristics of parents such as education and income had much more correlation with children's academic achievements than any school characteristics such as funding, curricula, degree of integration, facilities, and so on. Coleman's findings were substantially confirmed by the work of Christopher Jencks and his colleagues in the 1970s. His work is summarized in Robert Haveman and Barbara Wolfe in *Succeeding Generations: On the Effects of Investments in Children* (New York: Russell Sage Foundation, 1995), p. 62.

[6] Conclusions reached by a variety of authors and studies (an extensive study of seventeen thousand children in Great Britain; an National Institute of Health (NIH) study; sociologist Popenoe, author of *Life Without Father*; psychologist Nicholas Zill; sociologist Sarah McLanahan) as reported in "Some Worse Off When Parent Marries Again," *USA Today*, January 4, 1996, p. D1.

as partnership cooperation and stockholder cooperation are for business investment. There are alternative ways of doing things; but long-term, committed relationships between mothers and fathers have many inherent efficiencies for the project of investing time and resources in children.

Of the three basic forms of business organization – single proprietorship, partnership, and corporation – partnerships between mothers and fathers generally fare better than single proprietorships. What about the corporate model? Much of what has been proposed as "family policy" in recent years has been along the lines of a corporate model in which taxpayers become de facto investors in families. A collectivist approach of state-provided day care, mandated parental leaves, and governmental child allowances has been enacted in various degrees in most industrialized countries. Even in countries with the most generous family policies, however, fertility has fallen below replacement, and investments in the human capital of younger generations have been inadequate. Many governments are now facing a demographic crisis because families haven't produced enough workers with enough earning capacity to provide pensions and medical care for their aging populations,[7] an outcome generally predictable considering the nature of the problem.

As a general solution to the modern family's economic squeeze, the corporate model of family policy appears to have insurmountable problems because:

- Child-rearing is a very personal, hands-on job. No taxpayer or government agent will be there to relieve parents of the most critical jobs – the months of pregnancy and nursing, tending a sick child in the middle of the night, being on the spot to teach daily moral lessons, supervising homework and television watching, and so on.
- The enormous costs of doing the work of rearing one child to productive age in a modern economy as outlined previously are beyond the reach of any imaginable government initiative without compromising the basic incentives of a market economy. While many parents would probably say that some help from government is better than none and while government programs such as subsidized childcare can help to reduce the costs of family investment, it isn't possible for any public program to transfer from taxpayers to parents more than

---

[7] See, for example, "Population Implosion Worries a Graying Europe," *New York Times,* July 10, 1998, p. 1.

a fraction of the $1.4 million (the *U.S. News and World Report* estimate cited previously) in lifetime parental costs of rearing the average child.

If the problems of single parenting are often overwhelming and if a corporate-state approach is limited to providing marginal assistance to the process of investment in children's human capital, the parental-partnership model (marriage) stands out as the structure most likely to get the parental job done.

Marital Partnership and the Legal Infrastructure

Despite the potential advantages of marital cooperation for purposes of parental investment, many aspects of our economic system, tax system, and legal system make it difficult for mothers and fathers to function like a partnership. The essence of partnership efficiency is gains from specialization and exchange. It's rare in a business partnership that everyone does everything equally. Business partners typically specialize in production, marketing, accounting, and such, and share the gains of specialization according to partnership agreements protected by contract law. Beyond the biological specialization of pregnancy and nursing, the form of specialization that parental partners most often find necessary is specialization between breadwinning and caretaking (Becker 1981, Chapter 2). That particular form of specialization within marriage, however, carries extraordinary risks in modern economies.

Many modern parents are now dividing up breadwinning and caretaking work much more equally between mothers and fathers than their parents and grandparents did as a matter of economic necessity and/or personal preference. Regardless of preferences, however, practical considerations often prevent equal division of labor at home and in the workplace. For many practical reasons, ranging from geographical immobility to physical exhaustion, many families find that at least one parent has to make serious career sacrifices for the purpose of keeping a family together and for rearing children. Finding two equal jobs in the same place that allow enough flexibility for effective parenting by both parents, covering all of the parental bases especially if a child has special needs, and the exhaustion of working the "double shift" can be difficult barriers to labor market equality for even the most modern parents. Some degree of specialization in caretaking by one parental partner often proves to be a necessary fact of life. Over a lifetime, such sacrifices can be enormously expensive (Anne Crittenden 2001).

However useful and necessary it may often be for marital partners to specialize between breadwinning and caretaking to some degree in the project of child-rearing, the caretaking spouse is exposed to a 50 percent risk of divorce with relatively little legal claim on marital assets for being the caretaking partner. Solemn promises of lifetime love and support before roomfuls of witnesses frequently carry little weight in court when one spouse changes his or her mind. As a *Wall Street Journal* article has noted,[8] it's easier to get out of marital obligations than it is to get out of a car loan. Even in community property states where tangible property is divided equally in divorce, the caretaking spouse is often given short shrift because the dominant economic asset in most families is the earning capacity developed by the breadwinning spouse during the course of the marriage.[9] In addition to the "profit squeeze" on parental partners outlined in Table 14.1, there is also a daunting "risk squeeze" on the process of partnership specialization within marriage.

Why do modern societies provide so little protection and support for the functions of their major investment institution? Perhaps it's at least partly because the institution of marriage has been so invisible in economic theory.

MARITAL PARTNERSHIP IN MACROECONOMIC MODELS: READING BETWEEN THE LINES

The following paragraph is a quote from an essay on competitiveness:

Higher living standards depend on rising productivity, and in any economy the rate of productivity growth is principally determined by the size of domestic investments in plant and equipment, research and development, skills and public infrastructure, and the quality of private management and public administration (Lester C. Thurow 1994, p. 22).

Reading between the lines of the preceding quote, one could:

- Interpret the need for "research and development" as meaning that the economy needs motivated and disciplined people
- Think that "skills and public infrastructure" include such things as the honesty and responsibility of the citizenry

---

[8] "No-Fault Divorce Law Is Assailed in Michigan and Debate Heats Up," *Wall Street Journal*, January 5, 1996, p. 1.

[9] See Chapter 4 by Leslie Whittington and James Alm in this book for more on this topic.

- Believe that the quality of managers and administrators is affected by their health, judgment, social skills, and emotional stability

Since discipline, motivation, honesty, responsibility, health, social skills, and emotional stability are qualities that are largely developed in the early years of childhood and adolescence, parental investment of time and resources plays a crucial role in determining the competitiveness of a population. Prominent corporate leaders and entrepreneurs have stated that while their fathers "brought home the bacon," their mothers taught them their most important leadership qualities, such as determination, self-improvement, accountability, overcoming obstacles, hard work, staying level-headed, and doing the right thing.[10] Surely, our macroeconomic models would provides a better understanding of economic processes if something as important as parental investment weren't hidden between the lines.

Marriage for employment has cyclical implications, including how workers enter and leave the workforce (see Chapter 10 by Shoshana Grossbard-Shechtman and Shoshana Neuman in this book), but the major tie between parental partnership and the macroeconomy is in the area of long-run growth, where capital accumulation is particularly important. The dominant models of economic growth for most of the twentieth century have been some form of $Y = f(K,L)$, where Y is output, K is capital, and L is labor, with natural resources held constant and technology treated as an external variable that can shift the function over time. A practical drawback of such models has been that more actual growth has been generated outside the models by technology than by variables within the models and that actual growth trends across countries haven't correlated very well with model predictions.

As a reaction to the limitations of the dominant growth models, a body of theory known as endogenous growth theory has developed recently to try to incorporate more of the process of economic growth. A major focus of the new growth models is on why some economies absorb new technology more rapidly and more efficiently than others. The conclusion is that economic growth isn't just a mechanical relationship between inputs and outputs narrowly defined but is instead a process that is sensitive to social policy (Torben M. Anderson and Karl O. Moene 1993).

---

[10] Reported in "For Many Executives, Leadership Lessons Started with Mom," *Wall Street Journal*, May 16, 2000, p. B1.

Theory is confirmed by empirical studies across countries indicating that such functions as the maintenance of law and order, protection of property rights, and provision of infrastructure are significant determinants of growth rates (Robert J. Barro 1997). A conspicuous message of the new models is the importance of human capital in a society's ability to absorb technology (Paul M. Romer 1990). Attention has also been directed to the general ethics of a population that can raise or lower transactions costs, which become increasingly important as an economy becomes more specialized (Douglass C. North 1981).

General ethics and the ability to absorb technology would appear to be where marital partnership, as the primary creator of basic human capital, enters the growth theory picture. Any parent who has had the task of teaching morals and manners to the young and has undertaken the job of convincing a child that reading substantive books and working math problems are more fun (or at least more important) than watching television or playing computer games knows where ethics and the ability to absorb technology come from; they come primarily from parents who invest the time and resources needed to instill values, motivation, and learning skills in the next generation. Parental partnership plays a linchpin role in preparing the next generation to absorb technology and in transmitting the personal skills (morality, sociability, reliability) needed to reduce the transactions costs of economic specialization in a high-tech economy. Parents also play a major role, by teaching and by example, in preparing their children for family roles as the spouses and parents who will produce the next generation of workers.

Putting parental investment explicitly into growth models poses interesting conceptual questions. In his previously cited presidential address, Becker compared the Malthusian model of economic growth with the neoclassical models used by modern analysts. In Malthus's famous model that predicted persistent population pressure on food supply, resources including capital (K) are assumed to be constant or to grow relatively slowly while fertility (L) adjusts to the available resources. In the more modern versions of $Y = f(K,L)$, it has been the other way around. Fertility (L) has been taken as given, and investment (K) has been the important adjustment variable. If the major form of investment in modern economies is in fact parental investment in reproduction and the human capital of children, however, the L in growth models and the major part of K are both a result of the parental-investment process. L and K are bundled together within the family in a way not envisioned by either Malthus or the neoclassical model.

Bringing parental investment out from between the lines of growth theory requires putting it explicitly into models at the simplest level where analysts start to organize their thoughts about economic growth and progress. For instance, $Y = f(P, B)$, where P = parental investment and B = business investment, or $Y = f(F, P, B)$, where F = fertility, P = parental investment after birth, and B = business investment, would be a more realistic starting point than any model that doesn't explicitly recognize the critical role of parental investment in creating an economy's capital stock. Some sophisticated models have been constructed that do treat investment in human capital at the family level as the major engine of economic growth (for example, Becker, Kevin M. Murphy, and Robert Tamula 1990), but there is little indication as yet that the implications are widely understood or implemented in economic policy.

INTRODUCING MARRIAGE TO MACROECONOMICS

Returning to the speculative questions posed at the beginning of this chapter, what if:

- Economic theorists made parental investment such a conspicuous variable in the simplest economic growth models that no analyst could miss the message.
- The Federal Trade Commission reported that marital partnership has many efficiency advantages over single proprietorship or corporate-state organization for facilitating investment of parental time and resources in the human capital of the next generation of workers.
- The Securities and Exchange Commission reported that in terms of costs, returns, and risks to marital partners, the financial climate for parental investment has deteriorated enormously in recent decades to the point of transforming specialization in caretaking within marriage into an act of economic heroism.

If such an analysis were made of business investment, the reaction would surely be one of urgency and a perceived need to do something fairly drastic; but what can policy makers do about marriage? The protracted public hand wringing about "family values" has been conspicuously lacking in solutions that have the same dimensions as the problem.

At the theoretical level, what seems to be needed is a well articulated and widely understood union between the New Home Economics (NHE) that has introduced economic rationality into models of family decision making, as described in several chapters in this book, and the "new institutional economics" that emphasizes the role of institutions in growth theory and macroeconomic performance. Given that rational individuals now have to make decisions about marriage and family in an environment that has lost most of the traditional infrastructure that has supported families historically, taking the institution of marriage that forms the bedrock basis of any economy for granted and keeping it hidden between the lines of economic theory is a serious distortion of reality.

At the practical level, the "profit squeeze" and the "risk squeeze" on parental partnership need to be addressed directly; perhaps a better way to say it is that the risk and expense of parental partnership need to be reduced substantially. How likely is it that the institution of marriage will be able to just float along on a romantic cloud through the next century without a more supportive legal and economic base? The degree of imbalance in the way society treats work in various forms of business partnership versus work within marital partnership needs to be addressed in ways that are commensurate with the problem. The modern family needs an infrastructure appropriate for the conditions under which it now has to function.

Barro's (1997) findings about the importance of law and order, protection of property rights, and provision of infrastructure surely apply to marital partnerships as much as to any other institution in the economy. Marital partners shouldn't be forced to operate in an environment that is the legal equivalent of the Wild West – that is, a legal system that maintains relatively little law and order. Basic law and order means keeping people from (1) doing violence to each other, (2) stealing from each other, and (3) breaking contracts with each other. Consider the following:

(1) While more attention is now being paid to domestic violence, women are still more likely to be killed by the men in their lives than by any other assailant. Intimate relationships between the sexes can be as dangerous as robbers, muggers, and serial killers.[11]

(2) For all of the lip service paid to "family values," society has become increasingly callous about taking things from families. Large socialized retirement systems that depend on the wages of the next generation of

---

[11] Some experts are reported to believe that 50 to 70 percent of female homicides are perpetrated by men with whom the victim had a romantic relationship. "When Women Find Love Is Fatal," *New York Times,* February 15, 2000, p. D1.

workers to transfer large quantities of resources between generations are a form of expropriation from the family on a massive scale. The only source of support for an older generation in such programs is the wages of the next generation of workers, and yet the parents who invest the resources required to produce a younger generation have no claim on the system except by working outside the family. People who don't have children, people convicted of abusing and neglecting children, deadbeat parents who don't pay child support – all have as much claim (frequently more) on the next generation of children through collective pension systems as the most dutiful parents who have produced the workers to support the system. Parents have literally been disinherited from the economic returns of investing in their children.

The amount of wealth transferred out of the family via Social Security is an astronomical number. The "present value"[12] of what the U.S. Social Security system expects to transfer during the lifetime of people currently in the system (workers and retirees) was estimated at the end of fiscal 2000 to be over $25 trillion (Social Security Administration 2000, p. 56), a number roughly equivalent to the total tangible wealth in the U.S. economy! It's like asking farmers to bear all of the expenses, take all of the risks, and do all of the work of producing a crop but then telling them that they have no claim on the results – if they want to eat, they have to hold a job in a factory as well.

(3) Because the essence of investment is that it requires a commitment of resources over extended periods of time, the business economy would be thrown into chaos if it were forced to operate without reliable enforcement of long-term contracts. Parental investment has similar characteristics and requirements. Unlike other formal commitments, however, the partnership contract between spouses frequently carries little legal weight and provides little protection for the form of partnership specialization that parents most often find necessary. Given the high risk of divorce, any marital partner who compromises career development to invest in family caretaking takes a serious risk of being adandoned in midlife with few marketable skills, needing both to care for children and to earn a living simultaneously, and facing old age with few assets or pension claims.

---

[12] "Present value" is a financial term. In this context, it means that more than $21 trillion would have to be invested now at current interest rates in order to pay the future claims of people already in the system (workers and retirees) by current earnings and benefit formulas.

In order for the increasingly risky and expensive institution of parental-investment partnership to remain economically viable in the future, it will surely need more of the protections that are provided for the rest of society – that is, protection from violence, theft, and breach of contract. While much of what has happened to families in recent decades has been due to technological changes that are irreversible, some substantive actions could be taken. In addition to increasing protection against domestic violence and putting more legal teeth into the marriage contract for protection of caretakers, one way that significant support could be restored to parental partnerships would be to convert socialized old-age insurance programs to parental dividends.

In the United States, for example, if children's Social Security taxes were put into retirement trust funds for their own parents, it would have the effect of making parents shareholders in their own families and restoring $25.5 trillion (in 2000 dollars) of economic equity to the parental balance sheet – a sum that is on the same numerical scale as the family's economic problem. Restoring substantial economic value to parental investment in human capital would recognize the major investment role that families play in a realistic and tangible way. Surely part of the violence against economically dependent spouses and much of the willingness of parents to abandon their children to the poverty and stresses of single parenthood is the result of a social system that implies that work within marriage has no economic value.

Clearly, many questions, both practical and philosophical, would have to be addressed before anyone would conclude that reprivatizing so much family wealth is a workable and benign proposition.[13] Among the most obvious concerns that can be briefly addressed here are: (1) the distastefulness of putting a market price on the value of children to their parents and (2) the fact that younger generations would have to pay twice for retirement – once for their parents' retirement and again for their own, either by rearing their own children to generate a parental dividend for themselves and/or making other kinds of investments.

With respect to the distastefulness of putting a price on children, the situation can perhaps be compared to the life insurance industry in its early stages in the mid-nineteenth century. Prominent ministers initially condemned life insurance as a sin and a sacrilege for putting a price on a human life (Viviana A. Zelizer 1983). As economies industrialized, however, and as a worker's earning capacity replaced land as the major

---

[13] For an extensive discussion of relevant issues, see Burggraf (1999).

economic asset, a wage earner's death increasingly left widows and children to be dependents on society. The same ministers came to see buying life insurance as a responsible thing to do.

Although life insurance is still banned in some places (Syria, Libya), no one in an advanced society would confuse the value of a person's life insurance with putting a price on the value of the person as an individual. Life insurance is simply a way of using a market mechanism to take care of an important dimension of family business, a dimension made necessary by changing economic conditions in the nineteenth century. Changing conditions require new ways of thinking about things and new ways of doing things.

Concerning the issue of "double billing" younger generations, requiring people both to support their parents in old age and to provide for their own retirement would be a return to economic reality in many countries. Taking care of *both* the young and the elderly is what family members of working age have always had to do. It's what any society has to do, and the two functions are inextricably tied together within the family. There isn't any way to take care of either a young generation or an old generation without the other. That basic fact of life can't be made to go away either by economic models that ignore parental investment or by a welfare state that expropriates old-age insurance from parents on a massive scale while throwing relatively small bones to families to defray the costs of child-rearing.

Structural changes that accompany economic growth inevitably encompass the family as well as the market economy. However unaccustomed and untraditional it may seem and however expensive it may be to construct a realistic infrastructure that can support the basic functions of marriage and caretaking, the alternative is likely to be worse. Given the economic crunch that marital partnership is experiencing, omitting the linchpin role of parental investment from economic models and providing relatively little legal protection for society's major investment institution threatens the relevance of economic analysis and the long-run prospects of the whole economic system.

REFERENCES

Anderson, Torben M. and Moene, Karl O., eds. *Endogenous Growth*. Oxford, UK: Blackwell, 1993.
Barro, Robert J. *Determinants of Economic Growth: A Cross-Country Empirical Study*. Cambridge, MA: MIT Press, 1997.

Becker, Gary S. *A Treatise on the Family*. Cambridge, MA: Harvard University Press, 1981.

Becker, Gary S., Murphy, Kevin M. and Tamula, Robert. "Human Capital, Fertility, and Economic Growth." *Journal of Political Economy,* October 1990, *98*(5), Part 2, pp. S12–S37.

Beller, Andrea H. and Graham, John W. *The Economics of Child Support.* New Haven, CT: Yale University Press, 1993.

Burggraf, Shirley P. *The Feminine Economy and Economic Man: Reviving the Role of the Family in the Postindustrial Age*, rev. ed. Reading, MA: Perseus Books, 1999.

Crittenden, Anne. *The Price of Motherhood.* New York: Henry Holt and Company, 2001.

Joshi, Heather. "The Cost of Caring," in Carol Glendenning and Jane Millar, eds., *Women and Poverty in Britain: The 1990s.* New York: Harvester Wheatsheaf, 1992.

Korenman, Sanders and Neumark, David. "Marriage, Motherhood, and Wages." *Journal of Human Resources*, May 1992, *27*(2), pp. 233–55.

Minge-Klevana, Wanda. "Does Labor Time Decrease with Industrialization? A Survey of Time-Allocation Studies." *Current Anthropology,* June 1980, *21*(3), pp. 279–98.

Mulligan, Casey B. *Parental Priorities and Economic Inequality.* Chicago, IL: University of Chicago Press, 1997, pp. 277–305.

North, Douglass C. *Structure and Change in Economic History*. New York: W. W. Norton, 1981.

Romer, Paul M. "Endogenous Technological Change." *Journal of Political Economy*, 1990, *98*, pp. S71-S103.

Scarf, Maggie. *Intimate Worlds*. New York: Random House, 1995.

Social Security Administration. "Social Security Accountability Report for Fiscal Year 2000." Office of Financial Policy and Operations, SSA Pub. No. 31-231, November 2000, p. 56.

Thurow, Lester C. "Microchips, Not Potato Chips," in *Competitiveness: An International Economics Reader*. New York: Council of Foreign Relations, Inc., 1994.

U.S. Department of Agriculture, Center for Nutrition Policy and Promotion. *Expenditures on Children by Families: 1999 Annual Report.* Miscellaneous Publication Number 1528–1999. Washington, DC.

U.S. Department of Human Services. March 26, 1999, press release cited by Art Cleveland in "Lessons in Parenting: Actively Developing Stable Families," *Tallahassee Democrat*, March 29, 2000, p. 4B.

Zelizer, Viviana A. Rotman. *Morals and Markets: The Life Insurance Industry in the United States*. New Brunswick, NJ: Transaction Books, 1983.

Index

adjusted gross income (AGI), and income tax, 83

Agarwal, Bina, 113

age: of children and risk of divorce, 63; and control of income in marriage, 119–20, 123–4; and delays in childbearing, 41; and determinants of probability of divorce, 59, 67–9; and marital differentials in paid employment, 241–2; median at first marriage, 39, 40f. *See also* children; elderly

Aid to Families with Dependent Children (AFDC), 76–8, 177, 180–1, 226. *See also* welfare

Akerlof, George, 49

Alderman, Harold, 108

alimony, and child support, 165

Allen, Douglas W., 91n11, 92, 94t

Alm, James, 19, 83, 86, 88t, 89t

Amato, Paul R., 61

American Bar Association, Section on Family Law, 162–3

Anderson, Patricia, 265n14

Apps, Patricia, 110

Argys, Laura M., 171

assets, and wealth differences across household types, 135–6. *See also* savings and investments

Australia: definition of married and unmarried households in, 294; and Gross Household Product of married

households in, 306–16; life stages and types of households in, 295–8, 299t, 300–6

Australian Bureau of Statistics (ABS), 300, 307–8

awards, of child support, 159, 162

Bagnoli, Mark, 47

Bane, Mary Jo, 180, 183, 187, 189

bank accounts, marriage and ownership of, 114–18, 124

bargaining models: and control of money in marriage, 106; and housework, 203

Barro, Robert J., 334

barter, and compensation for Work-in-Marriage, 7

Bassi, Laurie, 183

Becker, Gary S.: and Coase Theorem, 91; and concept of implicit price, 8n21; definition of human capital, 11n26; on housework and time allocation, 204; and investments in marriage-specific human capital, 61–4; and market models of marriage, 203; and matching model of marriage, 44–6, 56; and New Home Economics, 3–4; on parental investment, 318–20, 325, 332; and "rotten kid theorem," 110; and theory of divorce, 19

Beckman, Martin, 44

Beller, Andrea H., 20–1, 165–6, 171–2, 266